Surveillance and the Vanishing Individual

Surveillance and the Vanishing Individual

Power and Privacy in the Digital Age

Juan D. Lindau

ROWMAN & LITTLEFIELD
Lanham • Boulder • New York • London

Published by Rowman & Littlefield
An imprint of The Rowman & Littlefield Publishing Group, Inc.
4501 Forbes Boulevard, Suite 200, Lanham, Maryland 20706
www.rowman.com

86-90 Paul Street, London EC2A 4NE

British Library Cataloguing in Publication Information Available

Library of Congress Cataloging-in-Publication Data

Names: Lindau, Juan David, author.
Title: Surveillance and the vanishing individual : power and privacy in the digital age / Juan D. Lindau.
Description: Lanham, Maryland : Rowman & Littlefield, [2023] | Includes bibliographical references and index.
Identifiers: LCCN 2022037734 (print) | LCCN 2022037735 (ebook) | ISBN 9781538173503 (Cloth : acid-free paper) | ISBN 9781538173510 (Paperback : acid-free paper) | ISBN 9781538173527 (epub)
Subjects: LCSH: Privacy, Right of--Cross-cultural studies. | Electronic surveillance--Cross-cultural studies. | Globalization--Cross-cultural studies. | Personal information management--Cross-cultural studies. | Privacy--Cross-cultural studies.
Classification: LCC JC596 .L56 2023 (print) | LCC JC596 (ebook) | DDC 323.44/8–dc23/eng/20221021
LC record available at https://lccn.loc.gov/2022037734
LC ebook record available at https://lccn.loc.gov/2022037735

Dedicated to my children, Paul, Rachel, and Sasha, and to my granddaughters, Zoe and Lily. You are the sun, the moon, and the stars.

Contents

Acknowledgments

I thank Nathalie Reinstein for her work copyediting the original version of this manuscript. The book benefited as well from the extensive commentary provided by Sandi Wong, a wonderful colleague and companion, and from the suggestions that came from anonymous reviewers. Additionally I offer particular thanks to Diane Alters, whose insights when we coteach our Secrecy, Surveillance, and Democracy course continue to enrich my views of this subject. Michael Kerns and Elizabeth Von Buhr at Rowman & Littlefield provided invaluable assistance as well.

Introduction

Although their proponents claimed that digital innovations, beginning with the computer and the Internet, empowered individuals, giving them hitherto unimagined capacities, these same tools ended up producing an unprecedented increase in the power and capacity of already huge organizations, especially governments and secondarily a relatively small number of private corporations. While the size of these corporations and their practice of surveillance engendered particular attention, their rise does not match the significance of the state's deployment of these digital surveillance tools and capacities. Unlike corporations, states can justify surveillance in the name of national security and cloak their surveillance in almost impenetrable secrecy. Moreover, states tend to exempt themselves, or circumvent regulations designed to protect privacy, given expansive understandings of national security and raison d'état.

Digital innovations transformed mass surveillance in particular into a simple and inexpensive process, even as artificial intelligence and machine learning made the mining of the metadata that this surveillance produced more probing and intrusive. And both democratic and authoritarian states, albeit to different degrees, succumbed to the allure of this technological ability since it promised greater security, control, certainty, and predictability. The deployment of these tools and practices, however, shrank the previously private inner world of individuals in previously unimaginable ways, making them smaller and more vulnerable. As states grew more searching and probing, individuals inevitably shrank both in relative and absolute ways. For their part, corporations transformed personal information into the "new oil," monetizing its appropriation, sharing, and sale. In this process they contributed enormously to stripping away and mining a critical portion of human freedom, the private inner world of each person, always the locus of the greatest personal sovereignty and choice.

Our current surveillance society, economy, and political system reflect revolutionary technological and ideological changes that came about during the late twentieth and early twenty-first centuries. A few seminal developments during the twenty years between 1990 and 2010 transformed mass surveillance into a central, indeed fundamental, feature of the modern digital age. The reification of the threat of terrorism after the attacks of September 11, 2001, in the United States certainly played a critical role in this development, since digital surveillance technologies seemed uniquely capable of finding terrorists who presumably used these networks and devices. Sweeping natural security bureaucracies developed during the Cold War eventually found a raison d'être in other "wars"—first against the drug trade and subsequently against terrorism.

Because terrorists, drug dealers, and other malefactors operate in the shadows, states, in the grip of collective post-9/11 fear, pursued increasingly expansive and unrestrained surveillance of both their populations and each other. In a world where hidden, seemingly existential threats lurked everywhere, surveillance seemed like a categoric necessity, promising safety and greater control. Concurrently, the online world emerged and expanded, as did innovations in digital surveillance technologies. These last tools promised to deliver unprecedented clairvoyance and omniscience, enabling states to "see" and confront these threats. Fear of terrorism reified security concerns, sweeping away legal restraints and attachments to privacy and civil liberties. Those who raised concerns about these ills were dismissed as hopelessly naive and unpatriotic. Cloaked in the language of patriotism and national security, and justified on the grounds of the highest national interest, mass surveillance grew unchecked, escaping serious public scrutiny in the decade after 9/11.

While a few political leaders in the United States voiced strong opposition—notably Senators Russ Feingold (D-WI), Mark Udall (D-CO), and Ron Wyden (D-OR)—they were voices in the wilderness. In fact, Feingold and Udall lost reelection bids to opponents who were uncritical supporters of the national security apparatus. Entities like the National Security Agency (NSA) in the United States and the Government Communications Headquarters (GCHQ) in the United Kingdom, along with their counterparts around the world, received enormous budget increases and hired many of the finest computer scientists during the decade after 9/11. This led to the creation of mass state surveillance on a scale previously unknown in human history.

In a world that combined ignorance, passive acquiescence, and outright support for measures that promised to root out terrorists and other "bad actors," mass surveillance became a norm, indeed a commonplace governing practice. Although police states were especially enthusiastic users of this type of surveillance, some democratic countries, especially the United States and the United Kingdom, engaged in notably extensive warrantless mass surveillance. This surveillance produced a tidal wave of data, requiring the adoption of algorithmic metadata mining resting on the presumption that states possess virtually unlimited ownership of hitherto private personal information.

On the commercial front, a set of fateful decisions in the years between the mid-1990s and the early 2000s created "surveillance capitalism," to use Shoshana Zuboff's felicitous terminology.[1] Even as states gathered more and more private personal information, two corporate entities, Google and subsequently Facebook, developed business models based on the logic of personal data accumulation and mining. In a remarkable sleight of hand, these corporations transformed their users/consumers into both their product and their raw material. These corporations deliberately kept users in the dark about both the form and extent of their commodification. Hidden behind labyrinthine terms of service, frequently couched in the densest legalese, this appropriation of private information for profit transformed growing swaths of the personal lives of users effectively into the property of these corporations.

The founders of these entities insisted that their profound ethical commitment to ever-greater connectivity and access drove them to offer a free service. However, the freeness of the service impelled them to rely on advertising in order to become viable for-profit operations. But these claims disguised the self-interest driving their provision of a free service. The monetization of users' private information offered profits that fees for service could never equal. Throughout, two imperatives informed their decisions—expanding the number of users and increasing the amount of time they spent on sites. Growing numbers of users increased the amount of data available for mining; and more data enabled the development of more sellable microtargeted ads. Time spent on the sites yielded additional insights into the lives, desires, appetites, and opinions of users, permitting the multiplication of revenue streams.

Despite claiming to empower people through connection to each other, the founders of Google, Facebook, and Amazon, among others, made vast fortunes reliant on an ever-growing pool of users whose activities, thoughts, desires, and feelings could be analyzed and manipulated. The founders of these companies, whatever their original intentions, clearly did not assign any value to the personal, private lives of their users. The founders of Facebook did not exhibit any understanding that they had designed a vehicle capable of spreading propaganda more effectively than Joseph Goebbels and Nazi Germany could ever have dreamed, while creating epistemic chaos, undermining democracy, and impoverishing social existence.

The founders of these platforms did not start out to create sites based on behavior modification—at least from what we know. This only came later, when they discovered that such manipulations increased traffic to their sites, creating opportunities for more advertising and other profitable activities. These companies hired behavioral scientists to promote the addictive use of digital devices and networks. While claiming that their goal was the promotion of human connection, Facebook and the other social networks instead deepen isolation and encourage antisocial behavior. More and more people spend many of their waking hours using their devices, reading and seeing things designed to arouse their individual fears and animosities while hardening their prejudices. In an additional equally consequential irony, these entities, even as they manipulate their users, become subject to manipulation themselves, as bots, bogus accounts, deepfakes, and fake news proliferate. Manipulation and falsehood flow in every direction.

Not to be left behind, governments engaged in their own form of mass manipulation, trafficking in fear through relentless threat amplification. The government's and the media's discussions of terrorism elevated it into the largest issue confronting humanity, dwarfing other matters. More and more intelligence spending, ever-larger national security and military budgets, and greater surveillance naturally resulted. Movies, television, and certain news outlets garner benefits from the public's fear of terrorism, as well. Raison d'état, especially the appetite for expanded powers, drives state actions. The inflation of threats demonstrates an old truth: fear is to feeling power as oxygen is to fire.

And what of the individual? Do the activities of these enormous private and public organizations make individuals safer? Do informed consent and choice accompany the transfer of personal information to these colossal public and private entities? What does this new digital surveillance reality, this "Brave New World," mean for human agency, dignity, and personal sovereignty? What does the appropriation of so much of the private mean for human existence? Is privacy an essential human right, or can individuals sacrifice it without much consequence? Is privacy only valuable to those "who have something to hide," as insisted the most enthusiastic traffickers of personal information and designers of surveillance capitalism, like Google's former CEO Eric Schmidt?

All these questions and more led to the writing of this book. While I am deeply worried about the impact of surveillance capitalism on human existence, I am even more concerned about the surveillance activities of states, given their unique ability to legitimately use violence and force against people and to deprive them of liberty.[2] Although surveillance capitalism contains several harmful elements, it cannot destroy civil rights. Only states can do that.

More generally, during the digital age surveillance became a key source of power, granting more capacity to the strong. Large organizations, both public and private, used surveillance to become even more powerful. Digital tools, contrary to their professed promise, facilitated the development of the oligarchical, indeed plutocratic, structures of power and wealth dominating the world in the early twenty-first century. Even in ostensibly democratic countries, surveillance defended the status quo, preventing change and preserving the power of the already rich and powerful. Moreover, everywhere, mass surveillance and other tools of the digital age were systematically used to monitor dissent. Private digital companies, for their part, engaged in an enormous economic taking from their users while paying nothing for this appropriation. In this regard, surveillance capitalism constituted a perfect extension of a practice central to the neoliberal economic agenda—an "accumulation by dispossession," to use David Harvey's terminology.[3]

A very few people elevated mass surveillance's centrality during the early digital age. The watchers, monitors, collectors, exploiters, and manipulators of data share many similarities. Those who approve of the state's mass surveillance reflect the consensus views of national security establishments and share a set of common understandings of the ends and purposes of state power. They tend, in addition, to define threats and security in similar ways. For this reason, governments that are ostensibly attached to civil rights protection adopted mass surveillance with little internal dissent or opposition—excepting in the cases of a few whistleblowers. The computer scientists and engineers in the employ of the state who develop these tools are similar to each other as well; their private sector counterparts are no more diverse. These groups, without the participation of other voices, effectively determined the limits of human privacy and the nature and form of social existence in the first decades of the Brave New Digital World.

Although the attack on human privacy with digital tools began during the last decades of the twentieth century, the attacks of September 11, 2001, on the United States transformed small and incipient measures into central and widespread governing practices. In the wake of 9/11, the Bush administration, in a foretaste of things to come, appointed Admiral John Poindexter of Iran Contra fame to create "Total Information Awareness." TIA, as it was known, aimed to see and know everything in the world in real time. Beyond all the other disturbing features of this enterprise for individual privacy, this governing project's desire to attain a *totality* of information provokes disturbing memories of other all-encompassing projects during the twentieth century. Though the revelation of TIA's intentions occasioned enough of an outcry to prompt its termination, it did not disappear. Instead, behind the veil of secrecy cloaking the security and other operations of the US state, the program migrated across the bureaucracy and led to the Five Eyes agreement. Within the American government, the NSA and the country's sixteen other intelligence agencies pursued TIA's ends. The conjoining of Canada, the United Kingdom, Australia, and New Zealand with the United States in the Five Eyes agreement facilitated this task. These five countries agreed to not spy on each other while collaboratively spying on everyone else and sharing the fruits of their labors. All of this produced a raft of vertically and horizontally integrated surveillance programs designed to fulfill TIA's goals of complete global surveillance.

Many of these activities occur behind a wall of ever-expanding state secrecy, with classification practices spreading to more and more areas as states try to hide their capacities from real and putative adversaries. Even portions of government far removed from activities related to national security routinely classify many of their actions. The extent of state secrecy fundamentally undermines governmental accountability, a key feature of any democracy, while simultaneously inverting the proper relationship between the individual and the state. Through mass surveillance, the government seeks to make individuals transparent while insisting on its right to keep its actions secret and consequently resistant to proper democratic oversight or accountability. This informational inequality contributes to growing power inequalities. The state as watcher becomes more powerful and opaque, while the population as the watched loses agency and becomes increasingly translucent. Watchers are always more powerful than those they watch, just like predators are more powerful than their prey; prey can only hide.[4] All of this is inimical to civil rights and to democratic accountability.

Especially during the first decade after 9/11, public concerns about mass surveillance lagged far behind fears of terrorism. Many during these years and subsequently dismiss the consequence of surveillance, asserting that they have "nothing to hide." Others say that they do not care about surveillance because "I do not matter to the government." Both arguments reflect the belief that conventionality and inconsequence constitute the best shield against the state. In many authoritarian countries, remaining irrelevant often constitutes the only way of avoiding the state. But these arguments reveal much about life in the digital age when voiced in a liberal, constitutional democracy.

These arguments stem, in part, from the failure to realize how much of the personal has been surrendered or taken. This inability to grasp the size of this loss and the ubiquity of digital surveillance comes from the passive, invisible nature of data collection and the effective disguise of this enterprise. The words used to describe this activity deliberately soften and shroud its intrusiveness. *Metadata*, for example, sounds vast and distant from the personal, obscuring the stunningly intimate information about the self that it reveals.

Other deceptive terms of art suffuse the surveillance enterprise. These usages deliberately undermine and negate commonsense understandings of words. As will be discussed later, and to mention just a few examples, in the world of US government surveillance, the word *targeted* does not mean "targeted," *collection* does not mean "collection," and *surveillance* does not mean "surveillance" when the watchers discuss their activities. The public, unaware of the ways that officials use these terms and shade their meaning, cannot evaluate the scope of the state's surveillance.

In addition, the lack of greater concern over mass surveillance flows from the sense of distance accompanying digital interactions. Communicating through a screen creates a sense of both distance and anonymity. Messages once "deleted" seemingly disappear into the ether. Although, in another twist, they are never entirely gone. The illusion of control over what is preserved and what is excised lingers, even when one knows better. How many remind themselves every time that they send a missive about the permanence and lack of privacy of all their emails?

Global powers find surveillance especially attractive because of the range and number of their adversaries. So too do countries engaged in prolonged conflict or that inhabit particularly conflictual neighborhoods, such as the Middle East. But ultimately all governments are drawn to the omniscience and corollary control that surveillance promises.

China quickly became the most extreme expression of this new reality. The Chinese government created a surveillance system that now intrudes into almost every sphere of life. Individuals and groups deemed undesirable, including Uighurs and Tibetans, are then subjected to especially suffocating surveillance. At the end of the second decade of the twenty-first century, the Chinese effort to construct a total surveillance state was advanced yet not entirely complete, although rapidly evolving technology continued to bring them closer and closer to meeting this goal.

While China constitutes an extreme example of domestic state surveillance, Israel continues to play a disproportionately large role in the international surveillance market. Over the years their surveillance industrial complex created extraordinarily intrusive and sophisticated tools. These capacities, originally developed to surveil the Palestinian population and monitor adversaries, enabled the creation of an Israeli "Silicon Valley" devoted to the invention of increasingly powerful digital surveillance tools.[5] The companies that take part in this digital complex sell their wares to both democratic and nondemocratic governments around the world. Many of the largest and most enthusiastic purchasers have been incomplete democracies and authoritarian regimes with very problematic human-rights records. However, unlike China and Russia, the Israelis did place restrictions on the usage of their technologies, although nonenforcement makes the terms largely meaningless.

The United Kingdom deserves particular mention as well given its early embrace and continued usage of surveillance technologies. It first deployed an extensive network of CCTV cameras after IRA attacks on London during the Thatcher administration in the 1980s. The population, at large, supported this development, despite its erasure of privacy in public spaces. This support reflected both the fear dominating the country and widespread trust in the security organs of the British state—a vestige of World War II.

Subsequently the British government developed some of the most sophisticated surveillance tools in the world, deploying them against foreigners and its own population. For example, the British government routinely uses Stingray, one of the most powerful phone-tracking systems in the world, and developed the Matrix system to enable "predictive" policing—the overarching goal of all surveillance states. Matrix assigned people a color-coded "risk score" of red, amber, or green, then subjected them to differential levels of scrutiny based on their score. Several variables created the score, including prior offenses, social media activity, participation in social networks, and, finally, friendships. These things were only discernible through the systematic surveillance of the population, especially of those who resided in crime-prone areas. Often these areas contained disproportionate numbers of recent immigrants and people of color. In addition, as was true elsewhere in the world, this surveillance and the algorithms that mined its metadata suffered from high error rates, just like the famous No Fly List in the United States.

These examples and many others reveal the consolidation of an increasingly Orwellian reality around the world during the first decades of the twenty-first century. More intrusive surveillance has transformed and shrunk privacy beyond recognition. State surveillance facilitates oppression, including the repression of peaceful protests, while corporate surveillance encourages consumption and materialism.

As I began writing this book, the COVID-19 pandemic struck, promoting a headlong rush onto the online world, further accelerating already extant trends in this area. Surveillance found yet another raison d'être and was adopted in many countries to track and trace outbreaks of the pandemic. In authoritarian regimes, and some democracies, especially in Asia, use of tracking and tracing apps was either mandated or widely used. In contrast, many countries and especially the Western democracies opted for voluntary usage and designed products that masked individual identity. This approach, in turn, reflected a belated but important increase in public awareness about the extent of digital surveillance and growing concerns about privacy. However, infectious diseases and other maladies will continue to encourage the use of digital surveillance, enabling governments and private corporations to become privy to more and more private health information.

This book is organized into several broad sections. Chapter 1 discusses the broader context of the transition from industrial to digital society during the last decades of the twentieth century and the first twenty years of the twenty-first century. It explores the implications of this shift for privacy, and in turn for individual power, especially in comparison to the capacity of states and huge private corporations. Chapters 2, 3, and 4 contain an interdisciplinary exploration of privacy and discuss the legal architecture governing—or failing to govern—its protection, especially from states. Chapters 5, 6, and 7 examine the rise and scope of state surveillance in the United States and the laws regulating its use. The United States government's adoption of mass warrantless surveillance makes it an emblematic example of how democratic countries embraced this practice during the first decades of the twenty-first century. The United States exemplifies the further expansion of state secrecy during this period, as well. Most consequentially, the use of mass surveillance across democracies grants their governments capacities that fundamentally undermine historic understandings of liberalism and of limited government. Chapter 8 then turns to the uses of surveillance in the United States and certain other countries against particularly power-less groups, including migrants, refugees, minorities, and dissidents, while discussing how these practices foster even greater vulnerability. Chapters 9 and 10 explore global surveillance practices, including cross-regime and cross-regional differences. Chapters 11 and 12 analyze the rise of surveil-lance capitalism and its effects, while chapter 13 is a case study of the uses of surveillance during the COVID-19 pandemic. The conclusion offers some overarching observations about mass digital surveillance and its impacts on privacy and, by extension, on individual agency and power. In addition, here different approaches to regulation are examined, distinguishing between those that offer some prospect of circumscribing the behavior of large cor-porations and those that governments might impose on their own activities.

Throughout, this book explores the challenges to human dignity of digital technologies designed to make all parts of the world legible. Legibility cre-ates novel sources of wealth and power that are anchored, in part, on the ability to penetrate the inner world of people, fostering a widening gap in the capacities of individuals and huge organizations. In the domestic sphere, states use their greater clairvoyance to facilitate governability and increase social control, expanding the already enormous power of the modern state. In addition, states deploy digital technologies and capacities against each other, fueling the relentless growth of cyberwarfare and hacking. Various malignant actors exploit these tools, transforming hacking and identity theft into crimi-nal enterprises. For their part, a raft of other private corporations, and espe-cially, although not exclusively, the social media companies have adopted "surveillance capitalism," designed to use the legibility of personal and for-merly private information as a new source of vast revenues and profits. In the process, they discovered that behavioral manipulation, the creation of closed epistemic communities, and the further erasure of the formerly personal redounded to the benefit of their bottom lines. While digital technologies bring many, many benefits and facilitate, and improve, many human activi-ties, their negative consequences are as substantial as those accompanying the emergence of the Industrial Revolution. The speed of technological change deepens these problems, complicating the search for regulatory remedies. Precisely because many of the most beneficial fruits of these technologies are inextricably connected to their most problematic costs, the search for remedies proves difficult and elusive.

NOTES

1. See Shoshana Zuboff, *The Age of Surveillance Capitalism* (New York: PublicAffairs, 2019).

2. See Max Weber, "Politics as a Vocation," in *From Max Weber*, trans. and ed. H. H. Gerth and C. Wright Mills (New York: Oxford University Press, 1946).

3. David Harvey, *A Brief History of Neoliberalism* (Oxford: Oxford University Press, 2005), 178–79.

4. The creator of the metaphor is Bruce Schneier. See his *Data and Goliath: The Hidden Battles to Collect Your Data and Control Your World* (New York: W. W. Norton and Company, 2015).

5. Thomas Webster, "Israeli Surveillance Companies Are Siphoning Masses of Location Data from Smartphone Apps," *Forbes*, November 12, 2020, https://www.forbes.com/sites/thomashbrewster/2020/12/11/exclusive-Israeli-surveillance-companies-are-siphoning-masses-of-location-data-from-smartphone-apps/.

Chapter 1

The Transition from the Industrial to the Digital Age

A number of central strands connect the industrial and digital ages. Both celebrated progress and technological innovation. Science and technology promised to overcome the maladies besetting humanity, bringing forth a brighter world. And both encouraged the growth of the two emblematic institutions of the modern age: the state and huge private organizations. The sheer size of these organizations, conjoined with their resources and capacities, granted them unprecedented power.

As noted before, the digital age transformed the state's ability to accumulate information at a moment when the 9/11 attacks produced an intense desire to "see" the world. As part of this effort, and in response to the public's demand for more security, states acquired tools that promised to enable prediction and to diminish—and even eradicate—the risk of terrorism, crime, and other maladies. However, when actions and choices become foreseeable and consequently subject to manipulation or alteration, they become less free. Moreover, prediction requires the erasure of the secret, the personal, the ineffable, the unuttered, and the unshared, inevitably causing the shrinkage of the self. Everything that states do not know about individuals, whether as biological entities or as sentient, conscious beings, impedes their ability to predict behavior. Thus prediction requires the appropriation of the formerly private. States use digital tools to systematically assault any barriers shielding this inner self. Regulations preventing this wholesale appropriation, in the relatively rare places where they existed, were inherited from the analog age. This made them immediately obsolete, and grossly inadequate, in the digital age.

Throughout history an insatiable quest for information drove states. This drive reflects the intimate nexus between information and the ability to wield power. Thus, while the digital age did not change the motives or the ends of states in their pursuit of power, it did transform the means at their disposal. This transformation of means expands their power in startling ways.

This new power is enormously difficult to control. The technological changes increasing the state's capacities far outrun the ability to develop new norms, regulations, or understandings of the proper relationship between the individual and the state. Moreover, the secret development and deployment of many of these new technologies makes them harder to resist or regulate. In liberal democracies these developments fundamentally alter the tenuous balance between the individual and the collectivity and between the dictates of security and the preservation of liberty. Moreover, the sheer speed of technological change complicates the development of regulations and laws designed to protect this balance. The slow pace of legislative and regulatory change in democratic polities only deepens this problem.

During much of the twentieth century relatively slow changes in analog technology allowed a more gradual, deliberative approach to regulation. In the United States, for example, a series of Supreme Court decisions and legislative acts eventually created the regulatory architecture of the analog world, informing legal restraints on wiretapping and determining how and when the First and Fourth Amendments of the Constitution applied to analog information. These laws and regulations marched unaltered into the digital age, governing everything from the Internet to the behavior of search engines and social media companies. Not surprisingly, this architecture proved inadequate in the digital age, as had many of the regulations governing the use of horse-drawn vehicles following the invention and adoption of the automobile.

While the real and presumed dictates of national security made states reluctant to meaningfully regulate their own activities, impediments to the regulation of the private sector arose from the fear of stifling innovation. This enabled technology companies to resist regulation as countries tried to dominate new market niches. In several developed countries, technology companies constituted the most dynamic economic sector and a vibrant source of export earnings and employment. They were consequently seen as national champions, giving them enormous leverage over lawmakers, regulators, and the public at large. Moreover, because digital capacities were so intimately woven into the national security apparatus, the fear of falling behind adversaries further animated the state's reluctance to regulate the private sector. Outside of the European Union, the first region to enact significant measures designed to protect digital and informational privacy, and in a few other countries, legislative and regulatory action advanced glacially, if at all, throughout this period.

The founding and growth of digital companies, moreover, occurred during a period of regulatory shrinkage in much of the world. Thatcherism and the emergence of the so-called Washington Consensus led to the widespread adoption of neoliberal policies. The period witnessed a gravitational shift to the right in many countries, a pattern that continued throughout the 1980s and 1990s and into the first decades of the twenty-first century. This turn to the right included the retreat of the state from economic life along with the diminution of its regulatory and social welfare activities.

In the United States this regulatory retreat included a decline in antitrust actions. As a result, market concentration eventually marked every part of the US economy. By the first decade of the twenty-first century, two or three enormous firms dominated many sectors of the US economy, producing a new Gilded Age, the era of great fortunes, conspicuous consumption, and extraordinary inequality marking the last decades of the nineteenth century and the first part of the twentieth.

The founders and primary shareholders of the technology companies established in the 1990s and into the first decades of the twenty-first century amassed vast fortunes, while the income of most of the population stagnated or shrank. Films, biographies, and articles extolled the "tech titans" as the geniuses and heroes of the age, given the American love of wealth and entrepreneurship. These men (and they were all men) were initially perceived as being more civic-minded and progressive than their historical counterparts or their despised contemporaries on Wall Street or in sectors like oil. Most dramatically, Apple's Steve Jobs and Microsoft's Bill Gates attained the status of sages. However, unlike many of the other tech titans, Mark Zuckerberg became a widely detested figure. Facebook's manifestly toxic impact on vast spheres of life, conjoined with the company's resolute unwillingness to change or abandon one of the most problematic business models in corporate history, created this animus.

Despite growing disquiet about the rising inequality marking the Brave New World created by Thatcherite and Reaganite neoliberalism during the 1980s and 1990s, the technological savoir faire of these entrepreneurs—along with the view that many of them were much more enlightened than their predecessors during the industrial age—preserved their cult status in the United States. In addition, growing fears of climate change elevated the status of the technologists, since parts of the population harbored the hope that they could create innovations that could solve this crisis. The technology companies got bigger and bigger, operating in an American market that included few regulatory restraints while possessing a tax regime designed to foster economic accumulation. This situation persisted for decades, although it generated growing numbers of critics.

Encouraging this criticism, the founders of the technology companies unsurprisingly behaved just like other plutocrats. They used their wealth on vanity projects and engaged in conspicuous consumption, acquiring planes, mansions, and all the other appurtenances of the American plutocracy dating back to the enormous mansions in Newport, Rhode Island, built to celebrate wealth during the Gilded Age. And except for a few notable exceptions,

they proved to be no more philanthropic than many of the so-called rob-
ber barons who dominated that earlier era. While Bill Gates and a few
others made philanthropic contributions on a par with Andrew Carnegie's,
in the main they focused on the accumulation and preservation of their
already enormous fortunes.

Finally, the rise of the digital age occurred at a moment when governments
in many countries, and especially in the United States, were privatizing and
outsourcing government functions, in line with Reaganite and Thatcherite
neoliberal understandings about the role of the state. This development
eroded restrictions on who could collect and hold certain types of information. The line between the government and private corporations working as
contractors and subcontractors for the state became more and more blurry.
In addition, state acquisitions of digital technologies continue to drive the
growth of a "surveillance industrial complex." Moreover, governments have
ensured that they can "see" the data that private companies gather. States
require companies to create gaps in encryption or use their abilities to find
and take advantage of so-called *zero days*—software flaws that, once discovered, can be "exploited" to penetrate security and other protocols.

ADDITIONAL REASONS FOR THE FAILURE
TO CONFRONT THE CONSEQUENCES
OF THE DIGITAL AGE

Several other factors beyond the speed of technological change, the dominance of neoliberal understandings, and the extent of technological determinism make it hard to address the digital age's most harmful effects. Those
advocating regulatory reform at any given historical moment have always had
to confront entrenched economic and political interests. But these reformers
could sometimes count on significant grassroots movements to give their
demands greater weight. No such grassroots movement has arisen to fight
spreading digital surveillance or to advocate for the protection of privacy. The
absence of such a grassroots movement, beyond the activities of a number of
NGOs, reflects several factors, including the immateriality to many of this
assault on the self, conjoined with continuing fears of terrorism and crime and
the attachment to the conveniences flowing from the use of digital devices
and platforms.

Even though mass surveillance produces novel forms of information
inequality and enhances the power of enormous public and private organizations while diminishing individuals, disquiet has mostly focused on the
growing economic inequality marking the early digital age. In some ways
the battle against economic inequality during the industrial age parallels this

disquiet, reflected in the Occupy Wall Street protests after the financial crisis in 2008 and 2009 and in the support for Bernie Sanders during the 2016 and 2020 presidential elections. During the industrial age, after the spilling of much blood, reformers managed to change, or at least mitigate, some of the era's most problematic features—especially those revolving around the treatment of workers and, to some extent, the environment.

Factory and living conditions in the first century of the Industrial Revolution eventually, if fitfully, led to the development of significant labor movements and the rise of reformist forces. These groups pushed for the development of welfare states capable of addressing the intolerable social problems that accompanied previously unregulated capitalist accumulation. These changes included the creation of a more extensive regulatory environment as well. What Karl Polanyi called "embedded liberalism" came into being, a system wherein minimum wages, limits on the length of the workweek, the right to strike, pension schemes, and a host of other changes palliated modern industrial capitalism's most exploitative effects.[1] As noted earlier, the decline of these regulations and social protections led to a return to Gilded Age levels of inequality after the rise of Thatcherism and Reaganism in the 1980s. The pursuit of these neoliberal policies accelerated a precipitous decline in the size of the labor movement, transforming it into a far less effective and powerful voice for change. Eventually, however, more and more people began pressing for measures that lessened the extreme inequality plaguing many otherwise wealthy societies. At the end of the second decade of the twenty-first century, these demands had materialized in incipient but growing efforts to unionize companies, raise the minimum wage, and make the US tax regime more progressive.

In large part those pressing for change, including such figures as US Senator Bernie Sanders (I-VT), focused on one of the most problematic features of the digital age: its impact on the nature of work. The digital age's expansion in the number of part-time "gig workers"—independent contractors who do not receive benefits, are paid poorly, and are completely disposable—continued to arouse particular concerns given its impact on wage stagnation and inequality. In addition to this part-time workforce, the working and middle classes not only confronted stagnant wages but also the prospect of continued displacement and declining incomes from automation and developments in machine learning.

The effective destruction of labor unions during the 1980s reduced the efficacy of grassroots efforts to change this reality. However, the number of people confined to part-time work, the persistence and even worsening state of wage stagnation, and the growing objections to ever more extreme economic inequality produced a growth in grassroots activity. The Democratic

Party became the locus of both grassroots and elite pressures to diminish economic inequality.

In contrast, efforts to reform and regulate the digital age's commodification of the private and its normalization of mass surveillance will be the result of elite action rather than grassroots activity. NGOs, privacy activists, and members of the political and academic elite will be the loudest voices in this area for the foreseeable future, given the extent of public quiescence. And even many of those who object to these practices often succumb to fatalism, seeing them as insoluble problems since "the horse has left the stable." According to this view, people have already surrendered their privacy and can never retrieve what they have lost.

In addition, the sense of control over the technology, since one can presumably control one's own use and communications, increases the tendency to neglect thinking about what happens to online information. For example, people are unlikely to think of every one of their searches as part of an expanding and perfectly faithful record of their activities, interests, and thoughts in real time. Nor do most, I suspect, spend much time thinking about what it means to inhabit a place where everything is collected and stored. By extension, they are unlikely to know that extant interpretations of law make their online postings of personal memories, photographs, and other manifestations of the private the effective property of the private platforms that they are using.

So the sharing of the self continues, in ways unimaginable during the industrial age. This promiscuous use of digital products means that states and the technology companies do not have to struggle to extract information from unwilling subjects. Instead, their central technical challenge is to use their ever-accumulating stock of personal information in more efficient and profitable ways.

NEW CONFIGURATIONS OF POWER
IN THE DIGITAL AGE

In the Brave New World of digital surveillance a new power relationship has developed that cuts across and deepens extant inequalities. As mentioned earlier, Bruce Schneier's comparison of the relationship between surveillor and surveilled to the relationship in the natural world between predator and prey aptly captures this power dynamic: The predator seeks and watches, while the prey hides. The predator chooses the time and place of attack and enjoys most of the power and agency. Invisibility is the prey's greatest protection. Essential inequality characterizes the relationship between predator and prey. Those who are watched must make sure that their actions do not draw attention to them or else risk being transformed into prey.[2]

Those who are most cognizant about these technologies and their capacities experience their impact most acutely and immediately when they succumb to self-censorship. This self-censorship reveals itself in every word intentionally not uttered out of fear, in every digital search not made, and in every thought not written due to concern about the presence and reaction of outside eyes. Everything avoided because of the feeling of being watched, listened to, recorded, or photographed and facially recognized diminishes freedom, agency, self-determination, and choice. Self-censorship differs profoundly from self-restraint: Fear often drives the former, while the concern for others and for their feelings and well-being animate the latter. Volition and choice lie behind self-restraint, while a visceral reaction to danger and fear drive self-censorship. Because of these differences, self-restraint does not violate the self, while self-censorship comes from the intrusion of fear into one's properly private world.

The advocates of mass surveillance and data collection would reject this characterization, arguing that the only "prey" are those who have something to hide. But this defense elides its impact—as George Orwell so brilliantly captured—on all those who are watched and are aware that they are being watched, whether they are the intended prey or not. The monitoring of searches and online communications inevitably produces self-censorship on the Internet, just as eavesdropping transforms and chills conversation. The presence of an outsider alters all interactions. As Nadine Strossen writes,

> [Undue] secrecy and surveillance, propel a vicious spiral. The secrecy shields the surveillance from oversight, and both of them suppress free speech, dissent, and democracy. . . . Thanks to undue secrecy and surveillance, we have exactly the opposite information flow than we should have between We the People and those we elect—they have too much information about us, and we have too little information about them.[3]

And as Johann Cas, Rocco Bellanova, J. Peter Burgess, Michael Friedewald, and Walter Peissl note,

> The secret exertion of mass-surveillance is in itself a clear symptom of disesteem of democratic principles. . . . [For] essentially unlimited measures of surveillance, in terms of people affected, means used, data collected, and duration, the burden of proof is reduced to the existence of abstract, and as such always prevalent, security threats, without any need to provide evidence for the effectiveness of measures of bulk surveillance.[4]

Outside of the United States, concerns about the extent of inequality plaguing many countries during the last decades of the twentieth century and the first decades of the twenty-first century also primarily revolved around the economic gap between the global billionaire class and the remainder of the world's population. However, unlike in the United States, and especially in Europe, the informational gap between individuals and huge organizations was recognized as a serious and invidious problem. The most notable information gap revolved around access to metadata. And those with this access possessed a particular power that lent itself to abuse.

Although regulatory restraints can and do reduce the potential abuses flowing from the concentration of information in a few hands, amassing this volume of data in and of itself creates problems. Information can be weaponized, leaked, or stolen. It is in the logic of metadata collection to gather increasingly minute information on everyone. Everybody's information consequently can become the object of these abuses.

Due to the extent of secrecy regarding information collection, noninsiders cannot gauge state capacities, distorting perceptions of the government's abilities. Mystery about government power, known since the Roman Empire as *arcana imperii*, adds to the state's majesty since the unknown excites reverence, fear, and compliance. The perception of this exalted capacity significantly depends on the opacity of the government and its illegibility. This mystery grants it the appearance of invulnerability. As a result, even as states insist that their secrecy protects the common good, they demand the right to penetrate the private world of individuals also in the name of the common good.

Although arcane knowledge, symbols, and practices always accompany ruling power, modern states—and especially modern states possessed of substantial digital capacities—develop even more elaborate mechanisms to facilitate governance. Highly detailed and expansive secrecy doctrines lie at the heart of this governing project.[5] The protection of information central to national security from the prying eyes of others typically justifies elaborate secrecy. Secrecy, however, regardless of the justifications underlying its use, inevitably deepens informational inequality between state and individual. While the former can use reason of state to cloud its operations, the individual cannot claim an equivalent right or power.

The rarity of leaks and other revelations about the scope of informational appropriation and surveillance prevent the public from accurately understanding the evolution of state powers in this area even though they are broadly aware that these powers keep growing because of technological innovations. For their part, states insist that the preservation of national security requires secrecy and an absence of transparency. As a result, the only way that the public learns about these activities occurs when whistleblowers leak information or journalists and NGOs expose state activities. The resulting ignorance about the precise extent of state powers and their use promotes contrary proclivities. Some fear these powers, others dismiss them, some feel protected, and yet others feel exposed and vulnerable. The limited nature of the glimpses into these powers fosters in some a tendency to inflate the scope of secret state capacities. At the extreme, some are figuratively inclined to wear "tinfoil hats" and brood over conspiracy theories about the nefarious activities of a "deep state."

In the United States, conspiracy theories flourish among those inclined to embrace these views of the world. These people believe in a "deep state" suffused with dark forces using vast digital capacities and other secret powers in nefarious, diabolical ways. As Richard Hofstadter brilliantly wrote in 1964 about this long-extant worldview informing the attitudes of conspiracy theorists, "I call it the paranoid style simply because no other word adequately evokes the sense of heated exaggeration, suspiciousness, and conspiratorial fantasy that I have in mind. . . . The paranoid style is an old and recurrent phenomenon in our public life which has been frequently linked with movements of suspicious discontent."[6]

While various American political movements, typically situated on the right, exhibited this "paranoid style" throughout the country's history, the digital age promoted the emergence of new groups exemplifying this proclivity. The "birther movement," built around the false claim that President Barack Obama was not born in the United States, perfectly reflected this set of understandings. So too did other assertions about him circulating among members of the conspiratorial right, including arguments that he was a closet Muslim bent on destroying the United States—a kind of "Manchurian Candidate." Donald Trump played a key role in propagating these paranoid falsehoods, helping animate the conspiracies that flourished during his subsequent presidency.

Believers in conspiracies see them everywhere: states, the powerful, and various minorities are thought to engage in activities that threaten "good, ordinary" Americans. And not surprisingly, the conspirators wield vast powers and engage in malevolent acts. While Hofstadter's "paranoid style" emerges again and again throughout American history, the reach of the Internet and social media companies allows conspiracies to spread more rapidly and gain more adherents. The sharing and "likes" of bizarre notions on these platforms makes them a crowd-sourced phenomenon. Endless repetition and encounters with others who hold the same views establishes their veracity even when bots generate much of this sharing of links or likes.

While many succumb to paranoid understandings of the state's digital capacities in the United States, even larger numbers of people accept, deny, or are resigned to this development. Some minimize or rationalize state surveillance powers and devote little thought to the implications of metadata mining or the consequences of the state's efforts to erase privacy, even as some of them become more apt to engage in large and small acts of self-censorship. Meanwhile, those who support the further expansion of state capacities, seeing them as guarantors of national greatness or security, advocate for increased surveillance and related activities. Given the centrality to American identity of the country's ability to exercise global dominance since World War II, those who favor more surveillance capacities enjoy the greatest power, occupying the apex of the system. Their power reflects their ability to frame an extraordinarily expansive understanding of national security and tap into a militaristic conception of patriotism.

All states, of course, and not just the United States, seek to retain significant definitional control over existing understandings of the common good in matters related to security. Although states are not monolithic actors, the bureaucratic, routinized logic and respect for hierarchy that informs their behaviors, conjoined with path dependency, tends to perpetuate established doctrines. Self-perpetuating coteries typically govern and define the security realm, further entrenching a set of largely unquestioned understandings about the measures required to preserve the nation.[7]

Given the tendency to conflate the common good with national security, states assert that their insatiable appetite for information reflects the imperative need to protect the public from manifold, ever-present threats. And they can argue that these same imperatives drive the need to intrude into the private. As Beate Roessler and Dorota Mokrosinska observe,

> The traditional view of privacy, in which protection of individual privacy is a means of protecting individual interests, has proved a weak basis for protection of privacy in political practice: When individual privacy conflicts with broader social interests such as law enforcement, public security, or the implementation of social justice, protecting individuals' interests seems to be a luxury that society can ill afford.[8]

In the main, democratic states insist that their intrusions into the private are minor, inconsequential, and carefully designed to shield the innocent. Problematically, the evidence that does emerge when the veil of secrecy shrouding these operations occasionally lifts reveals that the intrusions are not minor. Instead, these revelations show that many states are engaged in a systematic effort to collect everyone's private information.

As Max Weber predicted, the central feature of modern states is their bureaucratization and size. Their crushing weight and power compared to the smallness of average individuals in part explains alienation and apathy. In other words, feelings of powerlessness encourage conspiratorial thinking or complete denial and disengagement. The commonality of these two extremes in many modern countries serves as a profound indication of the problem of individual irrelevance. The rise of digital technologies makes the state and other huge organizations stronger but does not increase individual agency and capacity in equivalent ways.

The massive migration of people onto the online world, conjoined with their corollary willingness to share private information in the quest for intimacy, connection, or convenience, shrank and continues to shrink personal privacy. The nature of the Internet promotes the false conception that intimate communications remain private. People inaccurately imagine that they can protect their privacy if they place limits on the number of people who can see their information. They believe they have the power to determine what to share and with whom; nobody seems to exist except for the person receiving the communication. People do not think about the unseen presence behind all of these interactions—the online platforms gathering data and the states that can access this information virtually at will. Curiously, especially during most of the first two decades of the twenty-first century, people perceived entities like Facebook and many other comparable platforms as passive facilitators that merely enabled personal communications. People seemingly forgot that these were capitalist enterprises bent on the pursuit of profit—in this case through the appropriation and monetization of users' personal information.

Because people entered the digital age with sensitivities and understandings derived from the industrial-analog age, online interactions managed to seem both intimate and personal on the one hand and completely anonymous on the other. While inherently contradictory, these two impressions resulted from the physical distance and two-dimensional communication fostered through a screen; this made digital interactions feel somewhat impersonal or even disembodied. The indiscriminate sharing of the personal in the first decades of the digital age resulted, consequently, not from the disregard for privacy but from the widespread illusion of intimacy and anonymity.

Moreover, the privacy settings included on these platforms increased the sense that they structurally protected the personal, thus elevating the user's willingness to share information and increasing the disposition to communicate in unmediated, often incompletely considered ways. And while these settings protected information from other individuals, except when hacking occurred, as it did frequently, they never shielded it from the companies themselves. Under the circumstances, the surrender of privacy was not a genuinely considered and voluntary act but instead resulted from the platforms' deliberate deception.

Limited knowledge about the practices of these companies during the first decades of the digital age contributed to a false sense of online security. Few understood that their personal information was being used by platforms to refine behavioral manipulations designed to keep the user glued to their devices. In fact, the platforms systematically failed to provide information about what they were doing to their users. The provision of a free service amplified the impression that they were a mere conveyance, a tool, since users never had to pay a bill or consider the value of the service they were receiving.

For many years the tendency persisted to see search engines and social media companies as inert pathways to the Internet—mere highways, as it were. People gradually became aware that these companies were not passive transmission belts but actually were collecting everything and commodifying the personal and the intimate, although it took many years for this understanding to develop. However, this growing awareness did not lead to widespread changes in online behavior, diminution in the use of these search engines and social media platforms, or pressure for regulatory change. The desire for connection and convenience seemingly trumped the growing understanding that one was surrendering ownership of personal information in profound and unprecedented ways. By the time this awareness emerged, people had become addicted to these platforms and could not imagine life without their services. In fact, as noted before, rather than changing their behavior, people only developed more-expansive rationalizations designed to quiet reservations about the loss of privacy.

THE EMERGENCE OF NEW
DIGITAL ECONOMIC IDENTITIES

The shift from the industrial to the digital age inaugurated other changes beyond those noted at the outset of this chapter. One of the features of capitalism during the industrial age involved the emergence of a new identity— "the consumer." This identity contained new feelings of agency and personal power, in part explaining the love of shopping that came to mark modernity. This new understanding of the self emerged slowly, expanding in the wake of reforms like the forty-hour workweek, minimum wages, and other changes. Increased income and greater leisure time spread the benefits of industrial capitalism to broader swaths of the population. But mass consumption truly began with the invention of the credit card after the austerity of the Great Depression and World War II. The feelings of choice and agency that consumers enjoyed made mass consumption a natural expression of a democratic ethos.

People who acquired this new identity during the industrial age did not think of their thoughts and feelings as products or raw materials that could be exploited as sources of profit. Instead, despite the manipulations of advertisers, consumers believed that they retained choice and exercised agency over the things they bought and used. However, the digital age transformed this terrain in ways that undermined core features of this consumer identity.

People behaved indiscreetly on these platforms because they still saw themselves as "consumers" of a service who maintained choice and agency. They failed to understand their transformation into a raw material, the source of an invaluable commodity: personal, private information, the "new oil."[9] Complicating matters, people were users, consumers, and products at the same time, putatively empowered to make choices on the one hand, while simultaneously losing more and more control over their personal information on the other. In short, the transformation of people from users and consumers into products occurred without a corollary cognitive shift or changed self-definition. If customers and consumers enjoy power and agency while retaining decision-making capacity, products do not; products are mere clay, subject to the molding of others.

THE IMPACT OF THE INTERNET ON POLITICAL AND ASSOCIATIONAL ACTIVITY

Political protests and mass political action operate as critical forms of expression and dissent throughout human history. The use of online platforms to facilitate the organization of protests across the Middle East during the Arab Spring led many to see social media platforms and the Internet as novel and powerful emancipatory tools that individuals could use to confront authoritarian regimes and organize political protests. The use of these tools by protestors across the world during subsequent years seemingly confirmed this conclusion. However, as the second decade of the twenty-first century evolved, states learned to use these same platforms and digital capacities to discover, monitor, or manipulate protest behavior. While dissidents could use these technologies to communicate, governments could intervene in them, transforming them into tracking and monitoring tools that could find opponents and dissenters. While the Internet could spread information and news, it also provided an effective way for states to promote fake stories, spread misinformation, and manipulate public opinion. Moreover, the lack of efficacy of many protest movements raises the question of whether social media facilitates communication but diminishes extensive organizing.

Although the impact of the Internet and social media on political protests can be readily evaluated given the amount of information on the topic, it is much harder to discern their effect on associational activity, which remains the most widespread form of political activity other than voting in many democratic countries, especially the United States. The commonality of associational behavior in the United States first caught Tocqueville's eye during the 1830s. In an enduring insight, he argued that voluntary associations facilitated limited government, since they performed tasks that otherwise required state action. Moreover, associational activity magnified the power of individuals since collective action gave them greater voice in the polity.[10]

In part for this reason, robust associational activity became central to liberal understandings of the state. Rich associational activity, liberal theorists believed, helped to bind society together; these associations enabled people to meet and connect with those who shared their interests and commitments but might otherwise come from different social backgrounds. Extensive associational activity, especially if it involved participation in many different types of groups, created connections that sometimes cut across class and demographic lines, fostering greater social trust among a population.

However, the latter stages of the industrial age began to see a decline in associational activity, according to a few scholars, and especially Robert Putnam. In *Bowling Alone*, he explores several possible explanations for the steady and dramatic decline in associational activity in the United States that emerged in the last decades of the twentieth century.[11] After rejecting several possible answers, including such things as the entry of women into the labor force, he concludes that television explains this change. According to Putnam, the rise in television viewing that began in the 1950s and accelerated throughout subsequent decades as channels multiplied correlated strongly with declining participation in voluntary associations. People who had spent their leisure time participating in associations and groups increasingly cloistered at home, spending these hours watching television instead.

However trenchant in many ways, Putnam's analysis elides some critical contrary evidence. While many types of associational activity declined in the United States, such as bowling leagues, the Daughters of the American Revolution, and parent-teacher associations, other forms of associational behavior rose dramatically. In the 1960s, civil-rights groups proliferated despite ubiquitous television viewing, as did participation in all the social groups that emerged during this period. To cite another example, in later decades, despite continued high rates of television viewership, large numbers of Americans participated in sports leagues, organized to facilitate "travel sports" for their children. In these various youth travel leagues involving virtually every sport, they encountered others who came from different occupational backgrounds, creating precisely the kind of cross-cutting interactions that Tocqueville had once observed.

The Internet's impact on associational activity remained largely speculative and difficult to discern during the early decades of the digital age. On one hand, online activities are interactive, unlike television. Communication with others over the Internet increases political engagement and awareness while in many cases encouraging the descent into obsessive and conspiratorial understandings of the political world. The Internet, unlike television, also plays an enormous role in facilitating the organization of political activities, ranging from meetings to protests. On the other hand, while the Internet can inflame political obsessions and resentments, it simultaneously undermines face-to-face interactions and reinforces the tendency to only consume information that emphasizes already held viewpoints. In these regards it plays a role in destroying the broader social trust that traditional associational activity helped to foster. And like television, the Internet produces a pronounced tendency to isolate from others and stay home.

As a result, many associations continued to languish during the digital age. Neighborhood groups, PTAs, and the countless other voluntary entities that had widespread memberships before the advent of television did not reappear. Their shrinkage and disappearance in many cases ended a central wellspring of social trust. However, other cross-cutting associational activities such as sports leagues continue to flourish. So too does voluntary participation in a variety of charitable activities. But as was true after the advent of the television age, more and more people spend more and more of their lives at home, consuming the kind of content that does not create a sense of broader social connection. Tribalism, one form of engagement and activity, prospers in this environment, especially when anchored in identitarianism, while wider social trust and feelings of common humanity decline.

CONCLUSION

The industrial age, at least in its infancy, promised to end what Marx called the "idiocy of rural life," dragging people away from the poverty, economic somnolence, ignorance, and deprivation of rural life.[12] The transition from agrarian to industrial society touched every part of life, as would the subsequent transition from the industrial age to an informational and digital epoch. Both eras revolved around technological change—the former with the development and adoption of machines and eventually the assembly line, and the latter with the ability to appropriate and mine information. Both ages created extraordinary wealth and extraordinary inequality. Especially in their early stages, both eras fostered substantial immiseration despite high levels of growth.

Both ages glorified innovators and entrepreneurs and ridiculed or marginalized those who questioned the development of these technologies. And the apostles of technology insisted that these technologies would resolve intractable problems. The most fervent advocates of digital innovations believed that technology could reconcile economic growth with environmental preservation and eradicate disease, prolonging life. Digital technologies and online connectivity would drive down costs and increase global access to education, health care, and many other things, equalizing information and knowledge while diminishing inequality and poverty. And more generally, they said, the Internet and other digital innovations would empower individuals, giving them greater agency and control over their lives.

Both the Industrial Revolution and the digital age moved forward for decades without substantial regulation. The allure of the novel, conjoined with the availability of new sources of capital accumulation, encouraged a logic of precipitous adoption and only a slow and abbreviated effort to address the problems accompanying each epoch. In both ages, technological innovation was seen as inevitable and irresistible: human curiosity could not and should not be restrained. Moreover, technological change was tangibly beneficial. Among many other things, technology enabled the creation of new products and new activities. The previously unimagined became routine and the complicated could be simplified.

During the digital age this logic, along with economic self-interest, encourages the adoption of every new device, platform, and app. Those arguing for comprehensive circumscriptions on certain digital technologies and practices—including mass surveillance, facial recognition technology, the selling of personal information, and metadata collection and mining—are portrayed as hopelessly idealistic or outright obscurantists. Every innovation must be embraced if only to avoid "falling behind" the "bad actors" bent on exploiting these new capacities. And even as many worry about the employment and other effects of artificial intelligence, its further expansion, given the logic of technological determinism, seems irresistible.

This same insidious logic drove a substantial part of technological innovation and change during the industrial era. The culminating and most terrible invention of that age—the atomic bomb—was the fruit of this same set of understandings. The security dilemma and its concordant arms races simply did not permit inaction in scientific weapons development. Beyond the atomic bomb, the race for wealth and economic dominance during the industrial age encouraged the development and use of extraordinarily poisonous industrial chemicals subjected to little testing of their effects on human health and the environment—just as the business models of social media and other companies were not tested for their impact on social or political life before they were adopted.

In both epochs, the nature of work changed. During the early decades of the digital age, part-time work and self-employment increased. Labor unions declined during this period, as did the real wages of workers. The numbers of unionized workers, who enjoyed job security, a decent wage, and benefits that included health care and a defined benefit pension plan, continued to shrink during this period, although incipient unionization efforts emerged after the COVID-19 pandemic.

Blue-collar workers experienced transformations during the digital age as significant as those that occurred during the Industrial Revolution. In the first decades of the digital age, occupations disappeared due to either globalization or automation. As a result, the income premium for education rose precipitously, deepening inequality. While the working class largely supported parties of the left during the industrial age, its social resentments and feelings of exclusion made it more susceptible to xenophobic, anti-immigrant appeals from the right during the early digital age. In particular the working class's already strong antipathy to migrants in immigrant-receiving countries only became more intense, given the tendency to see them as job competitors who increased unemployment and drove down wages. In many countries the class-based partisan alignments characteristic of the industrial age gave way to a politics based on cultural, ethnic, and other cleavages, permitting the rise of populist leaders who channeled these sentiments.

While all the developments discussed above were discernible throughout the first decades of the digital age, their long-term implications remain difficult to gauge. In common with those who lived through the early decades of the transition from agrarian to industrial society, those who experienced the birth of the digital age can only vaguely glimpse its eventual contours. Almost from the outset, however, it has been evident that, whatever their many benefits, digital technologies have altered the texture of human existence in many negative ways. A number of these changes fly directly in the face of the expectations accompanying the birth of the Internet. Technologists, the high priests of the digital age, insisted from the beginning that the Internet would give people greater agency over their lives. They claimed as well that it would promote democracy, connection, community, and a host of other goods. While some of these things occurred, the Internet proved to be a double-edged sword, impacting each of these areas in extraordinarily negative ways.

Complicating matters, the benefits and costs of the digital age are inseparably linked to each other. For example, while individuals gain the ability to easily access hitherto unavailable information and communicate with each other in previously unimaginable ways, they pay for these things with a growing portion of their personal selves. While technology makes daily life, for those who can afford it, easier and full of previously unthinkable conveniences, vast wealth and power flows to those providing these services, deepening inequality.

The neoliberal policy framework enshrined during the Thatcher and Reagan administrations in the 1980s fostered inequality, and the digital age made it much worse. While some experienced economic empowerment and found new economic opportunities, others were pushed into part-time work, granted "flexibility" in exchange for the surrender of the economic security that the benefits accompanying full-time work provided. And machine learning and automation produced occupational obsolescence, ensuring—absent significant reforms and state intervention—greater levels of structural unemployment, economic dislocation, and inequality.

Calculating changes in relative power remains a difficult task. It is clear, however, that huge organizations, and especially states and corporations, used digital technologies to appropriate previously private elements of human existence in massive, ubiquitous, and largely unregulated ways. Consequently their power grew while the relative agency of individuals shrank. The digital age's fundamental imperative—the need to acquire and exploit increasing amounts of information—could have been regulated and directed in ways that avoided the development of mass surveillance and the surrender of privacy. However, this did not occur. But precisely for this reason and because privacy lies at the core of human existence, efforts to reestablish and protect it as technological change continues only grows more important.

NOTES

1. See Karl Polanyi, *The Great Transformation* (Boston: Beacon Press, 1954).

2. Bruce Schneier, *Data and Goliath: The Hidden Battles to Collect Your Data and Control Your World* (New York: W. W. Norton and Company, 2015).

3. Nadine Strossen, "Post-9/11 Government Surveillance, Suppression and Secrecy," in *Privacy, Security and Accountability: Ethics, Law, and Policy*, ed. Adam D. Moore (London: Rowman & Littlefield International, 2016), 223.

4. Johann Cas, Rocco Bellanova, J. Peter Burgess, Michael Friedewald, and Walter Peissl, "Introduction," in *Surveillance Privacy and Security* (London: Routledge, 2017), 6.

5. For a fascinating discussion of *arcanae imperii*, see Sissela Bok, *Secrets: On the Ethics of Concealment and Revelation* (New York: Vintage Books, 1989).

6. Richard Hofstadter, "The Paranoid Style in American Politics," *Harper's Magazine*, November 1964, https://harpers.org/archive/1964/11/the-paranoid-style-in -american-politics/.

7. Michael J. Glennon, *National Security and Double Government* (Oxford: Oxford University Press, 2015).

8. Beate Roessler and Dorota Mokrosinska, "Introduction," in *Social Dimensions of Privacy: Interdisciplinary Perspectives*, ed. Beate Roessler and Dorota Mokrosinska (Cambridge: Cambridge University Press, 2015), 3.

9. "The World's Most Valuable Resource Is No Longer Oil, but Data" *The Economist*, May 6, 2017, https://www.economist.com/leaders/2017/05/06/the-worlds-most -valuable-resource-is-no-longer-oil-but-data (paywall).

10. Alexis de Tocqueville, *Democracy in America*, translated by Harvey C. Mansfield and Delba Winthrop (Chicago: University of Chicago Press, 2002).

11. See Robert Putnam, *Bowling Alone* (New York: Simon and Schuster, 2001).

12. In section 1, "Bourgeois and Proletarians," of Karl Marx and Friedrich Engels, *The Communist Manifesto*, trans. Samuel Moore (London: Workers' Educational Association, 1848).

Chapter 2

Interdisciplinary Discussions of Privacy and Its Loss

A broad interdisciplinary literature emanating from philosophers, legal scholars, political scientists, and anthropologists explores privacy, revealing its centrality to freedom, choice, agency, and dignity. These disciplines contribute to an extraordinarily rich and multifaceted debate over privacy's consequence to human existence and its status as a human and civil right. Portions of this literature explore cross-cultural variations in the treatment and protection of privacy. And countless works of fiction explore the ways in which it can be protected and violated.

Milan Kundera's description of the Czech communist government's surveillance and prosecution of novelist Jan Procházka, whose private conversations the regime recorded and then broadcast as it worked to destroy his reputation, offers perhaps the most compelling insight into the importance of the private and the distinction between the private and the public. "Instantly Prochaska was discredited," Kundera writes,

> because in private a person says all sorts of things, slurs friends, uses coarse language, acts silly, tells dirty jokes, repeats himself, makes a companion laugh by shocking him with outrageous talk, floats heretical ideas he'd never admit in public, and so forth. . . . [That] we act different in private than in public is everyone's most conspicuous experience, it is the very ground of life of the individual. . . . [It] is rarely understood to be the value one must defend beyond all others. Thus only did people gradually realize . . . that private and public are two essentially different worlds and that respect for that difference is the indispensable condition, the sine qua non, for a man to live free; that the curtain separating these two worlds is not to be tampered with, and that curtain-rippers are criminals.[1]

The digital age attacked privacy in especially serious ways. Throughout human history, technological incapacity prevented states from systematically invading the private lives of their populations. They could target individuals but could never "see" everybody. Even surveillance states like the German Democratic Republic at the height of the Cold War had to rely on a blunter and much less sophisticated instrument: huge networks of informants. In other words, human beings had to put in the hours to surveil the population—a relatively inefficient undertaking when compared to contemporary surveillance. "Today, for the first time in human history, technology makes it possible to monitor everyone all the time," writes Yuval Noah Harari. "Fifty years ago, the KGB couldn't follow 240m Soviet citizens twenty-four hours a day, nor could the KGB hope to process all the information gathered. . . . But now governments can rely on ubiquitous sensors and powerful algorithms instead of flesh-and-blood spooks."[2]

In democratic countries, legal restraints govern such things as wiretapping, preventing states from arbitrarily hoovering up everybody's information. But digital mass surveillance capacities swept away or allowed states to frequently elide these restraints. For the first time, digital capacities enable states and huge private corporations to metaphorically turn entire populations inside out. And, most importantly of all, we can all be seen unless we choose to eschew all digital devices and avoid public spaces. Objections are swept away even though they involve fundamental transformations in social and political relations. Partly for this reason, little discussion occurs regarding the long-term implications of increasingly translucent existences, as these practices became institutionalized.

Before going further, *privacy* must be distinguished from *secrecy*. While the secret involves the deliberately hidden, the private encompasses the whole of the inner self. Nonetheless, many conflate the two. Secrecy can hide the discreditable, making its practice objectionable. This disrepute then extends to claims for privacy. As Sissela Bok notes, "Why should you conceal something, many ask, if you are not afraid to have it known? The aspects of secrecy that have to do with stealth and furtiveness, lying and denial, predominate in such a view."[3]

Despite the tendency to link privacy and secrecy, they differ in critical ways. To quote Bok again,

> Having defined secrecy as intentional concealment, I obviously cannot take it as identical with privacy. I shall define privacy as the condition of being protected from unwanted access by others—either physical access, personal information, or attention. Claims to privacy are claims to control access to what one takes—however grandiosely—to be one's personal domain. . . . But privacy need not hide; and secrecy hides far more than what is private. A private garden need not be a secret garden; a private life is rarely a secret life.[4]

Privacy and secrecy share one important similarity: the ability to maintain them comes from power. In authoritarian regimes, the elite and especially the leaders use their power to shroud themselves in secrecy while denuding their populations. Elites find it harder to shield themselves in societies with press freedom and other mechanisms designed to foster transparency, but their resources frequently allow them to secure types and forms of privacy beyond the reach of ordinary people.

In a speech about privacy to the American Library Association, Cory Doctorow captures the connection between power and privacy when he asserts that

> [The] decision . . . over when and under what circumstances your personal information is divulged tracks very closely to how free [you are] and how much power you have in a society. When you look at really stratified societies . . . the further up the ladder you go, the more raw power you have over this disclosure of your personal information. And the further down the ladder you go, the less power you have.[5]

While the apex of the American elite, for example, could not shield themselves from scrutiny as completely as Vladimir Putin in Russia or Xi Jinping in China, they could still erect formidable informational barriers around themselves. Paradoxically, several the founders of the most intrusive digital companies, whose fortunes come from the collection and exploitation of other peoples' most intimate information, assiduously guard many facets of their private lives or even do not permit their children to use their platforms. Eric Schmidt's declarations, and subsequently his actions, best capture this irony. In an interview in 2009, when he was still CEO of Google, Schmidt was asked if users should share their private information with the company as if it were a trusted friend. He replied, "If you have something that you don't want anyone to know, maybe you shouldn't be doing it in the first place." However, demonstrating the rampant hypocrisy of the technology tycoons, Schmidt subsequently blacklisted CNET reporters from Google after the tech news company published an article revealing his salary, the neighborhood where he lived, and his political donations and interests. CNET had gleaned all the information from Google searches, subjecting Eric Schmidt to only some of the intrusions that the company visited on all its users.[6]

Mark Zuckerberg, in turn, used some of the fortune derived from destroying the privacy of others to create complete physical privacy for his family, purchasing the four houses surrounding his Palo Alto home. He then tore them down, creating a compound designed to physically shield his household from the outside world. Zuckerberg and Schmidt exemplify the attitudes and behaviors of many tech tycoons. Long before Schmidt revealed his views about privacy, then-CEO of Sun Microsystems Scott McNealy said in 1999, "You have zero privacy anyway. Get over it."[7] In pithy form, at a time when Facebook did not yet exist and Google was still in its infancy, McNealy captured attitudes about privacy common among the technology entrepreneurs.

Bruce Schneier responds to these assertions and reaffirms the centrality of privacy to human existence, when he writes,

> For if we are observed in all matters, we are consequently under threat of correction, judgment, criticism, even plagiarism of our own uniqueness. We become children fettered under watchful eyes, constantly fearful that—either now or in the uncertain future—patterns we leave behind will be brought back to implicate us, by whatever authority has now become focused on our once-private and innocent acts. We lose our individuality because everything we do is observable and recordable.[8]

Another way of understanding the central importance of privacy to human existence comes from Erving Goffman's study of the effects of so-called "total institutions." Prisons constitute perhaps the most extensive modern total institution. To quote him,

> after being confined in such places . . . a kind of contaminative exposure occurs. On the outside, the individual can hold objects of self-feeling—such as his body, his immediate actions, his thoughts, and some of his possessions—clear of contact with alien and contaminating things. But in total institutions these territories of the self are violated; the boundary that the individual places between his being and the environment is invaded and the embodiments of the self profaned.[9]

Because of their scope and intrusiveness, digital technologies can, absent regulation and restraints, begin to replicate features of "total institutions."

As Goffman argues, because the interior world constitutes a central part of identity, it defines personhood. Some elements of this inner world are deliberately hidden and are consequently secret, but others are simply not expressed or shared. In this inner world, the individual enjoys true freedom and sovereignty. This sovereignty enables the regulation of social relations, the maintenance of the boundaries between the self and others, the development of degrees of intimacy and distance, and the ability to engage in unconstrained inner explorations.

Dreams, fantasies, thoughts, feelings, memories, hopes, and desires constitute some of the most essential parts of this inner world. Innovation and creativity require the unconstrained exploration that privacy permits. The knowledge that one is being observed invites self-censorship and the adoption of other protective and constraining behaviors. If outsiders, and especially those working for either governments or huge private corporations, can read everything one writes, hear everything one says, and even discern one's thoughts from browsing activities, then inner freedom, inner sovereignty, vanishes. There may be consolation for some in the view that individuals retain an inner core where privacy still resides—despite the collection of all their online activities and the cataloging of their public behaviors. This core consists of everything that is never expressed, manifested, or shown to others through an utterance or an action.

The preservation of this core depends on the practice of discretion, which involves the careful safeguarding of the personal and the exercising of judicious restraint over revelation. To quote Sissela Bok, discretion "is an acquired capacity to navigate in and between the worlds of personal and shared experience."[10] But in a world lived online, a world where promiscuous sharing and self-revelation are fostered through social media and other plat-forms, the exercise of discretion shifts. Discretion is both a learned behavior and a reflection of personal disposition. Discretion depends upon personality, culture, and social mores as well. Shifts in cultural and social practices produce equivalent changes in the exercise of discretion.

In many ways, technology transforms discretion. Mass surveillance and metadata mining erase the line between intended and unintended revelations. The smallest indicia, including keystrokes and scrolling patterns, are collected to ultimately reveal larger parts of the self. Digital footprints, always inadvertently left behind, enable the deconstruction of the private. Consequently individuals find it more and more difficult to discern how much of their inner selves remains private and just how much has been exposed. This profoundly alters the exercise of discretion, which rests on the ability to control information about the self.

Part of childhood involves learning to defend the self from unwanted intrusions. The best of intentions and curiosity typically drive the prying of parents and peers. As soon as they can speak, children hear a question that will follow them throughout their lives: "What are you thinking?" This question sometimes comes from a desire for closeness, sometimes from curiosity, and sometimes from a desire to overcome silence and spark a conversation. While almost always innocuous, this question constitutes an intrusion that children learn to manage, occasionally answering it but mostly parrying it with "Nothing."

Very young children indiscriminately share everything, given their incomplete sense of the boundary between themselves and others, most notably their parents. As the awareness of the difference between the self and others grows, the child begins delineating these boundaries through silence, withholding, secrecy, dissimulation, avoidance, evasion, and even lying. These practices increase requests and demands for transparency from others, especially parents. Nonetheless these practices become commonplace parts of every child's behavior.

The universal use of one or more of these stratagems eloquently testifies to the fundamental importance of the private in the construction and maintenance of the self. And because children lack power, they learn to use these stratagems to defend themselves. In a world suffused with power differentials, the ability to shield the self from the more powerful constitutes an essential survival mechanism. Although frequently deplored and condemned, these behaviors and practices often seek to reduce personal vulnerability and ward off the more powerful.

The use of these stratagems reaches an apex in adolescence. During this period, the search for greater individual power and agency requires a more assertive defense of the self from those in authority, and especially from parents. Children and adolescents learn the consequences and rewards of sharing and withholding, of revealing the previously unspoken and of remaining silent. Negotiating the social world in adulthood requires additional honing of these skills, as relationships multiply, involving different degrees and types of distance and intimacy. Avoiding unwanted intrusions is a learned ability.

Unfortunately, none of these carefully cultivated skills is designed to confront hidden, omnipresent intrusions. The digital age precisely produces these types of assaults on the self. Its intrusions, perhaps because they are both hidden and routine, do not activate the defenses learned to protect the private. And surveillance becomes so tightly woven into daily life that it is then normalized. When everything is silently and indiscriminately watched, the intrusion feels less direct and personal. And in such a world, it is easy to avoid thinking about the loss of privacy, given all the overt conveniences flowing from digital technologies.

That said, eventually—although fitfully—awareness of the ubiquity of surveillance began to grow, as did awareness of the loss of privacy. Most remain unaware, however, of the extent of these problems, or else they accept them in exchange for conveniences. But growing numbers began using technical means to protect their privacy, including virtual private networks, browsers like Tor, and applications that included end-to-end encryption. Companies arose to provide these services, seeking to profit from business models that promised to value and protect user privacy. As privacy became a scarce good, it became more of a market opportunity. In the Brave New Digital World both the appropriation of the private and its protection from outsiders became opportunities for enrichment. A larger and larger cybersecurity industry requires the continued existence of hackers, ransomware attacks, and other threats to ensure its further growth.

SOCIOCULTURAL UNDERSTANDINGS OF PRIVACY

In many cultures, silence and the capacity to preserve confidences indicate strength and personal virtue. The taciturn are reliable, strong, and stoic, while the loquacious lack the capacity for self-restraint and are weak and untrustworthy. The loquacious reveal too much about themselves and cannot be trusted to protect others. The colloquial phrase "strong and silent" captures the essence of this understanding.

The unauthorized revelation of the private occasions universal revulsion, beginning in childhood. The word *tattletale* captures the childhood view of those who "tell on" others, "ratting" to figures of authority. Their "tattles" are an unauthorized sharing of something that belongs to another; through this act, they make someone else vulnerable while seeking a status reward from those with greater power. In addition, the tattletale derives a certain sadistic satisfaction from getting others into trouble with authority figures. Children despise tattletales, seeing them as unworthy of trust and friendship. Tattletales appropriate a key part of individual power and agency, the decision as to what to reveal and what to withhold. In later life, other words express the revulsion that children first feel toward the tattletale. *Gossips, narks, rats, informants, snitches,* and *grasses* are just a few English terms of opprobrium for those who engage in this behavior. The term *indiscreet,* although less pejorative, describes this unacceptable behavior in a more socially acceptable way.

The agents of the coercive apparatuses of states cultivate informants, using them to uncover the clandestine, but nobody sees them as virtuous or worthy of trust and friendship. Just like the tattletale, the informant tries to gain a personal advantage through the sharing of the information of others. And those whose information they appropriate and share see them as traitors and thieves. Even those who employ informants frequently despite them, since their willingness to betray others makes them unworthy of trust.

Other languages contain similarly condemnatory language for those who share the private information of others and who consequently engage in a theft of the private. In Spanish, for example, the word *chismoso,* a mix of "gossip" and "tattletale," captures many of these meanings. In French, the term *commère* conveys similar sentiments. In German, *petze* describes the tattletale and is linked in adulthood with the verb *verraten,* or "to betray." Hindi, Mandarin Chinese, and most other languages contain similar words with similar connotations. And many languages have appropriated *tattletale* to describe the thief and unauthorized sharer of the private.

Elaborate linguistic practices preserve the private in traditional societies, regulating social relationships and helping establish closeness and distance. In addition, language reflects and preserves hierarchy, itself a structure that relies on distance. Changes in linguistic practices reflect and encourage shifts in broader social attitudes toward hierarchies and other types of social distance. The change in these attitudes and corollary shifts in the mechanisms regulating social interactions eventually impacts privacy as well. For example, the use of the formal *usted* began to decline in Mexico and then partially in other Spanish-speaking countries about thirty to forty years ago, while the use of the informal *tu* grew. Numerous factors caused this change. The enormous growth in the number of young, educated people in these countries grew, and like the young everywhere, the members of this group rejected hierarchy and embraced an egalitarian ethos.

As the twenty-first century advanced, *usted* largely disappeared, replaced with *tu* in virtually all social interactions. *Usted* provides a way to address strangers and recognize elders and social superiors, but above all it indicates mutual respect in all interactions. *Tu* was used between friends and particularly those who are equal; consequently, the rejection of *usted* involved a repudiation of hierarchy and the embrace of a more egalitarian ethos. However, the ritualized distances embedded in *usted* protect distance and privacy. *Tu* contains in and of itself the possibility and promise of sharing and revelation. *Usted*, in contrast, emphasizes "proper" distance, thus protecting privacy. One does not ask intrusive questions in *usted* relationships or speak in unguarded ways. These restraints do not exist in *tu* relationships.

The diminution of *usted* reduces a deeply established form of privacy protection. Closeness and distance become more confusing and difficult to regulate. "Inappropriate" questions become more commonplace, and traditional understandings of politeness and civility decline, creating uncomfortable social situations even as they indicate the rise of a less rigidly regulated society and the emergence of more egalitarian norms. *Usted* relationships did not require choices about when and what to reveal and when and what to withhold. Its abandonment forces people to negotiate a new social terrain that involves engaging in choices about when to preserve silence, discretion, and distance and when to "open up," complicating the regulation and protection of the private.

In many cultures silence, discretion, and reticence embody ideal typical constructions of masculinity and especially *machismo*. The "strong" man, through his silence, remains aloof to his surroundings. The strength of the *macho* derives from his hermeticism. This hermetic carapace enables the *macho* to remain closed off and hence invulnerable. Opening and sharing, the process of revealing the self to become intimate with another, involves the acceptance and embrace of vulnerability. The "open" is weak for these very reasons, while hermeticism reflects strength. The association of the open with weakness and vulnerability then suffuses understandings of gender and of gender roles.

In Mexico the traditional conception of femininity, known as *marianismo* because of its link to understandings of the Virgin Mary, celebrates stoicism as the highest virtue, seeing the capacity to endure suffering as strength.[11] A *macho* can never allow himself to *rajar* (crack), a term synonymous with cowardice. At all costs, the *macho* must preserve impenetrability to remain strong. Women can transcend the weakness of being "open," demonstrating their strength and character through the capacity to silently endure suffering. Octavio Paz, Mexico's great poet, social commentator, and Nobel laureate, argued that these traditional norms and behaviors create a profound, collective solitude despite being adaptive responses to a hostile, violent history that included marginalization, subjugation, and conquest. Both *machismo* and *marianismo* are mechanisms that enable people to distance and protect themselves from the outside world. These ideal typical constructions constitute extreme expressions of the centrality of privacy to the preservation of personhood. However, since they wall off the self from the outside world, they also produce profound isolation and solitude.

The person who can endure the greatest travails in silence, according to these ideal types, possesses much more inner strength than someone who complains or whines. The person who reveals their inner feelings and consequently their weakness makes others uncomfortable. The strength of the stoic resides in their ability to remain confined within their inner private world while preserving a mask of impassivity. This ability to conceal feelings indicates great self-control, standing in juxtaposition to the person whose lack of restraint makes them untrustworthy.[12]

All of this reveals the weight that different cultures and societies place on the individual's ability to shield the private from others. And it indicates the presence of deep reservations about those who are incapable of protecting their own privacy or who wish to intrude into the privacy of others. In short, societies across the world have traditionally valued the private, discrete person over the voluble.

While silence enables the construction of a barrier between the self and others, it contains other virtues as well. As many monastic orders show, contemplation requires silence. Silence constructs a space apart, where reflection and creativity can flourish. Silence tends to facilitate the exploration of the inner self. And it also constitutes a necessary precursor to intimacy. Intimacy requires the breaking of silence, since it is a place reserved for only a few. In other words, silence functions as an essential regulatory mechanism, establishing and preserving social distance, but can also foster closeness after the silence has been broken.

The power that individuals exercise over their private world cannot be separated from their ability to regulate silence. Further, individual sovereignty and agency cannot exist without this ability, and personal identity requires the separation of the self from others through silence. The digital age includes a systematic attack on the individual's ability to regulate their use of silence. Indeed, digital tools undermine silence itself. Mass surveillance in particular compromises the individual ability to regulate silence. The insatiable quest for more extensive and intimate private information seeks to make everybody voluble—whether they are speaking or not. In this regard, digital technologies are engaged in a fundamental war with a human capacity—the ability to not reveal—that constitutes an essential component of a sane existence and the regulation of social relationships.

Cultural differences exist too in understandings of the relationship of the shameful to the private. Some frame privacy as a fundamental right, while others see it as instrumental. In Chinese, for example, the word most used for privacy is *yinsi*, which translates as "shameful secret." *Yinsi*, to quote Cao Jingchun, "does not equate with the Western concept of privacy. . . . *Yin* means 'hide,' and *si* means 'private.' It is this word which is most often used in [Chinese] legislation and is most familiar to Chinese lawyers. It is translated into English as 'privacy,' 'personal secret,' or 'shameful secret.' However, it usually means something negative."[13] Tiffany Li elaborates on these ideas when she wrote,

> Instead of viewing privacy as a reflection of personal liberty. . . . Chinese culture has traditionally understood privacy as more of an instrumental good—valued for objectives like protecting a person from shame. . . . For example, consider the difference between Chinese and American reactions to facial-recognition surveillance. In the United States, facial-recognition technology has faced intense backlash. . . . In China, the facial-recognition industry is booming. . . . Chinese citizens may be more willing to accept facial-recognition technology as an instrumental tool to enforce social norms.[14]

Space around the body constitutes another domain of the private. Unwanted touches and excessive physical closeness violate privacy as much as do intrusions into the inner self. While social and cultural mores in different societies govern the privacy of the body, all cultures recognize some measure of physical territoriality. To cite Sissela Bok,

> [People] guard, first of all, against others coming too nearby, protecting what has come to be called personal space and territoriality. To be sure, the boundaries of this space are differently envisaged according to culture and personality and imagination; but . . . most individuals do conceive of certain near-physical boundaries enclosing their bodies, some of the space immediately surrounding them. . . . Some people also sense boundaries around their names, their thoughts, their inventions, and what they have created. . . . In many cultures,

even minimal control over physical access can be hard to come by in the midst of communal and family life. . . . Many ways are then devised to create privacy. Villagers may set up private abodes outside the village to which they go for days or even months.[15]

Moreover, across cultures people find ways to safeguard their privacy even when their living circumstances limit physical space. In these circumstances people will use other means to preserve distance. As Robert Murphy notes,

> social distance pervades all social relationships though it may be found in varying degrees in different relationships and in different societies. . . . Inasmuch as social conduct implies limitations upon range of expectable behavior and closures upon other relations and behavior, the actor must insulate large portions of his social existence. . . . [Privacy] and withdrawal of the social person is a quality of life in society. That he withholds himself while communicating and communicates through removal is not a contradiction in terms but a quality of all social interactions.[16]

The regulation of social relations through withholding and sharing crosses all cultures, although the extent of the withheld and the shared varies enormously. Murphy's research on the use of the veil among the Tuareg people led him to ask,

> Why do Tuareg males cover their faces so completely that only areas around the eyes and nose may be seen? Short answer: by doing so, they are symbolically introducing a form of distance between their selves and their social others. The veil, though providing neither isolation nor anonymity, bestows facelessness and the idiom of privacy upon its wearer and allows him to stand somewhat aloof from the perils of social interaction while remaining a part of it.[17]

Murphy went on to write, "The social distance set in some societies by joking and respect or avoidance behavior toward certain specific categories of relatives is accomplished here through the veil."[18] Extending Murphy's conclusions, Sissela Bok asserts that "human beings find the most ingenious ways to protect their privacy, even under conditions of near constant physical proximity to others. . . . Many cultures have developed strict rules of etiquette, along with means of dissimulation and hypocrisy that allow certain private matters to remain unknown or go unobserved."[19]

Moreover, social and interpersonal privacy intrusions can arise even in the absence of very close physical proximity. This occurs whenever a person can be heard or observed. Many cultures see the fixed gaze, the stare, as an assault and an intrusion on the self. Staring can transmit a spell, putting an "evil eye" on someone; a person thus afflicted will experience many ills and misfortunes. Amulets, spells, and other magics are used to ward off the evil eye and thus protect the self.

At the very least, staring is discourteous. Those who experience stares feel scrutinized and consequently violated and uncomfortable. Stares, for these same reasons, can be interpreted as aggressive acts. For example, staring at a man constitutes a challenge because of *machismo*. In Mexico a common response to a stare is "No me mires!" (Do not look at me!) or "Que me ves?" (What are you seeing in me?). The stare is both a violation and a diminution of the person being observed. For these reasons, stares are assertions of dominance and power.

The significance of the look, the stare, testifies to the importance of eyes. Though capable of penetrating others, the eyes can also reveal the self. And for this last reason, in many cultures eyes are seen as sources of vulnerability. As Robert Murphy observed, writing in 1964,

> In contemporary society . . . defense and withdrawal is often achieved by wearing dark glasses. Sunglasses and tinted glasses are almost badges of office among West African emirs and Near Eastern potentates, and they have also become items of prestige in other parts of the world. They are commonly used in Latin America, where, indoors and out, heavily tinted glasses are the hallmark of the prestigeful [sic] as well as those aspiring to status, for they bestow the aloofness and distance that has always been the prerogative of the high in these lands.[20]

Tinted glasses hide the eyes, preserving the wearer's invulnerability while expressing their power.

Children learn about the power of eyes, believing that "looks" can "see" into the inner self. When a parent tells a child to "look me in the eye" to uncover a lie, the child begins to fear that their eyes betray their thoughts. This sense is reinforced through clichés like "the eyes are the windows into the soul." From early childhood, people learn to manage their eyes. They understand when to look down, when to avert their gaze, and how long they can look at someone before coming off as rude or aggressive.

While looks and stares can be perceived as violative, so too can questions. For this reason, cultures typically define the appropriateness of questions. Strictures on certain types of questions reflect shared understandings of privacy. In some societies, for example, questions about somebody's profession, aspects of their family life, or their past are deemed inappropriate, particularly during early encounters between people. In contrast, other places may see such questions as natural. Questions routinely asked in one society may never be voiced or even considered in another. And questions seen as entirely normal in one society are deemed intolerably "nosy" in another.

Precisely because questions impact social relations, their regulation tries to preserve harmony and prevent discomfort or conflict. This regulation of questions reveals much about hierarchies as well. Particularly in very hierarchical societies, upper-class people enjoy a power to ask questions that others lack. Thus questions both reflect and reinforce inequality. And in all societies the power to ask questions creates informational inequality. Those who can ask questions and extract information are much more powerful than those who lack this capacity. And even in relatively egalitarian societies, unequal possession of information creates social discomfort. No one wishes to be an "open book" around others who remain closed. In fact, the asking of questions and the sharing of information requires reciprocity to avoid social discomfort and conflict.

The person who questions without restraint and who consequently tramples on the boundaries of others can be despised as much as the informant. This is especially true if their intrusions cannot be resisted because of their power. When this occurs, they become an inquisitor—a person reviled across history. The Spanish Inquisition, the Holy Vehm in Germany, the Securitate in Nicolae Ceauşescu's Romania, the Stasi in the GDR, and the interrogation practices of the CIA during the "war on terror" all reflect the inquisitor's capacity to engage in an assault on the individual.

Across the world, different groups receive distinct privacy protections. One of the greatest differentials reflects the gap in the treatment of male and female privacy. Across a host of societies, men routinely subject women to catcalls, wolf whistles, comments, looks, stares, vulgar questions, and even more intrusive acts. These actions are rarely punished, indicating tacit social toleration of the behavior. Men do not experience this commonplace and invasive assault on their privacy and on their physical territoriality. Women lose a central part of privacy: "the right to be let alone."[21]

Social, interpersonal privacy differs from juridical privacy, the latter understood primarily, although not exclusively, as protection from the state. To extend Max Weber's analysis, states do not just enjoy a monopoly over the legitimate use of violence within a territory, but they are the sole human institution that can require and coerce the surrender of personal information. Effectively, this means that states become repositories of personal information that people would never otherwise share with each other. People, as a result, are much more legible to the state than they are to each other. In face-to-face interactions in the contemporary world, somewhat paradoxically, social and cultural conventions that disguise the self from others persist even as the surrender of information to states and huge private corporations accelerates.

RATIONALIZATION FOR THE LOSS OF
PRIVACY IN THE DIGITAL AGE

Most people during the first two decades of the twenty-first century continued to indiscriminately upload their private information onto every platform and application that requested or required this data. This was especially true of behavior on social media platforms, especially Facebook, where people shared virtually everything, including the most intimate details of their lives.

Even those who claimed to value privacy participated in these behaviors, leading scholars to label this phenomenon. As Krueger, Best, and Johnson write,

> The surveillance and privacy literature often finds that individual preferences for valuing privacy fail to translate into actions protecting privacy. . . . This disconnect . . . is described as the "privacy paradox." . . . For example, despite expressing support for the value of privacy and concerns surrounding privacy violations, individuals still submit personal information online or on nonanonymous surveys.[22]

In developed countries and wherever people have the means to purchase devices connected to the Internet, they demonstrate an insatiable appetite for the "Internet of things." This network of devices includes "smart" televisions, refrigerators, cell phones, doorbells, thermostats, and many other products. Most dramatically, it includes pure surveillance devices, like Alexa, that are explicitly designed to listen to what is going on in the surrounding environment. These devices fill homes, recording everything. The ubiquity of the Internet of things normalizes the presence and use of these devices, leading people to place them in the most intimate spaces of their residences, including their bedrooms.

The poor security of many of these devices and their susceptibility to hacking has not slowed their acquisition and use. And smartphones are extensions of people's bodies, serving as perfect monitoring, tracking, and listening devices. They are always carried, even though outsiders can exploit their cameras, microphones, and GPS features to learn everything about one's movements and interactions in real time. People tend to put information about every feature of their lives on these phones, transforming them into increasingly complete repositories of the self. They continue to do this even after revelations that outsiders can hack, remove, and scrub this data. In the name of convenience and the powerful desire to possess the "newest and the best," people not only accept and tolerate but, in fact, embrace a world that surrounds them with surveillance cameras and microphones. In all these ways, they reaffirm the "privacy paradox."

However, even as people surrender their private information to companies and states, a number of rationalizations emerged to make the loss of private information less disturbing. While most do not evidence concern about this loss of privacy, the many who do adopt one or all these rationalizations. These rationalizations fall into several categories, each seeking to minimize the impacts of the loss of privacy.

THE I-HAVE-NOTHING-TO-HIDE RATIONALIZATION

As noted earlier, many assert that mass surveillance and the collection and mining of personal data do not matter to them because they have "nothing to hide." This claim involves a remarkable conclusion about the self. First, it fundamentally reflects the view that one's behaviors and beliefs are so conventional that they are unworthy of notice. Second, it involves the dubious belief, probably based on a form of bravado or deliberate amnesia, that nothing about one can cause shame and embarrassment if revealed. As Jennifer Granick notes, however, "If you sit and think for even a moment, you know that everyone has something to hide. We've said things about people we wouldn't want them to hear. We've made mistakes or done embarrassing things we wouldn't want our children, our coworkers, or our mothers to know about. We may have even done something illegal."[23]

Put simply, the I-Have-Nothing-to-Hide claim negates reality. As any lawyer knows, the extraordinarily dense set of rules in many countries covering every aspect of human existence ensures that everyone, whether knowingly or not, has broken a rule, technically becoming a criminal. These rules cover everything from acts against others to behaviors involving mutual consent to those that affect only the self.

The United States, to mention one example, criminalizes a vast number of behaviors. By the end of the second decade of the twenty-first century, one in four Americans possessed a criminal record, and many, many, many more would bear this same stain if not for dumb luck or socioeconomic status and race. Extraordinarily unequal law enforcement anchored in racism and the tendency to neglect the arrest and prosecution of those with resources were the only reasons why American rates of incarceration were not even higher. What does mass surveillance mean in a country that prosecutes and jails more of its people and subjects them to longer sentences than any other developed country in the world? Indeed, as every American should know, the United States, with only 5 percent of the world's population, contained 25 percent of the human beings experiencing incarceration during the early decades of the twenty-first century.[24]

To quote Jennifer Granick again,

something closer to 100 percent of Americans have committed crimes other than mere driving infractions. We just haven't been caught. Most Americans participate in activities that are illegal: marijuana use, computer misuse, petty theft, eavesdropping, obstruction of justice, wire fraud. . . . Some criminal laws are so broad you could argue that almost anything is a transgression. US criminal laws can apply to common behaviors like smoking marijuana and loitering, which gives police and other government actors power over millions of individuals. Some laws are so vague that the line between innocent behavior and criminal conduct is unclear. And then there are the regulatory offenses that are so arcane you might be forgiven for not knowing that what you were doing was wrong. For example, it's a federal crime to possess a lobster under a certain size. When there are so many ways that the average person can transgress, prosecutors pick and choose whom to go after.[25]

In short, everyone has something to hide, even if it is just a peccadillo or something embarrassing. And no one's past is entirely blameless, void of mistakes, fraught decisions, regrets, and missteps. Everyone has been indiscrete or intemperate and said things in private that do not bear repetition in public. Unfortunately, as I have noted, the collected never disappears, enabling the weaponization of this information by anyone with access who wishes to inflict harm. The I-Have-Nothing-to-Hide claim often marches hand in hand with a second set of beliefs designed to assuage concerns about the surrender and appropriation of personal information. This rationale is best labeled the I-Am-Irrelevant claim.

THE I-AM-IRRELEVANT RATIONALIZATION

Feelings of personal inconsequence anchor the justification that even if the state appropriates one's information, and even if one is swept up in surveillance because of the use of extraordinarily broad selectors (queries of data), it does not matter; the irrelevance of one's data ensures that it will be ignored. This comfort comes from the difficulty of discerning the scope of selectors, given the secrecy enshrouding them, or on the lack of understanding of the precise nature of metadata mining. The rationalization also stems from the belief that the state will not expend resources looking at those who are "irrelevant," "ordinary," "law-abiding" citizens.

While nobody, except for those inclined to self-deception, can pretend to have never broken a rule or behaved with perfect discretion, the vast majority can legitimately claim to be ordinary and irrelevant, even though engaging in perfectly legal acts can transform this status. For example, participating in political protests and demonstrations that are both nonviolent and legal can still make one a target of drone and plane surveillance, ending "irrelevance."

This occurred, for example, during protests around the United States following the Minneapolis Police Department's murder of George Floyd in May 2020. Among other things, the government used facial-recognition technology connected to CCTV cameras to identify individual participants in these protests. And in a stunning display of the implications this technology has for privacy, the mayor of Saint Louis named protesters on television and provided their addresses. Irrelevance, thus, depends on one's willingness to remain politically inert.

In addition, this rationale assumes that a relatively high degree of precision and discernment, designed to distinguish the irrelevant from the relevant, informs the targeting of state surveillance. However, as Jennifer Granick wrote in 2017,

> Today that calculation—that I will only be investigated if there is a good cause to do so—is naïve. It's naïve because modern spying tools have dramatically reduced the cost and trouble associated with investigating someone. . . . No one has to bother to listen to your calls or read your emails. Instead, machines automatically analyze or search the data, highlighting just the interesting stuff for analysts to read. This is already easy for computers to do with text. It's getting increasingly easy to do with phone calls as voice-recognition software improves. Face- and image-recognition software is also getting very accurate. It will become trivial, for example, for computers to search a trove of images and find all of the people holding a joint or underage minors holding a can of beer.[26]

The frequently voiced claim that one is "a needle in a haystack" reflects similar feelings of irrelevance. The state's appropriation of everybody's information, according to this view, results in a mountain of data that transforms each person's private information into a speck of sand in the Sahara. Those who harbor this perspective ironically think that the erosion of everybody's privacy re-creates a measure of privacy protection derived from the anonymity that comes from being a drop in the ocean.

The final and most paradoxical rationalization is the claim that the discovery of everybody's mistakes, peccadillos, and morally and legally dubious acts make all these transgressions increasingly inconsequential. Growing public indifference to revelations detailing both the private and public misdeeds of public figures, including celebrities, provides the central proof for this argument. This indifference to torrents of revelations about public figures seems to render the collection and release of personal information increasingly irrelevant. This argument became more widespread after Donald Trump's presidential election, despite continuing revelations about his extraordinarily checkered past and participation in activities historically seen as socially, morally, and legally reprehensible. For this reason, I call this the Trump rationalization.

THE TRUMP RATIONALIZATION

Continuing revelations about Donald Trump's marital affairs, infidelities, acts of sexual harassment, and repeated lies and fabrications, along with the exposure of many of his other behaviors during his campaign for the US presidency, did not significantly impede his rise to power. Previously revelations of any of these things would have destroyed a presidential candidate. For example, in 1987 Gary Hart's campaign for the White House was destroyed by revelations that he had cheated on his wife. And less than a decade before Trump's rise, John Edwards's own campaign and his political career came to an end after revelations about his infidelity and his fathering of a child with his mistress. But in 2016 and subsequently, huge numbers of Americans shrugged off Donald Trump's behavior, seeing it instead as evidence of his "authenticity." And celebrities and others transcended the release of information that in an earlier era would have made them pariahs and ended their careers—although the #MeToo movement and modern "callout" culture constitute an important counterexample, leading to the sanctioning of previously tolerated behavior.

Despite these last exceptions, it is true that many revelations of personal failings do not occasion the same reaction that they produced in the past. The Trump rationalization rests on the belief that sins, peccadillos, and various failures of judgment are minimized due to a sort of numbing effect that results from sheer volume of revelations, often themselves the result of a prima facie privacy violation—such as when compromising photos are posted on the Internet.

On the other hand, as the #MeToo movement reveals, it is almost certainly a mistake to draw blanket conclusions about shifting social mores during the digital age. While some things no longer occasion the opprobrium they aroused in the past, public sanction condemns other things, often revolving around behaviors related to gender and race that were previously tolerated. In short, the revelation of something private in one area that might have led to ruin in the past, such as one's sexual orientation, might in the present occasion nothing more than a shrug, while evidence of depredations against women that would have gone undiscussed and unrevealed have become the object of revelation and punishment.

PUBLIC DEFENDERS OF MASS SURVEILLANCE

While many in the US government tacitly support mass surveillance and facilitated its expansion, most do not ventilate these views in public. The few public voices willing to publicly acknowledge, defend, and advocate mass surveillance consequently deserve particular mention. The most well-known member of the group is Judge Richard Posner, a legal scholar and judge on the Court of Appeals for the Seventh Circuit in Chicago.

Beyond defending mass warrantless surveillance, Judge Posner is an equivalently prolific critic of efforts to further entrench privacy protections and apply them more effectively during the digital age. For example, after independent NSA contractor Edward Snowden's 2013 revelation that the agency was engaged in the mass warrantless surveillance of Americans, Posner said, "If the NSA wants to vacuum all of the trillions of bits of information that are crawling through the electronic worldwide networks, I think that's fine."[27]

Judge Posner asserted as well that "much of what passes for privacy is really just trying to conceal the disreputable parts of your conduct. . . . If someone drained my cell phone, they would find a picture of my cat, some phone numbers, some email addresses, some email text. . . . What's the big deal? Other people must have really exciting stuff. Do they narrate their adulteries or something like that?"[28]

These last statements capture the claims of those who believe they have nothing to hide because their online activities are ordinary, innocuous, inconsequential, and perfectly conventional. And of course Judge Posner mentioned his cat, since nothing makes a person seem more innocuous and conventional than the ownership of a household pet. Judge Posner did not note that the elements shielding him from scrutiny had little to do with the conventionality of his online behavior. Instead, he is primarily shielded because of his race, background, education, profession, and wealth. In addition, his position as a defender of the status quo and of the social and political order makes him unlikely to be one of the watched. Judge Posner has never been a dissident or questioned the social order in ways that eliminated the "invisibility" conferred by conventionality and acceptance of the extant political reality.

Judge Posner reflects the views of those who are prone to elevate security over privacy. This group typically includes the national security establishment and the supporters of its weltanschauung across the polity. Adam Moore divides the arguments about why privacy should always yield to security into "just trust us" claims: the "you have nothing to worry about if you have nothing to hide" assertions, the bald "security trumps privacy" argument, and the claim that citizens have "consented" to these privacy intrusions.[29] Not surprisingly, these arguments in favor of mass surveillance reflect the most common rationalizations about the loss of privacy in the digital age.

CONCLUSION

From the outset, the digital age produced many benefits and made many parts of life easier and more convenient. But this new epoch in the history of human and social development included some extraordinarily problematic features as well. States for the first time gained the capacity to engage in the mass surveillance of entire populations and availed themselves of all of these tools, vastly expanding their power and ability to "see" the society and intrude into the inner world of individuals. As a result, this development assaulted privacy in unprecedented ways.

Different cultures across the world possess elaborate mechanisms to protect privacy, indicating its importance to social existence. While these protections often safeguard hierarchy and can reduce accountability, as will be discussed in the next chapter, they also play a central role in constructing a space where individuals can separate themselves from others. In their absence, vulnerability grows. As a result, the loss of privacy, although possibly making the powerful more accountable and less capable of hiding egregious behaviors, increases the vulnerability of those who already lack power and agency. It is a measure of the disquiet that the wholesale loss of privacy occasions that several rationalizations designed to disguise and minimize the magnitude of this loss have arisen during the digital age.

NOTES

1. Milan Kundera, *The Unbearable Lightness of Being* (New York: Harper and Row, 1984), 261.
2. Yuval Noah Harari, "Yuval Noah Harari: The World after Coronavirus," *Financial Times*, March 19, 2020, https://www.ft.com/content/19d90308-6858-11ea-a3c9 -1fe6fedcca75.
3. Sissela Bok, *Secrets: On the Ethics of Concealment and Revelation* (New York: Vintage Books, 1989), 8.
4. Bok, *Secrets*, 10–11.
5. Doctorow as quoted in Richard Esguerra, "Google CEO Eric Schmidt Dismisses the Importance of Privacy," Electronic Frontier Foundation, EFF.org, December 10, 2009, https://www.eff.org/deeplinks/2009/12/google-ceo-eric-schmidt-dismisses -privacy.
6. Esguerra, "Google CEO Eric Schmidt."

7. McNealy as quoted in Polly Sprenger, "Sun on Privacy: 'Get Over It,'" *Wired*, January 1999, https://www.wired.com/1999/01/sun-on-privacy-get-over-it/.

8. Schneier as quoted in Esguerra "Google CEO Eric Schmidt."

9. Erving Goffman, *Asylums: Essays on the Social Situation of Mental Patients and Other Inmates* (New York: Doubleday, 1968), 23.

10. Bok, *Secrets*, 41.

11. For a brilliant discussion of this topic and especially of *machismo* and *marianismo*—the conception of women embedded in these understandings—see Octavio Paz, *The Labyrinth of Solitude and Other Writings*, trans. Lysander Kemp, Yara Milos, and Rachel Phillips Belash (New York: Grove Press, 1985).

12. Paz, *Labyrinth of Solitude*.

13. Cao Jingchun, "Protecting the Right to Privacy in China," *Victoria University of Wellington Law Review* 36, no. 3 (2005): 646, https://ojs.victoria.ac.nz/vuwlr/article/view/5610/4977.

14. Tiffany Li, "China's Influence on Digital Privacy Could Be Global," World Post Opinion, *Washington Post*, August 7, 2018, https://www.washingtonpost.com/news/theworldpost/wp/2018/08/07/china-privacy/.

15. Bok, *Secrets*, 11–12.

16. Robert Murphy "Social Distance and the Veil," *American Anthropologist* 66, no. 6 (December 1964): 1271, https://anthrosource.onlinelibrary.wiley.com/doi/epdf/10.1525/aa.1964.66.6.02a00020.

17. Murphy, "Social Distance," 1257, as quoted in Leila Silvana May, *Secrecy and Disclosure in Victorian Fiction* (New York: Routledge, 2017), 156, accessed online at https://books.google.com/books?id=HoyuDAAAQBAJ&pg=PA156&lpg=PA156&dq=%22do+Tuareg+males+cover+their+faces+so+completely+that+only+areas+around+the+eyes+and+nose+may+be+seen%22&source=bl&ots=HkTx8u3nCz&sig=ACfU3U1pUSvs1yF3d64wMBm3ZcqpJOf3Jg&hl=en&sa=X&ved=2ahUKEwj7qOOQn9vvAhUXCc0KHSuwDvIQ6AEwAHoECAMQAw#v=onepage&q&f=false.

18. Murphy, "Social Distance and the Veil," 1270.

19. Bok, *Secrets*, 12.

20. Murphy, "Social Distance and the Veil," 1272.

21. Samuel D. Warren and Louis D. Brandeis, "The Right to Privacy," *Harvard Law Review* 6, no. 5 (December 15, 1890): 193–220, archived at https://archive.org/details/jstor-1321160/page/n1/mode/2up.

22. Brian S. Krueger, Samuel J. Best, and Kristin Johnson, "Assessing Dimensions of the Security-Liberty Trade-Off in the United States," *Surveillance and Society* 18, no. 1 (2020): 114, https://ojs.library.queensu.ca/index.php/surveillance-and-society/article/view/10419/9159.

23. Jennifer Stisa Granick, *American Spies: Modern Surveillance, Why You Should Care, and What to Do about It* (Cambridge: Cambridge University Press, 2017), 128.

24. Michelle Ye Hee Lee, "Does the United States Really Have 5 Percent of the World's Population and One Quarter of the World's Prisoners?" Fact Checker, *Washington Post*, April 30, 2015, https://www.washingtonpost.com/news/fact-checker/wp/2015/04/30/does-the-united-states-really-have-five-percent-of-worlds-population-and-one-quarter-of-the-worlds-prisoners/.

25. Granick, *American Spies*, 129.

26. Granick, *American Spies*, 129.

27. Posner as quoted in Glenn Greenwald "What Bad, Shameful, Dirty Behavior is Judge Richard Posner Hiding? Demand to Know," *The Intercept*, December 8, 2014, https://theintercept.com/2014/12/08/bad-shameful-dirty-secrets-u-s-judge-richard -posner-hiding-demand-know/.

28. Greenwald "Bad, Shameful, Dirty Behavior."

29. Adam D. Moore, "Why Privacy and Accountability Trump Security," *Privacy, Security and Accountability: Ethics, Law and Policy*, ed. Adam Moore, chap. 9 (London: Rowman & Littlefield International, 2016), 171–82.

Chapter 3

Philosophical Debates about Privacy

Philosophers have produced the most profound exploration of privacy. This is especially true of liberal philosophers. The focus on the individual and on limited government in this tradition promotes the exploration of privacy while tying it frequently to individual power and dignity. The liberal tradition's emphasis on limiting the power of the world's most overwhelming institution, the government, in order to foster the flowering of individual freedom naturally made it turn to the examination of privacy.

However, the discussion of the private and of its centrality to human existence did not begin with liberal thinkers. Initial conceptions of privacy emerge in Aristotle's separation of the *polis*, the public sphere, from the *oikos*, the personal, family domain. This classical distinction separating the public world from the home that Aristotle, Confucius, and a number of other philosophers explore, does not address the central modern conception of the private—the world of the inner self. This conception flows naturally from the liberal tradition's understanding of the individual. In contrast, the older private/public distinction limits its identification of the private to the part of human life occurring within the home and the family. However, the recognition of a private sphere separate from the public world became fundamental to future understandings about the proper limit and scope of state power and the existence of a space protected from external intrusions. As Daniel Solove observes, "People have cared about privacy since antiquity. The Code of Hammurabi protected the home against intrusion, as did ancient Roman law. The early Hebrews had laws safeguarding against surveillance. And in England the oft-declared principle that the home is one's castle dates to the late fifteenth century. . . . [And] eavesdropping was long protected against in English common law."[1]

But the modern conception of privacy requires the liberal understanding that individuals possess fundamental rights. This naturally led to explorations of other essential components of individual personhood that needed to be protected from society and the polity. Individual privacy—understood as comprising the world of the inner and outer self and extending to such matters as the ability to control personal information—also came to be seen, although not without controversy, as being an essential part of personhood that required protection. And understandings about the distinction between the private and public spheres continues to influence views of the difference between private and public acts and behaviors. This includes all the norms and regulations informing differences between home and work, between the house and the street, and between public and private professions.

The liberal arguments influencing modern discussions of privacy effectively begin with John Locke. His discussion in *The Second Treatise on Government* of the natural right to property fostered the eventual understanding of individual privacy as a form of private property flowing from the ownership of one's body.[2] But John Stuart Mill probably did more than anyone else to create the modern understanding of privacy. In a famous passage in *On Liberty* he wrote that "the only purpose for which power can be rightly exercised over any member of a civilized community, against his will, is to prevent harm to others. His own good, either physical or moral, is not a sufficient warrant."[3] This argument about the difference between the self-regarding and the other-regarding joined to Mills's corollary rejection of tutelary laws (laws that advance "proper" moral and physical conduct in areas that do not damage others) established the foundation for the liberal assertion that public authorities could not violate individual privacy except to prevent harm to others.

In marked contrast to the liberals, the communitarians throughout the eighteenth and the middle of the nineteenth centuries rejected the modern understanding of privacy. Notable communitarians included the followers of Robert Owen and groups like the Oneida Community. In their quest for solidarity and harmony, these groups opposed behaviors commonly understood as private or exclusive acts, seeing them as mere expressions of the selfish and the self-interested.

However, Hegel provided the most powerful rejection of claims about the importance of individual privacy. As Glenn Negley notes,

> Hegel's definition of *moralitat*, as referring to individual private judgment, and *sittlichkeit*, the definition of obligation in terms of duties defined by the corporate, institutional order, is, of course, the classic example of political philosophy which argues that the claim of privacy is simply an exhibition of caprice, triviality, and irresponsibility. . . . Such a view allows little controversy in respect to the right to privacy, since the rights and duties of individuals are determined by

the existing corporate orders in which he participates, the highest form of which is the state.[4]

In the late 1950s and early 1960s, philosophers and other scholars began defining the right to privacy more expansively. As Ferdinand Schoeman observes, "Despite the fact that privacy has been identified by contemporary philosophers as a key aspect of human dignity, or alternatively as something even more basic than rights to property or than rights over one's person, there was no major philosophical discussion of the value of privacy until the 1960s." Schoeman then taxonomizes the philosophical literature on privacy into three categories: "attempts to define privacy, discussions that emphasize the centrality of privacy to morality, and essays that are morally skeptical about the value of privacy."[5]

An early example of this scholarship is the work of Clinton Rossiter, who in 1958 wrote that

> privacy is a special kind of independence which can be understood as an attempt to secure autonomy in at least a few personal and spiritual concerns, if necessary in defiance of all of the pressures of modern society. . . . It seeks to erect an unbreachable wall of dignity and reserve against the entire world. The free man is the private man, the man who still keeps some of his thoughts and judgments to himself, who feels no overriding compulsion to share everything of value with others, not even those he loves and trusts.[6]

In 1964 Edward J. Bloustein extended Rossiter's connection of privacy to human dignity.[7] He wrote, "A man whose conversations may be overheard at the will of another, whose home may be entered at the will of another, whose marital and familial intimacies may be overseen at the will of another, is less of a man, has less human dignity, on that account. He who may intrude upon another at will is the master of the other."[8]

For his part, Glenn Negley asserted in 1966 that

> the nature of the political and legal decisions required, such as the assessment of homosexual behavior, of the extent of the right to counsel, or of privacy invasion by electronic means, is a sharp demonstration that the most pressing demand upon our philosophy is for a consideration of the moral and political obligations, duties, and rights within a corporate social order that evidences none of the characteristics of a relatively simple, decentralized, face-to-face society. . . . If privacy is defined as an essential requirement for the achievement of morality, then privacy is a right that the law must protect and provide.[9]

The rise of surveillance in the 1960s in the climate of the Cold War and the presence of widespread protest and dissent explains a significant portion of the discussion on privacy since then. More and more, these discussions revolved around the topic of informational privacy, since it was this part of privacy that confronted growing assaults. In 1967 Alan Westin asserted the argument for informational privacy, writing that it is "the claim of individuals, groups, or institutions to determine for themselves when, how, and to what extent information about them is communicated to others." He also saw four "basic states of individual privacy: solitude, intimacy, anonymity, and reserve." He defined *reserve* as "the creation of a psychological barrier against intrusion."[10]

A number of scholars during the subsequent decade added to the understanding of privacy and of its centrality to human existence. For example, writing in 1970 Charles Fried associated privacy with control over information about the self. In common with many other scholars, he argued intimacy cannot occur without privacy, as "intimacy is the sharing of information about one's actions, beliefs and emotions which one does not share with all, and which one has the right not to share with anyone. By conferring this right, privacy creates the moral capital which we spend in friendship and love."[11] Indeed, without privacy, intimacy is difficult to imagine. The mutual trust embedded in intimate relationships requires the preservation of a cocoon of privacy. Within this cocoon, confidences can be shared and people can reveal themselves, becoming vulnerable. The shattering of this cocoon destroys trust and, with it, intimacy.

James Rachels also emphasized the central role that privacy plays in the regulation of social relations. "If we cannot control who has access to us, sometimes including and sometimes excluding people," he wrote in 1975, "then we cannot control the patterns of behavior we need to adopt . . . or the kinds of relations with other people that we will have." In particular, he discussed the centrality of privacy to friendship: "The relation of friendship, for example, involves bonds of affection and special obligation, such as the duty of loyalty, which friends owe to one another; but it is also an important part of what it means to have a friend that we welcome his company, that we confide in him, that we tell him things about ourselves, and that we show him sides of our personalities which we would not tell or show to just anyone."[12]

Stanley Benn also linked privacy to mutual human dignity and respect, writing in 1971 that "to respect someone as a person is to concede that one ought to take account of the way in which his enterprise might be affected by one's own decisions. By the principle of respect for persons, then, I mean the principle that every human being . . . is entitled to this minimal degree of consideration."[13]

The concerns about informational privacy, evident since the 1960s, accelerated in the 1990s as digital technologies expanded. In 1995, William Parent wrote that privacy was:

the condition of a person's having undocumented personal information about herself not known to others. Undocumented information consists of all facts about someone that are not part of the public record and, as such, available for public inspection. "Personal information" designates facts either that most people in a given situation choose not to reveal about themselves (except to close friends, family, counselors, etc.) or about which a particular person is especially sensitive and which therefore he does not choose to reveal about himself (expect to close friends, family, etc.).[14]

This same concern with digital intrusions marks Jerry Kang's understanding of privacy. His definition perhaps best captures the necessary boundaries of the private in the digital age. Privacy, he writes, involves "the extent to which an individual's territorial solitude is shielded from invasion by unwanted objects or signals," "an individual's ability to make certain significant decisions without interference," and "an individual's control over the processing—i.e., the acquisition, disclosure, and use—of personal information."[15]

As the digital age continues to unfold, scholars return to these themes while reiterating older arguments about the categoric centrality of privacy to the preservation of human dignity. For example, Luciano Floridi writes that "the protection of privacy should be based directly on the protection of human dignity, not indirectly, through other rights such as that to property or to freedom of expression. . . . [The] protection of privacy [is] protection of personal identity: 'my' in 'my data' is not the same 'my' as in 'my car'[;] it is the same as 'my' as in 'my hand,' because personal information plays a constitutive role of who I am and can become."[16]

Adam Moore's work reflects a particularly profound understanding of the impact on privacy of the evolving and multiplying intrusions embedded in the digital age. To quote him,

> Privacy protects us from the prying eyes and ears of governments, corporations, and neighbors . . . [Privacy] rights stand as a bulwark against governmental oppression and totalitarian regimes. . . . Arguably, any plausible account of human well-being or flourishing will have a strong right to privacy as a component. Controlling who has access to ourselves is an essential part of being a happy and free person. This may be why "peeping Toms" and rapists are held up as moral monsters—they cross a boundary that should never be crossed without consent.[17]

In a subsequent work written with Michael Katell that reflects the evolution of digital intrusions during the decade spanning 2005 and 2016, Moore elaborates on this prior definition of privacy while discussing requirements for its defense. Katell and Moore write that

> We favor what has been called a "control" based definition of privacy. A right to privacy is a right to control access to, and uses of, places, bodies, and personal information. . . . Privacy also includes a right to choose, within limits, the scope of control over information. Sharing information with others does not necessarily render it public and no longer subject to any privacy rights. . . . If access is granted accidentally or otherwise, it does not follow that any subsequent use, manipulation, or sale of the good is justified.[18]

These definitions of privacy highlight the critical importance of consent. Consent, because it is an essential part of personal power and agency, cannot be separated from the protection of privacy. Consent is the only thing that can transform a privacy intrusion and violation into an acceptable act. Privacy disappears in the absence of consent. Without consent, any act affecting the self is an a priori privacy violation, although such violations can range from the minor to the extensive. The power to consent and to withdraw consent constitutes a key component of individual power and of the ability to preserve the private.

Both consent and privacy serve as brakes on power, imposition, and force. They are grounded in an understanding of reciprocity and mutual respect. The respect for privacy and the insistence on consent reflect a recognition of equal rights and common humanity and the understanding that these things guarantee mutual well-being. The differential ability to exercise consent constitutes one of the most problematic features of unequal power relationships. Because of the intimate relationship between privacy and control, the inability to fully consent leads to the loss of a central component of human dignity—agency over the self. This is why those who strip away or manipulate consent commit moral abominations; they violate a fundamental right lodged in every human being: the right to have control over the self. No one, and certainly not states or private corporations, has the right to inflict these harms on human dignity.

These harms arise repeatedly from the actions of many digital corporations. Deliberate obfuscation about their operations constitutes the core of these harms. But these manipulations of consent pale in comparison with the behavior of governments that engage in mass surveillance and other indiscriminate violations of privacy. States cite raison d'état, the imperatives of national security, and the need for secrecy in their avoidance of securing consent. In republics, elected representatives should, in theory, express the public's consent to these measures. However, given the power of national security understandings, elected representatives in these polities often provide ritualized and contentless consent, serving instead as rubber-stamp bodies. The modest oversight that legislatures provide in many countries makes their activities in this area little more than a veneer, since legislators are typically unwilling to question the protectors of national security. In fact, the debility of such oversight in many democratic countries makes these legislatures seem more like servants than masters of their respective intelligence and national security apparatuses.

ARGUMENTS ABOUT PRIVACY'S SUBSIDIARITY TO OTHER RIGHTS AND INTERESTS

The contemporary philosophical argument against the existence of a fundamental right to privacy originally came from Judith Jarvis Thomson, who argued that it is a "derivative" or "composite" right. For Thomson, interferences with or violations of privacy subvert fundamental rights to physical security and property.[19] Julie Inness contests Judith Jarvis Thomson's arguments about privacy, asserting that

> I believe that [Thomson's] claim stumbles on two points. First, assuming that the right to privacy consists of such a composite, there remains the question of which shared feature identifies these rights; a shared feature would reveal that privacy claims are at least conceptually separable from property or personhood claims as a whole. . . . My second point is that the value we accord to privacy does not derive necessarily from the value we accord other rights. Hence Thomson fails to establish that talk about privacy can be reduced to talk about the nature and value of other concepts without conceptual or moral loss.

Julie Inness then moves beyond critiquing Thomson to establish the fundamental importance of privacy to intimacy and to autonomy, writing, "intimacy claims are claims about the motivations of persons, not the nature of actions, and since they embody the personal point of view, claims to control intimate decisions—that is, privacy claims—are claims to possess autonomy with respect to the expression of love, liking, and care."[20]

Ruth Gaviscon rejects what she calls Thomson's "reductionism," as well. She wrote,

> I begin by suggesting that privacy is indeed a distinct and coherent concept. Our interest in privacy, I argue, is related to our concern over our accessibility to others: the extent to which others have physical access to us, and the extent to which we are subjects of others' attention. This concept of privacy as a concern for limited accessibility enables us to identify when losses of privacy occur. Furthermore, the reasons for which we claim privacy in different situations are similar. They are related to the functions privacy has in our lives: the promotion of liberty, autonomy, selfhood, and human relations, and furthering the existence of a free society.[21]

Gaviscon's definition of privacy refutes claims that other "more fundamental" rights can encompass it or that its breadth and diversity render it formless and incoherent. In other words, the debate between Thomson and her critics revolves around whether other rights subsume privacy or privacy claims conflate disparate issues. Ferdinand Schoeman describes this debate, which informs a significant part of the literature on privacy, in the following way:

> What emerges in the continuing debate over privacy are two questions about the reducibility of privacy to other interests or rights. First, does an analysis of privacy in terms of a variety of interests rather randomly associated do justice to our conception of privacy? . . . Second, does an analysis of privacy in terms of other interests point to anything distinctive about privacy, in contrast to other values we find it important to protect? . . . [Authors] can and have argued that the interests protected under the rubric of privacy are important but not distinctive; such authors think that privacy represents just one way of pointing to interests or values already recognized as significant under different labels.[22]

An even more critical view of privacy than Thomson's comes from a strand of feminist scholarship. Most famously, Anita Allen juxtaposes claims to privacy with the need for accountability. She argues that,

> Accountability for private life is pervasive, wide-ranging, and essential. Individuals are accountable for their private lives to the extent that they are obligated or impelled, whether by internal or external norms, to perform acts of reckoning with respect to nominally personal matters. . . . In our society, moral, ethical, legal, and other imperatives require that individuals not only reckon or account in the senses of (1) reporting, (2) explaining, and (3) justifying acts and omissions but also that they (4) submit to sanctions and (5) maintain reliable patterns of behavior.[23]

The #MeToo movement perfectly encapsulates the argument that accountability trumps privacy claims. Writing roughly a decade and a half before the Harvey Weinstein case would come to trial, Anita Allen asserted that

> Accountability for private life has become a salient feature of contemporary American culture. The New Accountability is bold, democratic, and superpowered by technology. . . . The New Accountability reflects overdue public response to the social consequences of harmful conduct in nominally private spheres of sex, family, and health. After 1980, concerns about rampant domestic violence, sex crimes, and gender inequality intensified accountability demands.[24]

In a summary of the feminist critique of privacy claims, Judith DeCew writes, yet it can be said in general that many feminists worry about the darker side of privacy and the use of privacy as a shield to cover up domination, degradation, and abuse of women and others. Many tend to focus on the private as opposed to the public rather than merely informational or constitutional privacy. If distinguishing public and private realms leaves the private domain free from any scrutiny, then these feminists . . . are correct that privacy can be dangerous for women when it is used to cover up repression and physical harm to them by perpetuating the subjugation of women in the domestic sphere and encouraging nonintervention by the state.[25]

Nondisclosure agreements perfectly embody these feminist critiques, revealing the most problematic features of categoric privacy claims. NDAs, when designed to prevent accountability for bad behavior, constitute a clear abuse of arguments for privacy protection. While these feminist critiques about the problematic relationship between privacy and accountability are irrefutable, they do not explore the consequences to intimacy, human dignity. and autonomy of a world that requires everyone to be effectively translucent. Most importantly, while they appropriately explore the worst side of privacy claims, they avoid confronting the worst features of the extreme transparency resulting from the reification of accountability.

Privacy practices like NDAs can hide odious behaviors that damage others. But the wholesale pursuit of accountability can inflict terrible harms as well, exposing people to the needless and potentially deadly release of private information. Just as the reification of privacy reflected in the abuse of NDAs creates a multiplicity of problems, so too does the pursuit of complete transparency. The practices of Julian Assange and Wikileaks embody this extreme understanding of transparency. Their insistence on making everything transparent in the name of creating true accountability inevitably produced extraordinary harms, most famously when one of their information dumps revealed previously private details about the rape of a girl in Saudi Arabia. Given the nature of Saudi society, Wikileaks's failure to adequately consider the harm to this girl and to her family of this disclosure constitutes an intolerable violation of the privacy rights embedded in her personhood. As this example reveals, although a perfectly transparent world might make the powerful more accountable, it inevitably makes the powerless translucent at the same time, increasing their vulnerability.

A different criticism of privacy assertions comes from those who see them as secondary to the imperatives of security. For example, Kenneth Einar Himma argues that "[the] right to informational privacy relative to our interests in security . . . must yield to these interests in the case of direct conflict. . . . [Utilitarian] and contractarian justifications of state authority entail that when privacy conflicts with the most important security interests, those security interests trump the privacy interests." All of this leads him to conclude that "since privacy interests lack significance in the absence of adequate protection of security interests, it seems reasonable to infer that security interests deserve, as a moral matter, more stringent protection than privacy interests."[26]

The complication with this argument rests in the difficulty of establishing utilitarian necessity. First, those advancing this claim must, yet often don't, establish that the depth of the threat to security merits the abrogation of a right. Fear, moreover, typically prevents a dispassionate analysis of the magnitude of threats while making people more inclined to surrender rights.[27] States, in addition, possess strong inclinations to inflate threats, since fear enhances their power and enables them to extract more resources from the society. Politicians often face significant costs if they potentially underestimate a danger to security but benefit from threat amplification, since it often leads to outpourings of popular support, sustained by patriotic fervor.

Ruling elites frequently assert that they need to adopt sweeping measures and powers to meet the existential security threats lurking everywhere while claiming that these same threats require the preservation of the strictest secrecy, preventing them from providing information about these activities. For example, the US government adopted mass surveillance without a public discussion (and even lied repeatedly about its use of this practice), even though this surveillance diminished privacy, a fundamental right, while knowingly subjecting many innocent people to warrantless searches in contravention of the Fourth Amendment. To add insult to injury, there is little evidence that mass surveillance has played a central role in uncovering terrorist plots, although it undermined a human right.[28]

CONCLUSION

The central argument dividing liberal philosophers during the last part of the twentieth century revolved around whether privacy was a primary right or a "derivative," flowing from a broader right to property. In the main, however, philosophers reject this second claim and assert that privacy is primary because it is essential to human dignity. As these philosophers note, privacy lies at the heart of identity, intimacy, friendship, and the ability to have agency over one's life. The ability to lead the good life rests on the preservation of human dignity, and this dignity in turn depends upon the capacity to protect the self.

Since the 1960s, but especially after the 1990s, a growing body of philosophical thought has focused on informational privacy, given the multiplication of intrusions into this sphere. The digital age's appropriation and commodification of personal information produces a historically unprecedented, systematic, and ubiquitous assault on the self. Concerns about the implications of this assault for human dignity have animated philosophical inquiries into this subject throughout the first decades of the twenty-first century.

During this period, and in opposition to much of the scholarship establishing the human right to privacy, feminist philosophers powerfully juxtaposed it with accountability, highlighting the profound, indeed intrinsic, conflict between these two goods. Much like the intrinsic tension between liberty and security, the tension between privacy and accountability reveals the importance of balance. At the extreme, all these goods produce personal, social, political, and other ills, while balancing them requires enormous nuance and art.

NOTES

1. Daniel J. Solove, *Nothing to Hide: The False Tradeoff between Privacy and Security* (New Haven: Yale University Press, 2011), 4.

2. Locke's *Second Treatise* was first published in John Locke, *Two Treatises of Government: In the Former, The False Principles, and Foundation of Sir Robert Filmer, and His Followers, Are Detected and Overthrown. The Latter Is an Essay Concerning The True Original, Extent, and End of Civil Government* (London: Awnsham Churchill, [1689]).

3. John Stuart Mill, *On Liberty*, intro. Gertrude Himmelfarb (New York: Penguin, 1974), 68.

4. Glenn Negley, "Philosophical Views on the Value of Privacy," *Law and Contemporary Problems* 31, no. 2 (Spring 1966): 321, https://scholarship.law.duke.edu/cgi/viewcontent.cgi?article=3111&context=lcp, emphases original.

5. Ferdinand Schoeman, "Privacy: Philosophical Dimensions of the Literature," in *Philosophical Dimensions of Privacy: An Anthology*, ed. Ferdinand Schoeman (Cambridge: Cambridge University Press, 1984), 1, 8.

6. Clinton Rossiter, "The Pattern of Liberty," in *Aspects of Liberty: Essays Presented to Robert E. Cushman*, ed. Milton R. Konvitz and Clinton Rossiter (Ithaca, NY: Cornell University Press, 1958), as quoted in Adam Moore, "Intangible Property: Privacy, Power and Information Control," in *Information Ethics: Privacy, Property and Power*, ed. Adam Moore (Seattle: University of Washington Press, 2005), 183–84.

7. Edward J. Bloustein, "Privacy as an Aspect of Human Dignity: An Answer to Dean Prosser," *New York University Law Review* 39, no. 962 (1964).

8. Edward J. Bloustein, *Individual and Group Privacy*, intro. Nathaniel J. Pallone (New York: Routledge, 2018).

9. Negley, "Philosophical Views," *Duke Law Scholarship*, 325.

10. Alan F. Westin, *Privacy and Freedom* (New York: Atheneum, 1967), 7, 31–32.

11. Charles Fried, *An Anatomy of Values: Problems of Personal and Social Choice* (Cambridge, MA: Harvard University Press, 1970), 140, 142.

12. James Rachels, "Why Privacy Is Important," *Philosophy and Public Affairs* 4, no. 4 (Summer 1975): 331, 327–28.

13. Stanley I. Benn, "Privacy, Freedom, and Respect for Persons," *Nomos* 13 (1971): 9.

14. William A. Parent, "Privacy: A Brief Survey of the Conceptual Landscape," *Santa Clara High Technology Law Journal* 11, no. 1 (January 1995): 23, https://digitalcommons.law.scu.edu/chtlj/vol11/iss1/4/.

15. Jerry Kang, "Information Privacy in Cyberspace Transactions," *Stanford Law Review* 50, no. 4 (April 1998): 1202–3.

16. Luciano Floridi, "On Human Dignity as a Foundation for the Right to Privacy," *Philosophy and Technology* 29 (2016): 308, https://doi.org/10.1007/s13347-016-0220 -8.

17. Adam Moore, "Intangible Property: Privacy, Power and Information Control," *American Philosophical Quarterly* 35, no. 4 (1998): 365–78, 373.

18. Michael Katell and Adam Moore, "Introduction," in *Privacy, Security and Accountability: Ethics, Law and Policy*, ed. Adam Moore (London: Rowman & Littlefield, 2016), 3–4.

19. Judith Jarvis Thomson, "The Right to Privacy," *Philosophy and Public Affairs* 4, no. 4 (Summer 1975): 295–314.

20. Julie C. Inness, *Privacy, Intimacy and Isolation* (Oxford: Oxford University Press, 1992), 8, 10.

21. Ruth Gaviscon, "Privacy and the Limits of Law," *Yale Law Journal* 89, no. 3 (January 1980): 423.

22. Schoeman, "Privacy," 17.

23. Anita L. Allen, *Why Privacy Isn't Everything: Feminist Reflections on Personal Accountability* (Lanham, MD: Rowman & Littlefield, 2003), 15.

24. Allen, *Why Privacy Isn't Everything*, 15–16.

25. Judith DeCew, "Privacy," *Stanford Encyclopedia of Philosophy* (Spring 2018 ed.), ed. Edward N. Zalta, at 2.4, https://plato.stanford.edu/archives/spr.2018/entries /privacy/.

26. Kenneth Einar Himma, "Privacy versus Security: Why Privacy Is Not an Absolute Value or Right," *San Diego Law Review* 44, no. 4 (2007): 859, 919, https://digitalsandiego.edu/sdlr/vol44/iss4/10.

27. See, for example, Alan Brinkley, "Past as Prologue," in *Liberty Under Attack: Reclaiming Our Freedoms in an Age of Terror*, ed. Richard C. Leone and Greg Anrig Jr. (New York: PublicAffairs, Century Foundation, 2007), 25–49.

28. Many sources document this failure. See, for example, Jennifer Stisa Granick, *American Spies: Modern Surveillance, Why You Should Care, and What to Do about It* (Cambridge: Cambridge University Press, 2017), 90–98.

Chapter 4

Privacy as a Legal and Constitutional Right

Even as nineteenth-century liberal philosophers, building on earlier thought, explored the importance of privacy, American jurisprudence remained silent on the topic until the very last part of the century. At that time, privacy emerged in the discourse of a coterie of influential lawyers as the "right to be let alone." This definition, enunciated by Judge Cooley in 1888, animated Warren and Brandeis's famous and seminal discussion of a right to privacy and strongly influenced subsequent understandings. As Warren and Brandeis wrote in 1890,

> From corporeal property arose the incorporeal rights issuing out of it; and then there opened the wide realm of intangible property, in the products and processes of the mind, as works of literature and art, goodwill, trade secrets, and trademarks. . . . The common law secures to each individual the right of determining, ordinarily, to what extent his thoughts, sentiments, and emotions shall be communicated to others. . . . The principle which protects personal writings and all other personal productions, not against theft and physical appropriation but against publication in any form, is in reality not the principle of private property but that of an inviolate personality.[1]

This last concept, that of an "inviolate personality" lying at the core of the need to protect the private, constitutes an especially enduring part of Warren and Brandeis's seminal article. The notion that intangible property comprises feelings, thoughts, and products of the mind has resonated across the decades as well.

The definition that Warren and Brandeis provided established privacy as a right of noninterference. "There is something very seductive about attempts to equate privacy with noninterference, or being let alone," writes Arthur Schafer, "what philosophers call 'negative liberty.' The standard cases which the phrase 'invasion of privacy' brings to mind do commonly take the form

of coercive interferences with or intrusions upon the individual."[2] Warren
and Brandeis were primarily concerned about protecting individuals from
the encroachments of the press, especially the yellow press—something they
saw as an intolerable privacy violation. However, their argument could be
extended to an individual right to control information about the self, a concept
now known as *informational privacy*.[3]

William Prosser, perhaps the most important legal expert on privacy in the
United States in the seventy years after the publication of the Warren and
Brandeis article, argued that there are four "rather definite privacy rights: (1)
intrusions upon a person's seclusion or solitude or into his private affairs,
(2) public disclosure of embarrassing private facts about an individual, (3)
publicity placing one in a false light in the public eye, and (4) appropriation
of one's likeness for the advantage of another."[4] As Judith DeCew writes:

> Warren and Brandeis were writing their normative views about what they felt
> should be protected under the rubric of privacy, whereas Prosser was describ-
> ing what courts had in fact protected in the seventy years following publication
> of the Warren and Brandeis paper. . . . [Privacy] as control over information
> about oneself has come to be viewed by many as also including unwarranted
> searches, eavesdropping, surveillance, and appropriations and misuses of one's
> communications.[5]

Yet another interpretation of the difference between Warren and Brandeis and
Prosser comes from Ferdinand Schoeman. He wrote,

> Although Prosser seems to concede Warren and Brandeis their primary legal
> claim—that there is a unified concern that involves the interest private indi-
> viduals have in keeping their private lives out of the public light—there is a
> difference in emphasis regarding what is at stake in violations of this sort. For
> Brandeis and Warren, at issue is something sacred, connected with inviolate
> personality. For Prosser, the issue is reputation and protection from emotional
> distress.[6]

And writing in 2006, reflecting the growth in legal explorations of privacy,
Daniel Solove noted,

> In 1960, the famous torts scholar William Prosser attempted to make sense of
> the landscape of privacy law by identifying four different interests. But Prosser
> focused only on tort law, and the law of information privacy is significantly
> more vast and complex, extending to Fourth Amendment law, the constitutional
> right to information privacy, evidentiary privileges, dozens of federal privacy
> statutes, and hundreds of state statutes. Moreover, Prosser wrote over forty years
> ago [now over fifty], and new technologies have given rise to a panoply of new
> privacy harms.[7]

THE FOURTH AMENDMENT AND PRIVACY

The Fourth Amendment of the US Constitution holds that "the right of the people to be secure in their persons, houses, papers, and effects against unreasonable searches and seizures shall not be violated and no warrants shall issue but upon probable cause supported by oath or affirmation and particularly describing the place to be searched and the persons or things to be seized." Although the Fourth Amendment is the legal wellspring for the protection of privacy in the country, it does not include the word *privacy*—although many of the elements that it singles out for protection constitute parts of the private sphere. Reflecting this understanding of the meaning of the text, in 1965 the US Supreme Court's decision in *Griswold v. Connecticut* asserted that privacy was a "penumbral right" emanating from the Fourth Amendment. *Griswold* overturned the convictions of a doctor and of the director of Planned Parenthood for distributing contraceptive information and other services to married couples. In his decision, Justice William O. Douglas argued that a "penumbral right" "emanating" from the Constitution created a privacy zone that covered the sexual relations of married couples. The reasoning contained in *Griswold* would subsequently influence the legalization of interracial marriage and the possession of pornographic material at home. Most famously, the reasoning contained in *Griswold* led to the *Roe v. Wade* decision in 1973 that legalized abortion in the United States. Once Donald Trump's appointments to the Supreme Court created a strong conservative majority, *Roe* was overturned in 2022, raising the danger that all of the decisions based on the notion of a "penumbral right" to privacy "emanating" from the Constitution would be subject to potential reversal, as well.

Bowers v. Hardwick in 1986 challenged the conception of a right to privacy protecting individual decisions related to marriage, lifestyle, or reproduction, when it rejected the effort to overturn Georgia's antisodomy laws on privacy grounds. However, *Lawrence v. Texas* in 2003 overturned *Bowers v. Hardwick* when it decided that a Texas statute that banned some same-sex behaviors violated both liberty and privacy as well as due process.[8]

A second body of Supreme Court decisions interpreted the Fourth Amendment throughout the twentieth century in ways that would dramatically influence privacy protections during the first decades of the twenty-first century. Early in the twentieth century, the Court interpreted the Fourth Amendment as only applying to intrusions into physical space. Notably, the 1928 *Olmstead v. US* decision established that wiretapping did not violate the Fourth Amendment because it did not involve entry, search, or seizure. In *Katz*, however, rendered in 1967, the Court overturned *Olmstead*. The *Katz* ruling asserted that "the Fourth Amendment protects people, not places. What a person knowingly exposes to the public, even in his own home or office, is not a subject of Fourth Amendment protection. But what he seeks to preserve as private, even in an area accessible to the public, may be constitutionally protected."[9]

In his concurrent opinion on *Katz*, Associate Judge John Harlan asserted that the Fourth Amendment regulates whether "an actual (subjective) expectation of privacy" exists that the "society is prepared to recognize as 'reasonable.'"[10] This concurrent opinion in *Katz* thus established the still extant interpretation of when and where the Fourth Amendment applies. And it only does so when "a reasonable expectation of privacy" exists.

This effectively means, as Daniel Solove observes, that

> using privacy instead of physical trespass was supposed to broaden Fourth Amendment protection [through the overturning of *Olmstead* by *Katz*], not constrict it. The reason privacy has led to such a narrow scope of Fourth Amendment coverage is [because] . . . the Supreme Court conceives of privacy as a form of total secrecy. Under this view, if you share your information with other people—even people you trust a lot—you can't expect privacy. If you expose your information in any way—even if the government has to go to great trouble and expense to discover it—then you can't expect privacy.[11]

And as Solove notes elsewhere, "a privacy violation occurs when concealed data is revealed to others. If the information is not previously hidden, there is no privacy interest implicated by the collection or dissemination of the information. In many areas of law, this narrow view of privacy has limited the recognition of privacy violations. Tort law is generally consistent with this approach."[12]

Legislative silence on the Fourth Amendment and Supreme Court interpretations permit unconstrained video surveillance in public. Again, to quote Solove, "In Fourth Amendment law, courts frequently conclude that surveillance in private places implicates a reasonable expectation of privacy whereas surveillance in public places does not."[13] Reflecting these understandings of the proper bounds of privacy, American cities utilize a growing number of cameras to surveil their streets and public areas.

"So here is where the law stands," Solove writes, reflecting on this dearth of privacy protection. "The Fourth Amendment will provide you with protection only when you're at home or in a private place. If you're in [a] park or a store or restaurant, you have no Fourth Amendment protection from video surveillance."[14] And this video surveillance, in the years since he wrote in 2011, has been transformed with the spread of facial-recognition technology.

To make matters worse, the Supreme Court created an environment during the analog age that enabled mass private corporate surveillance through the establishment of the third-party doctrine. Several Supreme Court decisions established this legal doctrine. While the *Katz* decision in 1967 enshrined the principle of a "reasonable expectation of privacy," *US v. Miller* in 1976 established that this expectation did not apply to bank records.

Because these records were voluntarily surrendered to another party, the government could access them without a warrant. *Smith v. Maryland* in 1979 took this reasoning a step further, establishing that the Fourth Amendment did not cover phone numbers—so-called "pen registers"—in the hands of telecommunications companies. Although the *Katz* decision had already protected the content of phone calls, *Smith v. Maryland* established that Fourth Amendment protection only applied to content. As a consequence, *Smith v. Maryland* created the legal basis for metadata collection during the early decades of the digital age while cementing the principle that information voluntarily turned over to "third parties" lost the "reasonable expectation of privacy."

This loss of a "reasonable expectation of privacy" began with banks and moved to phone companies and other providers, before being extended after the dawn of the digital age to Internet service providers, email services, social media platforms, and every entity that requires the provision of personal information in exchange for receipt of a service. Turning over this information qualifies as a voluntary act, ending the "reasonable expectation of privacy." *Smith v. Maryland*'s extension to the digital world, and especially its distinction between "pen registers" and content, represents another case of technology outpacing law. In fact, as anyone who understands metadata knows, "pen registers" *are* content. In fact, they can reveal as much as if not more than content. And metadata did not exist and could not even have been imagined in 1979 when *Smith v. Maryland* became law. While technology advances rapidly, law and regulation move slowly.

On the other hand, the US Congress did recognize in 1974 that the exploding trove of personal data in the hands of the federal government, even during the analog age, had to be regulated to preserve privacy. This awareness was reflected in the passage of the Privacy Act that year, designed to govern the treatment and sharing of the personal information of individuals between federal agencies. However, even though the Privacy Act regulated this activity, the impact of the subsequent establishment of the third-party doctrine along with the understandings derived from *Katz* meant that this act, despite its name, did not protect anything beyond a small privacy zone. Even this privacy zone came under assault after 9/11, when US government data, especially in the law-enforcement and national security realms, became less segregated, ending many of these protections.

However, law finally began to catch up with digital technology belatedly and very partially in the *Carpenter* decision in 2018. Here the Supreme Court somewhat altered the precedent that *Smith* had established when it ruled that the government must seek a warrant to obtain cell phone location information. For the first time this meant that information given to a third party (the cell phone provider) was subject to Fourth Amendment protection. In *Carpenter* the Court established five tests, without making any of them dispositive, or giving them different weight, that determine the requirement for a warrant: "The intimacy and comprehensiveness of the data, the expense of obtaining it, the retrospective window that it offers to law enforcement, and whether it was truly shared voluntarily with a third party."[15] In addition, in its decision the Court asserted that it was not overturning *Smith* and did not extend its reasoning to other digital technologies. Chief Justice John Roberts wrote, "the majority's opinion only applies to 'seismic shifts in digital technology' while it did not question conventional surveillance techniques and tools, such as security cameras."[16] This means, for example, that absent additional jurisprudence on the topic, *Carpenter* does not apply to facial recognition unless courts eventually determine that it represents a "seismic shift in digital technologies" and meets the tests that *Carpenter* established. At the time of this writing, it is still too early to tell whether or not evolving jurisprudence will meaningfully constrain the third-party doctrine, since *Smith* remains in place.

More fundamentally, *Carpenter* did not deal with the fundamental problem plaguing *Smith* and the third-party doctrine. Is the surrender of private information to third parties really a voluntary act in the modern age? As Thurgood Marshall noted in his brilliant dissent to *Smith*, it was already almost impossible to live in the 1970s without having to "voluntarily" surrender information to banks and to telephone companies.[17] Moreover, "voluntary surrender" means less and less in the twenty-first century. Does the idea of a "voluntary surrender" have any meaning or content in a digital world that *requires* such a surrender to engage with any service or platform? Accustomed to engaging daily in "voluntary surrender" in order to complete the most mundane tasks, most think little about what they have lost or how it is eroding any remaining vestiges of Fourth Amendment protection, since this ostensibly voluntary act ends "the reasonable expectation of privacy." One can only ask if something can be understood as being voluntary when the only choice is to eschew digital interactions and live in a cave. Few know about the third-party doctrine, and fewer still understand its logic or how it applies to their activities on Facebook and other apps and platforms. For example, the almost indiscriminate uploading of photographs indicates that people often do not know or think about the fact that the third-party doctrine grants these companies effective ownership of these personal items, enabling them to monetize these images along with everything else uploaded to their sites.

In addition, people are unlikely to consider that the state can readily access all of the information "voluntarily" submitted to Facebook and other entities. Few are likely to understand that a "reasonable expectation of privacy" does not apply to the messages they send to loved ones, the things that they share with intimates, the photos they upload, and their searches. Nor do many think about or know that the steady decline in the cost of data storage means that, absent data-retention regulations, these organizations have the capacity to hold all of this information forever, creating a world in which these entities increasingly know everything and are designed to forget nothing, while individuals know little and inevitably forget much. The only thing that might constrain some of the state's practices in areas such as the collection of searches will be jurisprudence on *Carpenter* and interpretation of its five tests.

In tandem with the Supreme Court decisions interpreting the extent of Fourth Amendment protection and establishing the third-party doctrine, a long debate between different schools of constitutional interpretation suffuses the discussion of the existence of a constitutional right to privacy and of its form and extent. Conservatives and so-called "textualists," who eventually clustered themselves into the Federalist Society, ground their arguments in what they term "original intent" and reject the understanding of privacy flowing from the *Griswold* decision—with their reasoning becoming, as noted before, most explicitly manifest in the overturning of *Roe*. On the other side, the defenders of *Griswold* and other, similar decisions reject "textualism" and the effort to discern the "original intent" of the drafters of the Constitution in the late eighteenth century—instead insisting that the United States has a "living" Magna Carta, designed to be adaptable and capable of being interpreted in light of social and historical change.

In many ways, Robert Bork is the father of the modern "textualist" understanding of the Constitution. Ronald Reagan nominated Bork to serve on the Supreme Court in 1981, leading to a nasty and conflictual Senate confirmation process. This confirmation battle, and the eventual rejection of Bork's nomination, prefigured and encouraged the very polarized partisan confirmation fights accompanying Supreme Court nominations during subsequent decades. In addition, it fueled the growth of the Federalist Society—an organization whose power, conjoined to its doctrinal rigidity, contributed to the Supreme Court's transformation into a completely partisan body during the Trump administration.

Bork argued that *Griswold* was a deeply flawed interpretation of the Constitution. According to him, *Griswold* departed from the text of the Fourth Amendment, reading rights into it that were not enumerated. In so doing, the Court in *Griswold* had carried the institution into social and cultural issues. Bork objected as well to the imprecision of a right to privacy. To quote Andrew Koppelman on Bork,

Far more devastating is his claim that the right is indeterminate, so that there is no way to know what liberties are or are not protected. For example, Bork maintained that *Griswold v. Connecticut*, which held that married couples had a right to use contraceptives, "did not indicate what other activities might be protected by the new right of privacy and did not provide any guidance for reasoning about future claims laid under that right."[18]

As an extension, the "textualist" view rejects the notion of a right to privacy fundamentally emanating from the Constitution; or at least it sees privacy claims as being a subset of liberty claims. It is around this matter that many of the disputes over privacy between the "living constitution" school and the "textualists" arise. As Judith DeCew writes,

In response to Bork's complaint that constitutional privacy protection is not at all about privacy but only concerns liberty or autonomy, it has been successfully argued that while we have multiple individual liberties such as freedom of expression, many do not seem to be about anything particularly personal or related to the types of concerns we might be willing and able to see as privacy issues. If so, then liberty is a broader concept than privacy and privacy issues and claims are a subset of claims to liberty. . . . [Privacy] protects liberty, and . . . privacy protection gains for us the freedom to define ourselves and our relations to others.[19]

As mentioned previously, perhaps the most well-known contemporary opponent of a privacy right is Judge Richard Posner, whose views on mass surveillance were discussed in the previous chapter. In the wake of the Boston Marathon bombing, and in response to Mayor Michael Bloomberg's announcement that he intended to expand surveillance in New York City, Judge Posner wrote an opinion piece entitled "Privacy is Overrated" in *The New York Daily News* on April 28, 2013. In this piece, he asserted that

Neither the word "privacy" nor even the concept appears anywhere in the Constitution, and the current Supreme Court is highly sensitive, as it should be, to security needs. . . . There is a tendency to exaggerate the social value of privacy. I value my privacy as much as the next person, but there is a difference between what is valuable to an individual and what is valuable to society. . . . ["Privacy"] is really just a euphemism for concealment, for hiding specific things about ourselves from others. . . . I am not suggesting that privacy laws be repealed. I don't think that they do much harm, and they do some good. . . . But I don't think they serve the public as well as civil libertarians contend, and so I don't think that such laws confer social benefits comparable to those of methods of surveillance that are effective against criminal and especially terrorist assaults. More than effective: indispensable.[20]

This last claim is, as I have argued, false. The advocates of mass surveillance repeat this claim, as they did about torture, despite the absence of evidence that the mass surveillance of the US population plays a significant role in uncovering terrorist threats. Furthermore, in a fundamental misunderstanding of the digital age, Judge Posner argues that mass surveillance is not Orwellian because it occurs in public. In addition, he extols the virtues of deploying even more technology, presumably to create an all-encompassing surveillance system. Writing in 1984, Richard Wasserstrom advanced arguments that are deeper and more nuanced than Posner's but arrived at a similar conclusion. He asserted that

> The withholding of personal information about the self is presumptively improper because it bears the color of deception. The need for privacy arises from shame about elements of the self that the individual considers rare and unique and not broadly shared. In turn, this shame is culturally constructed i.e., enculturated. The desire for privacy thus represents our discomfort with ourselves, leading us to act hypocritically and deceitfully.[21]

There is a deep problem with the arguments that Posner and Wasserstrom advance. Inevitably, in their absolutist arguments for transparency, they fall into the same trap as the feminist advocates of full accountability. In both cases, abuse is inevitable. The perfectly transparent person will experience, in the digital age, the evaporation of their inner world and particularly acute problems with identity theft, hacking, and the commodification of especially large amounts of their formerly private information. Moreover, neither Posner or Wasserstrom considers the profound consequences for individual freedom, agency, and control of a world suffused with historically unprecedented informational inequalities.

Ferdinand Schoeman adds another critique of Posner's and Wasserstrom's arguments, when he writes,

> The picture that both Posner and Wasserstrom . . . present of human nature is something like this: People are really and fundamentally unitary. We act either authentically or inauthentically as we present ourselves in various contexts. If we do not reveal all of what we are to those who have reason to interact with us, we are being partially deceptive. . . . For both Posner and Wasserstrom, what we are private about relates presumptively to matters we wish to conceal because of the different images of ourselves that would be projected through such a disclosure."[22]

The Manichaeism of Posner's and Wasserstrom's arguments caricatures the choices that humans confront in their interactions with others, including not just strangers and acquaintances but intimates as well.

Behind both Posner's and Wasserstrom's arguments lies the view that the United States adequately protects privacy. Moreover, because the two equate deception with privacy, they question the need for protections designed to ensure its preservation. Neither, however, addresses the hollowing out of the Fourth Amendment because of technological change and Supreme Court interpretations. As Daniel Solove writes, "Increasingly the answer to whether the Fourth Amendment provides protection is 'not at all.' The Fourth Amendment applies only when a person has a reasonable expectation of privacy, and the US Supreme Court understands privacy in a very antiquated manner. According to the Court, something is private only if it is completely secret."[23]

The weakness of Supreme Court privacy protection and its effective evisceration of the Fourth Amendment, despite the *Carpenter* decision, does not cause discernible public disquiet given the general silence on the topic. While people are aware that digital technologies assault their privacy, they seemingly do not know (or, more disturbingly, care) that the Fourth Amendment, despite the *Carpenter* decision, still does not protect them broadly from digital intrusions since the core of *Smith*, the notion of "voluntary surrender" ending the "reasonable expectation of privacy," remains largely undisturbed. An amendment that only completely protects the never spoken and the never written is a quaint anachronism in a world that requires the continual disgorging of increasingly intimate personal information. Moreover, metadata mining and other technological changes, including surveillance whose capacities reveal the powers of AI and machine learning, along with the development of such things as the metaverse, promise additional and even more expansive assaults on privacy in the years ahead.

Reflecting shifts in its composition since 2018, the current Court might have rejected *Carpenter*, which was only decided by a five-four majority (with Chief Justice Roberts joining the four liberal members of the Court— Breyer, Ginsburg, Kagan, and Sotomayor). All the other conservatives on the Court, including Alito, Kennedy, Gorsuch, and Thomas, dissented from the majority. After the *Carpenter* decision the Court veered far to the right when Donald Trump appointed a member of the Federalist Society, Brett Kavanaugh, to replace the retiring and less-doctrinal Anthony Kennedy. Textualist supremacy was assured when Ruth Bader Ginsburg died, to be replaced by a doctrinally Borkian jurist, Amy Coney Barrett, with the enthusiastic approval of the Federalist Society. As noted before, the overturning of *Roe* is an inevitable result of this development, which also undermines all the other decisions reflecting the reasoning contained in *Griswold*. The dominance of judges aligned with the Borkian view of the world makes it unlikely that Americans will find constitutional remedies to the multiplying digital appropriations of the self for the foreseeable future. Instead, such protections, if they arise, will have to come out of the legislative branch (as it perhaps more properly should in a republic), despite the national Congress's continuing inaction in this area, save for the efforts of a few senators.

In this environment, the overturning of *Roe* inevitably pushed decisions about abortion rights to the states, producing a patchwork of laws around the country. Some states are even offering cash bounties to those who report violators, including providers, of this law. The enforcement of bans on abortion within state boundaries and the effort to prevent residents from seeking this procedure in states where abortion is legal promises to increase the surveillance of women's bodies. This prospect prompted Senator Ron Wyden (D-OR) to make a speech on the floor of the US Senate on May 11, 2022, after Republicans blocked the Women's Health Protection Act.

> With abortion criminalized, women's personal data is going to be weaponized against them by bounty hunters and the government. . . . Shady data brokers are already tracking women who go to Planned Parenthood Clinics [because of the availability of location data taken from cell phones], and they will sell that data to anyone with a credit card. Imagine for a moment what not just prosecutors but these deranged right-wing vigilantes will do with this data. . . . In short, this is 'uterus surveillance.'"[24]

These developments also prompted Zeynep Tufekci to write:

> Surveillance made possible by minimally regulated digital technologies could help law enforcement track down women who might seek abortions and medical providers who perform them in places where it would become criminalized. Women are urging one another to delete phone apps like period trackers that can indicate they are pregnant. But frantic individual efforts to swat away digital intrusions will do too little. What's needed, for Americans, is a full legal and political reckoning with the reckless manner in which digital technology has been allowed to invade our lives.[25]

The overturning of *Roe*, however, may finally drive a greater public awareness of the implications of the *Griswold* decision for privacy and freedom and impel the American public to confront the consequences of their erosion. This might increase activism, beyond its current pallid levels, designed to counteract the shrinkage of the Fourth Amendment. Armies of Americans fund lobbying efforts to defend the Second Amendment and vote for candidates whose platforms hinge on the protection of largely unrestricted gun ownership. The First Amendment occasions strong passions as well, frequently becoming the subject of discussion and debate. The Fourth Amendment, in comparison, seems almost invisible. It does not occasion the discussion that surrounds the First Amendment or the lobbying and voting activity that surrounds the Second Amendment, although the overturning of *Roe* may finally change this reality.

THE LEGAL AND CONSTITUTIONAL PROTECTION OF PRIVACY IN OTHER COUNTRIES

Different polities, for sociocultural, historical, or political reasons and because of their distinct legal development, treat privacy in markedly distinct ways. In the contemporary era, however, the United States has become an increasingly notable laggard, especially when compared to Europe, in the effort to protect privacy from proliferating intrusions. Beyond the Supreme Court decisions discussed in the previous section, the power of American private corporations and the country's especially strong attachment to the free market during the first decades of the digital age have ensured regulatory debility. As a result, the US government throughout this period did not circumscribe the surveillance, collection, or mining of personal information. And it used its extraordinary resources to continually expand its own capacities in these areas, given the scope of its national security concerns and doctrine. As Judith DeCew writes,

> The US has generally stood behind efficiency arguments that business and government need unfettered access to personal data to guarantee economic growth and national security, whereas the EU has sent a coherent signal that privacy has critical value in a robust information society because citizens will only participate in an online environment if they feel their privacy is guaranteed against ubiquitous business and government surveillance.[26]

Reflecting these understandings and the view that privacy is essential to human dignity, on April 14, 2016, the European Union passed the General Data Protection Regulation. Article 88 specifically mentions human dignity—echoing the writings of Stanley Benn and other philosophers who wrote decades earlier—asserting that the GDPR "shall include suitable and specific measures to safeguard the data subjects' human dignity, legitimate interests, and fundamental rights."[27]

In this same vein, the European Data Protection Supervisor noted in 2015,

> better respect for, and the safeguarding of, human dignity could be the counterweight to the pervasive surveillance and asymmetry of power which now confronts the individual. It should be at the heart of a new digital ethics. . . . Privacy is an integral part of human dignity, and the right to data protection was originally conceived in the 1970s and '80s as a way of compensating the potential for the erosion of privacy and dignity through large scale personal data processing.[28]

These understandings of the need to expand privacy protections spread to the rest of the world—even as the United States continued to resist them. As DeCew writes, "European-style privacy-protection regulations have spread rapidly across the industrialized world, with the United States as a major exception, and have transformed and led the global privacy debate."[29] Paradoxically, despite continuing to pursue unrestrained and especially extensive state surveillance, in August 2021 even China moved to restrict and regulate the activities of corporations before the United States took action, passing a data-privacy law that included many of the elements contained in the GDPR.

Unlike the United States, many countries explicitly recognize privacy in their constitutions, including South Korea, Brazil, and South Africa, while other countries specify an implicit privacy right, including Canada, France, Germany, Japan, and India.[30] The following summary of practices captures the state of constitutional protections for informational privacy. Koops, Newell, Timan, Skorvanek, Chokrevski, and Galic write,

> Constitutional law protects personal data in most European countries—although not in Italy—as well as at the European level. Most jurisdictions use the term "personal data," though some use the term "personal information." It is a stand-alone right, being regulated in a provision separate from that containing the right to privacy, most famously in the EU Charter but also in Poland and Slovenia. The Czech Republic and the Netherlands also regulate the right to data protection in a separate paragraph of the provision containing the general right to privacy. . . . [In addition,] Russia protects "information on the private life" of persons against processing without consent, while Spain protects "data processing in order to guarantee the honour and personal and family privacy of citizens." . . . Some jurisdictions formulate data protection as a negative liberty, most clearly seen . . . in the Swiss provision: "[every] person has the right to be protected against abuse of personal data." Poland has a special form of negative liberty: "[no] one may be obliged, except on the basis of statute, to disclose information concerning his person." . . . In contrast, Germany phrases data protection as a positive liberty: the right to informational self-determination. . . . [Informational] privacy is constitutionally recognized in Canada as well, in the form of the Charter protecting (intimate) information that touches on a person's "biographical core."[31]

As the list above reveals, the degree of data protection varies considerably across countries, as does the extent of their protection of informational privacy. Enforcement of these provisions differs as well. Authoritarian regimes like Russia's may constitutionally protect privacy while eliding these protections in the name of raison d'état or the inclinations of the leadership. Democracies, as revealed by the war on terror pursued since September 11,

2001, are not immune to these problems either. And the initial reaction to the COVID-19 pandemic caused many countries, as will be discussed in a later chapter, to adopt measures at odds with these protections.

Beyond these variations, other questions arise about whether these regulations serve to adequately protect individuals from intrusions into their private lives. While several countries—particularly those that are members of the European Union—increasingly use these measures to restrict the activities of private corporations and regulate their data collection and retention practices, most states are not subject to these restraints on their activities. Democratic states mostly embed at least some putative privacy protections in their most egregious and intrusive practices, but digital capacities frequently overwhelm these protections. The most common of these protections are so-called "minimization" procedures—measures ostensibly designed to "mask" those whose information is accidentally or improperly collected. However, "minimization" as Jennifer Granick notes, does not actually hide identity, given the power of digital tools to disassemble these procedures.[32] Moreover, and perhaps most importantly, governmental exploitation of zero days and other circumventions of security protocols enables effectively unregulated and commonplace privacy violations.

And across the world, the intelligence and security apparatus in most countries pursues the collection of personal data on a massive scale, with most of their operations hidden behind a wall of secrecy. Additionally, states use their increasingly sophisticated digital capacities to surveil widening social, political, and economic spheres. Inevitably, capacities once reserved, at least ostensibly, to the national security apparatus are extended to domestic law enforcement and then to other areas. In sum, regardless of current protections, national security and other imperatives will shrink privacy further until legislation or international treaties require states to begin meaningfully regulating themselves.

INTERNATIONAL LAW AND PRIVACY

The recognition of the fundamental importance of privacy led to its explicit inclusion in the Universal Declaration of Human Rights. International definitions of fundamental human rights are more broadly expansive than those contained in most domestic constitutions but are less enforceable than these local provisions. Article 12 of the Universal Declaration asserts that "no one shall be subjected to arbitrary interference with his privacy, family, home, or correspondence, nor to attacks upon his honour and reputation. Everyone has the right to the protection of the law against such interference or attacks."

In a nearly verbatim echo of the Universal Declaration of Human Rights, the International Covenant on Civil and Political Rights, ratified by 164 countries as of 2014, states in Article 17 that "no one shall be subjected to arbitrary or unlawful interference with his or her privacy, family, home, or correspondence, nor to unlawful attacks on his or her honour and reputation."

The UN Office of the High Commissioner for Human Rights' Special Rapporteur on Freedom of Expression and Opinion, David Kaye, published a report in 2014 detailing "The Right to Privacy in the Digital Age."[33] Approved and released by the UN General Assembly, the report is worth quoting at length, since it constitutes the most important and comprehensive analysis to date of international privacy law. Most importantly, this report establishes a strong prima facie case, grounded in the International Covenant on Civil and Political Rights, against several governing practices that violate privacy.

The United Nations categorically asserts that state uses of several digital capacities lead to systematic assaults on privacy, constituting extraordinarily widespread violations of a central human right included in both the Universal Declaration of Human Rights and the International Covenant on Civil and Political Rights. The practices producing the most serious violations are mass surveillance, third-party data retention, access to bulk data, the use of secret rules and secret interpretations, and policies that discriminate between nationals and foreigners, since privacy is a universal human right. Most states, including liberal constitutional democracies, engage in these practices, thus violating a universal human right.

The introduction of the Special Rapporteur's report to the General Assembly notes that "technological advancements mean that the State's effectiveness in conducting surveillance is no longer limited by scale or duration. Declining costs of technology and data storage have eradicated financial or practical disincentives to conducting surveillance. The State now has a greater capability to conduct simultaneous, invasive, targeted, and broad-scale surveillance than ever before."[34] In common with much of the jurisprudence on privacy, the report of the Special Rapporteur does not define the precise scope and reach of this right. However, it does enumerate interferences with privacy in the digital age, establishing a de facto definition of informational privacy.

Reflecting its focus on informational privacy, the report asserts that

> any capture of communications data is potentially an interference with privacy and, further, that the collection and retention of communications data amounts to an interference with privacy whether or not those data are subsequently consulted or used. . . . The very existence of a mass surveillance programme thus creates an interference with privacy. The onus would be on the State to demonstrate that such interference is neither arbitrary or unlawful.[35]

The UN Human Rights Committee, in turn, asserts that lawful interference occurs when it is authorized "on the basis of law, which itself must comply with the provisions, aims, and objectives of the [International Covenant on Civil and Political Rights]." Further, "the expression 'arbitrary interference,'" argues the Special Rapporteur, "is intended to guarantee that even interference provided for by law should be in accordance with the provisions, aims, and objectives of the Covenant and should be, in any event, reasonable in the particular circumstances."[36]

In addition, the report establishes that surveillance must meet the tests of necessity and proportionality:

> Any limitation to privacy rights reflected in article 17 must be provided for by law, and the law must be sufficiently accessible, clear, and precise so that an individual may look to the law to ascertain who is authorized to conduct data surveillance and under what circumstances. The limitation must be necessary for reaching a legitimate aim, as well as in proportion to the aim and the least intrusive option available. Moreover, the limitation placed on the right (an interference with privacy, for example, for the purposes of protecting national security or the right to life of others) must be shown to have some chance of achieving that goal. The onus is on the authorities seeking to limit the right to show that it is connected to a legitimate aim.[37]

The report makes an especially strong case against mass surveillance and third-party data retention, arguing that they do not meet basic requirements of necessity and proportionality. It argues that "mass or 'bulk' surveillance programmes may thus be deemed to be arbitrary, even if they serve a legitimate aim. . . . In other words, it will not be enough that the measures are targeted to find certain needles in a haystack; the proper measure is the impact of the measures on the haystack, relative to the harm threatened—namely, whether the measure is necessary and proportionate."[38] However, as is true of other conclusions of the report, governments retain enormous discretion in determining whether the measures have produced an impact on the haystack, "relative to the harm threatened." The ability of governments to define threats—whether from terrorism and crime to pandemics—in apocalyptic, existential terms enables them to insist that their actions are necessary and proportional.

A set of similar arguments guide the report's analysis of third-party data retention policies. "Mandatory third-party data retention—a recurring feature of surveillance regimes in many States—where Governments require telephone companies and Internet service providers to store metadata about their customers' communications and location for subsequent law enforcement and intelligence agency access—appears neither necessary nor proportionate."[39]

And although it is clearly the case that third-party data retention constitutes a systematic violation of privacy, since it gathers the personal information of all—guilty and innocent alike—to facilitate the government's ability to investigate anybody on whatever grounds the state has established, governments retain the absolute capacity to define *necessity* and *proportionality*. And as is true of surveillance and the other practices discussed in the next chapter, national security and public safety are the essential rationales behind claims of categoric necessity, enabling the framing of extreme actions as proportionate and acceptable.

The report does try to set grounds for establishing proportionality, asserting that

> what is done with bulk data and who may have access to them once collected [determines proportionality]. . . . The absence of effective use limitations has been exacerbated since 11 September 2001, with the line between criminal justice and protection of national security blurring significantly. The resulting sharing of data between law enforcement agencies, intelligence bodies, and other State organs risks violating article 17 of the Covenant.[40]

Unfortunately, the crossing of this line has now become so routine that it is virtually institutionalized. In the case of the United States, some remnants of the so-called "wall" between criminal justice and national security investigations still exist, as evidenced in the jurisdictional battles during the impeachment investigations of Donald Trump. However, this "wall" has become far more porous. The extent of this porosity is sometimes difficult to discern, given the secrecy surrounding national security investigations and the FBI's use of so-called "national security letters" (that prevent all those contacted during an investigation from publicly revealing that an investigation exists).

This last example reflects the repeated violation of two of the other injunctions contained in the Special Rapporteur's report. Secret rules and interpretations dominate the practice of mass surveillance, metadata mining, and other state practices—even though this secrecy flies in the face of not only the International Covenant but also of a basic principle governing the rule of law: laws must be published and publicly accessible. Absent this element, compliance becomes impossible and enforcement completely discretionary.

The adjudication of law and judicial proceedings must meet minimal tests of transparency to ensure fairness and accountability. In addition, secrecy destroys due process, with the government becoming the sole party in court proceedings. As the Special Rapporteur writes in a trenchant summation of this problem, "secret rules and secret interpretations—even secret judicial interpretations—of law do not have the necessary qualities of 'law.' . . . The secret nature of specific surveillance powers brings with it a greater risk of arbitrary exercise of discretion, which, in turn, demands greater precision in the rule governing the exercise of discretion, and additional oversight."[41]

Democratic countries around the world professing their attachment to the rule of law routinely violate this injunction. Typically these governments cite the imperatives of national security for their practice of secrecy. Given the capaciousness and expansiveness of national security doctrines, rationales for the creation of secret rules and interpretations grow across time, and especially during periods of conflict. Superpower rivalries, along with fears of other threats, encourage this expansion.

Finally, most governments systematically and extensively discriminate between nationals and foreigners, although some countries respect "person-hood" more than others. The willingness to see rights as being embedded in universal "personhood" reveals itself most powerfully in the treatment of migrants. This discrimination constitutes a prima facie human-rights viola-tion, since the rights established in the International Covenant do not stop at international boundaries. Despite this rather obvious fact, governments only extend privacy protections to citizens or legal residents where these protections exist, excluding foreigners from safeguards. In the world of nation-states, the parochial usually trumps the universal, and the already pal-try protection of the privacy rights of citizens becomes even more attenuated when it comes to safeguarding the privacy rights of foreigners—even though they are "persons."[42]

CONCLUSION

The legal protection of privacy varies significantly around the world. The United States created the earliest constitutional provision protecting many elements of privacy when it included the Fourth Amendment in the Bill of Rights. However, the Fourth Amendment's failure to specifically use the word *private* and make privacy an explicit right ensured enduring controversy over the subject in subsequent centuries. In practical terms, as was true of much of the Bill of Rights, the question of a right to privacy remained legally dormant in the United States throughout the nineteenth century until Warren and Brandeis published their seminal article on the subject.

Throughout the twentieth century, however, Supreme Court decisions, conjoined to a vivid debate between "textualists" and believers in the "living constitution," expanded and shrank the right to privacy in the United States as new decisions replaced older determinations and the ideological composition of the Supreme Court changed. Most significantly, privacy protections were further circumscribed with the understanding that the "reasonable expectation of privacy" only applies to the never spoken, never written, and never said, conjoined to the establishment of the "third-party doctrine" in *Miller* and *Smith*. This occurred before digital technologies facilitated the appropriation of unprecedented amounts of formerly private information.

Ironically, the country in the world most suffused with classic liberal understandings became a laggard when it came to protecting privacy in the digital age. While the *Carpenter* decision in 2018 opened up a door to greater privacy protections by modestly circumscribing the third-party doctrine, the more textualist Borkian cast of the Supreme Court after the Trump administration, conjoined with the likelihood of continuing legislative inaction—for reasons that will be explored later—makes it likely that the United States will continue to lag behind other developed democratic countries when it comes to the enactment of measures designed to protect individual privacy. In fact, unlike the United States, most countries in the rest of the liberal West increasingly shared an understanding that mass digital intrusions represented a fundamental attack on human dignity. Consequently, they moved to pass restrictions on a number of digital practices, including such things as data retention. The United States, however, resisted moving in this direction, afraid of limiting its ability to surveil the world—a necessity for a country bent on remaining the world's dominant military power—or afraid of circumscribing innovation and capital accumulation, even if it produced virtual monopolies.

Despite these contemporary differences over privacy and its protection in the liberal West, a liberal rights discourse, and the influence of these states at the end of World War II, found voice in the Universal Human Rights Declaration. This declaration and the International Covenant that enshrined it in treaty form govern the treatment of privacy in international law. Because of its specific mention as a fundamental right in the declaration, privacy possesses greater international legal standing than it receives in many domestic legal regimes.

The speed of technological change and the slowness of legislative action and regulatory development made the first decades of the digital age an especially challenging period for those who valued privacy. Rapid technological change overwhelmed efforts to moderate the worst effects of the digital age throughout this period, with serious consequences for societies and the individual. At the start of the third decade of the twenty-first century, the gap between the speed of technological change and the development of a regulatory architecture continued. Technological determinism dominated discourse; and the fear of inhibiting "innovation" or falling behind others, especially China, in the race for the greater legibility of everything, limited adequate regulatory change, especially in the United States.

NOTES

1. Samuel D. Warren and Louis D. Brandeis, "The Right to Privacy," *Harvard Law Review* 6, no. 5 (December 15, 1890): 193–205, archived at https://archive.org/details /jstor-1321160/page/n1/mode/2up.

2. Arthur Schafer, "Privacy: A Philosophical Overview," in *Aspects of Privacy Law: Essays in Honour of John M. Sharp*, ed. Dale Gibson (Toronto: Butterworths, 1980), 6–7, archived at https://umanitoba.ca/faculties/arts/departments/philosophy/ ethics/media/privacy_-_a_philosophical_overview.pdf.

3. Judith DeCew, "Privacy," *Stanford Encyclopedia of Philosophy* (Spring 2018 ed.), ed. Edward N. Zalta, at 1.1, "Informational Privacy," https://plato.stanford.edu/ archives/spr.2018/entries/privacy/.

4. William Prosser, "Privacy," *California Law Review* 48 (1960): 389.

5. DeCew, "Privacy," at 1.1, "Informational Privacy."

6. Ferdinand Schoeman, "Privacy: Philosophical Dimensions of the Literature," in *Philosophical Dimensions of Privacy: An Anthology*, ed. Ferdinand Schoeman (Cambridge: Cambridge University Press, 1984), 17.

7. Daniel J. Solove, "A Taxonomy of Privacy," *University of Pennsylvania Law Review* 154, no. 3 (January 2006): 478, editorial mine.

8. For an excellent discussion of the legal history, see DeCew, "Privacy."

9. *Katz* as quoted in Daniel J. Solove, *Nothing to Hide: The False Tradeoff between Privacy and Security* (New Haven: Yale University Press, 2011), 98–99.

10. Solove, *Nothing to Hide*, 99, parenthetical original.

11. Solove, *Nothing to Hide*, 100–1.

12. Solove, "Taxonomy of Privacy," 497.

13. Solove, "Taxonomy of Privacy," 496.

14. Solove, *Nothing to Hide*, 177–78.

15. Laura Hecht-Felella, "The Fourth Amendment in the Digital Age: How *Carpenter* Can Shape Privacy Protections for New Technologies," Brennan Center for Justice at New York University School of Law, March 18, 2021, p. 3.

16. Supreme Court of the United States, "Syllabus: *Carpenter v. United States*," October Term 2017, no. 16–402, argued November 29, 2017, decided June 22, 2018, see p.3.

17. Hecht-Felella, "Fourth Amendment in the Digital Age," 5.

18. Andrew Koppelman, "The Right to Privacy?" *University of Chicago Legal Forum* 2002, no. 1, art. 6 (2002): 106–7, https://chicagounbound.uchicago.edu/cgi/ viewcontent.cgi?article=1318&context=uclf.

19. DeCew, "Privacy," at 2.3.

20. https://www.nydailynews.com/opinion/privacy-overrated-article-1.1328656.

21. Richard Wasserstrom, "Privacy: Some Arguments and Assumptions," in *Philosophical Dimensions of Privacy: An Anthology*, ed. Ferdinand Schoeman (Cambridge: Cambridge University Press, 1984), chap. 14.

22. Schoeman, "Privacy: Philosophical Dimensions," 29–30.

23. Solove, *Nothing to Hide*, 94.

24. "Wyden Delivers Floor Speech after Republicans Block the Women's Health Protection Act," Wyden.Senate.gov, May 11, 2022, https://www.wyden.senate.gov/new/press-releases.

25. Zeynep Tufekci, "We Need to Take Back Our Privacy," *New York Times*, May 19, 2022 https://www.nytimes.com/2022/05/19/opinion/privacy-technology-data.html.

26. DeCew, "Privacy," at 1.1, "Informational Privacy."

27. As recounted by Luciano Floridi, "On Human Dignity as a Foundation for the Right to Privacy," *Philosophy and Technology* 29 (2016), https://doi.org/10.1007/s13347-016-0220-8.

28. European Data Protection Supervisor, "Opinion 4/2015 Towards a New Digital Ethics, Data Dignity and Technology," EDPS/Europa.eu, accessed May 20, 2021, https://edps.europa.eu/sites/edp/files/publication.

29. DeCew, "Privacy," at 1.1, "Informational Privacy."

30. Solove, *Nothing to Hide*, 3.

31. Bert-Jaap Koops, Bryce Clayton Newell, Tjerk Timan, Ivan Skorvanek, Tomislav Chokrevski and Masa Galic, "A Typology of Privacy," *University of Pennsylvania Journal of International Law* 38, no. 2 (2017): 537–39, parentheticals original.

32. Jennifer Stisa Granick, *American Spies: Modern Surveillance, Why You Should Care, and What to Do about It* (Cambridge: Cambridge University Press, 2017), 24.

33. David Kaye, "The Right to Privacy in the Digital Age," Human Rights Council, 27th sess., agenda items 2 and 3, in *Annual Report of the United Nations High Commissioner for Human Rights*, United Nations General Assembly, June 30, 2014.

34. Kaye, "Right to Privacy in the Digital Age," para. 20.

35. Kaye, "Right to Privacy in the Digital Age," para. 20.

36. Kaye, "Right to Privacy in the Digital Age," both quotations drawn from para. 21.

37. Kaye, "Right to Privacy in the Digital Age," para. 23, parenthetical original.

38. Kaye, "Right to Privacy in the Digital Age," para. 25.

39. Kaye, "Right to Privacy in the Digital Age," para. 26.

40. Kaye, "Right to Privacy in the Digital Age," para. 27.

41. Kaye, "Right to Privacy in the Digital Age," para. 29.

42. For other discussions of international law and privacy, see Kristian P. Humble, "International Law, Surveillance and the Protection of Privacy," *International Journal of Human Rights* 25, no. 1 (2021): 1–25; Vivek Krishnamurthy, "A Tale of Two Privacy Laws: The GDPR and the International Right to Privacy," *American Journal of International Law Unbound* 114 (2020): 26–30, https://www.cambridge.org/core/journals/american-journal-of-international-law/article/tale-of-two-privacy-laws-the-gdpr-and-the-international-right-to-privacy/8F51BC461CEC2B557962643B6E24D390; and "International Privacy Standards," Electronic Frontier Foundation, accessed August 23, 2022, EFF.org, https://www.eff.org/issues/international-privacy-standards.

Chapter 5

National Security and the Expansion of Digital Surveillance

Surveillance, and watching and eavesdropping, have occasioned revulsion throughout recorded history. The origin of the term *Peeping Tom* reveals this disgust. The term dates from England in 1050, when Lady Godiva rode naked through Coventry to protest taxes. A man named Tom stared at her naked body and in punishment for his intrusion was blinded, while earning the nickname "Peeping Tom." Although her ride was a public act, Tom's act violated social conventions and the understanding that inviolable privacy surrounds the naked human body. Peeping Toms are socially ostracized and despised for intruding, without consent, into somebody else's privacy. The Peeping Tom tries to see the hidden, violating all privacy norms. In particular, the Peeping Tom derives forbidden sexual satisfaction from surreptitiously observing people who are undressed or engaged in private acts. Peeping Toms, consequently, steal the privacy surrounding the body, even as they try to penetrate the self. *Peeping*, just like surveillance, involves watching without consent in a hidden, clandestine fashion. However, digital surveillance surreptitiously "sees" everything with a minuteness beyond the reach of any ordinary Peeping Tom.

Surveillance in all its forms raises the same problems and promotes the same disquiet that informs views of the Peeping Tom. Both penetrate the private and try to "see" things that are not voluntarily shared or relinquished. Because surveillance constitutes such an intrusive act, liberal polities never portray it as a good in and of itself but only as a necessary means to a greater end—typically security. *Surveil* and *pry* are synonyms, and both describe actions that inappropriately violate boundaries. Those who pry and surveil often derive satisfaction from penetrating another's inner world while preserving their own privacy. For this reason, prying and surveilling always involve assertions of dominance.

In liberal constitutional societies anchored in respect for fundamental rights, surveillance's intrinsic assault on individuals, and on their freedom and agency encouraged efforts to circumscribe governmental uses of this tool. These efforts led to the imposition of warrant requirements to ensure that surveillance was targeted, confined, and focused. Mass surveillance, by definition, involves the indiscriminate use of this tool against entire populations. Mass surveillance tries to see everything, including the most intimate. The state agents who conduct mass surveillance acquire even greater powers over ordinary people, hollowing out the content and practice of democracy.

Concerns about surveillance, watching, and eavesdropping did not abate after Lady Godiva's ride or during subsequent centuries. Daniel J. Solove quotes William Blackstone's definition of *eavesdropping* as "[listening] under walls or windows, or the eaves of a house, to hearken after discourse, and thereupon to frame slanderous or mischievous tales."[1] Blackstone captured in this definition the enduring view of the eavesdropper, or the person engaged in surveillance, as acting in a surreptitious, deceitful fashion who appropriates something that is not theirs and then uses the appropriation with malicious intent.

The development of communications technology in the nineteenth century created the first modern worries about surveillance. The fear that these communications were subject to interception worried people from the outset. And they were right to be worried, since the ability to intercept communications accompanied their development and adoption. "As early as 1862," Solove writes, "California prohibited the interception of telegraph communications. Soon after telephone wiretapping began in the 1890s, several states prohibited it, such as California in 1905. By 1928, over half the states had made wiretapping a crime. Justice Holmes referred to wiretapping as a 'dirty business,' and Justice Frankfurter called it 'odious.'" Despite this, as noted before, in 1928 the Supreme Court ruled in *Olmstead* that the Fourth Amendment did not prohibit wiretapping. However, the US Congress made it a federal crime in 1934, before the Supreme Court overruled *Olmstead* in 1967 in *Katz*.[2]

Scholars, for centuries, have explored the impact of surveillance on individuals and on social and political life. Surveillance increases the capacity to control others. The first and most enduring expression of this understanding came at the end of the eighteenth century, when Jeremy Bentham proposed the panopticon. In 1791, Bentham produced an architectural design for a prison, which he called the panopticon, a term used ever since to describe a surveillance regime. Bentham's panopticon was a circular structure surrounding a central observation tower designed so that all the cells faced the tower. The guards in the tower could always see every prisoner. Even more importantly, while the guards could see the prisoners, the prisoners could not see the guards. This was designed to produce the so-called *panoptic effect*, a critical part of many surveillance systems: Every prisoner assumed that they were being continually watched. Pretty soon, the guards could stop watching, but the prisoners would continue acting as if they were being constantly observed. Bentham believed that the panoptic effect constituted an effective method of governance. It is for this very reason that utilitarianism has been seen to contain a totalitarian strand.

Michel Foucault, for his part, explored the diminution in the power of the individual and the expansion of government control after the transition during and after the nineteenth century from what he termed a "culture of spectacle" to a "carceral culture." The "culture of spectacle," characterizing the period before the impacts of the Enlightenment, preserved social control through public displays of hanging, torture, and other punishments, including dismemberment. In contrast, the "carceral culture" that followed used the panoptic effect to internalize conformity while spreading this compliance to formerly private spheres of life. As Foucault wrote, the Panopticon

> is polyvalent in its applications; it serves to reform prisoners but also to treat patients, to instruct schoolchildren, to confine the insane, [and] to supervise workers. . . . In each of its applications it makes it possible to perfect the exercise of power. It does this in several ways: because it can reduce the number of those who exercise it, while increasing the number on whom it is exercised. . . . The panoptic schema makes any apparatus of power more intense: it assures its economy (in material, in personnel, in time); it assures its efficacy by its preventative character, its continuing functioning and its automatic mechanisms.[3]

Writing in 1967 before Foucault, Alan Westin captures another effect of being systematically watched, writing, "Knowledge or fear that one is under systematic observation in public places destroys the sense of relaxation and freedom that men seek in open spaces and public areas."[4] It is this, along with its other effects, that makes the growing use of CCTV and especially facial recognition so problematic. Daniel J. Solove trenchantly captures the impact of the Panoptic effect and of surveillance when he writes,

> Surveillance limits our freedom. It can tie us to our past by creating a trail of information about us. It can make it difficult for us to speak anonymously. It can make our behavior less spontaneous and make us more self-conscious about where we go and what we do. Surveillance's inhibitory effects are especially potent when people are engaging in political protest or dissent. . . . Surveillance is a sweeping form of investigatory power. It extends beyond a search, for it records behavior, social interaction, and everything that a person says or does. . . . Moreover, unlike a typical search, which is often performed in a once-and-done fashion, electronic surveillance goes on continuously. Surveillance gives significant power to the watchers. Part of the harm is not simply in

being watched but in the lack of control that people have over the watchers. Surveillance creates the need to worry about the judgment of the watchers. Will our confidential information be revealed? What will be done with the information gleaned from surveillance? . . . Whether in public or in private, government surveillance can chill speech, dissent, and association; it provides great power to the watchers; it can be abused.[5]

Julie Cohen advances a similar argument about the impacts of surveillance on the individual but focuses on the way it induces conformity and conventionality. She writes,

Pervasive monitoring of every first move or false start will, at the margin, incline choices toward the bland and the mainstream. . . . [It shrinks] the acceptable spectrum of belief and behavior . . . [producing] a subtle, yet fundamental, shift in the content of our character. . . . [It consequently] threatens not only to chill the expression of eccentric individuality but also, gradually, to dampen the force of our aspirations to it.[6]

In addition, modern mass surveillance fosters a key element of the panoptic effect: people know of its existence but are unaware of how and when it is being used or if they are being observed at any moment. Part of this comes from the startlingly rapid development of the technology. As Yuval Noah Harari writes, no one "knows exactly how [they] are being surveilled and what the coming years might bring. Surveillance technology is developing at breakneck speed, and what seemed science fiction ten years ago is today old news."[7]

As previously noted, mass surveillance became a coterminous and intrinsic part of the digital age. Indeed, although often called the information age, it is equally appropriate to call this era the surveillance age. A long series of events and technological breakthroughs enabled this development. Perhaps the most salient was the successful British deciphering of the Nazi code machine Enigma during World War II. To decipher Enigma, Alan Turing, the most important figure at Bletchley Park, the British cryptography center, invented his own machine—the progenitor of the modern computer.

The work of someone else at Bletchley Park, Gordon Welshman, was perhaps even more important to the development of modern mass surveillance and metadata mining. Welshman created "traffic analysis," the lineal precursor to network analysis. These inventions facilitated the defeat of the Nazis while influencing the United States' creation of the Mitre Corporation—the entity established by the US government to develop digital surveillance capacities. For its part, the Mitre Corporation was as intimately connected to the development and expansion of the National Security Agency, the US surveillance agency, as Bletchley Park was to the genesis and evolution of the Government Communications Headquarters, the British signals intelligence agency.

The surveillance tools developed by these agencies were primarily directed at foreign adversaries during the Cold War. Even from the beginning, however, the capacious definition of *adversaries*, be they communists, presumed communists, leftists, or dissidents, including civil rights and other activists, drove the expansion of surveillance to more and more areas. Adversaries lurked overseas and at home and had to be watched and monitored. Surveillance spread from efforts to penetrate adversary states to the systematic observation of nonstate actors, who were seen as agents, both witting and unwitting, of these adversaries, and then to the monitoring of domestic political actors, especially dissidents. State efforts to "see" and monitor larger parts of individual lives drove them to push for regulatory and technological changes that made modern forms of communication more easily penetrable.

The development of the Internet was critical to the expansion of digital surveillance. US government research played a fundamental role in this area as well. The Advanced Research Projects Agency (ARPA) attached to the Department of Defense began the ARPANET project in 1966. In 1969 the first computers were connected. These links spread over the next few years, becoming the military computer network. DARPA (Defense Advanced Research Agency), attached to the Pentagon, not only participated in the genesis of the Internet but also played a critical role in the development of other innovations related to the security realm, including those that multiplied surveillance capacities. Access to the technologies that ARPA created expanded steadily, first manifesting themselves in the Computer Science Network (CSNET) in the 1980s. For its part, the National Science Foundation funded the National Science Foundation Network (NSFNET), which connected universities for the first time. By the time ARPANET ended in 1990, the private sector was heavily involved in the development of the World Wide Web, the current Internet. Once fully formed, the Internet became a conduit of boundless amounts of hitherto inaccessible information, permitting surveillance on a scale previously unimaginable.

While surveillance capacities grew steadily throughout the Cold War, it would take another "war," this time against nonstate actors, to bring the modern surveillance state into full bloom. After the attacks on the United States on September 11, 2001, state surveillance grew, and any distinctions between foreign and domestic surveillance largely evaporated in the search for terrorists scattered throughout the world. While dissidents and other opponents of states had long experienced surveillance, these efforts spread to entire populations, as governments sought to find what they described as "needles in haystacks." And as these digital capacities continued to evolve, an even broader use of surveillance became discernible, especially in the countries with the most developed digital sectors. This was the use of surveillance to make society more predictable. Such capacities theoretically enable the state to foresee and consequently control and largely eradicate crime, terrorism, and other social ills.

In China, an all-encompassing surveillance state sought to substitute an all-knowing and all-seeing governmental apparatus for citizen voice. An all-knowing government could not only provide perfect security and prosperity but could also substitute information for democracy. A virtually clairvoyant state, after all, did not need to seek either individual or collective expressions of preference, since its clairvoyance enabled it to understand the needs of the population better than they understood themselves.

Yuval Noah Harari describes this new type of monitoring as "under-the-skin surveillance." What marks this surveillance is the unprecedented ability to "hack" human beings and not only gather biometric and health information but also penetrate their emotional and cognitive states.[8] Harari thus raises the specter that haunts the development of the digital age: What does it mean to live in a world where machines, thanks to AI and machine learning, know us as well or even better than we know ourselves and where nothing remains personal and private? He describes the most baneful effects of this new world.

> If you know, for example, that I clicked on a Fox News link rather than a CNN link, that can teach you something about my political views and perhaps even my personality. But if you can monitor what happens to my body temperature, blood pressure, and heart rate as I watch the video clip, you can learn what makes me laugh, what makes me cry, and what makes me really, really angry. It is crucial to remember that anger, joy, boredom, and love are biological phenomena just like fever and a cough. The same technology that identifies coughs could also identify laughs. If corporations and governments start harvesting our biometric data en masse, they can get to know us far better than we know ourselves, and they can then not just predict our feelings but manipulate our feelings and sell us anything they want—be it a product or a politician.[9]

Despite all of these problems with surveillance, a powerful logic drives its continuing expansion. The architects of the digital age and their many employees and devoted followers tend to see and frame issues as information problems. The generalized faith in the emancipatory power of metadata available for mining drives surveillance in other areas. Surveillance, after all, constitutes one of the best ways to address issues whose resolution requires more information. CCTV and the tracking and monitoring capacities of phones, along with other devices that collect data, facilitate crime solving and contact tracing during pandemics, among other things. The question is whether these virtues override all the vices detailed above. Moreover, surveillance's greatest alleged "virtues" are its largest vices, since the finding of one, a few, or some requires intrusions into all and the appropriation of everybody's personal information.

NATIONAL SECURITY AND STATE SURVEILLANCE

In the United States, in common with many other countries, the extension and preservation of national security constitutes the most important rationale for surveillance. The power of this rationale rests on the primordial desire for safety and security. And the intensity of this desire, along with the presence of real and imagined threats, makes national security a naturally expansionary doctrine, especially in a country that seeks global dominance and that perceives ever-proliferating external and internal threats.[10]

The National Security Strategy documents that each US administration issues capture the expansiveness flowing from the deep conviction of American Exceptionalism—the belief in US greatness, universalism, and global destiny. In the last few decades, the most soaring expression of these understandings and vision came from the George W. Bush administration (2001–2009). The administration released "The National Security Strategy of the United States of America" in June 2002, less than a year after the 9/11 attacks. The overview of this document declared that "the US national security strategy will be based on a distinctly American internationalism that reflects the union of our values and our national interests. The aim of this strategy is not just to make the world safer but better."[11] The document then details several measures to achieve this goal. In addition, this Bush administration embraced the idea of preventive war, a doctrine with limitless implications. As Andrew Bacevich wrote, "the [second Bush] administration's response demonstrates how little the unprecedented attack on the World Trade Center and the Pentagon affected the assumptions underlying US foreign policy; the terrorists succeeded only in reinvigorating the conviction that destiny summons the United States, the one true universal nation to raise up a universal civilization based on American norms."[12]

Although the hard lessons of failure in the Iraq War and the War in Afghanistan somewhat tempered, if only temporarily, some of these inclinations and ambitions, US officials continued to see the country as an indispensable nation with an essential global role. Almost twenty years after Bush released his strategy, on March 3, 2021, Joe Biden's administration produced an "interim guidance" on national security strategy, designed to reassert the US global role after the chaos and unilateralism that marked the Trump administration. In the cover letter the president wrote:

The United States must renew its enduring advantages so that we can meet today's challenges from a position of strength. We will build back better our economic foundations; reclaim our place in international institutions; lift up our values at home and speak out to defend them around the world; modernize our military capabilities, while leading first with diplomacy, and revitalize America's unmatched network of alliances and partnerships.[13]

Even though this strategy was not as expansive as the second Bush administration's, elements of continuity in the US view of itself and of the centrality of its military predominance are more notable than differences over such things as preventive war and the importance of diplomacy.

In the United States, the definition and pursuit of national security receive little critical attention, given the power of fear and the corollary desire for safety. Moreover, patriotism's emotive power envelops invocations of national security, diminishing critical scrutiny and fanning popular support. Because of the power of conventional understandings of patriotism, a significant portion of the population accepts the state's claims that mass surveillance and secrecy promote the common good. As Solove writes, "'National security' has often been abused as a justification not only for surveillance but also for maintaining the secrecy of government records"—and, I would add, actions—"as well as for violating the civil rights of citizens."[14]

Nation-states with global ambitions, such as the United States, focus on external threats as much as countries who share borders with adversaries. Ironically, although their circumstances differ, both such states suffer from feelings of vulnerability. The latter fears attack from its neighbors, but the former, despite all their power and military capacity, do not manage to feel more secure and only become more acutely aware of the range of threats that they confront. These threats, in turn, are the result of the pursuit of hegemony, which requires continual intrusions and aggressions against others.

The reification of threat narratives heightens the power and consequence of the coercive organs. The US government allocates the largest budgets in the world to its military, its intelligence agencies, and its domestic law-enforcement and police apparatus, since fears of internal disorders and especially crime often accompany fears of outsiders. These agencies will deploy any tools, including mass surveillance, that promise to help them ferret out old and new threats. Despite all these efforts, however, and the aggregate expenditure of trillions of dollars over the years, feelings of security remain elusive, encouraging ever-larger budget allocations to the coercive apparatus and the deployment of even more intrusive surveillance tools. And these entities, because of their position, play a critical role in labeling and identifying threats and consequently help frame the parameters of the country's national security doctrine.

The coercive agencies of the state intrinsically privilege security over civil rights and liberties. This is especially true if certain rights and liberties inhibit the pursuit of activities, including mass, warrantless surveillance, undertaken in the name of security. In the United States, despite the modest number of "Islamic" terrorist attacks on American soil in the decades after September 11, 2001, terrorism drove many of the country's foreign and domestic policies, consumed trillions of dollars, and led much of the population to accept government intrusions on their rights, including the deployment of mass, and consequently indiscriminate, surveillance.

The informational appetite of the US government fundamentally, and perhaps fatally, undermines historical understandings of limited government. The state's growing omniscience gives it previously unimagined capacities. Metadata mining makes all state activities more efficient but also more minute, searching, and intrusive. As noted before, the effort to "see" and "hear" everything creates a totalizing governing project given the extremity of its penetrations into the private lives of entire populations.

The state's sense that its capacities, no matter how large, are insufficient not only undermines regulatory efforts but also explains the reluctance to restrict the use of mass surveillance and other digital tools. Jane Harmon is the former congressional representative from California who devoted a large part of her time in Congress to the Intelligence Committee before leaving to become head of the Woodrow Wilson Center, a leading think tank and academic center. She perfectly reflects the view that the state's capacities, no matter how enormous, remain inadequate. "While our intelligence community is the most impressive in the world," she writes, "we can't see and know everything. No nation can."[15] Enduring feelings of insufficient clairvoyance, even as mass surveillance covers more and more areas of life, ensures the continuing search for even more powerful and intrusive digital tools, along with ever-expanding budgets.

Much of the US population, moreover, does not think in terms of a trade-off between privacy and security or the cost to their rights in the context of the "war on terror." Although some feel that they have surrendered privacy while gaining little in terms of security, others think that these policies advance security without compromising privacy. For example, a study by Krueger, Best, and Johnson reveals that a "nationally representative survey of US residents demonstrated that the vast majority of Americans do not think of counterterrorism policies in terms consistent with the assumptions of the liberty-security values trade-off. Respondents typically thought that these either do not effectively reduce terrorism but do violate privacy or do effectively reduce terrorism and do not violate privacy."[16]

Other studies take a different approach, exploring factors that influence the population's views on liberty and security. Darren W. Davis and Brian D.

Silver, who studied the US population's willingness to trade civil liberties for greater personal security in the wake of the 9/11 attacks, conclude that

> the greater people's sense of threat, the lower their support for civil liberties. This effect interacts, however, with trust in government. The lower people's trust in government, the less willing they are to trade off civil liberties for security, regardless of their level of threat. . . . Liberals are less willing to trade off civil liberties than moderates and conservatives, but liberals converge toward the position taken by conservatives when their sense of the threat of terrorism is high.[17]

Other scholars argue that the desire for security overwhelms the protection of privacy. For example, Johan Cas, Rocco Bellanova, J. Peter Burgess, Michael Friedewald, and Walter Peissl write that

> [Security incidents] . . . usually directly [impact] the concerned persons; privacy violations, on the other hand, can happen in an unnoticeable manner. The consequence of such violations may only become visible with long delays. . . . Security incidents, in particular if they are related to terrorism, immediately get highest attention from media and policymaking. In contrast, only very large-scale privacy infringements make it to the headlines and are hardly followed up by policy debates on concrete actions.[18]

In the aftermath of a crisis, the public clamor for security grows, and with it demands for state action.

STATE CONSTITUENCIES FAVORING SURVEILLANCE IN THE UNITED STATES

The expansion of the national security apparatus in the United States during the Cold War created a powerful constituency pushing for the adoption and use of technologies that enhanced state capacities. Those connected to the formulation and implementation of national security policy share a remarkably similar view of the country's role in the world, regardless of whether they are Republican or Democrat. This explains the extraordinary continuity in many American policies. As Michael Glennon trenchantly asks, "Why does national security policy remain constant even when one president is replaced by another who as a candidate repeatedly, forcefully, and eloquently promised fundamental changes in that policy?"[19] Glennon asks this question to explore the continuity in both the definition and practice of national security during the George W. Bush and Obama administrations.

President Obama, despite criticizing many parts of the Bush adminis-tration's "war on terror," completely ended only one of his predecessor's policies—torture. The Obama administration continued to practice "extraor-dinary rendition"—a euphemism for state-sponsored kidnapping and torture by proxy. His administration pursued some paltry and unsurprisingly failed efforts to close the Guantánamo prison and continued to hold detainees with-out trial in military prisons. In addition, it significantly expanded several of the Bush administration's other programs, notably its drone war—the practice of remote, state-sponsored assassination. Finally, to pursue national security whistleblowers, the Obama administration used the Espionage Act (a law dating back to the apex of xenophobia during World War I) more frequently than did *all* his predecessors combined during the previous century. And what were these whistleblowers trying to reveal? The Obama administration's con-tinuing pursuit of the mass, indiscriminate, warrantless surveillance initiated by George W. Bush.

Despite denouncing surveillance (derived from his claim that the Obama administration had spied on his campaign), Donald Trump did not end this practice. Moreover, even though Trump was a disruptive figure, attacking the national security apparatus as the "deep state," Bush and Obama's "war on terror" policies continued, particularly the drone war. Trump's retreat from long-established global engagements and treaties and presumed attachment to Vladimir Putin alienated parts of the national security apparatus and virtu-ally all the foreign policy elite, as did several of his other policies, includ-ing the abandonment of the Kurds in Syria, his approach to North Korea, and his anti-NATO rhetoric. All of this reveals the extent of the consensus at the apex of the US foreign policy establishment, regardless of political party affiliation, about American Exceptionalism—the "indispensability" of its global role and the desirability of its possession of a vast military and national security establishment.

However, though the foreign policy elite objected to Trump, after his elec-tion in most ways little changed. Vast military spending, always a priority of this establishment and the national security apparatus, grew under Trump. The reauthorization of surveillance with the president's support, as will be discussed later, occurred, as well. So did the deployment of US troops all over the world, even though Trump initiated the precipitous end of the American military intervention in Afghanistan that culminated in the calamitous and chaotic withdrawal of remaining US and NATO troops in 2021 during the first year of the Biden administration. Moreover, Trump continued and even expanded several establishment priorities, including the large financial and military commitment to Israel and continued closeness to Saudi Arabia along with hostility toward Iran. Throughout his time in office, Trump professed the desire to expand Guantánamo and resume torture, although he failed to fulfill these goals, in part because of opposition from large parts of the Congress and from the CIA, the primary practitioner of torture during the second Bush administration. The latter was particularly concerned about the reputational costs of waterboarding and its other "enhanced interrogation" techniques.

However, Trump's rhetoric and bombast, conjoined with his departures from orthodox foreign policy positions, in particular toward NATO, and his alleged closeness to Vladimir Putin caused the foreign policy establishment to oppose him and support Joe Biden during the 2020 presidential campaign. This establishment hoped that Biden's victory would allow a speedy return to the status quo ante. After winning the election, Biden demonstrated his continuing attachment to many of this establishment's understandings of the world, picking representatives of the "national security consensus" to serve, respectively, as his secretary of state and as his national security adviser. Many of his other appointments come from this foreign policy establishment, as well.

Joe Biden himself was a representative member of this group, sharing its views about the desirability and necessity of an expansive US role in the world. Throughout his long career in the Senate, he repeatedly voiced this consensus perspective, particularly during his tenure on the Senate Foreign Relations Committee. During the George W. Bush administration, Biden supported the country's response to the 9/11 attacks, including the cornerstone of that reaction, the USA PATRIOT Act.

In addition, then-Senator Biden voted for the open-ended Authorization for Use of Military Force of 2001 that ratified the second Bush administration's decision to invade Afghanistan and Iraq. This AUMF not only permitted the calamity that subsequently unfolded in Iraq but also the numerous military actions and interventions that the US undertook throughout the Middle East during the Obama and Trump administrations. Even though Joe Biden came to oppose the Iraq War and argued against Barack Obama's troop "surge" in Afghanistan, he never wavered in this support for the notably wide-ranging American role in the world or the alliance structure that emerged after World War II.

It was for these reasons that Republican members of the foreign policy establishment joined their Democratic counterparts to support Biden's 2020 presidential campaign. They used their positions in foreign policy organizations, think tanks, and lobbying groups to criticize the Trump administration throughout the campaign. Biden's rhetoric and general approach, especially toward allies, immediately earned the approval of members of this establishment after he won the 2020 election. Many in this establishment objected to his decision to withdraw American troops from Afghanistan and criticized the implementation of this policy but in general supported his advocacy of a notably robust global role and a "tilt" toward addressing China and Russia. They also applauded Biden's reinvigoration of the NATO alliance in response to the massing of Russian troops on the borders of Ukraine during late 2021 and his reaction to Vladimir Putin's subsequent invasion of the country in 2022. After this invasion, they supported the administration's response, limiting their rare criticisms to calls for even more extensive arming of the Ukrainian army than the United States was already pursuing.

Additionally, this establishment applauded Biden's rejection of the isolationism that occasionally characterized Trump's "America first" rhetoric. Moreover, they widely favored the Biden administration's immediate assertions that the United States intended to "reengage" and remain the "indispensable" global hegemon and "lead" the world. Part of this enterprise, of course, required the maintenance of the country's huge military and national security expenditures. President Biden's support for the foreign policy status quo indicated a corollary unwillingness to push for the circumscription of mass surveillance since it had become a central pillar of the maintenance and extension of global power.

Writing in 2015, Michael Glennon provides an especially nuanced analysis of the persistence of US national security doctrines and practices across different administrations. He argues that the US possesses a "double government"—adopting Walter Bagehot's memorable description of the British state in the nineteenth century. Bagehot had argued that the British government included what he termed "dignified institutions," notably the monarchy and the House of Lords, and "efficient institutions"—those bodies that actually conducted the business of government. Glennon applies this to the United States, calling the "dignified" institutions "Madisonians," a group that includes the presidency, Congress, and the courts, while calling Bagehot's "efficient institution" the "Trumanites."

The Trumanites populate or are connected to the expansive bureaucratic apparatus devoted to national security that the United States created during and after World War II. The core of this Trumanite group

consists of the several hundred executive officials who sit atop the military, intelligence, diplomatic, and law-enforcement departments and agencies that have as their mission the protection of America's international and internal security. Large segments of the public continue to believe that America's constitutionally established, dignified institutions are the locus of governmental power. . . . But when it comes to defining and protecting national security, the public's impression is mistaken. America's efficient institution makes most of the key decisions concerning national security, removed from public view and from the constitutional restrictions that check America's dignified institutions.[20]

One might add as well that Trumanites share the consensus views of the rest of the foreign policy establishment about the necessity and desirability of an extraordinarily robust American role in the world.

The maintenance of social place, professional recognition, and prestige fuels adherence to a dominant paradigm. And its wide adoption gives it the status of a presumptive, established truth—a status enhanced through endless repetition, encouraging the excoriation and marginalization of dissenters. This network extends out of the bureaucracy to much of the country's foreign policy establishment, clustered in think tanks and academic institutions. Continual circulation between these spheres reinforces the shared view of the United States and its role in the world discussed above as well as virtual consensus over both the proper definition of national security and the means required to protect the country and its power.

This shared view, as noted above, transcends party affiliation. Thus neoconservatives in this establishment, like Max Boot and William Kristol, and liberal internationalists, like Samantha Power, Susan Rice, and Hillary Clinton, possess similar understandings about the desirability of dominant, and overwhelmingly expensive, American global military power and favor activism and intervention—although they differ on the proper ends of these interventions. In addition, as noted before, they shared a profound loathing of Donald Trump. Trump's characterization of the Trumanites as part of the "deep state" not only aroused their ire but also confirmed the power of Glennon's analysis. Of course, Trump's bombast and incoherence and the enormous gap between his words and deeds clouded matters, since he excoriated the "deep state" on the one hand while on the other appointing generals to an unprecedented number of top positions in the government. More generally, the internal and national security apparatus of the American state did not experience any diminution in their centrality or capacity during the Trump administration. His disdain for the "dignified institutions" of the US government clouded matters further, making him odious to many of the Trumanites even as he continued to pursue their budgetary priorities.

Michael Glennon summarizes the specific features of the Trumanite worldview and their approach to policy, when he writes that

> Their objective is to be *uncategorizable*—neither predictably hardline nor predictably soft-line, weighing options on their merits but remaining always—for it is, after all, national security that is at stake—tough. . . . One must always retain credibility, which counsels against fighting losing battles at high credibility costs, particularly for a policy that would play in Peoria as a weak one. . . . It is the appearance that matters, and in appearance the policy must seem hard-hitting. . . . The Trumanites thus define security in military and intelligence terms rather than political and diplomatic ones.[21]

A global hegemonic role ensures the continual presence of threats. Surveillance promises the early, indeed preemptive, discovery of threats, enabling their "neutralization." Problematically, the Trumanites and their coreligionaries in the military and the intelligence apparatus, as well as in Congress, the media, and the defense and surveillance industry, need persistent and even escalating threats to preserve their power, prestige, and budgets. The Trumanites, in addition, work assiduously to preserve their status as indispensable experts. This status comes from their unique, indeed esoteric, understanding of the exigencies of national security, since they and just a relatively few others are privy to the nation's secrets.

Michael Glennon writes that the incentive structure of the Trumanites

> encourages the exaggeration of existing threats and the creation of imaginary ones. The security programs that emerge are, in economic terms, "sticky down"—easier to grow than to shrink. The Trumanites sacrifice little when disproportionate money or manpower is devoted to security. . . . The Trumanites, however, reap the benefits of that disproportionality—a larger payroll, more personnel, broader authority, and an even lower risk that they will be blamed in the event of a successful attack.[22]

It is also true that the Trumanite position does not merely reflect personal and professional self-interest. Instead, a shared belief in American Exceptionalism and a common conviction that US global hegemony and "full-spectrum dominance" advance human well-being animates them as well. More generally, the incentive to exaggerate rather than minimize putative threats explains why national security understandings tend to expand to new objects while resisting contraction.

The framing of issues in military terms inexorably drives the United States toward ever-greater militarism. Several elements distinguish militarism from the mere maintenance of military power. First, it includes the elevation of the soldier over the citizen, as Andrew Bacevich argues.[23] One symptom of militarism is the transformation of the US military into the most prestigious institution in the society, along with the corollary perception that soldiers embody the best of the natural character, whose "service" makes them more virtuous and self-sacrificing than the rest of the citizenry. And ordinary citizens, along with pundits and others, repeatedly extol this "service," ratifying the superior virtue of the soldier over the citizen.

In addition, the tendency to frequently use force as a first rather than a last resort and to participate in frequent warfare reflect a militaristic conception of the world. Finally, notably large and unquestioned military budgets and the centrality of military strength and power to national identity define militarism. Ronald Reagan's glorification of the military, and his ability to recast

the narrative of the Vietnam War, played a large role in developing militarism. So too did the culture wars roiling the United States after the 1960s.
These culture wars pushed American evangelicals and the military together
as defenders of "traditional America" and of the country's "heritage." During
and after the Reagan administration, unceasing and voluble praise for the
military became a central feature of public discourse.

The inevitable outcome of the militaristic self-definition that captured the
United States was the creation of the largest military budget in the world—
estimated to exceed the military expenditures of the next largest ten military
spenders, including both allies and adversaries, combined. As a global hegemon and the "indispensable country," the United States requires an intelligence and surveillance apparatus of a size, capacity and intrusiveness to
match its ambitions and role. Both the military and the country's enormous
intelligence and internal-security apparatus created as parts of this enterprise
are voracious consumers of digital technologies, seeking to weaponize them
in as many ways as possible.

Andrew Bacevich's books on American militarism and Michael Glennon's
discussion of the implications of double government are part of an older literature examining the consequences of "standing armies" and their corollary
national security agencies for democracy. The US founding fathers argued
in *The Federalist Papers* that union would vitiate the need for a "standing
army," an institution that they saw as inimical to the carefully balanced
republic that they were trying to construct. In their view, such a military not
only required increased taxation but also concentrated power in the federal
government, reducing the power of states. It also increased the scope and
power of the executive branch. Finally, "standing armies" elevated the soldier
over the citizen with negative consequences for democracy. These themes
reemerge again and again in the work of a broad range of scholars across
American history.

For example, in 1941, during World War II, one of the country's seminal
sociologists and political scientists, Harold Laswell, wrote about what he
defined as the "garrison state." A military logic and a militarized understanding of the world dominated such states. Thus he undertook "to consider the
possibility that we are moving toward a world of 'garrison states'—a world
in which the specialists on violence are the most powerful group in society.
From this point of view the trend of our time is away from the dominance of
the specialist on bargaining . . . toward the supremacy of the soldier."[24]

Not long thereafter, writing in the mid-1950s, C. Wright Mill asserted that
"what is being promulgated and reinforced is the military metaphysics—the
cast of mind that defines international reality as basically military."[25] And
Justice William O. Douglas worried deeply during the Cold War about the
growing influence of the military on US foreign policy.[26] Furthermore, in an

analysis that in some ways parallels Andrew Bacevich's arguments about US militarism, James Carroll wrote in 1965 that "for the first time in American history, military assumptions undergirded America's idea of itself."[27] Finally, one long-standing member of the foreign policy establishment, Leslie Gelb, acknowledged in 2009 that his initial support for the Iraq War was "symptomatic of unfortunate tendencies within the foreign policy community—namely, the disposition and incentives to support wars to retain political and professional credibility."[28]

Although several scholars worried about militarism and the corollary growth of the national security establishment along with its handmaidens, secrecy and mass surveillance, a much larger group supported the pursuit of overwhelming American military power and intelligence capacities. This group completely dominated public discourse after the 1980s, when the foreign policy consensus acquired its contemporary form. A critical moment occurred after the fall of the Berlin Wall in 1989, with the collapse of the Soviet Union, the adversary whose existence justified unparalleled military and intelligence spending.

The United States, despite the end of the Cold War, only shrank the budgets of some of the coercive organs of the American state. Instead, the shared conviction that the United States was the linchpin of the world order—a world order designed to protect the country's economic and political interests—drove a continuing quest for "full-spectrum dominance," the establishment and preservation of preeminence in every conceivable military domain, ranging from conventional warfare to space and cyber. After 2001 and the 9/11 attacks, the Trumanite view of the desirability and indispensability of US global hegemony did not change but only directed itself to new ends and instruments. In particular, the conduct of an asymmetric war against a clandestine nonstate actor required the development and deployment of new tools.

The coincidence of 9/11 with the emergence of digital innovations, including the capacity to surveil everyone and to monitor and track people in previously unimaginable ways, animated the adoption of these digital tools to fight the "war on terrorism." Some expressed concerns about the use of these tools, but most, reflecting the country's zeitgeist after 9/11, supported their adoption or remained politically disengaged. Edward Snowden's revelations in 2013 about the NSA's mass, warrantless surveillance of both Americans and foreigners did spark outrage against the state's practices and especially its appropriation of all the personal information flowing over the Internet and its collection of everybody's private data. However, this scrutiny declined in the last years of the second decade of the twenty-first century, shifting away from the surveillance activities of the US government.

During this period, continuing revelations about the practices of corporate actors, and especially Facebook, consumed much of the attention devoted to exploring the negative consequences of digital technologies. Moreover, scrutiny of the US government's cyber activities was further diminished by a long-running controversy, embodied in the fraught, contested, and obsessively reported Mueller investigation about the Russian use of digital tools to interfere in the 2016 US presidential election in support of Donald Trump (or, more precisely, against Hillary Clinton). Additionally, widespread hacking operations against Americans originating in Russia and China along with other countries drove Snowden's concerns further from the headlines. So too did the increase in the number of ransomware attacks originating in Russia against American corporations during the Biden administration. Continual media coverage of these activities shifted attention away from the surveillance practices of other Western democracies as well. Simultaneously, continuing revelations about the practices of the Chinese state made US government surveillance seem small and inconsequential in comparison.

However, diminished attention did not reflect a decline in mass warrantless surveillance protected by a wall of secrecy. Neither did it indicate the US government's retreat from extraordinarily extensive collection and data mining. Furthermore, discussions about cyberattacks against the United States rarely explored American cyberattacks against others. To read the American press, one might imagine that the United States lacked the capacities of its adversaries in this area. These discussions rarely noted that the United States and Israel inaugurated state-sponsored cyberwar when in 2007 they deployed the Stuxnet virus against Iran's centrifuges, with the intention of disabling the country's nuclear program. The scope of this attack began to be revealed in 2010 and 2011. Not surprisingly, state adversaries responded in kind. Effectively, this new mode of attack against the United States began in 2014. During that year, the Iranian government hacked the Las Vegas Sands Corporation to punish its owner, Sheldon Adelson, for suggesting that the US drop an atom bomb on Iran. North Korea took a page from this book when it hacked Sony Entertainment to prevent the release of *The Interview*, a comedy revolving around the assassination of the country's dictator, Kim Jong-un.

The ensuing and escalating media coverage of these and other attacks during the rest of the decade typically did not explore the global cyber activities of the United States and its allies. In fact, in the wake of large hacks during late 2020 and early 2021, many clamored for more extensive spending on cyber capabilities and urged the United States to take more aggressive cyber action against Russia, in particular. As usual, many in the national security establishment argued that the United States had failed to spend enough and allowed its capacities to languish—even though its spending on cyber exceeded the budgets of its adversaries by several orders of magnitude. Simultaneously, the government had to escalate its cyber activities to confront adversaries and address the activities of criminal organizations targeting American networks.

THE LEFT AND THE RIGHT AND
MASS SURVEILLANCE

Whatever its other impacts, and for the first time in several years, the presidential election in 2016 witnessed a brief reemergence of public discussion about US government surveillance. As noted before, Donald Trump claimed that the Obama administration had surveilled his campaign, weaponizing this capacity. Evidence that the US government had surveilled Carter Page, an advisor to the Trump campaign, provided proof to Trump sympathizers that the "deep state" was targeting him because of his political affiliations.

All of this caused a scrambling of political alignments on the issue of government surveillance. The American left and libertarians on the right had long opposed surveillance and many of the national security apparatus's activities. However, after the 2016 elections, while libertarians largely retained their staunch objection to surveillance and to many of the activities of the national security state, a significant portion of the left abandoned their historic reservations about the CIA and the FBI and other parts of the "deep state." Instead, these entities were suddenly seen as allies in the struggle against Donald Trump. Former high-ranking members of these agencies became common pundits on news outlets like MSNBC and CNN, lavishly extolled and thanked by hosts for "their service" and asked to opine on the misdeeds of the Trump administration.

Hosts such as Rachel Maddow on MSNBC lauded these long-standing former members of the CIA, the NSA, the FBI, and the DEA for their virtue, their probity, their selfless patriotism, and their attachment to the country. Conveniently forgotten were torture, Guantánamo, extraordinary rendition, the war on drugs, and other actions that violated civil and human rights. No mention was made, when interviewing former high-ranking members of the CIA, of their role in approving or providing legal justification for the agency's activities during the "war on terror." Their anti-Trump sentiments established their manifest probity and unquestioned virtue.

Some of the frequent guests on these shows—all of whom shared the Trumanite view of the world—included Leon Panetta, former head of the Department of Defense and the CIA during the Obama administration, and his chief of staff, Jeremy Bash. These guests could be counted on to express horror about the Trump administration's violation of hallowed and virtuous foreign policy practices even though they themselves had worked in an agency whose actions repeatedly violated human-rights and international law. Another pundit and guest on Rachel Maddow's show and other programs was Chuck Rosenberg, former acting head of the DEA. By virtue of his leadership of this organization, Rosenberg had played a significant role in advancing a policy that the left had historically, and accurately, seen as saturated with racism—the drug war. Moreover, his roles in the Department of Justice had made him a part of a legal apparatus that transformed the United States into the largest carceral state in the world, a development that the left rightly deplored as well. But all was forgotten with Rosenberg's stalwart opposition to Trump.

An additional favored interlocutor on both MSNBC and CNN was General James Clapper, another Trump critic. Director of National Intelligence during the Obama administration, Clapper was a particularly public defender in this role of the US conduct of mass warrantless surveillance, of the drone war, and other national security policies that the American left had criticized during the George W. Bush administration. Both CNN and MSNBC used a stable of other generals as foreign policy commentators. Unsurprisingly, all of them reliably voiced the consensus informing the Trumanite view of the world. An especially notable member of this group was General Mike Hayden, a central architect of the US surveillance regime and its national security policies. As head of the NSA during much of the "war on terror," General Hayden had been a critically important champion of the mass warrantless surveillance system that Edward Snowden revealed in 2013. But like the others mentioned above, Hayden was a critic of the Trump administration. Ironically, many of these guests on certain "left-wing" media outlets were otherwise staunch conservatives, who had never supported progressive causes and whose sympathies, before Trump, had lain with the Republican Party.

Unlike libertarians, conservatives had always been supporters of the national security apparatus and of ever-expanding military and intelligence budgets. While many criticized the Trump administration, its inconsistency split many of them. Undoubtedly, some were offended by a number of its actions, but others strongly supported its tax cuts, its appointment of conservative judges, its culture wars, and the priority it accorded to military spending.

Although mass state surveillance has remained a largely dormant political issue at the time of this writing, during the first years of the third decade of the twenty-first century, an important group of NGOs and political figures continues to press for change in this area. The Electronic Frontier Foundation, for example, a longstanding advocate of digital privacy and a critical voice against mass surveillance and other state practices that use digital technologies in constitutionally dubious ways, remains active. Other notable NGOs that pursue these same ends include the ACLU, the Center for Democracy and Technology, Privacy International, Freedom of the Press Foundation, the Center for Humane Technology, the Tor Project, and the Electronic Privacy Information Center.

CONCLUSION

Despite being reviled as an odious practice across different cultures and societies, mass surveillance grew inexorably after the dawn of the digital age. The marriage of novel technological capacities with ubiquitous fear in the wake of the September 11, 2001, attacks in the United States transformed government practices in this area. The vast national security apparatus created during World War II and expanded during the Cold War found a new raison d'être after 9/11 and rushed to embrace digital technologies.

Up until Edward Snowden's revelations in 2013, the bulk of the US population remained unaware of the scope and reach of mass warrantless surveillance and of the state's appropriation of everyone's personal and formerly private information. A constituency spanning the US national security apparatus and foreign policy establishment supported this practice, seeing it as essential to the preservation of national security. The continual invocation of patriotism and national security ensured the support of large segments of the population.

A broad consensus about American Exceptionalism, the indispensability of its global dominance, and the undesirability of isolationism and other doctrines framed the discussion about the need for mass surveillance and the use of other tools. Much of the media did not question the broad lineaments of the US policy consensus mentioned above, even though these understandings often drove the country to adopt practices or participate in interventions that produced serious violations of human and civil rights. A few dissenting politicians, as noted before, such as Senators Ron Wyden (D-OR) and Mike Lee (R-UT), objected to the centrality of mass warrantless surveillance in the conduct of the "war on terror," but most were willing to trade liberty for security, to the extent that they thought about this at all as a trade-off.

Concerns about mass warrantless surveillance reached a peak after the Snowden revelations but then receded, although they did not disappear, replaced by worries about hacking, the behavior of social media companies, and other matters. Declining attention did not mean that the state's activities diminished. Indeed, as revealed by the US government's reaction to the Capitol riot on January 6, 2021, the FBI was already surveilling many of those who might have been inclined to participate in the riot and had knocked on their doors long before the event to dissuade them from traveling to Washington, D.C. It prevented others from flying to Washington, demonstrating the extent of its awareness of the movements of those who belonged to these groups. This came on top of its long-running surveillance of those the FBI labeled "Black identity activists" (including supporters of BLM) and other dissidents, peaceful and violent alike. Despite this, in the wake of the

Capitol riot, officials claimed that the law—or the absence of law—hampered their ability to fight "domestic terrorists," arguing that the powers and punishments from the "war on terror" should be extended to domestic groups. They, of course, did not discuss how this would add impetus to domestic mass warrantless surveillance.

NOTES

1. William Blackstone's *Commentaries on the Laws of England*, no. 169, as quoted in Daniel J. Solove, "A Taxonomy of Privacy," *University of Pennsylvania Law Review* 154, no. 3 (January 2006): 492.

2. Solove, "Taxonomy of Privacy," both the quotation and the discussion found on 492.

3. Michel Foucault, *Discipline and Punish* (New York: Vintage Books, 1977), 205, 206, parenthetical original.

4. Alan F. Westin, *Privacy and Freedom* (New York: Atheneum, 1967), 31.

5. Daniel J. Solove, *Nothing to Hide: The False Tradeoff between Privacy and Security* (New Haven: Yale University Press, 2011), 178–80.

6. Julie E. Cohen, "Examined Lives: Informational Privacy and the Subject as Object," *Stanford Law Review* 52, no. 1373 (2000): 1426.

7. Yuval Noah Harari, "Yuval Noah Harari: The World after Coronavirus," *Financial Times*, March 19, 2020, https://www.ft.com/content/19d90308-6858-11ea-a3c9-1fe6fedcca75.

8. Yuval Noah Harari in an interview with Stephen Sackur, "Yuval Noah Harari—Israeli Historian and Best-Selling Author," *HARDtalk BBC*, April 27, 2020, https://www.bbc.co.uk/programmes/m000hx95.

9. Harari, "World after Coronavirus."

10. For some trenchant analyses of this phenomenon, see Benjamin Friedman, "Alarums and Excursions Explaining Threat Inflation in US Foreign Policy," Cato.org, June 17, 2020, https://www.cato.org/publications/alarums-excursions-explaining-threat-inflation-us-foreign-policy. In addition, an especially excellent collection that explores this same topic is Andrew Bacevich, ed., *The Long War: A New History of US National Security Policy Since World War II* (New York: Columbia University Press, 2007).

11. National Security Council, George W. Bush White House, "The National Security Strategy," September 2002, https://georgewbush-whitehouse.archives.gov/nsc/nss/2002/.

12. Andrew Bacevich, *The New American Militarism: How Americans Are Seduced By War* (New York: Oxford University Press, 2005), 13.

13. Joseph R. Biden, *Interim National Security Strategic Guidance*, March 2021, https://www.whitehouse.gov/wp-content/uploads/2021/03/NSC-1v2.pdf.

14. Solove, *Nothing to Hide*, 66.

15. Jane Harmon, "Editorial," *New York Times*, February 24, 2020.

16. Brian S. Krueger, Samuel J. Best, and Kristin Johnson, "Assessing Dimensions of the Security-Liberty Trade-Off in the United States," *Surveillance and Society* 18, no. 1 (2020), https://ojs.library.queensu.ca/index.php/surveillance-and-society/article /view/10419/9159.

17. Darren W. Davis and Brian D. Silver, "Civil Liberties vs. Security: Public Opinion in the Context of the Terrorist Attacks on America," *American Journal of Political Science* 48, no. 1 (January 2004): 28.

18. Johann Cas, Rocco Bellanova, J. Peter Burgess, Michael Friedewald, and Walter Peissl, "Introduction," in *Surveillance Privacy and Security* (London: Routledge, 2017), 7.

19. Michael J. Glennon, *National Security and Double Government* (Oxford: Oxford University Press, 2015), 3.

20. Glennon, *National Security and Double Government*, 6–7.

21. Glennon, *National Security and Double Government*, 19–20.

22. Glennon, *National Security and Double Government*, 19–20.

23. For an excellent analysis of American militarism, see Andrew Bacevich's discussion of this topic in *New American Militarism*.

24. Harold D. Laswell, "The Garrison State," *American Journal of Sociology* 46, no. 4 (January 1941): 455.

25. C. Wright Mill, *The Power Elite* (New York: Oxford University Press, 1956), 222.

26. William O. Douglas, *The Court Years, 1939–1975: The Autobiography of William O. Douglas* (New York: Random House, 1980), 292.

27. James Carroll, *House of War: The Pentagon and the Disastrous Rise of American Power* (Boston: Houghton Mifflin, 2006), 29.

28. Lesley H. Gelb, "Mission Not Accomplished," with Jeanne-Paloma Zelmati, *Democracy*, no. 13 (Summer 2009), https://democracyjournal.org/magazine/13/mission-not-accomplished/.

Chapter 6

The Legal Architecture Governing Mass State Surveillance in the United States

Because the US Constitution and some Supreme Court and statutory decisions occasionally threaten to obstruct the operations of the American national security apparatus, interpretations must be found that create legal cover for these actions. In recent decades, the Office of Legal Counsel attached to the White House and the chief legal officers of entities like the CIA and the NSA have provided this service, finding ways to legally justify mass surveillance and other actions. The OLC became famous during the George W. Bush administration after issuing opinions justifying the practice of torture. Even though the United States had promoted and signed the International Convention against Torture, the OLC elided this "problem" through the redefinition of torture. According to its redefinition, actions leading to the failure of organs resulting in death constituted torture; anything short of these measures, including internationally recognized acts of torture, were acceptable US government practices.

In general, the OLC issues opinions comporting with the "unitary executive" theory. As a result, OLC opinions expand presidential power and seek to restrict limitations on the executive. For example, beyond enabling torture, the OLC legally authorized the mass warrantless surveillance of the US population during the George W. Bush administration. Another famous or infamous OLC opinion established that presidents enjoy complete immunity during their tenure in office. According to the OLC, impeachment or the invocation of the Twenty-Fifth Amendment could remove a president from office, but they are otherwise immune from judicial sanctions during their tenure.

In the main, however, the national security apparatus did not have to rely on controversial interpretations to pursue surveillance, given the weakness of US laws in this area, even before 9/11. As Stephen J. Schulhofer notes when writing about a period when mass warrantless surveillance of the American population was not a state practice:

> American surveillance laws set a very low standard for court orders that autho-
> rize . . . [the monitoring] . . . of telephone numbers (but not the content) of a
> suspect's incoming calls. Officials must certify that the information sought is
> considered relevant to an ongoing investigation, but they need not present any
> facts indicating an objective basis for suspicion, much less probable cause.
> Before 9/11, however, the law was unclear as to whether comparable surveil-
> lance of email (monitoring origin and destination addresses) was subject to the
> same regime, was more strictly regulated, or was not regulated at all. . . . The
> Patriot Act solved this puzzle by providing that email and Internet addresses . . .
> [were] subject to the same low standard applicable to phone numbers. Although
> this approach is superficially logical, it ignores the fact that routing identifiers
> for email and Internet browsing (such as Web site URLs) convey much more
> sensitive information than the number of an incoming or outgoing phone call.[1]

Moreover, the regulatory architecture governing state surveillance enshrines secrecy, as noted before. The foundation of the so-called "state secrets privilege" came from a seminal Supreme Court case, *United States v. Reynolds*, decided in 1952. In *Reynolds*, three widows brought a case against the military seeking accident reports on the crash of a B-29 bomber that killed their husbands. The military argued that releasing the details would reveal the plane's secret mission, threatening national security. The Court sided with the government, although it limited the invocation of the privilege, writing that it could only be invoked where "there is a reasonable danger that disclosure [of evidence] will expose military matters which, in the interest of national security, should not be divulged." And the invocation of the privilege had to come from "the head of the department which has control over the matter."[2]

Over time, interpretations of law and frequent invocation erased even these modest restrictions. The state secrets privilege extended to an increasing number of government activities far removed from the protection of national security. Eventually, the state secrets privilege, along with the commonplace classification of documents, transformed secrecy into a routine part of governance. Ironically, or perhaps not so ironically, given the frequent abuse of the privilege and the general extent of classification and secrecy after the 9/11 attacks, information eventually emerged that the government had lied to the Supreme Court in *Reynolds*. This deception became evident after the 2000 declassification and release of the documents about the B-29 crash. These documents showed that the plane had not been involved in a secret mission. Instead, the crash was the product of negligence given the poor condition and shoddy maintenance of the aircraft. So the "state secrets privilege" was the fruit of a tawdry effort to cover up malfeasance rather than protect the "precious secrets" of the nation.

Daniel Solove captures the insidious impact of secrecy on due process and the rule of law. "After the September 11 attacks," he writes, "the government began using a tactic called the 'state secrets privilege' to exclude evidence in a case if it will reveal a classified secret. Even if the government isn't a party to the case, it can swoop in and invoke the privilege. Many times, the case gets dismissed because a person can't prove her case without the evidence."[3] This might be less serious if classification were not so generalized.

Jewel v. NSA captures all the problems embedded in the invocation of the state secrets privilege. The Electronic Frontier Foundation brought this case on September 18, 2008, on behalf of Carolyn Jewel, a customer of AT&T, after Mark Klein, a whistleblower who was an AT&T technician, revealed that the NSA was vacuuming up all the telecommunications data of the company's customers. Subsequent revelations showed that the NSA was appropriating the telecommunications data of the customers of all the other US telecoms as well. In January 2010, Judge Vaughn Walker dismissed the case, claiming that the plaintiffs were bringing a "general grievance" against the government and consequently lacked legal standing. On appeal, the Ninth Circuit Court of Appeals reinstated the case in December 2011. The US government, having failed in its other efforts to get the case dismissed, invoked the state secrets privilege. In July 2013, Judge Jeffrey White refused to dismiss the case on these grounds, but the NSA continued to assert the state secrets privilege.

An even longer legal struggle began after 2013. The plaintiffs tried to stop the NSA's destruction of evidence, using temporary restraining orders, while the government continued to insist that the state secrets privilege covered all this evidence. In February 2015, Judge White ruled in favor of the government, dismissing the plaintiffs' claims that the NSA's UPSTREAM collection, the program that vacuumed up all the communications of people using AT&T, Verizon, and other companies, was unconstitutional. He also asserted that the adjudication of this matter would require the "impermissible disclosure of state secret information."[4]

However, in a partial reversal of his earlier decision, on May 19, 2017, Judge White ordered the NSA to provide "all relevant evidence necessary to prove or deny that plaintiffs were subject to NSA surveillance via tapping into the Internet backbone."[5] But in 2019, the Court sided with the government again. To quote Cindy Cohn about this ruling,

> despite the enormous amount of direct and circumstantial evidence showing our clients' electronic communications [were] likely swept up by the NSA dragnet surveillance to establish legal "standing," no public court can rule on whether this surveillance is legal. The Court agreed with the government that our claims

were caught in a state secrets privilege catch-22: no one can sue to stop illegal surveillance unless the court first determines that they were certainly touched by the vast surveillance mechanisms of the NSA. But the court cannot decide whether any particular person's email, web searches, social media, or phone calls were touched by the surveillance unless the government admits it—which the government will not do.[6]

However, this ruling set up yet another review by the Ninth Circuit Court of Appeals.

The evident catch-22 that the state secrets privilege creates makes it effectively impossible for anyone to secure remedies against illegal government surveillance. Government secrecy makes it difficult to establish that surveillance took place or to show that potential plaintiffs were swept up in its net. Without this proof, plaintiffs cannot establish legal "standing" and hold the government accountable. *Jewel v. NSA* is well into its second decade, revealing another advantage of the state secrets privilege to the government. The invocation of this doctrine, even when it does not result in the dismissal of a case, can slow proceedings to a crawl and prolong them almost indefinitely. For all these reasons, the state secrets privilege effectively makes it almost impossible for individuals to use the court system to challenge the government's use of mass surveillance.

THE FOREIGN INTELLIGENCE SURVEILLANCE ACT OF 1978

The Foreign Intelligence Surveillance Act of 1978 governs the US government's conduct of mass surveillance. FISA, as it is known, sought to regulate the practice of surveillance in the wake of revelations of widespread abuse, particularly during the 1960s. These revelations showed that the NSA had monitored, in clear violation of its mandate, American civil-rights activists and the antiwar movement.[7] The NSA was supposed to face outward, and it was statutorily restricted to monitoring foreign threats to the United States. The revelation that it had faced inward and monitored the domestic electronic activities of Americans, conjoined with information about the domestic spying activities of the FBI and other agencies against dissidents, increased congressional concerns about the behavior of the national security apparatus throughout the late 1960s and early 1970s. This, along with information about CIA activities around the world, culminating in the agency's role in the overthrow of Salvador Allende's government in Chile in 1973, led the Select Committee to Study Government Operations with Respect to Intelligence Activities to conduct Senate hearings in 1974.

This committee subsequently became known as the Church Committee, named after its chairman, Senator Frank Church (D-ID). In another indication of the extensive monitoring of Americans, revelations subsequently proved that Senator Church had been the object of surveillance as well. In a prophetic declaration made decades before the enactment of the USA PATRIOT Act, Senator Church said that "[the NSA's] capability at any time could be turned around on the American people, and no American would have any privacy left: such is the capability to monitor everything—telephone conversations, telegrams, it doesn't matter."[8] One can only begin to imagine what he would have thought of the NSA's use of digital technologies, which did not exist in the mid-1970s, to surveil, monitor, and collect the private information of the entire American population.

Enacted in the wake of the Church hearings, FISA prohibited the government from surveilling Americans' electronic communications without a judicially sanctioned warrant. FISA created the Foreign Intelligence Surveillance Court (FISC) to provide judicial oversight over foreign intelligence operations and approve and reject requests for warrants to conduct surveillance. Because of its purview, FISC was a secret court. This would subsequently prove to be its greatest, arguably its fatal, flaw since suffocating secrecy subverted its mandate. Secret arguments where only one side could present evidence, secret deliberations, and secret decisions created an environment that destroyed accountability and real judicial oversight—its ostensible purpose.

In part for this reason, even before 9/11, when all its inadequacies became exposed, FISC had developed into nothing more than a rubber-stamp body, exercising negligible oversight over the intelligence apparatus. The extent of its institutional capture and ineffectiveness can be seen in the following data on its performance. Between 1979 and 2013, FISC received 35,333 requests for surveillance warrants, granting all but twelve. *Twelve!* Moreover, FISC did not just rubber-stamp surveillance requests. In 2004, in a particularly significant decision, Chief Judge Colleen Kollar-Kotelly, in a secret ex parte order, authorized the bulk warrantless collection of Internet data.[9] In addition, during the Obama administration, FISC approved a warrant request from the FBI to monitor and collect the records and communications of reporters working for the Associated Press, a flagrant violation of the First Amendment. All of this revealed the extent of FISC's subordination to the national security apparatus and its failure to provide effective judicial oversight.

As previously discussed, even the modest restrictions on surveillance that existed at the time of the September 11, 2001, attacks were too constraining for the George W. Bush administration. It consequently turned to the OLC, as it did in other areas, to circumvent even these small constraints and to grant the color of law to mass warrantless surveillance. FISC subsequently lent its juridical approval to this practice in the Kollar-Kotelly decision.

In 2008, Congress reformed FISA when it passed the Foreign Intelligence Surveillance Act of 1978 Amendments Act of 2008 (FISAAA). The most significant part of this new law was Section 702, which ostensibly protected Americans from warrantless surveillance since it limited this activity to foreigners overseas. However, in practice, Section 702 gave broad legal cover to retrospective and prospective surveillance practices that impacted millions of Americans. Under Section 702, Americans could be surveilled without a warrant if they talked with foreign targets, if they talked to foreigners about foreign targets, or if they were mistaken for foreigners. Many Americans inadvertently strayed into this terrain, becoming the object of precisely the type of warrantless surveillance that Section 702 was designed to prevent. In effect, Americans engaging in any kinds of interactions with "non-US persons" were subject to surveillance. FISAAA contained sunset provisions but was routinely reauthorized and remains in effect, despite clear evidence that it has led to the warrantless surveillance of millions of Americans.

The failure of FISA, FISAAA, and FISC to effectively circumscribe state surveillance and prevent the monitoring and collection of the data of Americans and protect their civil and privacy rights encapsulates the problems of trying to regulate state behavior in the national security realm. Once created, these governing practices become institutionalized, and path dependency takes over. Moreover, FISA and FISC are vestiges of an analog world. Their resulting weaknesses and lacunae, since their analog assumptions and premises do not adequately address digital realities, make them notably poor guardians of the privacy of Americans. The executive branch, not surprisingly, continually blocks genuine reforms of this manifestly obsolete legal architecture since the latter's deficiencies expand the former's discretionary latitude.

EXECUTIVE ORDER 12333

In 1981 President Ronald Reagan issued Executive Order (EO) 12333, whose term of art is "twelve triple three," making it another legal pillar of the US government's surveillance regime. EO 12333, along with other regulations— some public and some classified—governs the conduct of the profusion of US intelligence agencies and their foreign spying activities, including their use and sharing of information. To protect Americans, EO 12333 establishes "minimization" procedures that remain in effect to this day, designed to protect the identity of "US persons" who are inadvertently caught up in the surveillance of foreign targets, an event that most commonly occurs when Americans are communicating with anybody outside the United States.

However, as Jennifer Granick writes

Minimization procedures are full of loopholes that allow the intelligence community not only to collect but also to use, analyze, and share Americans' communications data opportunistically collected as part of foreign spying. [Minimization rules] are generally classified, can be changed in secret, and are inordinately complex. There are effectively no remedies for violations of minimization procedures.[10]

As is true of much of the regulatory architecture governing US government surveillance, EO 12333 was issued decades before current technologies had expanded the state's capacities in previously unimaginable ways. Digital technologies limit the efficacy, if they do not totally erase, EO 12333's "minimization" rules, as does the presence of mass surveillance and the development of increasingly sophisticated metadata mining along with the use of machine learning and AI. To cite Granick again,

When EO 12333 was issued, the world was a different place. EO 12333 [is consequently] vast, multifaceted, top secret, and poorly understood. The FISC does not approve it, and Congress does little or nothing to oversee it. Historically EO 12333 collection has always been extensive, but it's growing. The Internet easily connects people with others around the world, communicating on Facebook, in chat rooms, and via instant-messaging applications. When Americans talk with people in other countries and the data is collected overseas in bulk or while targeting foreigners, the weaker EO 12333 rules, and not FISA's, apply.[11]

In fact, given technological changes, it is extremely unlikely that EO 12333 "minimization" disguises the identity of an inadvertent target, given the "unmasking" features of digital tools. The advantage of secrecy, of course, is that it makes it impossible for outsiders to categorically prove that this is the case, while enabling the government to continue to insist, without providing evidence, that "minimization" works. Even if a whistleblower eventually emerges who reveals widespread failures with "minimization," nobody could sue, since the state secrets privilege makes it impossible to establish that one is a victim, as *Jewel* and other national cases have demonstrated. Secrecy does not allow potential plaintiffs to establish standing and sue to protect their rights. It is hard to imagine a more perfect writ of immunity than the one this catch-22 provides to the US surveillance apparatus. For the state, as is true of FISA and FISC, it is better to keep an obsolete structure in place precisely because this obsolescence increases flexibility and the discretionary uses of state powers. The government can insist, as well, that it is protecting the civil rights of Americans by using these "minimization" procedures, even though digital technologies have destroyed their efficacy.

SECTION 215 OF THE USA PATRIOT ACT

Section 215 of the USA PATRIOT Act, passed in the wake of 9/11, allowed the government to collect the "call detail records" of Americans, including the phone numbers they received and called, and the date, time, and length of the call. As will be discussed in greater detail later, the government still claims, despite the enormous evidence to the contrary, that the exclusion of content from this collection protects privacy. In particular, the nature of metadata and of metadata mining completely erase the distinction between "call detail records" and content. In effect, metadata and metadata mining mean that "call detail records" can reveal as much if not more than content.

Consequently, Section 215 enabled the mass warrantless state surveillance of Americans for the first time in American history. Given the extraordinary powers that it conferred, Section 215 contained sunset provisions that required its periodic reapproval. At the time of this writing, twenty years after 9/11, the US Congress has never constrained the powers that Section 215 established. Even indications of widespread abuse have not prompted Congress to sunset these capacities. The most serious of these abuses revolve around the continuing release of information indicating the NSA's and CIA's domestic-surveillance activities. For example, under the leadership of General Mike Hayden the NSA used Section 215 authorities and approval from FISC to collect the phone number of every party in every call, the location in which the call was made, and the time and length of every call.[12]

As noted before, because its mandate is foreign surveillance, the NSA is banned from spying on Americans. However, a 2005 article in the *New York Times* revealed that the NSA had been illegally wiretapping Americans through a program called STELLAR WIND. Initiated without legislative approval immediately after 9/11, this surveillance program enlisted all US telecommunications companies leading them to hand over the "call detail" records of all their customers to the US government. Glenn Greenwald first revealed this practice in an article in the *Guardian.*

Greenwald showed that Verizon was turning over the "call detail" records of all its customers to the FBI. In turn, the FBI was passing them on to the NSA in direct violation of the strictures preventing the NSA from participation in domestic surveillance. As Alan Rubel wrote, under Section 215 of the USA PATRIOT Act, the NSA's bulk collection of telephone metadata

> is not simply a legal problem (though it is one); it is not simply a privacy problem (though it is one); and it is not simply a secrecy problem (though it is one). Instead, the importance of the metadata program is the way in which these problems intersect and reinforce each other. . . . [Because] the privacy loss was secret (both in fact and in legal interpretation), persons were denied the full value of

their privacy rights. In other words, the metadata program is not merely about privacy loss but the inability to actually make use of privacy rights because people did not know their privacy was diminished.[13]

A further prophetic analysis of the impact of Section 215 on civil rights and on the law came from Jacob Lilly. In 2005, he wrote that

> On September 20, 2001, President George W. Bush declared, "We're in a fight for our principles, and our first responsibility is to live by them." History shows, however, that when we are fighting for our principles, we have frequently failed to live by them. Previous constitutional tests applied during times of crisis have resulted in large-scale constitutional infringements and deprivations. Moreover, the USA PATRIOT Act and terrorism in the electronic age provide ever-developing challenges in a legal setting that has difficulty keeping up.[14]

A right stolen in stealth and without the right holder's awareness of its appropriation constitutes an especially egregious governmental act. The right holder loses any chance to assert the right's violation. This robs people of agency, preventing their taking action as they lose a constitutional protection. And the secret purloining of rights not only prevents the defense of these rights but actually destroys any chance of holding the thief accountable. Because the national security apparatus acts in secret, few revelations emerge about its rights violations, ensuring that the perpetrators of these violations escape accountability.

THE SNOWDEN REVELATIONS AND THE USA FREEDOM ACT

Although evidence of the mass warrantless surveillance of American citizens periodically emerged during the decade after 9/11, it took until 2013, after Edward Snowden's detailed release of the NSA's activities, for the public to learn the scope and intrusiveness of this practice. National security whistleblowers are not afforded the same protections as other whistleblowers under federal law. Whistleblowers elsewhere in the federal government can avail themselves of protections, especially when they are revealing the existence of fraud and abuse. Those involved in national security, however, receive clearances and must maintain strictest confidentiality. Leaking national security information constitutes a presumptively traitorous act, even when it is not released to a foreign adversary and is designed to unmask the wholesale abuse of the civil rights of Americans. Such leaks are treated as federal felonies, and whistleblowers are subject to lengthy prison sentences. It is for this reason that Snowden's decision to provide journalist Glenn Greenwald and documentary filmmaker Laura Poitras with extensive data on the surveillance activities of the United States and its partners in the Five Eyes agreement constituted a courageous, indeed heroic, act.

Edward Snowden's information incontrovertibly revealed that the US government was not just gathering the "call detail records" of Americans and others but was continuously vacuuming up all the information traveling through the global infrastructure of the Internet. The NSA had developed a global blanket surveillance regime designed to collect all emails, searches, browsing histories, and other personal information that traveled across the World Wide Web.

Although the public, or at least those who were paying attention, knew about the NSA's STELLAR WIND program, Edward Snowden's documents revealed the details of a previously unknown agency program called PRISM, in use during both the second Bush and Obama administrations. PRISM gathered all of users' private information from Facebook, Google, and several other search engines. Snowden's whistleblowing also showed how Sections 215 and 702 facilitated the government's mass surveillance of Americans despite the Bush and Obama administrations' repeated protestations to the contrary. Indeed, when it came to the topic of mass warrantless surveillance, Barack Obama proved just as willing to lie and dissemble about the activities of the national security state as George W. Bush.

Problematically, Edward Snowden's revelations about the scale and intrusiveness of NSA surveillance made this agency the sole focus of concerns about the government's practices. The surveillance practices of other agencies largely escaped notice, even though the raft of organizations comprising the US coercive apparatus all engaged in this behavior. As Alan Rubel wrote, "Once the NSA has gathered metadata in bulk, smaller (though still pervasive) collection of communications information hardly seems so bad. . . . [Gathering] of metadata by other law-enforcement and security agencies, even on a limited basis, does not seem to raise an eyebrow."[15] And the amount of data they collect and access is, in fact, not limited. For example, other federal agencies and local law enforcement routinely use digital surveillance technologies, while "fusion centers" ensure the sharing of all this information.

Many non-Americans found Edward Snowden's revelations about the extent of US surveillance of foreigners especially shocking. Snowden's information showed that the United States captured the cell phone data of the leaders of allied countries, including Angela Merkel of Germany and Dilma Rousseff of Brazil, and was surveilling the digital lives of ordinary citizens of many countries. Europeans, and especially Germans, given their history, reacted particularly strongly to the information contained in the documents that he released. The revelation that the NSA was secretly appropriating everything traveling along the backbone of the Internet and on the platforms of global monopolies like Google caused outrage around the world.

Because of the nature of the Internet, the United States holds huge amounts of the personal data of non-Americans, raising even deeper concerns about protections of this data, given the long history of US government disregard for privacy. Europeans object especially strongly given their greater attachment to privacy protection. The EU consequently threatened to end data sharing unless it received guarantees that the personal information of Europeans would receive adequate privacy protection. The result of this conflict was a new data-sharing agreement called the EU-USA Privacy Shield that ostensibly provided this protection. However, privacy advocates in Europe immediately objected to the inadequacy of the agreement and advocated for its abrogation. And on July 16, 2020, the European Court of Justice agreed with privacy advocates and ordered the cancellation of the agreement on the grounds that it did not adequately protect the privacy rights of Europeans, constituting a violation of their human rights.

In the wake of Edward Snowden's revelations, the Obama administration and its national security apparatus, along with most of Congress, attacked him and labeled him a traitor. The Trumanites and their Madisonian allies, and indeed much of the foreign policy and national security establishment, insisted that Snowden's "betrayal" had visited untold damage on American intelligence collection and compromised US operations abroad, putting lives at risk. More generally, they launched a concerted and coordinated effort to impugn him, attacking his background, character, education, and motives, while studiously avoiding serious discussions about the US government's use of dragnet, warrantless surveillance against both its residents and citizens and non–"US persons."

They insisted, as well, that Edward Snowden was working for China and was consequently a spy rather than a whistleblower, since he had fled through China after meeting with Greenwald and Poitras in Hong Kong. When he ended up in Russia after the United States canceled his passport and impeded his travel to other places that offered refuge, they accused him of being a Russian agent. In addition, they argued that a true patriot and whistleblower would return to the United States and face a "fair" trial. This last assertion was particularly questionable, since "fair" trials do not really exist in the national security area. Because they deal with classified information, such trials are closed processes, wherein the preservation of state secrets transforms the adversarial process designed to find the truth into a mockery since the defense cannot engage in real discovery or call witnesses and question the government.

Although the charges that Edward Snowden damaged American national security were serious, unlike the more numerous ad hominem attacks on his character, none was ever proved. Indeed, after nearly a decade there was still no evidence that Snowden's revelations put American lives in jeopardy or that the United States' digital probing of the world and of its own citizens declined. It is certainly true that the US government suffered reputational harm since Edward Snowden showed that the NSA was engaged in mass warrantless spying on everyone—a practice that reflected a deeply Orwellian and consequently proto-totalitarian disposition rather than an attachment to civil and human rights.

Although media and public attention faded during subsequent years, the awareness that Edward Snowden sparked did not disappear, becoming lodged in the popular consciousness. However, especially during and after the 2016 presidential election in the United States and the Brexit plebiscite in the United Kingdom, it was almost completely displaced by outrage over the activities of Facebook and other platforms. And continual hacks and ransomware attacks drove the activities of the US government from the news.

However, in the immediate aftermath of Snowden's whistleblowing, the intensity of the international and domestic reaction forced the Obama administration and US Congress to respond with at least some reforms. The USA Freedom Act, passed on June 2, 2015, captures in its very name the proclivity of the American state to conflate security and liberty even when it engages in practices that diminish civil rights. The USA Freedom Act preserved and, in some cases, modestly altered several provisions of the USA PATRIOT Act, which the government had allowed to sunset on the previous day.

According to President Obama, the USA Freedom Act remedied the government's most egregious surveillance practices. Despite his claims about the consequence of this reform, actual change was modest. One reform, at least at the time, seemed important and responded to criticisms of the government's practices. Before the passage of the USA Freedom Act, the NSA had been building a huge data center in Utah at the cost of $10 billion to store the yottabytes of data that flowed from its bulk collection. Critics argued that this gave the NSA excessive, centralized control over too much information, which facilitated abuse and other problems. These critics argued that the providers who originally collected this information, such as telecommunications companies, should keep it in storage and release it to the NSA in response to specific requests. The USA Freedom Act included this change, resulting in the mothballing of the Utah Data Center despite the already enormous sunk cost of the project.

In practice, however, all that happened was that the retention of data flowing from bulk collection shifted from the NSA to private companies, notably telecoms whose metadata remained available to the American surveillance apparatus. The USA Freedom Act did not include data-retention policies, further reducing its consequence. As a result, this change, advertised as a fundamental reform of Section 215 of the USA PATRIOT Act, had no impact on the practice of bulk collection. And the NSA could still mine metadata at will. Although the agency was supposed to use "targeted selectors" to access this data, the scope of these changes allows the NSA to continue most of its earlier practices.

A second, marginally more consequential reform was the limiting of surveillance to two "hops," where one hop involves the surveillance of everyone the target contacted, while a second hop involves the surveillance of everyone that these people, in turn, contacted. However, even this restriction still led to the collection of a vast number of records on people who had nothing to do with the original target. As the Center for Democracy and Technology revealed in 2018, only fourteen orders were issued to telecoms for the call-detail records of eleven targets. While this seems modest and indeed "targeted," the breadth of the selector defining the target involved handing over 440 million call-detail records to the NSA.[16] The classification of selectors makes it impossible to analyze their precise content, but the fact that eleven targets produced 440 million records indicates breadth rather than focus.

In addition, the Obama administration added a "special advocate" to FISC charged with defending privacy interests. Given the secrecy surrounding this court, it is very difficult to tell if the change has had a material effect. And the most important part of FISAAA, Section 702, remained unchanged. As a result, the US government's ability to engage in mass surveillance and bulk collection did not diminish.

For its part, in the years after the passage of the USA Freedom Act the US Congress focused on symbolic reforms and recharacterization of activities while limiting substantive changes. Congress's continual reauthorization of Sections 215 and 702 indicates the depth of resistance to change after 9/11. A few senators, mentioned before, tried unsuccessfully over the years to circumscribe the surveillance powers embedded in Sections 215 and 702. Their efforts repeatedly failed because a significant portion of Congress was unwilling to regulate or restrict programs portrayed as intrinsic to national security.

The absence of action did not indicate a complete lack of debate. For example, in 2015 Section 215 and other provisions temporarily expired as Congress debated the USA Freedom Act. Ultimately, the still-extant portions of the USA PATRIOT Act were reauthorized for four more years. Even when provisions expired, however, loopholes allowed the continuation of existing operations, so the delay did not pause surveillance activities.[17] Another iteration of this process occurred during the first half of 2020. Section 215 expired on March 15 of that year after Congress failed to agree on a set of reforms to FISA. Although the House had passed the USA Freedom Reauthorization Act of 2020, extending Section 215 for three more years with some small reforms, Senate majority leader Mitch McConnell (R-KY) lacked the votes to pass the bill in his chamber. This forced him to pass a bill that extended all the expiring provisions of FISA, including Section 215, for seventy-seven days. The House, however, left town before voting on this extension, so Section 215 temporarily expired.

However, Senator McConnell managed to subsequently corral enough votes, and the Senate passed the Reauthorization Act on May 13, renewing the extensive government surveillance carried over from the USA PATRIOT Act. By one vote, the Senate failed to pass an amendment to the reauthorization prohibiting law enforcement from searching the Internet browsing history of individuals without a warrant. The office of Senator Wyden (D-OR), who along with Senator Steve Daines (R-MT) sponsored the amendment, put out a statement posing the question, "Should law-abiding Americans have to worry about the government looking over their shoulders from the moment they wake up in the morning and turn on their computers to when they go to bed at night?" In this same press release, Wyden added, "Every thought that can come into people's heads can be revealed in an Internet search or a visit to a website. Their health history and medical concerns. Their political views. Their romantic lives and friendships. Their religious beliefs. Collecting this information is as close to reading minds as surveillance can get."[18]

Four senators, Patty Murray, Bernie Sanders, Ben Sasse, and Lamar Alexander, missed the vote. If any one of them had voted in favor of the amendment, it would have passed. Even if their presence had not changed the outcome, their absence indicates a troubling indifference to a matter of such importance to individual privacy rights. The Senate did pass an amendment that Senator Mike Lee (R-UT) and Senator Patrick Leahy (D-VT) sponsored. This amendment added some modest legal protections to FISC. These changes increased the transparency of its operations, if only in an ex post facto fashion, authorizing the outside review of cases seeking warrants on US persons. Although seemingly quite significant, this amendment paled in comparison to the fact that the Reauthorization Act preserved the US government's most intrusive surveillance powers. Finally, the fact that Chief Justice John Roberts was careful to indicate in the *Carpenter* decision that its reasoning did not extend to the national security realm further weakens protections in this area.

Initially, at least, the same effort to pass the Reauthorization Act foundered in the House when it was scheduled for a vote on May 28, 2020. A few Democrats who had become more skeptical about mass warrantless surveillance during the Trump administration and who worried about the debility of civil-rights protections were joined by several Republicans after Trump threatened to veto the Reauthorization Act. As a result, House Democrats, who controlled the chamber, withdrew the bill. As always, it was hard to discern the position of the Trump administration given its rhetorical assaults on the "deep state" and its combination of "America first" isolationism with huge military spending, animus toward Iran and China, and unwavering support for Israel and Saudi Arabia. Moreover, given the tenor of the times, it was difficult to tell if those Republicans who suddenly objected to surveillance did so out of newly formed convictions about its undesirability or fear of acting against Trump's wishes.

In the end, the Reauthorization Act passed the House, and Trump did not veto the legislation. The opponents of sweeping government surveillance in the US Senate and House managed to delay the reauthorization but failed, yet again, to limit the collection authorities flowing from Section 215 and Section 702. Although the opposition to mass surveillance crosses partisan lines, so too does support for the practice. The deterioration of the US relationship with both Russia and China during the Biden administration and increasingly damaging state-sponsored cyberattacks strengthen support for these authorities and practices in the United States.

For its part, the US national security and law-enforcement apparatus lobbies vigorously against any reforms of Section 215 and Section 702 authorities. They continue to insist, as they always have, that reforms will catastrophically reduce their capacity to uncover terrorist plots and criminal activities while strengthening the hand of foreign adversaries. It made these claims about the modest reforms embodied in the USA Freedom Act and echoes these arguments every time there is a reauthorization. One must ask, however, why the number of attacks on the United States did not increase after the passage of the USA Freedom Act. In fact, despite continued claims about the indispensability of incredibly broad surveillance powers, there is no evidence that these practices have thwarted a single "Islamic" terrorist attack in the United States. John Demers, head of the Justice Department's National Security Division, voiced the agency's familiar and typical reaction to any reform. Mr. Demers complained that stricter requirements about the accuracy of FISA applications included in the Lee and Leahy amendment would be problematic and onerous.[19]

The press provided diverse perspectives on the consequence of the Lee and Leahy amendment. On one side, a typical article on CNN's website was headlined "Senate Votes to Increase Legal Protections to Targets of Surveillance Court."[20] In contrast, a less mainstream and consequently less predictably conventional source, *Vox*, posted an article on its website headlined, "The Senate Voted to Let the Government Keep Surveilling Your Online Life Without a Warrant."[21] Unlike CNN, however, *The Verge*, Business Insider, CNET, and the *Daily Mail* all highlighted the Reauthorization Act's continuing approval of the warrantless collection of Internet browsing. The *New York Times*, interestingly, did not devote attention in its online Morning Briefing to the reauthorization.

The next reauthorization was scheduled for 2023. Although vote margins have narrowed, odds favor its continuing passage. As noted before, most Democrats and Republicans share an animosity toward Russia and China that bonds them together despite the extent of partisan polarization. Consequently they are likely to continue pushing for the further expansion of cyber capacities. Such an effort will inevitably further enhance the ability of the coercive organs of the American state to engage in domestic surveillance as well. The continuing influence of Trumanites and their understandings, especially about the consequences of growing Chinese power and the ever-more-problematic relationship with Russia, make them supporters of the powers embedded in Section 215 and Section 702.

Despite the reforms made during the Obama administration and the creation of the Privacy and Civil Liberties Oversight Board (PCLOB) by the USA Freedom Act, bulk warrantless surveillance continued, especially in the form of broad queries of data that contained the information of Americans. EO 12333 was used to provide legal cover to this activity. These practices were revealed in mid-February 2022 when Senators Ron Wyden (D-OR) and Martin Heinrich (D-NM) released a letter from the PCLOB written in April 2021 detailing concerns about the CIA's bulk warrantless surveillance activities.

Just like the NSA, the CIA had violated its mandate—the gathering of foreign intelligence—and had engaged in the mass surveillance of "US persons." The letter and part of the PCLOB report were declassified in February 2022, almost a year after it had first been written. For its part, the CIA insisted that it was acting within the law (EO 12333) and that it had to keep the details of its activities secret to protect "sources and methods," the habitual rationale that the intelligence apparatus uses to resist demands for even a small measure of transparency.[22]

ADDITIONAL LEGAL DECISIONS RESTRICTING SURVEILLANCE IN THE UNITED STATES

Although the legal architecture governing mass surveillance in the United States remained expansive throughout the first two decades of the twenty-first century, some decisions and opinions have laid the foundation for a potentially more robust future regulatory regime. As early as 2001, Justice Antonin Scalia wrote in an opinion striking down warrantless thermal imaging that the Fourth Amendment should not be left to "the mercy of advancing technology." And as former director of the ACLU Nadine Strossen wrote in response to the Supreme Court's decision in 2012 striking down warrantless

GPS surveillance, "five justices expressly questioned whether *Smith* applies to new technology."[23]

In addition to this ruling, Strossen notes that several recent Supreme Court decisions revealed an incipient judicial understanding of the obsolescence of the regulatory regime governing the digital age. To quote her again,

> [In] a 2014 decision concerning cell phones, the justices unanimously recognized that, in effect, "digital is different," so that prior cases allowing searches and seizures incident to arrest do not apply to cell phones, given the vast differences between such digital devices and other items. The same conclusion applies to the *Smith* decision; it simply does not govern dragnet metadata collection. The argument that bulk metadata collection is not materially distinguishable from the *Smith* facts is wrong for the same reason that the Supreme Court in 2014 unanimously rejected the government's argument that cell phone seizures are "materially indistinguishable" from other seizures: "That is like saying a ride on horseback is materially indistinguishable from a flight to the moon."[24]

In an additional indication of the presence of reservations in at least some portions of the judiciary about mass surveillance, Judge Richard Leon, in a preliminary injunction issued in 2013 against the NSA's dragnet collection, wrote, "I cannot imagine a more 'indiscriminate' and 'arbitrary invasion' than this . . . high-tech collection and retention of personal data on virtually every single citizen . . . without prior judicial approval. Surely such a program infringes on [the] privacy that the Founders enshrined in the Fourth Amendment."[25] Textualists, of course, given their literal reading of the Constitution, disagreed strongly with Judge Leon's interpretation of the Fourth Amendment. At the time of this writing, the three justices that Donald Trump appointed to the Court have not heard a surveillance case. But their overturning of *Roe* has potentially ominous implications for rights anchored in privacy and due-process claims. Although it is hard to predict what they will do, their attachment to the Borkian tradition makes them very, very likely to interpret the Fourth Amendment narrowly, with ominous implications for privacy writ large. On the other hand, Justice Antonin Scalia's opinion in 2001 indicates that, at least occasionally, some of the textualists may be inclined to limit the ways that new technologies circumscribe even the very narrow readings of the Fourth Amendment that this school of constitutional interpretation prefers.

CONCLUSION

The George W. Bush administration, in power at the time of the 9/11 attacks, assiduously and secretly constructed a mass-surveillance regime. However, throughout President Bush's second term, whistleblowers and leaks began to reveal the scope of the US government's activities, alerting portions of the population to the existence of mass surveillance. After coming to power in 2008, President Barack Obama, despite having run on a platform critical of many of the Bush administration's approaches to the "war on terror," continued these measures, particularly mass warrantless surveillance and his predecessor's efforts to preserve and expand the power of the executive branch.

Although President Obama ended the use of torture, he significantly increased the number of drone strikes, using this technology first in Afghanistan and Pakistan and then in other countries, including Yemen. Drone strikes constitute an insidious form of state-sponsored assassination— since the drone operators control these weapons from centers thousands of miles away, killing remotely. People in the wrong place at the wrong time or who inadvertently communicated with a suspect or with someone who wasn't a suspect but had communicated with a suspect suddenly became "targets." And metadata mining drove the decision about whom to assassinate, lending an aura of mathematical objectivity to the Obama administration's expansive practice of state-sponsored assassination.

Paradoxically, Donald Trump availed himself of these powers when he came to office. Despite criticizing the "deep state" and the Obama administration, Donald Trump did not restrict mass surveillance. And drone strikes and other "war on terror" policies continued during his administration, remaining immune to criticisms about the number of innocents that they damaged or killed. The fact that drones violated the sovereignty of other states did not deter the United States either.

At the time of this writing, it seems unlikely that President Joe Biden will depart from his predecessors and surrender some of the extraordinary capacities that the American president has acquired, especially since 9/11. His administration shares the view of the foreign policy establishment that American global dominance is indispensable and desirable. Russia's war against Ukraine and widespread concerns about the growth of Chinese power make the United States even more determined to expand its military and intelligence capacities and exercise global power. The unitary executive theory facilitates the pursuit of this end since it asserts that the president possesses sole and complete sovereignty over foreign affairs. For this reason, Biden and subsequent presidents are likely to behave like their predecessors and push for the preservation and even the further expansion of the already vast powers vested in the office.

The continuity across administrations indicates the strength of the Trumanite consensus over foreign policy and national security at the top of the US government. This consensus frames the understanding of national security and informs perceptions of the United States' global role. This explains the unwillingness to regulate and restrict activities, such as mass warrantless surveillance, that advance the state's power, even if they impact civil rights. In part for these same reasons, the United States remains a laggard in the effort to protect digital privacy. Anything that might potentially fetter technological innovation or that might limit the powers of the national security state is ferociously resisted. In the early decades of the digital age, concerns about the importance of privacy and the need to protect it proved no match for the central imperatives informing US behavior, the quest for greater security, and the preservation of its global dominance. Ubiquitous fears of malign actors and of real and imagined threats prevented the development of more robust legislation designed to protect privacy.

NOTES

1. Stephen J. Schulhofer, "The Patriot Act and the Surveillance Society," in *Liberty Under Attack*, ed. Richard C. Leone and Greg Anrig Jr. (New York: New Century Foundation, 2007), 134–35.

2. As quoted in "State Secrets Privilege," Electronic Frontier Foundation, EFF.org, accessed June 2, 2020, https://eff.org.

3. Daniel J. Solove, *Nothing to Hide: The False Tradeoff between Privacy and Security* (New Haven: Yale University Press, 2011), 67.

4. Cindy Cohn, "Judge Orders Government to Provide Evidence About Internet Surveillance," Electronic Frontier Foundation, EFF.org, May 23, 2107, https://www.eff.org/deeplinks/2017/05/judge-orders-government-provide-evidence-about-internet-backbone-upstream.

5. Ibid.

6. Cindy Cohn, "*Jewel v. NSA*: On the Ninth Circuit; 2019 Year in Review," Electronic Frontier Foundation, EFF.org, December 28, 2019, https://eff.org/jewel-v-nsa.

7. Michael J. Glennon, *National Security and Double Government* (Oxford: Oxford University Press, 2015), 66–67.

8. Church as quoted in Glennon, *National Security and Double Government*, 66.

9. Glennon, *National Security and Double Government*, 68.

10. Jennifer Stisa Granick, *American Spies: Modern Surveillance, Why You Should Care, and What to Do about It* (Cambridge: Cambridge University Press, 2017), 24.

11. Granick, *American Spies*, 107–8.

12. Glennon, *National Security and Double Government*, 68.

13. Alan Rubel, "Privacy, Transparency and Accountability in the NSA's Bulk Metadata Program," in *Privacy, Security and Accountability*, ed. Adam Moore (London: Rowman & Littlefield International, 2016).

14. Jacob R. Lilly, "National Security at What Price? A Look into Civil Liberty Concerns in the Information Age under the USA PATRIOT Act," in *Information Ethics: Privacy, Property and Power*, ed. Adam Moore (Seattle: University of Washington Press, 2005), 436.

15. Alan Rubel, "Legal Archetypes and Metadata Collection," *Wisconsin International Law Journal* 34, no. 4 (2017): 848–49, parentheticals original.

16. Greg Nojeim and Mana Azarmi, "Revised USA Freedom Reauthorization Act of 2020: More Improvements Are Needed," Center for Democracy and Technology, CDT.org, March 11, 2020, https://cdt.org/insights/revised-usa-freedom -reauthorization-act-of-2020-improves-fisa-more-improvements-are-needed/.

17. India McKinney and Andrew Crocker, "Yes, Section 215 Expired, Now What?" Electronic Frontier Foundation, EFF.org, April 16, 2020, https://www.eff.org /deeplinks/2020/04/yes-section-215-expired-now-what.

18. Senator Ron Wyden, "Wyden Opposes Warrantless Government Surveillance of Americans' Browsing History," press release, Wyden.Senate.gov, May 13, 2020, https://www.wyden.senate.gov/news/press-releases/wyden-opposes-warrantless -government-surveillance-of-americans-internet-browsing-history-.

19. Betsy Woodruff Swann, "Trump Officials Detail Opposition to Federal Surveillance Bill," *Politico*, May 27, 2020, https://www.politico.com/news/2020/05/27/ trump-officials-fisa-bill-285387.

20. Jeremy Herb and David Shortell, "Senate Votes to Increase Legal Protections to Targets of Surveillance Court," CNN, last updated May 14, 2020, https://www.cnn .com/2020/05/14/politics/senate-vote-extends-fisa/index.html.

21. Sara Morrison, "The Senate Voted to Let the Government Keep Surveilling Your Online Life Without a Warrant," *Vox*, last updated May 14, 2020, https:// www.vox.com/recode/2020/5/13/21257481/wyden-freedom-patriot-act-amendment -mcconnell.

22. Senator Ron Wyden, "Wyden and Heinrich: Newly Declassified Documents Reveal Previously Secret CIA Bulk Collection, Problems with CIA Handling of Americans' Information," Wyden.Senate.gov, February 10, 2022, https:// www.wyden.senate.gov/news/press-releases/wyden-and-heinrich-newly-declassified -documents-reveal-previously-secret-cia-bulk-collection-problems-with-cia-handling -of-americans-information.

23. Both quotations found in Nadine Strossen, "Post-9/11 Government Surveillance, Suppression and Secrecy," in *Privacy, Security and Accountability: Ethics, Law, and Policy*, ed. Adam D. Moore (London: Rowman & Littlefield International, 2016), 237.

24. Strossen, "Post-9/11 Government Surveillance," 237.

25. Strossen, "Post-9/11 Government Surveillance," 235.

Chapter 7

Features of State Surveillance in the United States

Although patriotic motives and a genuine belief that mass surveillance enhances security animates the architects of this practice, persistent use of deceptive language indicates an awareness that many would object on civil-rights grounds. The greatest act of obfuscation occurred when General James Clapper lied to Congress about the activities of the US intelligence apparatus. During a Senate hearing in March 2013, Senator Ron Wyden asked General Clapper if the NSA collected any information at all on hundreds of millions of Americans. After a pregnant pause, Clapper replied, "No—not wittingly." In a subsequent interview, conducted after the Snowden revelations two months later revealed that the NSA was pursuing exactly the type of collection that he had denied, General Clapper said, "I responded in what I thought was the most truthful, or least untruthful manner, by saying no." This claim rested on the national security apparatus's convoluted definition of the word *collect* included in Senator Wyden's question. To quote General Clapper further, "There are honest differences on the semantics of what— when someone says 'collection' to me, that has a specific meaning, which may have a different meaning to him." He then added that *collect* did not mean "to acquire" or "to gather." Instead, he said that collection meant "taking a book off the shelf and opening it up and reading it." Moreover, "collection" only occurred when a human, rather than a machine or an algorithm, "read" or examined the "book."[1] The claim that collection did not mean to acquire or to gather but only occurred when a human being acted on information reflects the national security-apparatus' use of terms of art designed to obscure and deceive.

The development of arcane semantics and definitions at odds with generally accepted meanings of words extends beyond the understanding of the word *collection*. Former NSA director General Keith Alexander, famous for saying "Collect it all, sniff it all, know it all, and exploit it all," stunningly told Congress in another hearing that the NSA "[did] not hold data on US citizens."[2] The Obama administration subsequently tried to defend this bald-faced lie, insisting that the word *data* was fundamentally different from *metadata*. Of course, neither general, given the centrality of the national security apparatus to the United States' view of itself, faced any legal consequences for committing perjury when they lied to Congress.

The doublespeak and parsing of meanings extend to virtually every other intelligence activity as well. For example, when the intelligence apparatus uses the word *surveillance*, it only means *electronic surveillance*, itself a label that excludes the gathering of data like phone numbers—an activity that they might, perhaps, describe as "collection." "Collection" is itself subdivided into several categories, depending on the type and place of the gathered communication.

The misdefinition of other words not only seeks to misdirect but to minimize the scope and nature of surveillance as well. The words that the United States government uses deliberately promote the impression that its domestic-surveillance activities are surgical and precise, and designed to exclude the innocent. For example, as noted before, the use of the words *targeted* and *selectors* deliberately conveys the impression that narrow, focused criteria govern the querying of metadata. Instead, available information reveals that the breadth of these activities vitiates any common sense understanding that they are carefully limited, as the word *targeted* implies.

The government's use of deliberately obfuscatory language increases public confusion about the scope of its activities. As noted earlier, the word *metadata* implies something vast that is very distant and removed from the individual and the private. If "metadata" seems like an abstraction to most, so too does "cloud." To those without the requisite knowledge, it is a term as ethereally abstract as "heaven." Where is it located? And how does data reside there? And incomprehension about how algorithms work and how they are designed only adds to confusion about the nature and consequences of metadata mining.

Acronyms serve to obscure, as well, and exclude the uninitiated, while granting the status of expert to insiders. Experts in all fields favor acronyms, given their inclusionary and exclusionary features. Ironically, although acronyms are a form of shorthand designed to simplify, they can just as powerfully disguise. Not surprisingly, given these attributes, the architects of surveillance evidence a pronounced predilection for acronyms, which suffuse their communications. The deliberate construction of word meanings at odds with accepted understandings and the use of a vast letter salad of acronyms socializes insiders into an esoteric club. But the misleading portion of this language creates the ability to claim that one has not spoken untruthfully and lied to protect *arcana imperii*. Therefore, these practices are just another effort to construct the "plausible deniability" that became famous during the Iran Contra scandal. The maintenance of secrecy, seen as a good in and of itself because of its association with the preservation of security, justifies these deceptions. But there is no avoiding the fact that a government that deceives and lies to its citizens systematically undermines the transparency and accountability that the exercise of democracy requires. In the end it reduces trust, causing more and more people to doubt its motives and the veracity of its declarations. Distrust of government becomes more and more widespread as well.

THE US GOVERNMENT'S POLICING OF THE WORLD WIDE WEB AND THE GROWTH OF THE SURVEILLANCE INDUSTRIAL COMPLEX

From the earliest days of the Internet, the US government, in another assertion of American Exceptionalism, claimed the right to police the World Wide Web. Although the United States had been home to the development of the Web in the first place, its effort to claim de facto sovereignty over an international public good became the source of many difficulties. While the US government touted the World Wide Web as a place where information could flow freely, it used its power and technical capacities to access all this information through the enforced weakening of encryption and by tapping into global fiber-optic and other communications networks. Thus, even as the United States asserted that the Internet was a truly "free space," to quote Hillary Clinton—an enthusiastic supporter of the US national security apparatus—it ensured that it could spy at will on all online activities. As always, exceptionalism enabled the US government to simultaneously proclaim its universalism and beneficence while pursuing naked self-interest and "full-spectrum dominance."

Moreover, even as the United States promoted the World Wide Web, its regulatory regime deliberately rejected and undermined the assertion of any global human right to privacy. The US government's rhetoric about the Internet combines a message of global collective empowerment and mutual benefit with claims about the dictates of realpolitik. Realpolitik forces it to monitor and spy on Web users because other states spy. It conveniently does not mention that nobody else claimed the right to exercise sovereignty over the Internet. Not surprisingly, several of these others, and not just China, behind its "Great Firewall," began thinking about creating intranets. While economic and other incentives continue to support the World Wide Web, the pressure for greater sovereign control grows steadily. Deglobalization, in the wake of the COVID-19 pandemic and the supply-chain shortages that it revealed, could accelerate this trend.

Events at the very end of the twentieth century created the private-public partnership alluded to before, best described as the *surveillance industrial complex*, which accelerated the US government's capacity to surveil the World Wide Web. Immediately after the fall of the Berlin Wall in 1989, the US intelligence apparatus, although still enormous, temporarily shrank in size and capacity, especially when compared to its halcyon days during the Cold War. This shrinkage coincided with the explosive growth in Silicon Valley during the 1990s. The so-called dot-com bubble drew venture capital and computer scientists into technology start-ups during this decade. However, this bubble burst in March 2000, leaving a pool of human capital available for other employment. As Patrick Radden Keefe notes,

> [the] dot-com boom coincided with considerable downsizing within the US intelligence community. . . . So it was that the American government . . . in the months and years after 9/11 was obliged to turn, hat in hand, to the private sector. . . . As it happened, private technology companies were just as eager to collaborate. . . . [Many] were driven by a coincidence of timing; in the fall of 2001 the bubble had only recently burst on the Internet economy. Venture capital for tech start-ups had run completely dry, dot-com employees were being laid off in droves.[3]

The surveillance industrial complex began in earnest in a private-public collaboration after the creation of the Matrix, a tool that the US government acquired from a private company. Hank Asher inaugurated this complex when he founded the surveillance technology company Seisint. The company's tool, the Matrix, collected data on 450 million people culled from public and other records. Asher then subjected this trove of data to algorithms designed to identify the 9/11 attackers. These algorithms included a query about Muslim foreign nationals who had entered the United States in the recent past. This mining turned up two hundred names, which he sent to the FBI. When the FBI saw that five of the 9/11 attackers were on this list, they began a partnership with Seisint that ultimately earned the company millions of dollars in government contracts. A host of other surveillance entrepreneurs would subsequently follow Seisint's path to profitability.[4]

Subsequent surveillance start-ups not only developed more powerful and intrusive spying devices and technologies but also lobbied aggressively for their adoption and use. As Patrick Radden Keefe writes,

> It is all too easy, when considering the range of intrusive new surveillance technologies brought to bear by various agencies of the US government in the years since 9/11 to overlook that fact that the real driver behind these technologies is

not the government at all but, rather, private investors and entrepreneurs like Hank Asher. . . . The result has been the sudden emergence of what might be described as an espionage industrial complex: a rapidly growing technology sector that conjures up ambitious new programs and devices to assist the government in its War on Terrorism.[5]

In pursuit of greater revenues, many of these companies sell their wares to other countries and develop devices that the general population can use to spy on each other. More and more precise and powerful cameras are developed and sold to monitor all activities occurring inside and outside homes, along with tiny listening and recording devices for those inclined to spy on others. And the marketing of these wares exploits the same popular fears and vulnerabilities justifying growing state surveillance—concerns about terrorism, crime, and a raft of other real and perceived dangers.

The private companies that participate in the US surveillance industrial complex engage in the same linguistic disguises, obfuscations, and outright deceptions that mark the government's communications in this area. On occasion, however, the manifest falsity of their communications is exposed. For example, the technology start-up Dataminr, whose funding comes from the CIA and Twitter, unsuccessfully tried to manipulate revelations indicating that it had participated in the surveillance of Black Lives Matter protests after the killing of George Floyd. Although its activities were amply documented, the company repeatedly insisted that it did not provide its government customers with "any form of surveillance."[6] The declarations on the topic of one Dataminr executive vice president reveal the willingness to lie about surveillance practices. As Sam Biddle writes for *The Intercept*,

> [The] apparently glaring contradiction by Dataminr, still publicly claiming it would never engage in surveillance while simultaneously facilitating the surveillance of protests, hasn't been lost on the company's staff. At a virtual staff meeting . . . executive vice president Jason Wilcox['s] . . . defense of Dataminr was based on a sort of linguistic distinction: that relaying data to the police isn't a form of surveillance but a form of ideologically neutral newsgathering. In an alternate euphemism, Wilcox described the surveillance alerts forwarded to police as "situational awareness through real-time events, [in] many of which people's lives are at stake, and they can respond more quickly and save lives." This is generally the same reason Twitter and Dataminr PR teams describe this governmental product as a source of "news alerts," not intelligence—a rationale that largely obscures the major differences between what, say, a newspaper might do with rapidly updated information about a protest against policing versus what the police might want to do with the same data.[7]

However, a few digital companies, most famously Apple, have had somewhat more conflictual or at least occasionally tense relationships with the
US government over questions related to privacy. The largest conflict arose
over state access to Apple's iPhones following the December 2015 terrorist
attack in San Bernardino, California. The US government insisted that Apple
should enable its "cracking" of the passcodes that the attackers had used to
protect the data on their phones. Apple asserted that the granting of such
access would effectively destroy the privacy of its users, rupturing the company's contract with them. This conflict, although real, included a fair amount
of theater. Even though the US government could already penetrate digital
devices at will, Apple wanted to further advertise its efforts to protect privacy,
which were more extensive than other device makers but still inadequate.
Unsurprisingly, in the end the US government "cracked" the phones without
Apple's help, revealing yet again the extent of its capacities.

Other conflicts between the government and the largest technology companies continue to arise. In substantial measure these tensions reflect the
fact that these companies are multinational entities engaged in international
markets. These companies also must be sensitive to other regulatory environments and to the demands of foreign consumers, while the US government
insists on its absolute primacy. But these tensions pale in comparison to the
degree of cooperation that exists between the American technology companies and the US state. All cooperate, often quietly and discreetly, with the US
national security apparatus.

A TYPICAL EXAMPLE OF THE FRUITS
OF THE SURVEILLANCE INDUSTRIAL
COMPLEX: FACIAL RECOGNITION

Facial recognition is an intrinsic part of the surveillance industrial complex. In
common with many other technologies, the adoption of facial recognition did
not encounter significant regulatory barriers. Ex post facto concerns about the
technology did become more common as populations in a number of countries began to understand its implications. Nonetheless, facial recognition
benefited from the same forces driving the adoption of other technologies.
These included a logic of inevitability, entrepreneurs and private corporations
seeking to profit from its use, governments enamored of its potential to fight
terrorism and crime, and its promise to make life easier and more convenient.

In public spaces, facial recognition promises to enable the virtually complete tracking and monitoring of the population. When paired with networks
of CCTV cameras and the mining of the facial images that people post on
the Internet, facial recognition allows states to see and identify people. And

not surprisingly, given the authoritarian—indeed, in many ways totalitarian—nature of the Chinese polity, the Chinese government became the most enthusiastic user of facial-recognition technologies in the world.

In the United States, facial recognition expanded slowly but steadily. The first serious questioning of the technology arose when studies conducted in Detroit and other cities revealed its discriminatory design and effects. These studies showed that facial recognition misidentified African Americans and people of color more than Whites. In February 2018, the seminal study "Gender Shades," written by two of the foremost experts in the field, Joy Buolamwini and Timmit Gebru, provided indisputable evidence that commercial facial-recognition systems contained serious gender and racial biases. The worst system, IBM's, was 34.4 percent worse at classifying gender for dark-skinned women than for light-skinned men.[8]

Despite these problems, use of the technology expanded. While democratic countries insist that they will confine the technology to certain defined ends, it has become clear that it is being deployed against political protesters, to cite just one example. In effect, facial-recognition technologies strip all public activity of any remaining vestiges of anonymity. And in most polities, anonymity serves as the primary source of protection for protestors, including those engaged in nonviolent action. Without it, they are vulnerable to increasingly precise and targeted state repression.

Although many companies pursue facial recognition, Amazon soon became the largest provider of this technology to governments and especially law enforcement. This led a group of nearly seventy research and civil-rights organizations to write to Amazon's founder and executive chair, Jeff Bezos, demanding that the company stop selling this technology to the Trump administration, which was using it to track and deport immigrants. For its part, the ACLU delivered a petition to the company with 150,000 signatures and a letter signed by a number of shareholders, while Amazon employees voiced their concerns through an internal memo.[9]

These requests failed to move the company, and it continued to sell law enforcement agencies its system, named Rekognition, deepening its surveillance partnership with governments. For example, after it acquired the doorbell–turned–home surveillance company Ring, Amazon began sharing the information derived from Ring cameras with local police departments. The company's "innovations" and acquisitions indicate Amazon's intention to become the largest actor in the surveillance industrial complex.

Indeed, Amazon's ability to monitor private spaces through Alexa, and its other products that surveil public spaces, such as Rekognition, transformed the company into a surveillance machine that only trailed the very largest governments in scale and capacity. More remarkably, people willingly purchased the surveillance tools used to monitor them, like Alexa and Ring.

becoming participants in their own surveillance, while continuing to see Amazon as a benign and reliable friend—even as it sells instruments that facilitate potential oppression to governments.

In marked contrast to Amazon, after researchers revealed the racial bias embedded in IBM's facial-recognition tools, the company stopped sharing this information with law enforcement and withdrew its product. In addition, this decision reflected the pressures emanating from a generalized complaint about facial-recognition systems. The photos that all these companies amass to develop facial recognition are captured indiscriminately from the Internet. For example, IBM was appropriating photos uploaded on Flickr to fuel its facial-recognition system. While the application of the third-party doctrine in the digital age makes this a legal appropriation, this action occasions disquiet since it destroys people's control over a portion of themselves, the use of their image.

Unlike IBM, Amazon doubled down on Rekognition, despite Buolamwini and Gebru's revelations showing that its error rate was almost as high as IBM's. Amazon insisted that its own scholarship showed that Rekognition is accurate and that the research of the critics of the system was misleading. Moreover, like many other Big Tech companies, and especially Google and Facebook, Amazon uses the third-party doctrine to provide legal justification for all its appropriations.

The killing of George Floyd on May 25, 2020, transformed the political context surrounding the police's use of facial-recognition technology. Congressional democrats, as part of their larger police reform efforts, sought to limit law enforcement's use of this technology. On June 10 of that year, Amazon finally announced that it would place a one-year moratorium on police use of Rekognition.

But Amazon did not extend this moratorium to federal agencies, including US Customs and Border Protection (CBP) and Immigration and Customs Enforcement (ICE). The company's intention to dominate the facial-recognition market and become the largest player in the surveillance industrial complex explains its reluctance to move away from providing facial recognition to the coercive apparatuses of states. In contrast, after the George Floyd killing, Microsoft completely suspended its facial-recognition partnership with governments until the development of a regulatory framework. Moreover, it did this before Amazon announced its one-year moratorium on sales to police departments.

Additional, less famous, and even more unprincipled facial-recognition companies emerged in the United States during the second decade of the twenty-first century, becoming intrinsic parts of the surveillance industrial complex. A notable early entrant into this market in the United States was Clearview AI. Clearview exploited the third-party doctrine as well, appropriating and mining the images of people available everywhere on the Web. In consonance with Google, Facebook, Amazon, and the other participants in the private information market, Clearview insisted that it was not appropriating personal information because people had already surrendered these images. Furthermore, they argued, privacy was already dead, or on the way to its inevitable demise. And as a result, there was no practical or ethical reason not to profit from this information.

Like Amazon and IBM, Clearview sells its facial-recognition capacities to law enforcement agencies. As the *New York Times* wrote about Clearview AI and its founder,

> Mr. Ton-That—an Australian techie and one-time model—did something momentous: He invented a tool that could end your ability to walk down the street anonymously and provided it to hundreds of law-enforcement agencies. . . . His tiny company, Clearview AI, devised a groundbreaking facial-recognition app. You take a picture of a person, upload it, and get to see public photos of that person, along with links to where those photos appeared. The system, whose backbone is a database of more than three billion images [a number that grew to over ten billion by 2022] that Clearview claims to have scraped from Facebook, YouTube, Venmo, and millions of other websites—goes far beyond anything ever constructed by the United States government or Silicon Valley giants. . . . Until now, technology that readily identifies everyone based on his or her face has been taboo because of its radical erosion of privacy. . . . But without public scrutiny, more than six hundred law-enforcement agencies have started using Clearview in the past year. . . . The computer code underlying its app, analyzed by the *New York Times*, includes programming language to pair it with augmented-reality glasses; users would potentially be able to identify every person they saw. The tool could identify activists at a protest or an attractive stranger on a subway, revealing not just their names but where they lived, what they did, and whom they knew.[10]

Clearview AI's financial backers include Peter Thiel, founder of surveillance company Palantir and an avid supporter of Donald Trump. Richard Schwartz—who founded Clearview AI along with Mr. Ton-That—is a conservative who worked for Rudi Giuliani during his time as mayor of New York. The right-wing affiliations of Clearview AI explain its pro–law enforcement bias but not its cavalier assault on privacy or its development of a tool that intrudes so systematically on the individual. Even though much of the American right enthusiastically supports the coercive branches of the government, many, especially those who are libertarian, are skeptical about state surveillance given the value they place on individualism and individual rights.

The answer to this seeming contradiction can be found in the declarations of David Scalzo, another financial backer of Clearview. When interviewed about the company's business model, he said, "I've come to the conclusion that because information constantly increases, there's never going to be privacy. . . . Laws have to determine what's legal, but you can't ban technology. Sure, that might lead to a dystopian future or something, but you can't ban it."[11]

Scalzo's comments capture several aspects of the implicitly and sometimes explicitly Orwellian worldview of those involved in the surveillance industrial complex. The first involves the complete dismissal of privacy: if it is already gone, or inevitably destined to disappear, there is nothing wrong with producing tools that intrude in new ways on people. A second understanding, evident in every corner of the digital world, derives from the belief in the inevitability of technological change.

For the technological determinists, technology possesses the same irresistible qualities as death and taxes. Developers cannot be blamed, no matter how problematic the effects of a particular invention, since they are just participants in an inevitable process of innovation. Technological determinists do not think that the creators and financial backers of Clearview AI should entertain ethical qualms about creating and marketing a tool purpose-made for stalking and for dissuading peaceful protest and dissent and that can make people reticent to exercise their First Amendment rights. After all, the reasoning goes, if they do not develop this technology, someone else will.

In all these regards, Clearview perfectly exemplifies in especially vivid form the central logic of the digital age—the commodification of things previously understood as personal, such as images of the self. And the lack of regulation of facial recognition and the rapidity of its spread constitutes yet another example of the willingness to adopt the newest technology and only subsequently start to think about how to mitigate its worst effects. Moreover, despite growing criticism and lawsuits against the company, Clearview AI continued to amass images, announcing its intention to gather and exploit one hundred billion images by 2023, equivalent to almost fourteen photos for each inhabitant of the Earth, enabling it to make "almost everybody in the world identifiable."[12]

Law enforcement agencies continue to deploy facial recognition, despite its problems with bias discussed above, given the view that its mathematical underpinning makes it accurate and reliable. Yet again, the reification of security justifies ignoring an expanding threat to privacy. As is true of so much of the digital age where regulation lags far, far behind innovation and widespread adoption, law enforcement and a host of other entities deploy facial recognition in an environment with few limitations on its use. "There are two ways that this technology can hurt people," writes Deborah Raji. "One way is by not working: by virtue of having higher error rates for people of color, it puts them at greater risk. The second situation is when it *does* work—where you have the perfect facial-recognition system but it is easily weaponized against communities to harass them. It's a separate and connected conversation."[13]

A report published on August 24, 2021, by the US General Accountability Office that surveyed twenty-four federal agencies showed that ten planned to increase their use of facial-recognition systems by 2023. Despite the extent of public objections to facial recognition, and the problems previously discussed, eighteen of the twenty-four agencies used facial recognition as of 2020. The Departments of Agriculture, Commerce, Defense, Homeland Security, Health and Human Services, Interior, Justice, State, Treasury, and Veteran Affairs all intended to deploy additional facial-recognition systems. These ten agencies planned to use seventeen facial-recognition systems, thirteen of which would be owned by the agencies, two by local law enforcement, and two by Clearview AI. The US Air Force and the US Fish and Wildlife Service are portions of the agencies listed above that plan to use Clearview AI. Federal agencies share this information with each other and cooperate on these efforts, as well.[14]

To quote the Electronic Frontier Foundation, "This important GAO report exposes the federal government's growing reliance on face-surveillance technology. Most disturbing is its use by law-enforcement agencies. Yet face surveillance is so invasive of privacy, so discriminatory against people of color, and so likely to trigger false arrests that the government should not be using face surveillance at all."[15] But the larger logic informing state surveillance and secrecy discussed throughout this book will drive these practices forward despite the technology's injurious effects.

ANOTHER EXAMPLE OF A FLOURISHING SURVEILLANCE INDUSTRIAL COMPLEX PROJECT: CLOUD SURVEILLANCE

Yet another part of the surveillance industrial complex revolves around the growth of state monitoring of the cloud. Government surveillance of the cloud uses so-called "cloud-extraction technology," which accesses, extracts, analyzes, and retains data stored in the cloud. Cellebrite, one of the private companies comprising the Israeli surveillance industrial complex, moved beyond its specialization—the development and sale of technology designed to extract data from cell phones—when it created and marketed a tool called the UFED Cloud Analyzer. This tool uses log-in credentials "that can be extracted from the device to then pull a history of searches, visited pages, voice-search recording and translations from Google Web history, and view text searches conducted with Chrome and Safari on iOS devices backed up [on] iCloud."[16]

Oxygen Forensics and ElcomSoft, two other surveillance industrial companies, produce cloud-extraction tools as well. The worldview of those involved in cloud extraction, and indeed of all those seeking revenues from the appropriation and exploitation of the personal data of others, can be seen in this tweet from Oxygen Forensics: "Cloud forensics is one of the most important, and fastest growing, area [sic] in digital forensics. If you are not looking to the cloud for data, you are potentially missing a treasure trove of valuable information. Join our Cloud Investigator course here."[17]

The Detective, as Oxygen Forensics has named their tool, has a "cloud extractor" that "acquires data from the most popular cloud services. . . . Also, various social media services are supported [sic] to include . . . Facebook, Twitter, Instagram, and many more. . . . [It] supports [sic] . . . fifty-four different types of cloud services, ranging from file storage, to messengers, drones, health apps and social media."[18] The use of the word *support* to describe the functions of this tool captures other features of the mentality and approach of the surveillance industrial complex. What is "supported" is the state's ability to track, monitor, and surveil its population. Moreover, all these surveillance industrial companies sell their wares to all types of states, including some with the worst human-rights records in the world.

THE ROLE OF HIGHER EDUCATION
IN STATE SURVEILLANCE

Universities in the United States play an essential role in the surveillance industrial complex. Despite their presumptive attachment to humanistic norms, their need for research funding fuels their work in these areas. Long before the dawn of the digital age, universities were involved in research activities that resulted in the development of weapons of war and the creation of technologies that frequently violated fundamental human rights. Arms races and technological change, conjoined with the industrialization of war, created the extraordinarily close nexus between American universities and the government, and between universities and the state in other countries devoted to the development of cutting-edge military capacities and technologies. The subordination of academic inquiry to the dictates of state power occurred in both authoritarian and democratic polities, as did scholarship that increased the coercive and oppressive capacities of these governments.

For example, significant portions of academic departments in Chinese, Russian, American, British, French, and Israeli universities, to mention only the most notable cases, are extensions of their own military industrial complexes, conducting the kind of research that enables the development of ever-more-lethal weapons systems. In the United States, the Manhattan Project and the work on the nuclear bomb at Los Alamos constituted the most famous example of this cooperation. However, many other portions of American academia play a critical role in other parts of the US national security state. As is true in other societies with a militaristic bent and that contain an especially strong "will to power," a significant portion of American science is devoted to the extension of state power. This makes portions of American academia natural participants in the effort to construct a panopticon.

Just like an earlier generation of physicists lent their talents to the development of nuclear weapons, a later generation of computer scientists and mathematicians sell their talents and services to states—whether out of cupidity, nationalism, or a mix of both motives—despite the civil- and human-rights implications of mass surveillance. If nuclear weaponry could not have come into being without the research activities of academics, neither could the development of mass surveillance and collection.

Perhaps the most extensive research effort to develop the technologies that the US government uses to surveil the world occurs at the University of Maryland, whose centrality equals Technion's in Israel. That said, many, many other research universities, such as Carnegie Mellon, are involved in the creation of the panopticon. Stanford University, the seedbed of many Silicon Valley companies that participate in the surveillance industrial complex, merits particular mention as well.

The University of Maryland's proximity to the NSA and also to Fort Meade, a center of the US government's cyber activities, make it an enthusiastic and well-remunerated participant in the construction of the modern American surveillance state. Just like many other American universities, UMD's research on cyber and data analytics seeks to advance the effort to "collect it all, know it all, and exploit it all," to again quote General Keith Alexander. Although commonplace and barely questioned, the participation of educational institutions in activities that injure privacy and other civil rights raises especially serious ethical and moral questions, given that their fundamental purpose is to produce knowledge that improves the human condition. The terrible example of German scientists lending their talents to the Nazi regime and participating actively in the advancement of its designs did not, unfortunately, lead to sufficiently robust ethical guidelines designed to limit the pursuit of research activities that give states even greater capacities to undermine human rights. Everywhere, the nexus between science and war extended after the dawn of the digital age to the collaboration between the STEM fields and the state in the effort to construct a panopticon.

CONCLUSION

The government desire to know everything and see everything encourages the emergence and expansion of a surveillance industrial complex. This new surveillance industrial complex is the fruit of many of the dynamics that fueled the earlier and continuing growth of the military industrial complex and occasions the same worries that President Eisenhower voiced in his farewell address, when he famously warned the country that the development of this entity constituted a fundamental threat to American democracy.

Beyond its other features, a surveillance industrial complex reflects the privileging of national security over the protection of civil rights. Surveillance marches hand in hand with the militarization and securitization of the polity and corrodes its democratic institutions. The quest to become safer, or to at least feel safer, produces a corollary decline in liberty. The population typically remains unaware of this trade-off or demonstrates a willingness to surrender rights, especially those of others, to the presumed dictates of security. Government surveillance produces an especially pronounced form of power inequality, a result of the enormous informational capacities at its disposal compared to the limited information available to individuals. As surveillance expands, individuals shrink. And the content of democratic citizenship, and especially agency and choice, declines and constricts as Big Brother becomes increasingly powerful.

The wholesale adoption of surveillance during the "war on terror" reflected both a decline in social trust and a corollary desire to make the society more legible and predictable. As Shoshana Zuboff writes, "Acts of terror reject the authority of civilizational norms and reveal the impossibility of society without mutual trust. Governments now turn to . . . certainty machines that promise direct, reliable means of detection, prediction, and even the automatic activation of countermeasures."[19] Surveillance, in short, seemingly promises to increase order and control whatever the costs in liberty.

However, despite the expenditure of hundreds of billions of dollars on surveillance, terrorism and crime could not be extirpated. In fact, they morphed while other digital tools enabled the proliferation of a whole new set of malevolent activities, including child exploitation, sex trafficking, identity theft, and novel types of financial fraud. Ransomware and hacking, two previously unknown activities, became ubiquitous crimes, threatening the society and the population. The shifting tactics of terrorists, and especially their avoidance of digital devices subject to intrusion, along with the rise in the number of "lone-wolf actors," limits the ability to predict attacks, even as everybody suffers the privacy losses flowing from mass surveillance. For example, the British and French governments, despite possessing some of the most comprehensive, sophisticated, and intrusive surveillance systems in the world, could not stop or predict lone-wolf attacks in London, Paris, and Nice. Rather than changing direction, the advocates of surveillance blamed their failures to predict on excessively restrictive regulation and grossly inadequate funding. The fight against "bad actors" required the passage of laws granting even greater powers to the coercive apparatus and the provision of more funding to support "innovation" and staffing.

NOTES

1. All quotations and discussion of this issue drawn from Jennifer Stisa Granick, *American Spies: Modern Surveillance, Why You Should Care, and What to Do about It* (Cambridge: Cambridge University Press, 2017), 33–34.
2. Granick, *American Spies*, 34.
3. Patrick Radden Keefe, "The Espionage Industrial Complex," in *Liberty Under Attack*, ed. Richard C. Leone and Greg Anrig Jr. (New York: New Century Foundation, 2007), 152–53.
4. Keefe, "Espionage Industrial Complex," 147.
5. Keefe, "Espionage Industrial Complex," 149–50.
6. Sam Biddle, "Police Surveilled George Floyd Protests with Help from Twitter-Affiliated Startup Dataminr," *The Intercept*, July 9, 2020, https://theintercept.com/2020/07/09/twitter-dataminr-police-spy-surveillance-black-lives-matter-protests/.
7. Biddle, "Police Surveilled George Floyd Protests."
8. As recounted in Karen Hao, "The Two-Year Fight to Stop Amazon from Selling Face Recognition to the Police," *MIT Technology Review*, June 12, 2020, https://www.technologyreview.com/2020/06/12/1003482/amazon-stopped-selling-police-face-recognition-fight/.
9. Hao, "Two-Year Fight."
10. Kashmir Hill, "The Secretive Company that Might End Privacy as We Know It," *New York Times*, last updated February 10, 2020, https://www.nytimes.com/2020/01/18/technology/clearview-privacy-facial-recognition.html.
11. Hill, "Secretive Company."
12. "In Big Win, Settlement Ensures Clearview AI Complies with Groundbreaking Illinois Biometric Policy Law," American Civil Liberties Union, ACLU.org, May 9, 2022, https://www.aclu.or/press-releases/big-win-settlement-ensures-clearview-ai-complies with-groundbreaking-illinois-biometric-privacy-law.
13. Deborah Raji, as quoted in Hao, "Two-Year Fight," emphasis original.
14. Tate Ryan-Mosley, "US Government Agencies Plan to Increase Their Use of Facial Recognition Technology," *MIT Technology Review*, August 24, 2021, https://www.technologyreview.com/2021/08/24/1032967/us-government-agencies-plan-to-increase-their-use-of-facial-recognition-technology/.
15. Ryan-Mosley, "US Government Agencies."

16. "Cloud Extraction Technology: The Secret Tech that Lets Government Agencies Collect Masses of Data from Your Apps," Privacy International (website), January 7, 2020, https://privacyinternational.org/long-read/3300/cloud-extraction-technology-secret-tech-lets-government-agencies-collect-masses-data.

17. Privacy International, "Cloud Extraction Technology."

18. Privacy International, "Cloud Extraction Technology."

19. Shoshana Zuboff, *The Age of Surveillance Capitalism: The Fight for a Human Future at the New Frontier of Power* (New York: PublicAffairs, 2019), 385.

Chapter 8

Surveilling the Most Vulnerable

The State and Refugees, Migrants, Dissidents, and Minorities

The most vulnerable people in each polity—migrants—experience the most intense impact of state surveillance. Everywhere, refugees and migrants are subject to the greatest surveillance. States gather and share particularly intimate information about them and monitor them especially closely. The belief that terrorists and criminals lurk among migrants justifies this expansive scrutiny. Even countries with strong attachments to civil rights limit the enjoyment of most of these benefits to citizens and, to a lesser but significant degree, to legal permanent residents. Undocumented migrants, on the other hand, experience, at best, highly contingent and attenuated respect for the rights embedded in their personhood. It is consequently common for them to experience egregious violations of personhood rights. Countries that violate these protections, then, must elide the fact that *personhood* constitutes the wellspring of the rights that their own citizens enjoy. As Linda Bosniak writes about undocumented migrants in the United States,

> The country's constitutional commitment to *personhood* as the fundamental basis of rights has produced certain zones of protected status for the undocumented, notwithstanding their irregular status under the immigration laws. . . . On the other hand, the rights undocumented immigrants formally enjoy as persons and as residents are always held in the long shadow of the government's immigration-enforcement power. An undocumented immigrant worker can formally claim a right to receive the minimum wage, for example, but her willingness to press for the fulfillment of that right (assuming she is aware of it at all) is commonly undermined by her fear of coming to the attention of the immigration authorities and being subjected to deportation. And, like all aliens, the undocumented may be deported for otherwise constitutionally protected conduct (e.g., certain forms of speech and association).[1]

During the early decades of the twenty-first century, war, violence, climate change, and extreme economic deprivation produced the largest displaced population since World War II. This human calamity coincided with the development and deployment of the digital age's surveillance tools. In most "developed" countries, and particularly in much of Europe and in the United States, fears about the number and the ethnic or religious background of these migrants and refugees layered onto existing nativist angers and resentments.

Reflecting these attitudes, governments around the world have opted to confront the issue of human displacement with a raft of tools designed to manage, and more typically exclude, migrants. These tools strip people, who have lost everything except for their lives, of their privacy and other rights. These actions constitute a profound assault on the human dignity of migrants, particularly given their vulnerability and lack of agency. While governments must acquire information directly related to security concerns about those seeking legal entry to protect their societies, the scope and nature of their intrusions are so extensive that they constitute prima facie violations of the Universal Declaration of Human Rights and of the International Covenant, which imposes treaty obligations.

The use of these and other tools rose dramatically after September 11, 2001, when the fear of terrorists created a fortress mentality. States in migrant-receiving countries deployed increasingly sophisticated digital tools during the subsequent two decades designed to surveil, catalog, monitor, identify, and track this population. Those who experience the greatest scrutiny and consequent intrusion are refugees and asylum seekers. To gain legal entry, refugees and asylum seekers are required to trade all their privacy to the receiving state. This involves a double victimization, since refugees and asylum seekers are overwhelmingly driven to migrate after experiencing terrible and life-threatening traumas.

Refugee camps throughout this period grew larger and larger, and more and more desperate journeys ended in death and tragedy. Receiving countries devoted enormous resources to fortifying their borders and to developing and deploying increasingly sophisticated monitoring and tracking tools. And despite professing to care about the circumstances that compelled people to leave their countries of origin, efforts to ameliorate these "push factors" paled in comparison to those designed to regulate and prevent entry.

Nativism, xenophobia, and racism fueled popular demands in receiving countries to further restrict and even end migration. Right-wing populists, especially in Europe and the United States, have ridden anti-immigrant sentiments to power and made anti-immigrant rhetoric a centerpiece of their public discourse. They have also enacted a broad range of restrictive and punitive policies against these migrants. These measures are added on to the already extensive monitoring of the movement of people around the world.

Intrusive identity documents containing personal biometric information became required after 9/11, further reducing privacy. The digitization of this information, including the entry and exit information of travelers and their photographs, creates yet another repository of data in the hands of governments subject to sharing, data mining, and the prospective and retrospective application of facial-recognition technology to billions of photographs.

In 2020, roughly 258 million people were international migrants. If trends continue—and this seems certain, given climate change and other problems—this number is projected to rise to at least 450 million in 2050. Fears about this population and the effort to protect borders led governments to use their most intrusive and capable tools against those seeking to gain entry to their countries. As Privacy International notes, "governments are using migrants as the testing ground for many of their so-called innovations—biometric schemes, invasive mobile phone–extraction procedures, and more. . . . Migrants are now expected to hand over their devices, their social media passwords, and even their DNA."[2]

Many countries use these extraordinarily invasive practices, although the United States leads the Western world in the deployment of these technologies and measures. But others are just as willing to deny the personhood-privacy rights of migrants. For example, in 2017 the German government granted migration officials the authority to extract data from the smartphones, laptops, and tablets of asylum seekers—despite the state's otherwise relatively robust commitment to privacy protection. Similarly, in 2018 Austria began requiring asylum seekers to turn over their phones to authorities.[3]

The Israeli surveillance company Cellebrite, already an active participant in the effort to eliminate privacy from the cloud, markets its tool to governments wishing to surveil refugees, asylum seekers, and others.[4] Cellebrite's tool allows the circumvention of passwords on digital devices. And just like the other companies comprising Israel's surveillance industrial complex, Cellebrite sells its tools to an array of regimes. Countries with egregious human-rights records and histories of repression have acquired its tools, including Turkey, Russia, the United Arab Emirates, and Bahrain.

The United Kingdom purchased Cellebrite's tool as well. In May 2018 the UK Office of Immigration Enforcement made a payment of forty-five thousand pounds to Cellebrite for its technology. The company asserts that its technology is able to audit "'a person's journey to identify suspicious activity prior to arrival,' track their route, run a keyword and image search through their device to identify 'traces of illicit activity,' and review their online browsing and social media activity." And Cellebrite's tool can also retrieve deleted data.[5]

After 9/11 the United States primarily drove the effort to more closely surveil and document migrants. Post-9/11 fears about dangers presented by the movement of people across borders led the US government to use its power and international weight to push other states to construct a collective surveillance regime. For example, shortly after the 2001 terrorist attacks, the United States banned entry to individuals coming from countries that lacked proper biometric passports. This forced countries around the world to modify their passports and gather additional, formerly private information from their citizens.

In addition, the United States strengthened its borders using physical barriers and surveillance. Much of this effort focused on the country's southern border, given the number of refugees and migrants, primarily although not exclusively, from Central America and Mexico. Countries in Europe adopted similar measures, especially as the number of refugees fleeing conflict in Syria and Afghanistan and overwhelming poverty and conflict in Africa rose during the second decade of the twenty-first century. Countries comprising the Schengen Area, a region that permitted document-free travel among countries that were part of the European Union, faced popular pressures to restrict movement across previously unpoliced borders. And several countries in Eastern Europe, and especially Poland and Hungary, adopted extraordinarily restrictive measures designed to exclude migrants, accelerating their transformation into illiberal polities.

Surveillance activities in the United States related to border control and the monitoring of refugees and other migrants were only vaguely understood for years after 9/11. In June 2019, however, hackers seized and released the information of a subcontractor who worked for US Customs and Border Protection. This hack revealed for the first time the scope of US surveillance activities related to border control. The hack "disclosed tens of thousands of travelers' facial images, license plate numbers, and the technology used to capture this information, including facial-recognition cameras."[6]

In addition, in 2019, Olivia Solon in the *Guardian* reported that,

> On the United States–Mexico border, an array of hi-tech companies also purvey advanced surveillance equipment. Israeli defense contractor Elbit Systems has built "dozens of towers in Arizona to spot people as far as 7.5 miles away." . . . Its technology was first perfected in Israel from a contract to build a "smart fence" to separate Jerusalem from the West Bank. Another company, Anduril Industries, has developed towers that feature a laser-enhanced camera, radar, and communications system that scans a two-mile radius to detect motion. Captured images "are analyzed using artificial intelligence to pick out humans from wildlife and other moving objects."[7]

While Elbit is part of the Israeli surveillance industrial complex, Anduril Industries was established by Palmer Luckey, founder of Oculus and a Donald

Trump supporter, with funding from Peter Thiel. The activities of Anduril and Elbit accompany the US government's deployment of facial-recognition technologies that capture the images of people crossing the border. "Secretive tests of the system carried out in Arizona and Texas saw authorities collect a 'massive amount of data,' including images captured 'as people were leaving work, picking up children from school, and carrying out other daily routines,' according to government records."[8] These intrusions into the activities of Americans, in addition to migrants, are the inevitable result of US Customs and Border Protection's definition of the border as an area that extends one hundred miles into the United States.

Investigative journalists examining the activities of US Customs and Border Protection (CBP) discovered that Mexican authorities were cooperating with the US government and were surveilling journalists, activists, and attorneys who assisted Central American migrants. Both the US and the Mexican governments, including President López Obrador (elected in 2018), categorically denied participating in these practices. However, under pressure from civil-rights lawyers and groups of journalists, the CBP finally acknowledged these activities. Randy Howe, head of CBP's Office of Field Operations, made this acknowledgment in a letter written to Mana Azarmi, attorney for the Center for Democracy and Technology, the organization leading a coalition of one hundred groups seeking information about CBP's targeting of journalists.[9]

Howe's letter confirms that

> CBP partnered with the Government of Mexico and other law-enforcement agencies. . . . A number of journalists and photographers were identified by Mexican Federal Police as possibly assisting migrants in crossing the border illegally and/or having some level of participation in the violent incursion events. . . . CBP utilized various sources of information. . . . [These] varied sources of information helped identify a number of people involved in assisting migrants cross the border illegally. . . . Occasionally, CBP may inconvenience law-abiding persons in our efforts to detect, deter, and mitigate threats to our homeland.[10]

In response, Azarmi told *The Intercept*, "It cannot be a crime to advise asylum-seekers about their rights or to report the government's abuse of those rights. . . . DHS is criminalizing compassion." Further, Azarmi argued, "Lawyers, activists, and journalists who associate with asylum-seekers have every right to do so. . . . Surveilling them and searching their computers and cellphones could chill lawyers from providing necessary legal services and chill journalists who are reporting on the asylum system."[11]

Risk-analysis algorithms sift the data collected through the surveillance systems at the border. And to function most effectively, these algorithms require more and more metadata. Carlyn Greenfield wrote about this insatiable need for data: "In June 2019, for example, the US State Department announced a new requirement for foreign travelers seeking a visa and would-be immigrants to share social media account names and email addresses up to five years old." Data points are then assigned for things such as health, education, and financial and travel history, becoming a person's "data double." But, to cite her further,

> a data double is not a person: humans cannot be summarized through data because certain traits, such as ambition or respect for the rule of law, cannot be quantitatively measured and assured. Therefore, the system denies a holistic approach and instead opts for reinforcing assumptions about what certain data points mean. Indeed, algorithms are not only vulnerable to error and discrimination but may compound bias due to the nature of the system.[12]

Beyond these problems with the algorithms, the extent and type of the data gathered on migrants needlessly violates personhood rights to privacy. When data collection involves matters of clear concern to states or societies, it is defensible and important. But much of the information gathered on immigrants strays beyond whether or not they may become threats, into intimate areas that reveal sexual preference and other private matters. Even more than citizens, immigrants acquire a comprehensive digital "permanent record" that includes both the trivial and the consequential. To make matters worse, governments routinely share this data with other countries, extending this harm. For example, the United States and the United Kingdom began sharing all data on migrants and travelers in 2013. Migrants experience enduring injuries when misidentifications and mislabeling inevitably occur. This is especially problematic when such a mistake leads to the decision to deny entry to a refugee fleeing oppression.

The United States' reluctance to limit data retention deepens these problems. During the first decades of the digital age, the extant US policy and legal framework enshrined permanent retention while being married to a technology that significantly facilitated this task. And while it is indisputably true that sovereignty gives governments the categoric right to determine who can enter and who merits exclusion, the kinds of information that these tools gather are meant to deliberately "push borders out." In effect, these tools extend the border to every part of the migrant's journey and into their country of origin. The architecture of immigration law causes borders to spread inward as well. This becomes particularly evident when receiving states seek to find undocumented migrants residing inside their territories. Linda Bosniak writes, "as a practical matter, these national borders—whether confined to the territorial threshold or permitted to pervade all social relations—are not going to prevent large numbers of people from coming to this country and residing and working as undocumented immigrants."[13]

Moreover, fortified borders and the reification of the distinction between "insiders" and "outsiders" requires the collection of more information on insiders as well. Only such information can reliably show who can legitimately claim insider status. The greater the fear of immigrants and outsiders, the more data governments must collect on their own citizens. Many of those who favor more extensive restrictions on immigrants and even their complete exclusion largely seem to accept that the serious pursuit of these policies inevitably increases the appropriation of everybody's information. Perhaps they do not realize that the nativist's assertion of power over the much more powerless immigrant only renders the nativists themselves smaller and more translucent. Intrusions into the lives of insiders include the adoption of documents such as biometric driver's licenses along with verification of employment eligibility among other things. However, the fact that these measures are largely uncontroversial and even popular indicates the willingness of people to trade portions of their privacy for restrictions on migration.

In addition, little has been done to alleviate the conditions in source countries that cause migration. By way of example, the United States spends billions of dollars on border control while doing almost nothing, in comparison, to address the circumstances in Central America that drive migration. This is particularly problematic since the United States played a central role in transforming the region into one of the most violent places in the world. The extent of US intervention in the region's conflicts during the Reagan administration of the 1980s made it a critical player in conflicts that killed hundreds of thousands and displaced millions. Unsurprisingly, many of the region's contemporary problems date from this period. Honduras, Nicaragua, El Salvador, and Guatemala were the centers of this war and became the greatest regional sources of migration to the United States. Indeed, before the 1980s the migratory flow from Central America to the United States was minimal. Although the United States was not the architect of the natural disasters that played an additional role in driving migration during the last part of the twentieth century and the first part of the twenty-first century, it did create the drug war that aggravated all these problems and pursued a series of deportation policies that ensured exponential increases in violence, causing people to flee north. In short, American policy played a critical role in creating the economic and social disaster that drove migration from Central America.

In contrast to its expenditures on these interventions in the 1980s, subsequent US spending designed to promote economic development in the region, or to improve security, remained paltry. While the Central America

Free Trade Agreement negotiated during the Obama administration produced some growth, it could not counteract the devastation that other US policies created. Since then, aid of all sorts has continued to remain modest compared to spending on initiatives to fortify the border or complicate and deter migrant journeys in other ways.

STATE SURVEILLANCE OF AFRICAN AMERICANS, OTHER ETHNIC MINORITIES, AND A VARIETY OF DISSIDENTS

In addition to refugees and migrants, dissidents and those seen as domestic "others" face especially extensive surveillance. Long before the digital age, the US government began surveilling dissidents and "others," especially African Americans. While much has been written about the FBI's surveillance of the civil-rights movement in the 1960s, Simone Browne shows the much deeper roots of this practice, tracing it to the very beginnings of the slave trade. As she writes:

> transatlantic slavery [is] antecedent to contemporary surveillance technologies and practices as they concern inventories of ships' cargo and the cheek-by-jowl arrangement laid out in the stowage plan of the *Brooks* slave ship, biometric information by branding the slave's body with hot irons, slave markets and auction blocks as exercises of synoptic power where the many watched the few, slave passes and patrols, manumission papers and free badges, black codes and fugitive slave notices.[14]

The subsequent monitoring of the African American community, reflected in a raft of policies and practices, constitutes the continuation of this history. These practices involve the construction of panopticons in neighborhoods, including the especially ubiquitous use of cameras and racial profiling, as part of "predictive policing." It also involves the construction of a carceral state that disproportionately imprisons people of color, subjecting them to the most suffocating panopticon of all—the modern prison. The preservation of marginalization and subordination requires the development of an especially extensive panopticon.

Early in American history as well, the US government began officially monitoring "aliens" and dissidents. These efforts were first codified in 1798 after the passage of the Alien and Sedition Act during the "Quasi-War" with France. During World War I, in an echo of this earlier legislation, the Woodrow Wilson administration passed not only the Espionage Act of 1917, which President Obama later resurrected, but also the Sedition Act of 1918, which made it a criminal offense to use "any disloyal, profane, scurrilous, or abusive language about the form of government of the United States or the flag of the United States or the uniform of the Army or Navy." To quote Alan Brinkley, "this . . . law was particularly useful to the government as an instrument for suppressing radicals and labor unionists. The greatest number of prosecutions under the law was directed against members of the Socialist Party and its radical offshoot, the Industrial Workers of the World."[15]

During the Red Scare after the end of World War I, the US government continued and expanded its repression of dissidents and especially immigrants, the so-called "hyphenated Americans." Russian Americans, because of the Bolshevik Revolution, and Italian Americans, presumed to be followers of anarchist Luigi Galleani, were subjected to particular scrutiny and repression. Much of this oppression was engineered by US Attorney General A. Mitchell Palmer, although he was by no means the only architect of the mistreatment. Luigi Galleani's followers had carried out a May Day bombing campaign in 1919, including the unsuccessful attack on Palmer's house. In response Palmer created the Radical Division in the Department of Justice, appointing twenty-four-year-old lawyer J. Edgar Hoover to direct operations. Within a year, using informants and surveillance, Hoover had created dossiers on over two hundred thousand people. The Radical Division was the first domestic-intelligence unit created in peacetime to monitor broad swaths of the population.

In November 1919 the Palmer Raids began, directed against Russian labor unionists. As a result of these raids, over two hundred people were deported. In early January 1920 an even more extensive roundup occurred, with raids carried out in thirty-three cities, seizing some five thousand people. Those detained were herded into detention centers and held for weeks without warrants ever having been issued, while being deprived of their property. Ultimately it turned out that the overwhelming majority had been held without cause and had no connections to the violent bombing campaign. Revelations about this injustice "created popular alarm, where local abuses had not, largely because of the greater suspicion with which Americans viewed broad federal power. The Palmer Raids produced widespread denunciations in the press, destroyed A. Mitchell Palmer's political career, nearly crushed in the bud J. Edgar Hoover's prospects for bureaucratic advancement, and badly damaged the Wilson administration and the Democratic Party."[16]

Because of the lessons of World War I, World War II did not lead to the passage of laws equivalent to the Espionage Act and the Sedition Act, although the United States did, in a massive violation of civil and human rights, subject the Japanese American population to internment camps. The resurrection of the Red Scare during the 1950s, particularly during the McCarthy period, animated a febrile search for communists, particularly by J. Edgar Hoover's

FBI. However, even though the US government constructed dossiers on dissidents and undesirables, it did not engage in the roundups that had marked the Palmer period.

The civil-rights movement and other activism during the 1960s, however, led to especially extensive and intrusive FBI surveillance. While groups like the Weather Underground were targeted, as were participants in the antiwar movement, the FBI devoted particular attention to African American activists, revealing the ways that surveillance seeks to preserve existing racial hierarchies and control the marginalized and the excluded. As Alvaro Bedoya writes:

> There is a myth in this country that in a world where everyone is watched, everyone is watched equally. It's as if an old and racist J. Edgar Hoover has been replaced by the race-blind magic of computers, mathematicians, and Big Data. The truth is more uncomfortable. Across our history and to this day, people of color have been the disproportionate victims of unjust surveillance; Hoover was no aberration. And while racism has played its ugly part, the justification for this monitoring was the same we hear today: national security.[17]

Even as Martin Luther King Jr. was subjected to relentless FBI surveillance, this monitoring indiscriminately encompassed everyone else involved in the Southern Christian Leadership Conference as well as those who participated in the Black Panther Party and the Nation of Islam, to mention a few examples, despite the differences between these groups. Moreover, this brief list does not begin to encapsulate the ways in which the US state surveilled, tracked, and eavesdropped on African American activists. Given this history, it was not surprising that it used these same practices decades later against the Black Lives Matter movement (BLM) despite its status as a nonviolent organization.

Indeed, the increase in the number of surveillance tools at the government's disposal, including drones and fixed-wing planes capable of capturing cell phone data, make the BLM movement even more subject to intrusive surveillance than were previous protest campaigns. This was especially true during the Trump administration. In an apt indication of the views of the US coercive apparatus, the FBI issued an intelligence assessment in August 2017 labeled "Black Identity Activists Likely Motivated to Target Law Enforcement Officers." This assessment labels its targets as domestic terrorist threats. To quote the ACLU, "the intelligence assessment claims, without evidence, that Black people involved in unrelated police killings shared an ideology that motivated their actions. It also focuses on Black people who, in the bureau's own words, 'perceive racism and injustice in American society.'"[18] This last assertion is especially ironic and tragic, since the FBI's' targeting of these people evidenced the continuing power of racist understandings in the agency.

Although the FBI does not identify the groups that are "Black identity activists," one imagines, given its history, that its definition mostly includes nonviolent organizations. Recently, organizations like the Center for Constitutional Rights, Color of Change, and MediaJustice (formerly the Center for Media Justice) have filed Freedom of Information Act requests and lawsuits seeking information on the FBI's surveillance of Black activists participating in the BLM movement. And the FBI resists these requests, in keeping with its historic record. Yet again secrecy trumps transparency except in the rare cases where courts force the disgorging of information or whistleblowers appear. Moreover, the FBI refuses to withdraw its claim that "Black identity extremists" exist as an organized "terrorist" group, despite never having substantiated this allegation.

As noted earlier, various US agencies used aerial surveillance in 2020 during the huge and mostly peaceful protests that occurred around the United States after a Minneapolis police officer killed George Floyd. The surveilling of protestors occurred in at least fifteen cities and involved fixed-wing aircraft, helicopters, and drones.[19] To quote one CNN report,

> A small Cessna Citation jet flying straight into Washington's highly restricted airspace would typically be met with fighter jets on its wing. But when one flew over the nation's capital on June 1 and circled the White House 20 times, it was hardly an accident. The plane was one of several aircraft—both piloted and unpiloted—that CNN has been able to track flying over protests in Washington, Minneapolis, and Las Vegas. Government watchdogs fear the planes were used to track protesters and perhaps capture cell phone data. . . . [Nearly] three dozen Democrats in Congress want to know whether the planes—typically equipped with live video cameras and heat sensors—were used for "surveilling of Americans engaged in peaceful protests."[20]

While many of these different aircraft can take high-resolution images and possess facial-recognition capabilities, the extent of their data collection remains unclear. These allegations prompted the inspector general of the US Air Force to open an investigation into how its assets had been used.

Yet another equally troubling example of the government's surveillance of Black Lives Matter protesters came from Dataminr's activities, discussed before. Because of its relationship with Twitter, Dataminr had access to the platform's content stream, known as the "firehose." The firehose allows the scanning of every public tweet as soon as it is posted. Both Twitter and Dataminr repeatedly insist that monitoring the tweets of protesters does not meet the definition of surveillance—yet another example of linguistic obfuscation.[21]

Despite claiming that it did not engage in surveillance, Dataminr facilitated the monitoring of social media activity of BLM protesters. Their information flowed to fusion centers as well. To quote reporter Sam Biddle of the *Intercept*,

> Dataminr relayed tweets and other social media content about the George Floyd and Black Lives Matter protests directly to police, apparently across the country. . . . And despite Dataminr's claims that its law enforcement service merely delivers "breaking news alerts on emergency events, such as natural disasters, fires, explosions, and shootings" . . . the company has facilitated the surveillance of recent protests, including nonviolent activity, siphoning vast amounts of social media data from across the Web and converting it into tidy police intelligence packages. . . . According to internal materials reviewed by *The Intercept*, Dataminr meticulously tracked not only ongoing protests but kept comprehensive records of upcoming antipolice rallies in cities across the country to help its staff organize their monitoring efforts.[22]

CONTEMPORARY FBI SURVEILLANCE OF OTHER NONVIOLENT DISSIDENTS

The FBI assigns, from all the data, many of its surveillance resources to the monitoring of other nonviolent groups. Writing for *The Intercept*, Alice Speri notes that "while terrorism in the US is relatively rare, over the last decade most politically motivated violence has come at the hands of right-wing extremists. Despite that reality, the FBI has devoted disproportionate resources to the surveillance of nonviolent civil-society groups and protest movements."[23] This has occurred despite rules banning the FBI from investigating groups or individuals based solely on their political beliefs. The prohibition arose in the wake of a report from the Office of Inspector General released in 2010 detailing "how the FBI, particularly in the post-9/11 era, had inappropriately tracked activist groups such as Greenpeace and the Catholic Worker for engaging in nonviolent protest."[24]

In 2019 the NGO Defending Rights and Dissent published the first complete survey detailing the FBI's surveillance of dissenters and nonviolent movements dating from the 2010 release of the Office of Inspector General's report until the date of the survey's publication. In summary form, it found that the FBI's surveillance of peaceful groups continued undiminished. The report found that

[The] FBI has repeatedly monitored civil-society groups, including racial-justice movements, Occupy Wall Street, environmentalists, Palestinian-solidarity activists, Abolish ICE protesters, and Cuba- and Iran-normalization proponents. Additionally, FBI agents conducted interviews that critics have argued were designed to chill protests at the Republican National Convention or intimidate Muslim-American voters.[25]

The ACLU echoes these findings. "For more than a decade now," they've found, "Americans have repeatedly encountered illegal and unnecessary spying by local, state, and federal law enforcement on lawful and peaceful protesters. Targets of such surveillance have been on both the left and right and include antiwar, anti–death penalty, antiabortion, and animal-rights activists, along with members of the Occupy movement."[26]

The FBI's surveillance of people peacefully exercising their right to assemble occurred routinely along the United States–Mexico border during the Trump administration. For example, the FBI surveilled those who peacefully assembled to protest the human-rights atrocity involved in the separation of migrant children from their parents and their subsequent caging. Peaceful protests decrying a policy that tore preteens from their mothers and fathers and threw thousands into steel cages apparently constituted enough of a threat to US national security to merit FBI surveillance. In a rare moment of transparency, the FBI itself revealed these activities in an "external intelligence note."[27] Were these protesters, including members of religious groups, "enemies of the state" and threats to national security? Apparently they were, according to the Trump administration.

In another indication that these protesters represented a serious national security threat in the eyes of the coercive apparatus and the Trump administration, the US military monitored them, as well, in a clear violation of posse comitatus—the law banning military participation in domestic law-enforcement activities. A leaked Pentagon document sent to *Intercept* reporter Ken Klippenstein revealed the military's role. This document, he writes, included "a 'threat estimate,' an assessment detailing the risk of perceived border threats. Among those threats [were] protests by members of religious groups against 'the detention of families and children,' as well as anti-ICE protests and protests by 'anti-border-wall extremists.'" The religious group being monitored was called the Heartland for Human Justice and included several religious groups from Saint Louis, about half of them Jewish, who had organized to protest the mistreatment of migrants.[28]

Mark German, a former FBI agent who became a fellow at NYU, says that "it has been a feature of the post-9/11 counterterrorism by the FBI to focus on nonviolent civil disobedience and to prioritize it. . . . For several years after 9/11 the FBI called environmental activists the number one domestic terror threat, even though there's not a single homicide related to environmental 'terrorists" in the United States."[29]

Informatin about the government's framing of environmental activists as dangerous threats to the social order emerged as well from a Freedom of Information Act request filed in 2016 by *The Guardian*. The documents that it obtained detailed the FBI's monitoring of climate-change activists, including Bill McKibben's organization, 350.org, prompting McKibben to observe, "FBI's failure to distinguish between nonviolent civil disobedience and domestic terrorism [is] contemptible. . . . Trying to deal with the greatest crisis humans have stumbled into shouldn't require being subjected to government surveillance. . . . But [since] much of our government acts as a subsidiary of the fossil fuel industry, it may be par for the course."[30]

Despite the passage of rules designed to protect the peaceful exercise of civil rights, the FBI remains true to its past, continuing J. Edgar Hoover's practice of using the agency to monitor peaceful groups. Remarkably, given his highly problematic record on civil rights during his many decades as FBI director, the FBI memorializes Hoover's name on its headquarters. Except in rare instances, the FBI does not reveal its political surveillance yet argues that it needs even greater capacities to catch criminals and terrorists. Although defenses of FBI surveillance are rare in the academic literature, those who favor the practice reflect the perception that perpetual threats menace the society.

Exemplifying this perspective is Griffin S. Dunham, a staunch defender of the FBI's Carnivore program, whose name is designed to highlight its predatory intent. In 2000 the FBI created the Carnivore program to monitor the Internet. Dunham wrote that the program "enables law enforcement to take one small step to level a playing field [the Internet] currently dominated by criminals who can routinely break the law by using an extremely evasive and criminally propitious medium."[31] The argument that criminals dominate the Internet is serious, although no more problematic than the mass state and corporate surveillance plaguing the medium. Moreover, Dunham does not mention that the US government has systematically fought efforts to increase encryption so as to ensure its own access to everything on the Internet. This plays a critical role in creating the "backdoors" and other vulnerabilities in security protocols that enable criminal activity, since it allows malign actors to exploit these weaknesses as well.

Dunham's defense of Carnivore provides additional insights into the national security apparatus's belief in the necessity for increasingly expansive surveillance. He wrote,

We live in a world where criminals can remain undetected or vanish with the mere click of a mouse. Terrorists, whether foreign or US citizens, are undoubtedly plotting to bomb more American structures. . . . Pedophiles are pursuing and encroaching on innocent children every day. . . . The governments of foreign countries are deploying intelligence teams to crack the computer codes that harbor our most important resources—such as our electrical and water supplies, oil and gas reserves, and telecommunications—to exploit our vulnerabilities and to potentially cause catastrophic and deadly results. College students are writing viruses solely for the thrill of destroying others' computer files.[32]

This list of threats merits deconstruction. Belying Dunham's prophecy, written in 2005, in the subsequent decade and a half, foreign terrorists killed very few Americans. The advocates of mass surveillance draw a straight line between its use and the absence of more terrorist activity on US soil but provide no evidence to substantiate this claim. More generally, it is hard to argue that Americans are safer than the citizens of other societies who spend much, much less on security and do not engage in the same degree of surveillance.

Even though Dunham's concerns about foreign terrorists have proved to be overblown, constituting a typical example of threat inflation, right-wing White nationalist and supremacist groups in the United States did become an increasingly serious problem during the Trump administration. Donald Trump's courting of these groups along with his incendiary rhetoric emboldened and activated them. The extent of this danger was revealed on January 6, 2021, when a mob attacked the US Capitol. Because of the significance of this riot, many immediately labeled the mob "domestic terrorists" while lamenting the inadequacy of tools available to fight them. In addition, many criticized what they saw as insufficient spending and a failure to create cyber capabilities able to confront ransomware and other attacks, particularly from Russia, China, Iran, and North Korea.

Every time a new danger appears, justifications reemerge for the expansion of surveillance, especially of Internet communications, including emails, searches, and social media activity. Threats are cited to establish the fragility of security and the need to grant even greater powers to the coercive apparatus. Measures might be unpalatable but are necessary, it is said, given the extent of danger. And no matter how expansive the measure, law enforcement, national security agencies, and their defenders insist that their practices are tailored to avoid violations of civil rights. But upon examination of the long record of abuses against dissidents, nonviolent protesters, and others, these claims ring hollow.

CONCLUSION

The search for a decent life or safe harbor forces migrants and refugees to open every part of their lives to governmental scrutiny. Although desperation and the promise of legal status promote the "willing" surrender of private information, an inevitable loss of human dignity occurs. States do not limit their inquiries and intrusions, resulting in the revelation of the intimate and the most private.

States often share this information with other polities and retain it permanently. While a fundamental security obligation to police borders and regulate entry animates the behavior of governments, the scope of their intrusions into the private and nonmaterial, such as sexual preference and intimate personal and financial details, constitutes a clear violation of elemental privacy rights and of human dignity. In theory, personhood grants certain rights to migrants and refugees. However, the protection of personhood varies enormously, and it is continually subject to violation given the vulnerability of non-citizens. Moreover, the rights embedded in personhood always yield to the perceived dictates of security and the protection of national sovereignty.

Throughout history, dissidents and those seen as domestic "others" have experienced the heavy hand of the state, confronting surveillance and other measures more than the rest of society. African Americans are the domestic group in the United States subjected to the greatest monitoring and who have most frequently found themselves at the center of the US panopticon. Digital tools have enabled the addition of mass surveillance to earlier measures, increasing the vulnerability of those who are already marginalized and excluded. And those who dissent and wish to change the status quo become more vulnerable as well.

In part for these reasons, mass surveillance intrinsically undermines liberal constitutionalism since it alters the relationship between the state and dissidents and domestic minorities. Surveillance increases the state's ability to stifle voices calling for change and monitor and track those engaged in protest. And through the manipulation of the psychological pressures and fears embedded in the panopticon, the government can discourage legitimate and legal forms of political participation, including peaceful assembly. These actions can promote self-censorship as well, chilling speech.

NOTES

1. Linda Bosniak "The Undocumented Immigrant: Contending Policy Approaches," in *Debating Immigration*, ed. Carol M. Swain (Cambridge: Cambridge University Press, 2007), 86–88, emphasis and parentheticals original.

2. Privacy International, "Communities at Risk: How Governments Are Using Tech to Target Migrants," April 11, 2020, https://www.privacyinternational.org/news -analysis/2781/communities-risk-how-governments-are-using-tech-target-migrants.

3. Privacy International, "Communities at Risk."

4. Privacy International, "Surveillance Company Cellebrite Finds a New Exploit: Spying on Asylum Seekers," April 3, 2019, https://www.privacyinternational.org /long-read/2776/surveillance-company-cellebrite-finds-new-exploit-spying-asylum -seekers.

5. All quotations in this paragraph from Privacy International, "Surveillance Company Cellebrite."

6. Carlyn Greenfield, "As Governments Build Advanced Surveillance Systems to Push Borders Out, Will Travel and Migration Become Unequal for Some Groups?" Migration Information Source, Migration Policy Institute, March 11, 2020, https:// www.migrationpolicy.org/article/governments-build-advanced-surveillance-systems.

7. Olivia Solon, "'Surveillance Society': Has Technology at the US-Mexico Border Gone Too Far? *The Guardian*, June 13, 2018, https://www.theguardian.com /technology/2018/jun/13/mexico-us-border-wall-surveillance-artificial-intelligence -technology.

8. Solon, "'Surveillance Society.'"

9. Ryan Devereaux, "Border Official Admits Targeting Journalists and Human Rights Advocates with Smuggling Investigations," *The Intercept*, May 17, 2019, https://theintercept.com/2019/05/17/border-smuggling-journalists-activists/.

10. Devereaux, "Border Official Admits."

11. Devereaux, "Border Official Admits."

12. Greenfield, "Governments Build Advanced Surveillance Systems."

13. Bosniak, "The Undocumented Immigrant," 94.

14. Simone Browne, *Dark Matters: On the Surveillance of Blackness* (Durham: Duke University Press, 2015), 12.

Some other notable pieces on this subject are Ashley D. Farmer, "Tracking Activists: The FBI's Surveillance of Black Women Activists Then and Now," *The American Historian*, 2020, https://www.oah.org/tah/issues/2020/history-for-black-lives/ tracking-activists-the-fbis-surveillance-of-black-women-activists-then-and-now/; and Andrea Dennis, "Mass Surveillance and Black Legal History," *ExpertForum*, February 18, 2020, https://www.acslaw.org/expertforum/mass-surveillance-and-black-legal -history/.

And explore the proceedings of Georgetown Law School's fourth Color of Surveillance conference at https://www.law.georgetown.edu/news/georgetown-laws-fourth -color-of-surveillance-conference-covers-the-monitoring-of-poor-and-working -people/.

15. All quotations in this paragraph have been drawn from Alan Brinkley, "Past as Prologue," in *Liberty Under Attack*, ed. Richard C. Leone and Greg Anrig Jr. (New York: Public Affairs, The Perseus Group, 2007), 29–30.

16. Brinkley, "Past as Prologue," 35–36.

17. Alvaro Bedoya, "The Color of Surveillance: What the Surveillance of Martin Luther King Says about Modern Spying," *Slate*, January 18, 2016, https://slate.com

/technology/2016/01/what-the-fbis-surveillance-of-martin-luther-king-says-about
-modern-spying.html.

18. Nurat Choudhury and Malkia Cyril, "The FBI Won't Hand Over Its Surveil-lance Records on 'Black Identity Extremists,' So We're Suing," American Civil Liberties Union, ACLU.org, March 21, 2019, https://www.aclu.org/news/racial-justice/fbi-wont-hand-over-its-surveillance-records-black.

19. Zolan Kanno-Youngs, "U.S. Watched George Floyd Protests in 15 Cities Using Aerial Surveillance: From Minneapolis to Buffalo, Homeland Security Officials Dispatched Drones, Helicopters and Airplanes to Monitor Black Lives Matter Protests," *New York Times*, June 19, 2020, https://www.nytimes.com/2020/06/19/us/politics/george-floyd-protests-surveillance.html.

20. Pete Muntean and Gregory Wallace, "US Government Planes Monitored George Floyd Protests," CNN, June 12, 2020, https://www.cnn.com/2020/06/11/politics/spy-planes-george-floyd-protests/.

21. Sam Biddle, "Police Surveilled George Floyd Protests with Help from Twitter-Affiliated Startup Dataminr," *The Intercept*, July 9, 2020, https://theintercept.com/2020/07/09/twitter-dataminr-police-spy-surveillance-black-lives-matter-protests/.

22. Biddle, "Police Surveilled George Floyd Protests."

23. Alice Speri, "The FBI Has a Long History of Treating Political Dissent as Terrorism," *The Intercept*, October 19, 2019, https://theintercept.com/2019/10/22/terrorism-fbi-political-dissent/.

24. Adam Federman, "Revealed: FBI Kept Files on Peaceful Climate Change Activists," *The Guardian*, December 13, 2018, https://www.theguardian.com/us-news/2018/dec/13/fbi-climate-change-protesters-iowa-files-monitoring-surveillance-.

25. Chip Gibbons, *Still Spying on Dissent: The Enduring Problem of FBI First Amendment Abuse*, special report (Washington, DC: Defending Rights and Dissent, 2019), 1, https://drive.google.com/file/d/1z-i_XCoZub8ISKEe5DzjoMh0bPS5u1Xm/view.

26. American Civil Liberties Union, "Spying on Protesters," ACLU.org, accessed April 28, 2020, https://www.aclu.org/issues/free-speech/rights-protesters/spying-protesters.

27. Zack Budryk, "FBI Monitoring Nonviolent Immigration Protestors at the Border: Report," *The Hill*, September 4, 2019, https://thehill.com/homenews/administration/459962-fbi-monitoring-non-violent-immigration-protesters-at-border-report/.

28. Ken Klippenstein, "The U.S. Military Is Monitoring Interfaith Group Opposed to Child Separation, Leaked Document Reveals," *The Intercept*, November 11, 2019, https://theintercept.com/2019/11/11/border-protest-groups-surveillance/.

29. Mark German, as quoted in Budryk, "FBI Monitoring Nonviolent Immigration Protestors."

30. Bill McKibben, as quoted in Federman, "Revealed: FBI Kept Files."

31. Griffin S. Dunham, "Carnivore, the FBI's E-mail Surveillance System: Devouring Criminals, Not Privacy," in *Information Ethics: Privacy, Property and Power*, ed. Adam Moore (Seattle: University of Washington Press, 2005), 392.

32. Dunham, "Carnivore," 392.

Chapter 9

Global Digital
Mass-Surveillance Practices

The use of mass digital surveillance as a central tool of governance and instrument of ruling power across the world was a particularly ironic development, since the advocates of digital technologies, continued to proclaim that their innovations would have equalizing, counterhegemonic effects. The use of social media to organize protests seemed to confirm this view. But different governments soon deployed and exploited these tools to surveil, undermine, and frequently extinguish the same movements that communicated with these technologies. Moreover, and even more critically, the powerful used digital tools to deploy increasingly sweeping surveillance systems designed to monitor political activity.

Every flavor of authoritarian regime developed even more extensive surveillance, building on the more primitive capacities that these types of polities used before the advent of digital technologies. In affluent, nondemocratic countries, such as Saudi Arabia and the oil sheikdoms of the Persian Gulf, ubiquitous digital surveillance is paired with the provision of economic benefits to the population, effectively becoming another pillar of state power. Phrased differently, these regimes use economic performance and growing affluence to construct a measure of legitimacy while relying on mass surveillance to identify and permit the extirpation of real and potential dissent. China embraces this approach as well. But other nondemocratic regimes, ranging from Putin's Russia to Venezuela, use surveillance to secure their hold on power and monitor and repress opponents.

Democracies, however, have succumbed to mass surveillances' allure as well. Although in the main authoritarian regimes resort to this practice more extensively than democratic polities, it is sometimes difficult to discern differences in their appetite for surveillance. As noted before, the United States, Israel, and the United Kingdom, for example, continue to display a particularly strong enthusiasm for digital surveillance. From the earliest days of the digital age these countries used their technological capacities and resources to jump-start a frantic global competition in this area. Even before the previously mentioned Stuxnet attack on Iran, the US government used its cyber capacities to penetrate foreign databases. Subsequent years witnessed a growing number of large and small cyberattacks, hacks, and a variety of additional intrusions, as other countries engaged in the same behavior. And as cyber threats grew, so too did the deployment of digital surveillance designed to uncover them.

Cultural and social variables, rather than regime type, constitute a better explanation for differences in the extent of the embrace of state surveillance. Precisely because cultures differ in their framing and understanding of privacy, the relationship between the individual and the community, and between individuals and the government, different societies perceive surveillance differently. These understandings inform views of the proper distinctions between the public and the private realm as well. Phrased differently, cultural and social mores are more important to the protection of privacy and the practice of surveillance than any other factor. While regime type and the corollary legal architecture matter, they are more epiphenomenal than the deeper cultural and social features of particular polities.

For example, cultural differences more than existing legal regimes explain why some societies accept and embrace CCTV with facial-recognition capabilities while other populations resist these tools. These same differences, in part, explain why the population of one country might strongly support the adoption of an extraordinarily invasive tracking and monitoring app against a pandemic while another sees the use of the same tool as an intolerable assault on privacy.

These differences influence views of transparency as well. At one extreme, the Chinese state asserts its right to complete opacity while insisting on the perfect legibility, indeed translucency, of all its subjects. Countries with the most sweeping freedom-of-information statutes conjoined to the most robust privacy protections lie at the other end of the spectrum. Germany, in most ways, represents this extreme, generally protecting privacy from digital intrusions more than its democratic peers. In general, however, all polities have adopted digital-surveillance technologies. And once established, surveillance grows inexorably. Those charged with watching always insist that they need to see more to know more, predict more, and protect more, while technological changes increase their capacity to achieve these ends.

NATIONALISM, MILITARISM, AND
STATE SURVEILLANCE

The narratives underpinning a society's patriotic and nationalist understandings frame the context that invites or dissuades surveillance. If nations are "imagined communities," to use Benedict Anderson's famous phrase, then the content of their "imagination" matters enormously.[1] This imagination influences self-perception and the view of the other. The civic narratives taught to children about their history and present most powerfully reveal this imagination, as do each country's objects of patriotic veneration. In addition, this imagination helps frame understandings and perceptions of threats and create preferences about the best ways to address dangers.

The "we feeling" embedded in the imagined community includes self-celebratory elements and derogatory understandings of others, all of which increases the collective's feelings of pride. Nationalism consequently involves a potent mix of amour propre and "othering," a combination typical of identitarian movements as well. However, when this imagination enshrines the military and the national security apparatus as the greatest and most noble expression of the community and as the repository of its greatest virtues, the worldview and behavior of these institutions acquires particular centrality and legitimacy. In such polities, these institutions receive many more resources and security tools, in part explaining why countries like the United States, Russia, China, Great Britain, France, and Turkey maintain the largest armies and security budgets in the world.

Elites in such societies are significantly more disposed to use national security tools, including surveillance. Much of the broader population, imbued with this same set of understandings, is more likely to accept their use as well. The endless repetition of stories about the virtues of the military, the derring-do of national security agents, and the country's glorious past and destiny ensures significant levels of support from citizens fed these narratives since earliest childhood. Because of their emotive depth and power, patriotism and nationalism sweep away critical thinking. The collective and ritualized amour propre intrinsic to these sentiments creates several especially insidious predilections, including the unwillingness to question national tropes and the tendency to see dissenters and critics as disloyal and traitorous. The rhetoric of Trump, Hungary's Viktor Orbán, Brazil's Jair Bolsonaro, China's Xi Jinping, Russia's Vladimir Putin, India's Narendra Modi, and Turkey's Recep Erdoğan, to mention just a few examples, contained all these elements, exciting their followers.

Although countries with an especially strong historic "will to power," like the United States, the United Kingdom, France, Turkey, China, and Russia, share elements of this type of nationalism, they differ in significant ways given their distinct historical experiences. Although all six countries derive enormous pride and a significant part of their identity from either their present or historic power and from their military capacity, their expressions of this pride differ. Foreign armies, at least since 1812, have not invaded the United States (unless one counts Pancho Villa's attack on Columbus, New Mexico, during the Mexican Revolution), given the advantages of its geographic isolation from great power rivals. American nationalism, consequently, does not reflect either the experience of foreign invasion or of subordination to stronger countries, both of which are evident in the patriotism of several of these other nations. Nonetheless, American nationalism is at least as strident and voluble. American politicians, pundits, television commentators, and other public figures rarely start or end a sentence without proclaiming that "the United States is the greatest country in the world."

In fact, even when discussing a failure, such as the United States' hapless response to the COVID-19 pandemic in 2020, commentators puzzled about how this could happen in "the greatest country in the world." Russian and Chinese nationalisms are equally although differently voluble, since they contain an intensely revanchist element suffused with historic resentments given their historical experiences with foreign invasion and intervention. In contrast, Turkish, French, and British nationalisms revolve around the sense of their own continuing global importance and relevance, even as their relative powers decline. However, the historic will to power in all these countries ensures a steady supply of adversaries and a continuing need to develop tools to confront them. Given the extent of conflict flowing from the will to power, state-surveillance practices flourish. And because these countries experience fluid but repeated threats, they turn surveillance both inward and outward.

These countries, whatever their other differences, all assign a high priority to military spending and the pursuit of military capacity. Although they are not the only countries with significant militaries, they stand out for the extent of their capabilities in this area (along with countries like Iran, Saudi Arabia, North and South Korea, Israel, Pakistan, and India, all parts of this club for other reasons). Just like the United States, countries that invest heavily in their militaries deploy especially intrusive and extensive mass-surveillance systems. In 2019 the Carnegie Endowment for International Peace published the most extensive report to date about state surveillance around the world. Report author Steven Feldstein writes of the use of AI surveillance that "there is a strong relationship between a country's military expenditures and a government's use of AI surveillance systems: forty of the world's top fifty military-spending countries (based on cumulative military expenditures) also use AI surveillance technologies."[2] Moreover, significant military spending and the corollary use of surveillance reveals other features of a regime, including the expansiveness of its national security doctrine, its perception of threats, and its goals and ambitions.

Beyond China's and Russia's militarism, the authoritarianism of these regimes further expands their practice of mass surveillance. But the seductions of power encourage democracies to become increasingly illiberal as well. The emergence of illiberal practices in the United States, the United Kingdom, and France at different historical moments might lead one to postulate that surveillance in democracies expands in direct proportion to their global ambitions and the extent of their engagement in global military operations. Their global interventions create internal and external threats, causing feelings of insecurity and fear to rise.

As a result, these countries direct more and more resources to the various branches of their national security apparatus. And in pursuit of these threats, the national security apparatus becomes even more intrusive, destroying the privacy of ordinary citizens in its search for "bad actors." The adoption of profoundly illiberal tools and practices undermines these polities' liberal, rights-based foundations as well. If privacy is the price that individuals pay for the type of security that surveillance provides, then states must sacrifice a measure of their liberalism for the same end.

Democratic countries that neither confront threats arising from their global activities nor maintain large military and national security establishments engage in much less surveillance. Nonetheless, occasional terrorist attacks on such countries and domestic criminal behavior encourage surveillance, even if it is less extensive. The Scandinavian countries, the Netherlands, and Germany are such examples. These polities, given their concerns about terrorism and other threats, deploy surveillance in several ways, including in "smart city" and "safe city" initiatives. However, they use this practice less than France and the United Kingdom, given the much larger global role of these two countries and the corollary weight of their national security apparatuses.

On the other hand, despite differences between states, some commonalities mark state surveillance practices. All states possessing the requisite resources and technical skills expanded state surveillance in the early twenty-first century given the allure of digital tools. Although, as noted above, they deploy surveillance to differing degrees, all use it to facilitate governance. As technology advances, so too does state surveillance, even in countries that do not confront dangers from violent actors.

For all these reasons, the number of "surveillance states" proliferated during the first decades of the digital age. In 2007 Privacy International surveyed forty-one countries on their surveillance practices and privacy safeguards. At that time, it listed eight "endemic surveillance societies." The most egregious violations of privacy and unconstrained use of surveillance occurred in China, Russia, and Malaysia. The situation in Singapore and the United Kingdom was almost as bad, and Taiwan, Thailand, and the United States were not much better.[3] In March 2013, Reporters Without Borders published a "Special Report on Internet Surveillance" that listed five countries as "State Enemies of the Internet." The five countries were China, Iran, Syria, Bahrain, and Vietnam.[4]

Edward Snowden's revelations that same year indicated that the United States had become more of a surveillance society, and technological innovations ensure that all the countries Privacy International cited in 2007 engage in even more "endemic" practices. Furthermore, Snowden's revelations showed that the United Kingdom's signals-intelligence agency, GCHQ, was using a particularly intrusive surveillance tool called Tempora, making it part of the endemic-surveillance club. This, to the surprise of many, applies to Canada as well. The documents that Edward Snowden released showed that Canada, typically seen as a model liberal society, engages in extensive surveillance. For example, the Communications Security Establishment (CSE), Canada's signals-intelligence agency, intercepted free airport Wi-Fi services in a bulk, warrantless fashion, gathering the communications and tracking the movements of all travelers, even after they'd left airports. The CSE did this despite the existence of robust Canadian privacy laws that bar the interception of the private communications of Canadians on Canadian soil. The Canadian government's willingness to disregard its own laws in the name of national security mimics the behavior of its southern neighbor and partner.

A 2015 Freedom House report provides additional evidence about the expansion of state surveillance during the preceding decade. To quote the report's authors, Sanja Kelly, Madeline Earp, Laura Reed, Adrian Shahbaz, and Mai Truong,

> Surveillance has been on the rise globally, despite the uproar that followed the revelation [by Edward Snowden] of mass data collection by the US National Security Agency (NSA) in 2013. Several democratic countries, including France and Australia, passed new measures authorizing sweeping surveillance, prompted in part by domestic-terrorism concerns and the expansion of the Islamic State (IS) militant group. Bans on encryption and anonymity tools are becoming more common, with governments seeking access to encryption backdoors that could threaten security for everyone.[5]

Unfortunately, in the years since the report's publication, governmental insistence on encryption backdoors precisely produced these effects, facilitating hacking, identity theft, and other problems.

Moreover, an arms race has developed. As governments and corporations increase their surveillance of individuals, ordinary citizens seek out privacy tools such as virtual private networks (VPNs) and gravitate toward services like Tor. In addition, the desire for privacy becomes a market opportunity. Companies like Apple seek to differentiate themselves from entities known to engage in the especially extensive appropriation of personal information, most notably Facebook/Meta, through the development of products designed to increase user privacy. Other companies offer such things as end-to-end encryption. A number of governments respond with bans on encryption and the use of VPNs while developing increasingly sophisticated digital tools that can penetrate even these protections and intensifying their exploitation of zero days to enhance their surveillance capacities.

As Freedom House's 2015 report notes about this escalatory cycle,

> Given the mounting concerns over government surveillance, companies and Internet users have taken up new tools to protect the privacy of their data and identity. . . . In response, policymakers in the United Kingdom and the United States have called for companies to provide intelligence agencies with a "back-door" to users' data, circumventing encryption. . . . While encryption protects the content of communications, anonymity is necessary for securing the privacy of users' metadata. Tools such as . . . [VPNs], proxies, and Tor can disguise an individual's original [IP] address and other details that would reveal the identity or location of users.[6]

In the middle of the second decade of the twenty-first century, China banned VPNs, while several countries including Indonesia and Iran banned the use of Tor.

The speed and extent of this escalatory cycle make robust international treaties governing cyber activities increasingly indispensable. Such treaties offer the only way to eventually reduce the frequency and increasing serious-ness of cyberattacks and begin to develop a global regime that can confront identity theft and other criminal activities. Unfortunately, serious efforts to construct such treaties remain in their infancy. In their absence, innovation and global competition will cause an even more rapid multiplication of all the digital problems discussed above.

Circumscribing mass state digital surveillance will be particularly difficult given the speed of its spread. The 2019 Carnegie Endowment for International Peace report on state uses of AI surveillance shows its extraordinary ubiquity, less than twenty years after the 9/11 attacks caused this practice to explode. This report sampled the practices of 176 countries. In 2019, seventy-five of the countries surveyed actively used AI for surveillance; fifty-six countries used "smart city/safe city" platforms, sixty-four used facial-recognition sys-tems, and fifty-two used smart policing. Four Chinese companies, Huawei, Hikvision, Dahua, and ZTE, were providers of surveillance technology to sixty-four countries, with Huawei accounting for fifty of these cases.[7] Unsurprisingly, given its own highly problematic human-rights record and pursuit of a foreign policy grounded in the reification of state sovereignty, China placed no limits on who could acquire this technology.

Outside of China, the Japanese NEC Corp. was the largest purveyor of AI surveillance technology in 2019, selling tools to fourteen countries. Several American companies—notably IBM, Palantir, and Cisco—sold these tools to thirty-two countries. Other French, German, Israeli, and Japanese companies participated in this trade as well.[8] Governments frequently do not seek to restrain this trade but instead promote the interests of their own corporations. This, in effect, makes them complicit when governments with abusive human-rights records deploy these tools against political targets.

Examples abound of governments acting as sales agents for companies that are part of their surveillance industrial complex. The government of the United Kingdom, to cite one case, repeatedly approved the sale of surveillance equipment to the Hong Kong government, a puppet of the Chinese state, between 2014 and 2019. The Hong Kong government used this British equipment against the prodemocracy protests occurring in the city during this period. Specifically, the British government granted "an export license for 1.9 million pounds [in 2019] of 'telecommunications interception equipment' to Hong Kong. This license was the fourth that the UK government had approved since the protest movement broke out."[9] Despite having participated in the negotiation of the "one country, two systems" model designed to protect the rule of law and the protection of civil rights when it surrendered the Hong Kong colony in 1984 to China, the UK government promoted the sales of British surveillance technology to a government that was systematically violating this agreement as it repressed people exercising these rights.

Even as the British state publicly condemned the Hong Kong government's actions against these protesters and China's violations of the promises embedded in "the one country, two systems" agreement, it simultaneously helped British companies profit from the repression. Nick Dearden of Global Justice Now observed in *The Guardian* that

> Surveillance equipment is a weapon in the hands of many repressive governments, which can be used to monitor, to harass, and to imprison people who are campaigning, exposing injustices, or simply telling fellow citizens what's going on in their country. . . . If you sell intercept equipment to governments with a history of using that equipment to crack down on human rights, saying those governments gave you assurances they wouldn't use it in repressive ways, [it] is no defence. You are complicit in those human rights abuses.[10]

Virtually all democratic countries that are purveyors of surveillance technologies to regimes with problematic human-rights records use this same excuse despite its patent inadequacy. All fail, as well, to ensure compliance with the pledges they claim to have received about limiting the uses of these tools to terrorism and crime. And so the human-rights abuses continue, as does the sale of surveillance and other technologies developed in democratic countries to brutal autocracies.

The 2019 Carnegie Endowment for International Peace study further confirmed the already voluminous evidence that democracies were not just purveyors of surveillance technology to other countries but also continued to expand its use on their own populations. The study showed that 51 percent of those it labeled "liberal democracies," 37 percent of "closed autocracies," 41 percent of "electoral autocratic/competitive autocracies," and 41 percent of "electoral democracies/illiberal democracies" used AI surveillance. As Steven Feldstein notes in this report, "liberal democracies in Europe are also racing ahead to install automated border controls, predictive policing, safe cities, and facial-recognition systems. In fact, it is striking how many safe-city surveillance case studies posted on Huawei's website relate to municipalities in Germany, Italy, the Netherlands, and Spain."[11]

Numerous examples reveal the spread of these practices. To quote Steven Feldstein again,

> In France, the port city of Marseille initiated a partnership with ZTE in 2016 to establish the [chillingly named] Big Data of Public Tranquility project. The goal of the program is to reduce crime by establishing a vast public-surveillance network. . . . Similarly, in 2017, Huawei "gifted" a showcase surveillance system to the northern French town of Valenciennes to demonstrate its safe city model. The package included upgraded high-definition CCTV surveillance and an intelligent command center powered by algorithms to detect unusual movements and crowd formations.[12]

These findings are echoed by Freedom House. Authors Adrian Shahbaz and Allie Funk write in *Freedom on the Net 2019: The Crisis of Social Media*,

> Internet freedom is increasingly imperiled by the tools and tactics of digital authoritarianism, which have spread rapidly around the globe. . . . [A] startling variety of governments are deploying advanced tools to monitor users on an immense scale. . . . [Repressive] governments are acquiring social media surveillance tools that employ artificial intelligence to identify perceived threats and silence undesirable expression. Even in democracies, such mass monitoring is spreading across government agencies and being used for new purposes without adequate safeguards. The result is a sharp global increase in the abuse of civil liberties and shrinking online space for civic activism. Of the sixty-five

countries assessed in this report, a record forty-seven featured arrests of users for political, social, or religious speech.[13]

This Freedom House report lists Iceland as the strongest guarantor of Internet freedom in the world and identifies Kazakhstan, Sudan, and Brazil as the three countries experiencing the largest decline in this freedom.

Other studies substantiate these findings. "Unsurprisingly," Steven Feldstein notes, "countries with authoritarian systems and low levels of political rights are investing heavily in AI surveillance techniques. Many governments in the Gulf, East Asia, and South/Central Asia are procuring advanced analytic systems, facial-recognition cameras, and sophisticated monitoring capabilities." Saudi Arabia represents an especially telling example of how these regimes amass extraordinary surveillance capacities. "Huawei is helping the government build safe cities, but Google is establishing cloud servers, UK arms manufacturer BAE has sold mass surveillance systems, NEC is vending facial-recognition cameras, and Amazon and Alibaba both have cloud computing centers in Saudi Arabia and may support a major smart city project."[14]

THE UNDERSTANDINGS EMBEDDED IN SMART CITY/SAFE CITY INITIATIVES

As evident in the previous discussion, a central part of the global movement toward mass surveillance involves initiatives covered under the benign sounding "smart city/safe city" rubric. Countries all over the world continue to acquire technologies connected to this model, which primarily includes the deployment of an expanding network of facial-recognition CCTV cameras and other monitoring tools that feed data to so-called information centers. These centers are the "eye" of the panopticon, serving to direct the activities of state agents.

The use of the term *smart* in the digital age disguises the fact that it is surveillance that produces "smartness," in an Orwellian turn of phrase. Indeed, in another example of linguistic sleight of hand, the positive attributes embedded in the word *smart* come in substantial measure from wholesale intrusions into the public and private worlds of individuals. Governments and huge corporations create the algorithms that mine the data derived from mass surveillance, enabling smart decisions. For governments, the efficient pursuit of security, not justice or equity or anything else, constitutes the core component of smartness. Above all, smart decisions efficiently seek to maximize public order and tranquility.

These tools can, on the one hand, help to manage problems like traffic congestion and crime. On the other hand, the omnipresent monitoring of all public spaces enables governments to control civil disobedience and nonviolent protest and discourage unconventional behaviors. Smartness involves the capacity to predict, as well. Smart policing—known as "predictive" policing, which is pursued in many large metropolises—sounds efficient, cost-effective, and targeted. However, the algorithms that drive these predictions are no less prone to bias than were previous strategies like profiling or stop-and-frisk. Increases in crime and particularly rising fears of crime encourage the adoption of "smart city" technologies.

The pairing of the term *smart* city with *safe* city indicates some of these predispositions and prejudices. By definition, *smartness* elevates safety and security over other public and private goods and rights. Perfectly encapsulating this view is American technology start-up Knightscope, which went public in early 2022. Knightscope made "autonomous security robots," designed to police indoor and outdoor spaces. The company's goal, to cite its numerous commercials and its website, was to make the United States the "safest country in the world."[15] In these regards it echoed the ambitions of the most extreme surveillance society in the world, China.

Local elites and the purveyors of these technologies define security and safety according to their own interests and their particular understanding of the good society. The conflation of smartness with tranquility and public order reflects, more than anything else, a Confucian understanding of the good society, although these views are not limited to the Confucian world. Nonetheless, and not surprisingly, China was a particularly early developer and global purveyor of smart city/safe city technology and continues to be the largest seller of these tools.

The implications of the use of smart technologies to create safety and security are evident in Hong Kong, as noted before, although these issues arise in metropolises around the world. Smart city/safe city technology covers Hong Kong's territory. The government relied upon traditional Confucian understandings about the importance of harmony—understood as the absence of political conflict—to justify its savage repression of prodemocracy advocates. Judging from the vast demonstrations between 2014 and 2020, many of the people of Hong Kong profoundly and fundamentally disagreed with this understanding of social well-being. Rather than seeing the monitoring of all their activities by the smart city/safe city technology as protecting their security, they knew that these digital tools subjected them to state violence and repression. And protesters around the world, in cities large and small, experience the impact of smart city/safe city technology through the state's ability to increasingly suffocate dissent and monitor and frequently repress peaceful assembly.

THE DRUG WAR AND STATE SURVEILLANCE
IN LATIN AMERICA: A CASE STUDY

The United States started the modern global drug war in the early twentieth century and intensified this "war" in the late 1960s during the Nixon administration. Until that time, modest uses of illicit substances made drug control a secondary government activity. The rapid rise in domestic drug consumption in the United States during the countercultural movement in the 1960s transformed this situation. The "law and order" elements of Richard Nixon's platform during his campaign for the presidency included the more aggressive enforcement of extant prohibitions on drugs and the drug trade. The capstone of Richard Nixon's antidrug regime was Operation Intercept, a 1969 exercise that closed the United States–Mexican border for three weeks, successfully pressuring Mexico to initiate a series of drug-control measures designed to reduce the flow of drugs across the border.

But it was only after the election of Ronald Reagan to the presidency in 1980 that the drug war truly engulfed many countries in Latin America and acquired its modern form. The expansion of the "war" during the late 1980s and through the next four decades coincided, as did rising terrorism, with the spread of digital technologies, animating states to use them against those involved in the drug trade. As crime, and especially violent crime, increased, security became the overriding political concern in many Latin American countries. The drug war played a significant but not exclusive role in the explosion of crime rates. Deepening economic inequality in already the most unequal region in the world contributed to the increase in violence as well. Drug-producing and drug-transshipment countries experienced especially widespread anomic violence, while crime and the use of mood-altering substances increased across the region. Over time, murder rates rose significantly in many countries, transforming parts of the region into the home of the highest homicide rates in the world.

The United States initiated and drove every part of the drug war, while insisting on treating drug consumption as a law-enforcement rather than a health-care issue. The racist link between the drug consumption of "others" and crime joined the strong Calvinist strand running through American history. This Calvinist strain explains why punishment, and especially very harsh punishment, has been widely perceived in the United States as the most effective way to address wrongdoing and promote behavior modification. The conjoining of these Calvinist beliefs with racism ensured the United States' development of a particularly punitive sentencing philosophy. The primary objects and victims of this war were African Americans and other people of color in the United States along with those in the Global South involved in this trade. All these people became victims of the largest carceral apparatus in the world and were subjected to incredibly long sentences, and even the death penalty, along with unspeakable violence.

The country's consequent insistence on treating drug use as a law-enforcement issue and its efforts to eradicate use did not abate during the twentieth century. The US government divided its efforts into two areas: demand and supply reduction. Supply reduction had two prongs. The first involved eradication at the source and often utilized local forces including the military and the police to engage in manual crop eradication, the destruction of processing facilities, the aerial spraying of herbicides, and efforts to arrest members of drug-trafficking organizations. The US Drug Enforcement Administration and other US government agencies cooperated with these local forces, maintaining a large presence in these countries. A second prong relied on the US Coast Guard and the US Customs and Border Protection to interdict drugs before they entered the country.

Both eradication and interdiction required the gathering of intelligence on the activities of drug producers and drug traffickers, encouraging expanded surveillance. Cross-border sharing of this information produced human-rights violations, particularly in countries whose protections of these rights was weak to begin with. Both the United States and Latin American governments surveilled the residents of the region, reifying the drug war over the protection of the civil rights of Bolivians, Colombians, Peruvians, Mexicans, Hondurans, Guatemalans, and many others.

The intensification of the drug war after the late 1980s happened to coincide with a transition to democracy in many countries. Even as countries moved in a democratic direction, the drug war's violence caused many to preserve and even expand their national security apparatuses. These already-large apparatuses, constructed across the region during the Cold War with the assistance of the United States, found a new raison d'être. Moreover, the increase in crime prompted governments in drug-producing countries to expand the size of their police forces, prison complexes, and militaries. Surveillance cameras, seen as crime-reduction devices, proliferated in every major city. This initiative subsequently expanded with the purchase of smart city/safe city tools from foreign software and hardware developers. And as happened elsewhere, local entrepreneurs capitalized on increased indigenous digital capacities, creating start-ups destined to become parts of burgeoning domestic-surveillance industrial complexes.

The clandestine nature of the drug trade and its enormous logistical complexity encourages the development of large and better-resourced criminal organizations. Although production costs are low, the coordination of production, transportation, and distribution favors large organizations. Successfully transporting the product across more heavily fortified borders requires resources and skills. And the profits from the trade require the development of equally elaborate money-laundering abilities. The size and sophistication of these organizations requires governments to acquire and use especially advanced surveillance technologies against them.

To combat money laundering, governments expanded surveillance in other ways. For example, states passed laws, copying those in use in the United States, that required the more extensive monitoring of all financial transactions. Of course, this practice did not merely impact drug traffickers and their financial partners but actually diminished everyone's privacy. These measures came on top of the increased tracking of people in public spaces with CCTV cameras and their identification with facial-recognition software, along with the capture of the cell phone data of many.

Ironically, even though surveillance grew, drug use and crime did not decline. Rather than changing their approaches, governments doubled down on antidrug enforcement, increasing their use of digital surveillance. In part, this reflects the intrinsic nature of the drug trade. The largely consensual nature of the relationship between producers, sellers, and buyers means that governments, if they insist on treating this matter as an issue of law enforcement rather than public health, must use agents provocateurs, informants, and surveillance to uncover illicit activity. The state identifies the "victims" of the trade as those who consume illicit drugs. However, these victims are simultaneously defined as criminals since they are engaged in an illegal activity. Because buyers and sellers are involved in a consensual act, they are not prone to come forward and identify each other. The state cannot rely on drug consumers, whom it simultaneously and contradictorily defines as victims and criminals, to identify the even greater criminals—drug dealers. Moreover, the growers of these illicit crops are not likely to identify drug traffickers, since these producers are often poverty-stricken peasants who participate in the trade because they lack viable economic alternatives. Digital technologies, on top of the use of agents provocateurs and informants, encourage governments to expand mass surveillance and engage in data mining and facial recognition to find participants in both wholesale and retail drug transactions.

Simultaneously, the unprecedented violence that the drug war unleashed throughout many Latin American countries created a population whose desire for security trumped everything else. Few oppose the deployment of increasingly invasive surveillance tools, and many, if not most, welcome CCTV networks, believing their government's claims that these cameras deter crime and facilitate the arrest of criminals. Even though crime statistics indicate the modest impact of these surveillance efforts, generalized popular support for them continues.

In Latin America and in the United States, continual lurid coverage of crime in both print media and television heightens public feelings of insecurity and

increases fears of violence. And news shows, television dramas, and movies promote the use of surveillance, especially CCTV networks. A parade of
cop shows favorably depicts the role that video surveillance plays in solving
crimes. In fact, their protagonists almost always lament the absence of more
cameras, whether to "see" the crime or capture all the criminals' and victims'
movements.

A clear and consistent message marks most of these shows: problems arise
when there are too few rather than too many cameras. And these shows,
including US productions like *Homeland, Criminal Minds, The Bureau, 48
Hours*, and *Dateline*, to mention only a few examples, rarely explore the
abuse of these technologies. For every show exploring the negative effects of
the panopticon on human existence, dozens of shows depict law enforcement
using these technologies to keep "ordinary, law-abiding citizens safe" as they
track down a seeming army of criminals, drug traffickers, psychopaths, and
terrorists, helping to create a particular zeitgeist about these tools.

The desire for security increased authoritarian proclivities in several
Latin American countries. The preference for strong-man rule rose as well.
While the election of Jair Bolsonaro in Brazil represented the most extreme
example of this trend, right-wing authoritarian and proto-authoritarian leaders held power in several countries at the beginning of the third decade of the
twenty-first century. El Salvador and Guatemala were notable examples of
this type of government. All these right-wing leaders exhibited authoritarian
proclivities and an appetite for strong-man rule—especially when it came to
fighting crime.

Several leftist governments in the region, especially Cuba, Venezuela,
and Nicaragua, shared the authoritarianism of their counterparts on the right
and were equally or even more repressive. All these regimes, regardless of
their ideological coloration, use intrusive surveillance technologies in unrestrained ways. And as is true everywhere, surveillance tools once acquired
and deployed vastly enhance state power, making governments not only
loath to relinquish them but also more inclined to use them in an increasing
variety of ways.

The drug war and the corollary elevation of security concerns inevitably
produces a decline in democratic performance. For example, Colombia,
despite possessing a well-established democratic government, has constructed perhaps the most expansive and intrusive surveillance state in the
region, outside of Cuba and Venezuela. Revelations in January 2020 showed
that the Colombian military was spying on journalists, politicians, judges,
and others. To quote Paula Martins, "the Military Intelligence Support
Command . . . acquired the platform known as Invisible Man, which allows
for the installation of malware in hacked equipment, from a Spanish manufacturer. *El Espectador* reported on the use of Voyager by the army, a tool

produced by an Israeli company. Tactical mobile equipment, such as [cell phone capture tool] Stingray, was also allegedly employed."[16]

Other countries in the region use these same tools, although the secrecy surrounding their deployment makes it hard to establish the scope and extent of their uses. This is especially serious in environments with very weak historical protections for civil rights. As Paula Martins writes, quoting a number of civil-society groups in Argentina and elsewhere, "this trend is especially worrisome in a regional context marked by long-standing dictatorships, armed conflicts, and systematic and generalized violation of human rights." Fabrizio Scrollini of the Latin American Open Data Initiative observes that "the increasing scale of illegal surveillance in Latin America—enabled by state procurement of surveillance and hacking software—is raising urgent questions about its impact on civil rights."[17]

CONCLUSION

Governments around the world adopt digital surveillance since it expands their power while simplifying "governability." Despite this commonality, enormous variations exist in the extent of surveillance, its centrality to governing projects, constraints on its deployment and use, and the technological capacities and resources at the disposal of different regimes. China stands at one extreme. The Chinese government's surveillance tries to ensure that nothing that occurs in public, on any street or in any park, can escape the omnipresent stare of its cameras. And it seeks to discern everything people do, what they buy, where they go, all their interactions, and what they believe and advocate. This surveillance state seeks to provide people with the goods they need in lieu of providing them with democratic choice, while ensuring that they comply with all its dictates, conform to desired behaviors, do not dissent or oppose, and act in ways that ensure the preservation of the state's definition of order and tranquility.

The illicit drug trade and the nature of this trade has occasioned especially widespread surveillance, especially in Latin America, the locus of much of the drug war. Producers, buyers, and sellers participate consensually in most facets of the drug trade. As a result, governments must use particularly intrusive tools, including surveillance, to discover these activities. Even though the lack of interstate conflict in Latin America and the conclusion of the Cold War created an opportunity to shrink the military and national security establishments in many countries (while perhaps enabling them to direct these funds to economic development and poverty eradication), the US government's imposition of the drug war ended these hopes. Instead, these state agencies grew, as did their violations of human rights in the struggle against the drug trade. Country after country engaged in mass surveillance as their governments tried to fight the crime, gangs, drug cartels, gun traffickers, and money launderers that the drug war created. The indiscriminate nature of this surveillance, however, meant that everybody in the region experienced profound assaults on their privacy. In the end, the people in the region sacrificed their security and their privacy for naught. Drug consumption did not decline, and violence did not abate.

NOTES

1. Benedict Anderson, *Imagined Communities: Reflections on the Origin and Spread of Nationalism* (London: Verso, 2006).

2. Steven Feldstein, "The Global Expansion of AI Surveillance," working paper, Carnegie Endowment for International Peace, September 2019, https:// carnegieendowment.org/files/WP-Feldstein-AISurveillance_final1.pdf, p. 2, parenthetical original.

3. Privacy International, "Surveillance Monitor 2007: International Country Rankings," December 28, 2007.

4. Reporters Without Borders, "A Special Report on Internet Surveillance, Focusing on 5 Governments and 5 Companies 'Enemies of the Internet,'" RSF.org, March 12, 2013, https://rsf.org/en/special-report-internet-surveillance-focusing-5-governments -and-5-companies-enemies-internet.

5. Sanja Kelly, Madeline Earp, Laura Reed, Adrian Shahbaz, and Mai Truong, *Freedom on the Net 2015: Privatizing Censorship, Eroding Privacy* (Washington, DC, and New York: Freedom House, 2015), 1, https://freedomhouse.org/sites/default /files/FH_FOTN_2015Report.pdf, parenthetical original.

6. Kelly et al., *Freedom on the Net 2015*, 10.

7. Feldstein, "Global Expansion of AI Surveillance," 1.

8. Feldstein, "Global Expansion of AI Surveillance," 1–2.

9. Jamie Doward, "Anger at UK Spy Tech Sales to Hong Kong," *The Guardian*, July 20, 2019, https://www.theguardian.com/world/2019/jul/20/uk-surveillance-tech -sales-hong-kong-protesters.

10. Nick Dearden, as quoted in Doward, "Anger at UK Spy Tech Sales."

11. Feldstein, "Global Expansion of AI Surveillance," 2, 8.

12. Feldstein, "Global Expansion of AI Surveillance," 10–11.

13. Adrian Shahbaz and Allie Funk, *Freedom on the Net 2019: The Crisis of Social Media* (Washington, DC, and New York: Freedom House, 2019), 1, 2, https: //freedomhouse.org/sites/default/files/2019-11/11042019_Report_FH_FOTN_2019 _final_Public_Download.pdf.

14. All quotations in this paragraph from Feldstein, "Global Expansion of AI Surveillance," 14.

15. Knightscope, "Fighting Crime with Knightscope," accessed August 30, 2022, https://www.knightscope.com/crime/.

16. Paula Martins, "Unnecessary, Disproportionate and Widespread: The Normalization of Surveillance in Colombia and Latin America," IFEX, May 27, 2020, https://ifex.org/unnecessary-disproportionate-and-widespread-the-normalization-of-surveillance-in-colombia-and-latin-america/.

17. Fabrizio Scrollini as quoted in Martins, "Unnecessary, Disproportionate and Widespread."

Chapter 10

Representative Examples of State Surveillance around the World

At this point, most of the world's population lives under some form of mass surveillance, although the extent, sophistication, and invasiveness of these systems continues to differ. At the start of the third decade of the twenty-first century, protections from this mass surveillance vary just as widely. Differences in the extent and protection of broader privacy rights is just as great. And in many countries with constitutions enshrining a privacy right, effective protections from state intrusions do not exist given the ways these provisions are written. In general, privacy guarantees in constitutions contain language that enables their circumvention in cases of public need. Given the elasticity and breadth of this language, states can easily violate these rights by citing national security and other imperatives.

Additionally, secrecy enables the circumvention of legal restraints. This makes a vigorous free press even more important. In contrast, strong, independent judiciaries have still not provided much relief from surveillance in some countries, although they have played a significant role in others. Overall, however, whistleblowers and investigative journalists have done the most to reveal and partially restrain the practices of national security apparatuses. Not surprisingly, precisely because an independent press constitutes the most important brake on secret and illegal practices, journalists have been the targets of state surveillance in many places. Beyond an independent press, civil-society groups, especially NGOs devoted to the protection of privacy, constitute a counterweight to state abuse. The relative debility of these groups makes them much less consequential than an independent press, although they do produce valuable information about government activities, creating greater transparency while serving as privacy advocates.

The use of surveillance varies across different regions of the world. In North America, the United States uses this practice particularly widely. This is also true of several states in Europe. And the 2019 Carnegie Endowment for International Peace report notes that "the East Asia/Pacific and the Middle East/North Africa regions are robust adopters of these tools. South and Central Asia and the Americas also demonstrate sizable take-up of AI surveillance instruments. Sub-Saharan Africa is a laggard: less than one-quarter of its countries are invested in AI surveillance."[1]

The Middle East, arguably the most conflictual part of the world, has many countries with outsized militaries and equally large national security apparatuses using surveillance and other tools against perceived external and internal threats. Israel and its neighbors, despite all their differences, participate in particularly extensive surveillance. As noted above, state surveillance is not as widespread in Sub-Saharan Africa, perhaps because of resource and technological constraints. However, this lag is already diminishing given the ability to purchase these tools from the global surveillance industrial complex. And as discussed in the previous chapter, in Latin America anomic criminal violence, drug trafficking, and the monitoring of political opponents drives the growth of state surveillance. States insist that they are using these capacities to fight crime, and especially drug trafficking cartels and other criminal organizations, but country after country has ended up using these tools to monitor political opponents and others, including journalists and dissidents.[2]

The sampling of representative cases of surveillance in this chapter begins with the discussion of the two largest authoritarian regimes in the world, China and Russia. It then explores the behavior of the world's largest democracy, India, and a democratic country engaged in continual conflict, Israel. The remainder of the chapter analyzes differences in some of the major regions of the world. It begins with a comparison of three European countries, the United Kingdom, France, and Germany, and then discusses two Latin American cases, Brazil and Mexico, two African cases, Nigeria and South Africa, and two Southeast Asian cases, Vietnam and Thailand. All these cases reveal, despite their other differences, that surveillance has become an intrinsic and growing part of governance around the world.

CHINA

The Chinese elite, almost immediately after the dawn of the digital age, understood that digital capacities enhanced the state's power, enabling it to monitor the population in previously unimaginable ways. In part, China's surveillance regime reflects the lack of a philosophical tradition built around the primacy of individual rights and the corollary effort to limit government power. In fact, these liberal understandings run deeply counter to China's tradition. The country's historical and political experience inculcates a profound concern with the preservation of order and hierarchy. The pursuit of social peace advances the common good. Confucianism and the association of peace, tranquility, and social harmony with a strong central government informs the Chinese polity. These understandings favor the concentration of power in the hands of the state and reify the community over the individual, attenuating notions of inalienable individual rights, including privacy.

As a result, the Chinese government violates privacy, understood according to the definition contained in the Universal Declaration of Human Rights, more systematically than any other country in the world. The country's passage of a data privacy law in 2021 does restrict the behavior of private corporations but does not inhibit state practices. Given all of this, it is not surprising that China is home to the largest CCTV network in the world. The Chinese government uses facial-recognition technology more extensively than any other state as well. And this last technology has spread across society, transforming faces into debit cards, credit cards, and IDs. The Chinese government also routinely uses smartphones as monitoring, listening, and tracking devices. In 2017 China had more than 170 million cameras observing the population and deployed four hundred million more by 2020. This is one camera for every three people, a number that no other country in the world matches. And the number of cameras will continue to rise, given the Chinese state's desire to see and know everything, including the most minute.

Dissenters, ethnic and religious minorities, and anyone seen as a remote threat to the omnipotence of the Chinese state receive heightened surveillance. In addition to confining more than a million Uighurs in "reeducation centers"—which are, effectively, concentration camps—the Chinese government covers the Uighur region of Xinjiang and its capital, Ürümqi, with a particularly dense CCTV network, creating a truly suffocating surveillance regime designed to erase private, anonymous activities. Tibetans, those associated with religious movement Falun Gong, and political dissenters, including human-rights advocates, experience particularly intrusive surveillance as well.

Surveillance sustains the social-credit system, which instituted a unified record scheme that grades a person's "trustworthiness." An individual's score reflects a compilation of positive and negative grades received for engaging in certain behaviors, all captured through continual surveillance. People with "low" credits can end up facing certain exclusions and sanctions. A low score results from activities as diverse as playing loud music, jaywalking, missing a restaurant reservation, failing to recycle, or financial problems. People whose low score defines them as untrustworthy can be denied access to goods and services available to others, including such things as high-speed rail and airline tickets. It can take from two to five years to be liberated from these sanctions. Positive credits are granted for charitable activities, blood donations, and community volunteer work. And those with high credits can gain greater access to employment opportunities along with other benefits including shorter waiting times in hospitals and government agencies and discounts at hotels.

Although the Chinese approach to surveillance can be interpreted as a sui generis feature of its polity and society, it contains features that make it exceptionally appealing to the powerful in other polities. Political elites in many countries are likely to envy the Chinese government's capacity to impose and ensure compliance with its directives. The Chinese governing model marries materialism and consumer convenience with informational and other capacities in the hands of the state.

As noted earlier, Chinese companies benefit from surveillance capitalism and are among the largest, if not the largest, multinational purveyors of surveillance technology to the rest of the world. Chinese law, however, requires that they submit the data gathered to the state upon request. This enables the Chinese state to capture digital data more easily than most other governments.

The extensiveness of China's surveillance system indicates the elites' deep disquiet about real and putative opponents and the extent of their effort to substitute clairvoyance for the expression of popular voice and democratic choice. These imperatives contribute to an obsession with prediction. The unrestrained use of mass surveillance, facial recognition, and metadata mining promises a new scientific social and political clairvoyance. The regime's ability to perfectly "see" the population and know everybody's needs and wants while extirpating undesirables and removing nonconformists promises perfect control while making expressions of democratic choice obsolete. After all, a perfect panopticon enables the creation of a state that knows people better than they know themselves and consequently does not have to resort to elections to determine the popular will.

RUSSIA

Markedly different from China in its approach to the Internet and surveillance is Russia, which never built a "Great Firewall" designed to restrict the population's access to the World Wide Web and to platforms like Facebook and Google despite the authoritarian nature of its regime. Indeed, for the first part of Vladimir Putin's reign Russia in contrast to China was a textbook example of a "competitive authoritarian" regime, according to Lucan Way and Steven Levitsky's typology.[3] Over time, however, the Putin regime did become increasingly repressive, culminating in its suffocation of independent media, violent response to peaceful protests, and closure of social media and other platforms after its invasion of Ukraine in 2022. And like many other states, the Russian government monitors the social media and online activity of the population becoming more and more like China in this regard.

Even before the hardening of its authoritarianism, Russia did engage like China and many others in extensive monitoring of online activities and focused on ways to turn its substantial digital strengths into instruments of foreign policy. The growing closeness of the Russian-Chinese relationship may drive increased collaboration between the two countries, designed to facilitate the development of additional cyber capacities. Such a partnership constitutes a logical response to the Five Eyes agreement. But for ordinary citizens the further acceleration of an arms race in this area has ominous implications, since it assures assaults on their privacy from every front.

To leverage state capacities and utilize the talents of the large numbers of Russians possessing first-rate technical skills, the Russian government entered into a tacit agreement with local hackers early in the Putin regime. In exchange for free rein in hacking foreign targets, Russian hackers agree to refrain from domestic activities. Russia's world-class STEM education creates a large pool of skilled computer scientists and potential hackers available to serve the regime. While Russia became a hotbed of digital scams, identity theft, spear phishing, and financial theft visited on other countries, these hackers emerged as an extraordinarily effective arm of the Russian state. Some function like independent contractors, pursuing their own activities while serving the state on other occasions. Others possessing these skills work for the vast and various branches of the Russian national security establishment and military.

The Russian state not only deploys its substantial digital capacities against foreign adversaries but continues to expand a comprehensive domestic surveillance system as well. Although not as vast as China's, Russian surveillance covers the country and especially its cities. Moreover, in common with other countries with strong digital sectors, Russia contains a surveillance industrial complex. Some of its digital companies, especially Kaspersky Labs, are internationally known, although many less well-known start-ups exist. The Russian state nurtures this sector, acquiring the tools it develops and promoting their export.

NtechLab, for example, created Moscow's camera-surveillance system. A network of 178,000 cameras (that continues to grow) equipped with very advanced facial-recognition capacities constitutes the heart of this system. While ostensibly created to fight crime, this video-surveillance network is used to identify protesters and dissidents. Unsurprisingly, given the nature of the Russian regime, this network was immediately activated in the wake of the outbreak of the COVID-19 pandemic to track the population and monitor compliance with quarantine orders. This network is also used to monitor and identify protestors against the regime, including those that occurred after Russia's invasion of Ukraine.

The extraordinary extent of corruption in Russia creates certain particularly insidious problems with the data that this surveillance generates. Investigative journalists have discovered that they can purchase the surveillance information and videos from this network on the black market for as little as seventy dollars.[4] This means that disgruntled spouses, stalkers, and others have access to the products of a very sophisticated surveillance system that monitors movement while amassing personal information, including such things as the names and addresses of those identified through facial recognition.

INDIA

Despite its long democratic tradition, India moved in an increasingly illiberal direction after the 2014 election of Narendra Modi. Although India's surveillance regime lags China's and Russia's, the Modi government has significantly shrunk this gap. In 2015 Prime Minister Modi announced the "Digital India" plan. Subsequently, the government invalidated 86 percent of the cash in circulation to combat tax evasion and move the country toward a "cashless society." The most dramatic example of this effort was the implementation of Aadhaar, an identification program that collects the private information of every Indian citizen. This information includes physical identifiers like fingerprints and eye scans and is stored in a single database linked to every part of a person's digital footprint, including their bank accounts, income tax returns, and cell phone and voter information. This system amasses intimate private information on over a billion people, constituting an extraordinary assault on privacy.

Aadhaar became a single, all-encompassing passport to access everything, including school, social-welfare payments, bank accounts, and any other public activity requiring the documentation of identity. An enterprise of this magnitude in a country as vast and diverse as India became immediately suffused with error and misinformation, an issue that continues today. As a result, Aadhaar consequently manages to combine Orwellian intrusions and the illusion of "digital accuracy" with commonplace mistakes and misinformation. These errors, conjoined to the difficulty of correcting them in a country with an enormous, corrupt, and incompetent bureaucracy, has baneful effects on individuals, denying them access to essentials such as education.

Despite the country's resource constraints, the Modi government announced early in 2020 that it intended to spend $4 billion on CCTV cameras and facial-recognition technology. The government advertises these cameras as crime-fighting tools designed to reduce violence. But it is more likely that the construction of a surveillance state including Aadhaar and the targeting of the country's Muslim population flows naturally from the Modi government's roots in the RSS—India's version of the Black Shirts and other fascist organizations in Europe. The RSS organization is connected to the BJP, the ruling party during Modi's administration. Both advocate Hindutva, an intensely exclusionary and strident expression of Hindu nationalism. The Modi government's claims that its surveillance state seeks to reduce violence ring particularly hollow given its overt and tacit incitements of ethnic and religious hatreds. Many who inflame these hatreds and participate in communal violence are in state employ, including some with senior positions. And the Modi government has done nothing to reform India's police forces, which combine the powers derived from growing surveillance capacities with a voluminous record of venality, violence, abuse, and brutality.

The Indian state uses its digital capacities to monitor online behavior as well. As is true elsewhere, the Indian government surveils social media activity and penetrates cell phones and other devices. In addition, it continues to expand its ability to collect online searches and engage in metadata mining.

ISRAEL

Israel merits particular mention in any discussion of surveillance. Indeed, there is no country in the world with a larger surveillance sector relative to the size of its economy. This results from a deliberate economic strategy designed to transform Israel's military capacities into a high-tech market niche. This strategy has been extraordinarily successful, at least in economic terms. By the end of the second decade of the twenty-first century, Israeli companies ranked among the largest and most successful purveyors of surveillance tools around the world. While many Israeli companies produce and market intrusive surveillance tools, NSO Group Technologies has become particularly well-known and controversial.

Like the rest of the Israeli surveillance industrial complex, NSO sells its tools to governments with very poor human-rights records and who do not exhibit respect for liberal democratic norms. The company's most famous tool, Pegasus, can remotely activate a smartphone, turn on its microphone and camera, scrub its contents, and then disappear without leaving a trace. To protect itself, NSO requires that governments promise they will limit the use of Pegasus to investigations of criminals and terrorists but then does nothing to enforce these terms.

In fact, NSO and the other companies within the Israeli surveillance industrial complex continue to sell their tools to governments with histories of spying on, repressing, and killing journalists and dissidents. A consortium of journalistic organizations including the *Washington Post, Die Zeit, The Guardian,* and *Le Monde* along with human-rights organization Amnesty International investigated the use of Pegasus around the world, revealing their findings in July 2021. Using a leaked trove of fifty thousand phone numbers, including fifteen thousand from Mexico, they discerned the use of the tool. *The Guardian* reported that "the wider Pegasus project investigation found NSO has close links to the Israeli state and in 2017 was given explicit permission by the Israeli government to try to sell the hacking tools to Saudi Arabia in a deal reportedly worth at least $55 million."[5]

The surveillance technology that NSO sold to the Saudi Arabian government was used to spy on *Washington Post* journalist Jamal Khashoggi and those close to him. Consequently NSO, and the Israeli state by extension, were passive and very well-remunerated accomplices of those who subsequently murdered and dismembered Khashoggi in the Saudi consulate in Istanbul in October 2018. Additionally, the investigation revealed that Pegasus has been sold to countries like Hungary and India, whose governments have moved in an increasingly illiberal direction. International pressure after the publication of the results of the investigation caused the Israeli government to announce the creation of a task force to review the granting of export licenses to cyber tools. However, given the centrality of the surveillance industrial complex to Israel's economic strategy, significant reform remains unlikely.

Israel's market niche reflects the impacts of the country's siege mentality and the corrosive effects of the prolonged occupation of another population on the polity and the society. Continual conflict, including its War of Independence (which Palestinians call al Nakba), the 1967 War, the Yom Kippur War (or Ramadan War), the 1982 Lebanon War, and smaller almost numberless armed engagements mark the country's history. In addition, after its conquest of the West Bank and other territories in the 1967 War, Israel became an occupying power, ruling over a subordinated, hostile population. To govern them, Israel created, among other things, a comprehensive surveillance network covering the occupied territories, including not just cameras but the extensive monitoring of online activity as well. And to protect the country from terrorist attacks, surveillance and other security measures spread to the rest of Israel's national territory. Tragically, a country founded as a refuge and homeland for Jews became the antithesis of itself and of many of its founding ideals.

The refugee became the oppressor, and the persecuted became the colonizer. People whose history embodied all the horrors of racism and discrimination acquiesced—except for dissidents, of course—in the de facto and then the increasingly de jure construction of an apartheid system. And Israel, just like other countries, reveals militarism's destructive impact on the recognition and protection of universal human rights. Furthermore, "garrison states" inevitably acquire the traits of militarism, including an outsized respect for the soldier, viewing them and other security organs as the highest and finest expression of the nation. Security is elevated over the protection of civil rights, diminishing the commitment to liberal norms. In the case of an occupying power, this attachment to civil and human rights erodes further. The occupied experience the denial of the benefits of citizenship and full personhood, and the state embraces the principle of differential treatment, destroying an essential component of liberal democracy—equality of rights.

Due to decades of conflict, including terrorist attacks and the degrading effects of settler colonialism on the occupier, Israelis—with some notable exceptions, among them privacy activists and civil-rights advocates—have welcomed and become habituated to the presence of CCTV and other forms of surveillance. This might explain why in 2020 Israel became the first country outside of Asia to employ cameras and drones to monitor and track the population after the outbreak of the COVID-19 pandemic.

Israel exemplifies the old truism that people will sacrifice liberty for greater security, especially in an environment where continual concerns about security erode concerns about human rights. Privacy and other civil rights embedded in personhood, and not just citizenship, do not receive adequate protection in an environment suffused with existential fears no matter how rational or justified. These existential concerns and the reification of security coarsen the population and the elite, leading to an increased tendency to rationalize abuses against others.

Military service constitutes a core component of Israeli identity, and the Israel Defense Forces (IDF) are a central locus of national pride, "we feeling," and nationalism. Israel's political culture celebrates the soldier-citizen as the highest embodiment of the society and glorifies the military and the remainder of the security apparatus, including Mossad (Israel's equivalent of the CIA) and Shin Bet (the country's primary internal-security agency).

Alumni of Unit 8200, the cyber branch of the IDF, founded and staff NSO and the numerous other companies comprising the country's surveillance industrial complex. Beginning in high school, the IDF recruits the best math and computer science students in the country to serve in Unit 8200. Those recruited avoid ordinary military service and are effectively guaranteed a job in Israel's surveillance industrial complex after they complete their service in the IDF. The practice of recruiting the best students in subjects related to cyber while they are still in high school creates a disproportionately large pool of talent for both the IDF and the surveillance industrial complex. Technion, the country's internationally recognized technology university, plays a large role in the development of these capacities, as well. The companies that are part of Israel's surveillance industrial complex reflect this talent and training, developing world-leading digital-surveillance tools capable of stripping away all vestiges of privacy and individual control over personal information. The sale of these technologies to governments with atrocious human-rights records only makes matters worse.

THE UNITED KINGDOM

As noted before, the United Kingdom's embrace of surveillance stands out from most other European countries—and many other democracies. The critical and justly celebrated role of the British intelligence services in helping to defeat the Nazis gave a mythic status to these agencies. This mystique continued throughout the Cold War. Novels and movies celebrated MI5, the counterpart of the CIA in the United States, especially those that glorified the exploits of the fictional James Bond. The Bond films attained a global audience, elevating the status and visibility of British intelligence. And unlike the CIA, British intelligence, despite its active involvement in regime-change operations around the world, escaped the opprobrium that came from this activity. Even in subsequent years, despite the closeness of its alliance with the CIA, British intelligence largely avoided the taint of association with an agency that used waterboarding and extraordinary rendition while creating and maintaining black-box prisons. This was true of GCHQ, the British signals-intelligence agency, whose deep collaboration with the NSA was barely known or criticized.

Beyond its national security apparatus's celebrated role during World War II, the country's reliance on these agencies—and especially MI6, the domestic counterpart of MI5—during the long and fraught conflict with the Irish Republican Army (IRA) elevated their status. The IRA's bombing campaign against British cities from the 1970s through the 1990s terrorized the British population, creating a clamor for decisive police action and security. Al-Qaeda's 7/7 attacks on London in 2005 intensified these sentiments. These attacks killed fifty-six people, including the bombers.

Throughout these decades, the government developed and deployed a national CCTV network. By 2020 this network included more than five hundred thousand cameras in London and 4.2 million across the rest of the country. This was one camera for every fourteen people. Although this pales in comparison to China, this CCTV network made Britain the most surveilled large country in Europe. By comparison, according to the best-available evidence (a suspiciously low number), France had 1.65 million cameras and Germany 5.2 million, or one for every sixteen people. However, the United Kingdom still lagged far behind the United States, where there is 1 camera for every 4.6 people (although this number does not disaggregate private from public surveillance cameras, inflating it in comparative terms). However, unlike people in other democratic countries, and particularly the United States, where cameras remain very controversial, much of the British public welcomed them. As Jeffrey Rosen writes, the country's CCTV cameras are seen as "a friendly eye in the sky, not Big Brother but a kindly and watchful uncle or aunt."[6]

The first large crack in the reputation of these British services in the second decade of the twenty-first century came with Edward Snowden's revelations in 2013. The information he released detailed parts of GCHQ's domestic surveillance in Great Britain, especially its notably expansive monitoring of online activities. Many for the first time heard about the Five Eyes agreement and the scope of its collective vertically and horizontally integrated appropriations. For the first time, as well, people learned about the extent of GCHQ's collaboration with the NSA and of its technical capacities.

Imperfectly understood state surveillance activities became more transparent with the release of information about classification designations indicating the degree of cross-national surveillance collaboration—especially CANUKUS (an intelligence acronym designating that the material is for Canadian, United Kingdom, and United States eyes only)—and for the designation that covered all five "eyes." The outrage over documentary evidence showing that the NSA and its partners were surveilling, monitoring, tracking, and data mining the digital activities of everybody within their global reach not only tarnished the NSA but also GCHQ, its primary partner. Revelations that GCHQ was collecting Web searches all around the world in real time and was sharing this information with its partners in the Five Eyes agreement occasioned particular disquiet.

Even with Edward Snowden's revelations, however, it remains difficult to discern the precise contours of British mass surveillance or learn about the activities of the state's national security agencies. Britain's Official Secrets Act creates a cloak of secrecy even less penetrable than the one covering US national security operations. Under external pressure brief, partial, and rare flashes of transparency occur, permitting glimpses into these operations. In October 2016, for example, the Investigatory Powers Tribunal, a very rough equivalent of FISC in the United States, produced a decision in which it revealed that the British security services had illegally and without a warrant collected the financial information, phone call records, Web use, and other personal information of British citizens over the preceding seventeen years.

In response, in November of that year the British government passed the Investigatory Powers Act 2016. Just like the USA FREEDOM Act, this "reform," although containing changes of varying significance, primarily sought to quiet criticisms while preserving the security services' ability to surveil, collect, and mine. In fact, the act reaffirmed existing powers and revealed the extent of interference with electronic devices and the ubiquity of metadata mining. However, and importantly, the legislation's language did significantly change data-retention practices. The act requires ISPs and telecommunications providers to only retain pen-register information on their customers for twelve months. On the other hand, and problematically, police and intelligence agencies can access this data without a warrant as part of an investigation.

The latter half of the second decade of the twenty-first century witnessed a series of events promoting the further growth of mass surveillance. Continuing Islamic State–inspired terrorist attacks on London and other British cities fostered a climate of fear and concerns about security. The government, with the active support of the population, expanded and intensified surveillance as it tried to discover and prevent future attacks. Widespread fear about growing "knife crime," especially in London, added to this climate.

Brexit, conjoined with the closeness of the relationship between the United Kingdom and the United States, has serious implications for mass surveillance. The relationship between the United Kingdom and its Five Eyes partners, particularly the United States, promises to grow even more intimate as the country moves away from Europe. Moreover, Brexit ends an important restraint on the British government's ability to deploy additional digital intrusions, since it frees the country from EU data-privacy and human-rights laws.

In effect, prior to Brexit, the decisions of the Court of Justice of the European Union served as counterweights to the pressures for mass surveillance brought to bear by the United States. With Europe out of the picture, Britain will become more connected to the United States and more subject to American security needs and dictates. Moreover, the British public's long enchantment with their security services, the country's collective nostalgia for empire, and the consequent and continuing scope of its global military activities ensure enduring support for government activities in this area. And the country's insistence on preserving an outsized global role, despite its modest size, guarantees the emergence of continuing threats and attacks. And these attacks, just like the earlier ones from the IRA, ensure a continuing need for mass surveillance and the adoption of digital innovations in this area, along with the deployment of even more intrusive tools that impact the privacy of everybody in the country.

FRANCE

France uses mass surveillance extensively as well. The country's long tradition of strong central government and its lack of protection for habeas corpus facilitate its use of mass surveillance—although it protects other rights, notably and particularly, freedom from religion, much more strongly than other liberal societies. The country's continuing pursuit of global power and consequence produces repeated involvement in foreign conflicts and wars. In common with other countries with similar ambitions, this promotes the development of an outsized military and national security apparatus, particularly when compared to France's size. This apparatus, moreover, enjoys a comparatively free hand in the selection and implementation of measures designed to enhance security. Attacks in France since the Algerian War during the mid-1950s and early 1960s elevate concerns about domestic security, increasing the power and centrality of the security services.

Particularly during the second decade of the twenty-first century, Islamic State supporters carried out devastating terrorist attacks on France. The most notable were the January 2015 attacks on the offices of magazine *Charlie Hebdo* and on a kosher supermarket in which twelve people were killed; the attack on the Bataclan threater and numerous other sites including the Stade de France in November of that year, in which 130 people were killed; and a truck attack in Nice in 2016, that killed 86 and injured 458. Not surprisingly, ubiquitous fears of terrorism mark this period.

Amid this climate, in June 2015 French legislators passed an expansive surveillance law and other measures, granting extraordinary powers to the security apparatus. Despite opposition from the far left and human-rights activists, most legislators supported the new law. It enables the state security services to use a host of extraordinarily invasive practices with little to no judicial oversight. State agents can place cameras and recorders in private homes without having to secure prior judicial approval and are also now entitled to record computer keystrokes in real time. Furthermore, the law requires that ISPs and telecommunications companies install algorithms programmed to alert the authorities if users engage in "suspicious" activity, including viewing content deemed problematic. The state can retain recordings for a month and metadata for five years. The law permits data mining as well. These activities prompted intense criticism from Freedom House, who accused France of pursuing "problematic policies . . . such as restrictions on content that could be seen as an 'apology for terrorism,' prosecution of users, and significantly increased surveillance."[7]

In fact, the measures contained in France's June 2015 law exceed the provisions contained in the USA PATRIOT Act and the British responses to the 7/7 attacks. This prompted both the United Nations and the European Union to publicly condemn the law's Big Brother characteristics. On the other hand, even though they could not stop the law, France's vibrant and engaged civil society immediately participated in a wide-ranging and comprehensive public debate about these measures.

Beyond the June 2015 law, France possesses a constitutional order that facilitates the declaration of a state of siege. Article 36 of its constitution creates this power, while Law No. 55–385 of April 3, 1955, establishes the grounds for states of emergency. During a state of siege, the military authorities can assume police powers, during which the right of association, the searching of private places, and other basic rights can be circumscribed. During a state of emergency, or *état d'urgence*, the minister of the interior receives extraordinary powers, including the ability to order house arrests. In addition, prefects can limit movement and association and enact curfews, among other things. Despite already possessing the powers contained in the June 2015 law, the French government declared an *état d'urgence* after the November 2015 attacks at the Bataclan theater and kept it in place for the following two years.

By way of comparison, Article 1, Section 9, Clause 2, of the US Constitution asserts that "the privilege of the writ of habeas corpus shall not be suspended, unless in cases of rebellion or invasion the public safety may require it." Abraham Lincoln invoked this clause during the Civil War, becoming the only president in American history to nationally suspend these protections against summary imprisonment. Although President Grant invoked this clause during Reconstruction, he limited its reach to the former Confederacy. The last time the United States experienced the application of this constitutional provision occurred in Hawaii during World War II. The island's geographic location and especially its demography, given the depth of racist sentiments against anyone of Asian descent, occasioned this suspension. President George W. Bush tried to invoke this clause after 9/11, but the Supreme Court struck down his effort in *Hamdi v. Rumsfeld* on June 28, 2004. As this history reveals, the French constitutional order provides much more latitude to the government to impose extraordinary measures than the US Constitution affords US administrations.

GERMANY

Among large, economically developed democracies, Germany stands out in its relative resistance to the use of digital-surveillance tools. Because of its World War II history with the Nazis and with the Stasi in the GDR, Germany remains the greatest bastion in Europe, and perhaps the world, against expansive state surveillance. The country focuses more on the protection of privacy rights than its neighbors and promotes increases in the regulation of digital intrusions. Germans vividly recall the consequences they and others suffered under the use of unrestrained and coercive state powers conjoined with mass surveillance. As Tyson Barker writes,

Postwar Germany reacted to the experience of totalitarianism by establishing the principle of "informational self-determination," a strict notion of data protection as a human right. . . . Germany continues to have one of the lowest cloud adoption rates in Europe, owing, in part, to a suspicion of potential data abuse by outsiders, a perception reinforced for many by the US National Security Agency and Cambridge Analytica scandals. Many Germans—not just citizens but businesses and governments—prefer to keep their data physically close, be it in their phones, in on-site servers, or regulated through tough data-localization laws.[8]

In addition, Germany's protections have transformed Berlin into a home for "digital refugees" fleeing societies, including the United States, that resist efforts to significantly circumscribe state surveillance.

But even Germany has succumbed to some of the pressures driving the expansion of surveillance in other democracies. Its national legislature, in reaction to concerns about terrorist attacks, passed new surveillance laws in October 2016. One covers the retention of telecommunications data and the second the preservation of flight-passenger information. In both cases, data can be kept for five years, a period similar in length to other countries. Privacy advocates universally support shorter data-retention periods to limit intrusions and minimize abuse. In addition, a new Source Telecommunications and Online Surveillance Law expanded state and police capacity to use malware beyond just terrorism to intervene in mobile phones and the Internet. Additionally, a law on video surveillance expands the government's ability to use cameras to monitor public spaces. The law came into effect in May 2017, a few months after twelve people were killed in a truck attack on the Berlin Christmas market. While still not as extensive as the measures in place in other countries, these laws indicate that Germany has not escaped the insidious impacts on privacy that the fear of terrorism produces.

BRAZIL

In Latin America, Brazil originally imposed the strongest protections governing the state's ability to acquire and share data across different agencies. In 1995 Brazil created an Internet Steering Committee at a time when other countries were not thinking about the regulation and governance of the Internet. This committee included academics, members of civil-society groups, businesses, and government. After Edward Snowden revealed that the US National Security Agency was spying on Brazilian president Dilma Rousseff and many others in the country, the legislature passed a Marco Civil da Internet—a civil framework enumerating a sort of Internet "bill of rights," another unique innovation. And most importantly, in 1999 the

National Congress of Brazil passed the LGPD (Lei Geral de Protecao de Dados—General Law on the Protection of Data), a data-protection law much like Europe's General Data Protection Regulation.[9]

However, Brazil's relatively strong Internet- and data-protection regime frayed after the 2018 election of populist proto-fascist Jair Bolsonaro. After coming to power, Bolsonaro's government passed a series of measures that eviscerated these rules, revealing how rapidly an illiberal government can overwhelm rights protections in a democratic polity. In October 2019, Bolsonaro ordered federal agencies to consolidate much of their data, including health records and biometric information, into a single database, the Cadastro Base do Cidadão (citizens' basic register). As Richard Kemeny notes:

> Under the October decree, any federal body could start requesting and gathering data from others. Documents . . . revealed that ABIN, Brazil's national intelligence agency, had already used the decree to ask Serpro, a state-owned data company, for the records of the seventy-six million Brazilians who hold driver's licenses. . . . The scope for data acquisition under the decree is broad. Along with basic information such as name, marital status, and employment, the Cadastro will include biometric data such as facial profiles; voice, iris and retina scans; prints of digits and palms; even gait. There are no limits placed on how health data can be shared, and the list even includes genetic sequences.[10]

Ominously for Brazilians, these efforts echo the Modi government's activities in India.

In addition, a Central Data Governance Committee composed of members of the Bolsonaro administration oversaw the use of this data. The restraints and oversight that the Internet Steering Committee exercised, given its much broader membership and inclusion of diverse interests, disappeared.[11] And all these changes effectively subverted the privacy protections afforded by the LGPD.

All of this came on top of the Brazilian government's growing use of surveillance cameras and facial-recognition technology. The country's high rate of violent crime drives the adoption of these tools, as did its hosting of the 2014 FIFA World Cup and the 2016 Summer Olympics. As Richard Kemeny notes, in the MIT Technology Review,

> Surveillance camera networks installed for the 2014 World Cup and 2016 Olympics stayed in place after these events ended. . . . Last year Brazilian police arrested 151 people who'd been identified with the help of facial recognition. . . . The shortcomings of facial recognition are well documented—particularly the fact that existing systems, most of them developed in majority-White countries, disproportionately misidentify people of color.[12]

This last problem raises particular issues in Brazil, given the demographic composition of the country. These technologies are primarily used to surveil the residents of the shantytowns of major cities, where residents are disproportionately people of color. The addition of deeply biased facial-recognition technologies whose "precision" lends the color of scientific veracity to a system already saturated with racial profiling and discriminatory treatment, along with endemic judicial and police abuse, produces even greater injustices.

The next several years will witness a significant struggle in Brazil over data privacy and security. Those who strongly favor Bolsonaro's measures, including the military and the right, confront a strong and diverse civil society. This civil society contains many well-organized NGOs devoted to data-protection and privacy rights. The push and pull between these different sides of Brazil's polity will color the development of its still incomplete and increasingly fragile digital regulatory architecture.

MEXICO

The uses of surveillance and other digital tools in Mexico reveal the enduring hold of practices created during a prior authoritarian regime in a still relatively young democracy. Before Mexico's 2000 transition to a democracy that was electoral—though still not fully liberal constitutional—its previous authoritarian regime had developed a large and sophisticated national security apparatus that surveilled domestic political opponents, prominent figures in various social and political spheres, and the few independent journalists.

This regime had constructed a democratic veneer through the regular conduct of elections, even though the winners were predetermined. The ruling party, the Institutional Revolutionary Party (PRI), always won despite the presence of opposition parties, who were sometimes state subsidized to add a patina of legitimacy to the elections. Persisting economic problems, growing violence, and other serious issues extant throughout the 1990s finally created an environment that culminated in the 2000 presidential elections and the ruling party's loss for the first time in more than seventy years.

However, the opposition National Action Party (PAN) that came to power after the 2000 elections was infused with a conservative, Catholic, and pro–free market ideology and thus consequently would not countenance truly systemic change. Its unwillingness to fundamentally disturb the institutional order or to transform the bureaucracy and other parts of the previous regime, conjoined with the continuing power of interest groups devoted to the preservation of their privileges, enabled most state structures and many of their practices to survive unaltered.

The national security apparatus, including the police and much of the judiciary, remained particularly corrupt, violent, and prone to abuse. The intelligence agencies of the Mexican state, deeply involved with their counterparts in the United States, continued to surveil the same groups monitored during the authoritarian regime. Years before the revelations in 2021 about governmental uses of Pegasus around the world, investigative journalists and activists in Mexico had discovered that the Mexican state was using this tool to surveil different groups. Those most targeted were often these same journalists, dissidents, and activists. These revelations showed that the Mexican government had purchased Pegasus from NSO in 2011 for over $80 million. Throughout the latter parts of 2017 and into 2018, news organizations reported extensively on this subject, raising awareness for the first time of both the extraordinary capacities of Israeli surveillance tools and the Mexican government's use of this software to track dissenters and activists and to monitor the press.

The subsequent global press investigation in 2021 about the uses of Pegasus showed that Mexico's President Andrés Manuel López Obrador, along with much of his inner circle, had been monitored with Pegasus by his predecessor, Enrique Peña Nieto, who had served from 2012 until López Obrador's 2018 election.[13] The Peña Nieto government had been surveilling political opponents in addition to all the groups mentioned above. Although President López Obrador insisted in 2021 that these practices had ended, given his professed rejection of authoritarianism (despite using the Mexican military in unprecedented ways throughout his administration), privacy activists in Mexico City continue to voice concerns about the extent of surveillance. They have shown that fake antennas and so-called Stingray devices are being broadly used to surreptitiously capture cell phone information. Chilean privacy activists who monitor this activity around Latin America have discovered more Stingray devices in Mexico City than in any Latin American city other than Caracas.[14] Additionally, the Mexican state does not meaningfully circumscribe its surveillance of online behavior.

NIGERIA

State uses of surveillance vary across Africa. However, as noted before, surveillance developed later in the region than elsewhere, although it has expanded rapidly ever since. Nigeria reflects the experience of several other African countries in these regards.

In the decades after declaring its independence in October 1960, Nigeria struggled with corruption, internecine strife (especially the Biafran War), the natural resource curse, and eventually Boko Haram terrorism. Corrupt and frequently highly repressive military regimes and incomplete democracies governed the country throughout this period. Once digital tools became available, and under the guise of protecting national security, the leaders of this still problematic polity—beset by extraordinary corruption, in particular—began purchasing sophisticated surveillance equipment during the second decade of the twenty-first century.

In April 2013, for example, the Nigerian government spent $40 million on tools from Israeli surveillance company Elbit Systems. These tools enabled the Nigerian government to surveil the online activities of the country's then-forty-seven million Internet users. This purchase was secret, and Elbit announced the sale while hiding the name of the purchasing country.[15] As John Dada and Teresa Tafida wrote in 2014, "Nigeria does not yet have any data-privacy laws or legal provision for interception of communication. The current security challenges in the country are being used as the reason to take major security decisions and make national commitments without the necessary constitutional approvals."[16]

During subsequent years, some efforts to protect privacy advanced slowly, although Nigeria's regulatory architecture remained weak and notably incomplete. For example, as late as the start of the third decade of the twenty-first century, Nigeria lacked a truly comprehensive data-protection and privacy act. However, the National Information Technology Development Agency (NITDA) did issue a Data Protection Regulation in January 2019, which "governs the control and processing of personal data of natural persons residing in or outside Nigeria but of Nigerian descent. The Constitution of the Federal Republic of Nigeria (as amended) . . . guarantees citizens' privacy. Section 37 of the constitution protects citizens' homes, correspondence, telephone conversations, and telegraphic communications."[17]

Despite this regulation and the privacy guarantees in the Nigerian constitution, four concerning observations made in 2018 by Privacy International continue to apply:

[First,] the Nigerian state appears to have significant surveillance capabilities, but the legislation governing communications surveillance fails to abide by international human-rights standards. [Second,] increased monitoring of online activity by government actors creates an atmosphere of fear around controversial online speech and may endanger the right to privacy. [Third,] the absence of comprehensive overarching data-protection legislation and the lack of a central data-protection agency . . . fail to meet international standards and put privacy at risk. . . . [Fourth,] mandatory registration of all SIM cards, the establishment of a database containing information about users of mobile phone services, and mandatory data-retention requirements on Internet service providers are measures that contravene international human-rights standards on the right to privacy.[18]

SOUTH AFRICA

South Africa's approach to state surveillance and its regulation differs significantly from Nigeria's and makes it somewhat of an outlier in Africa, although
this is quite a recent development. South Africa adopted digital-surveillance
tools somewhat earlier than other countries in the region, including Nigeria
and delayed regulating them for years. However, the Zuma government's
aggressive use of mass digital surveillance between 2009 and 2018 elicited
strong objections from civil-rights groups, given the country's dark history of
surveillance used against dissidents and others during the apartheid regime.

Pressure from these groups, along with legal cases, finally led to a seminal judicial decision in 2019 that created the basis for a privacy-protection
regime that is more robust than others in the region. On September 16, 2019,
Judge Roland Sutherland of South Africa's High Court issued a blanket ruling
applying to the nation's intelligence agencies: "Bulk surveillance activities
and foreign signals interception undertaken by the National Communications
Centre (NCC) are unlawful and invalid."[19]

This decision came after years of complaints about the unchecked and
highly problematic surveillance of journalists and political opponents that
occurred under the Regulation of Interception of Communications and
Provision of Communication-Related Information Act (RICA) enacted in
2009. As Jane Duncan wrote in 2014,

> the act has insufficient guarantees for civil liberties online. . . . An added prob-
> lem is that foreign-signals intelligence gathering does not fall under RICA,
> which means that this practice is unregulated by law. This is particularly wor-
> rying as the state's bulk monitoring capacity is held by the interception centre
> that undertakes foreign-signals intelligence; so the state agency with the greatest
> capacity for mass surveillance is also the one that is least regulated by law. In
> 2005, the state's mass-surveillance capacity was misused to spy on perceived
> opponents of the then contender for the presidency, Jacob Zuma.[20]

Other cases of surveillance against investigative journalists during subsequent years revealed, to quote Jane Duncan again,

> just how easy it is to intercept journalist's communications . . . One of the most
> serious weaknesses is that no one is even informed that their communications
> have been intercepted, even after the investigation is complete. . . . Another
> problem . . . is the speculative nature of the grounds for issuing of interception
> directions using RICA. . . . Furthermore, the granting of directions is an inher-
> ently one-sided process, which means that the judge has to take the information
> that is given to him on trust. . . . The level of information provided by the des-
> ignated judge that is released is inadequate. . . . Furthermore, other democracies

have established independent commissions to oversee all monitoring and interception activities. . . . Yet in South Africa, the parliamentary reports are written by the very judge who took the decisions. . . . South Africa's act also does not recognise the right of journalists to protect their sources of information. . . . All these problems make for an act that is not human rights–compliant.[21]

Against this problematic history, South Africa's High Court finding in 2019 establishing the illegality of mass bulk surveillance is especially important while reflecting the depth of attachment to privacy in much of the country's population. This ruling has contributed in the last few years to the incipient creation of a regulatory regime that is much more developed than can be found elsewhere in the continent. In this area, South Africans exhibit similar proclivities to Germans: they lived through a regime that possessed the means to practice unrestrained surveillance and are consequently more prone to resist this practice than people in other African countries without this concrete modern historical experience and memory.

THAILAND

Many countries in Southeast Asia use digital surveillance particularly widely. In part, this is the result of their relatively advanced technological capacities along with the existence of a political environment that facilitates this enterprise. Despite these commonalities, the practice of mass surveillance varies across the region, reflecting each country's unique historical experience and contemporary circumstances.

Thailand's surveillance state reflects the country's history, political culture, and conflicts in especially interesting and revealing ways. Exceptionally strong lèse-majesté laws prohibiting criticism of the king act as a powerful constraint on freedom of expression in the country. In addition, intense political conflict and repeated military coups have created an environment that encourages those in power to use surveillance against their opponents. On the other hand, Section 32 of the Thai constitution, which was passed by a military government in 2016, declares that "a person shall enjoy the rights of privacy, dignity, reputation, and family. An act violating or affecting the rights of a person under Paragraph One, or the use of personal information for benefit by any means, shall not be permitted except by virtue of provisions of the law specifically enacted as deemed necessary for the public interests."[22]

In addition to this explicit privacy protection in the constitution and in marked contrast to the laws of neighboring Cambodia and Vietnam, Thailand has specific regulations governing the interception of digital, postal, and telephonic communications. This regulation, written into Section 25 of the Special Case Investigation Act, requires the Department of Special Investigation to seek authorization from a judge before obtaining these forms of information. The interception of communications cannot last for more than thirty days, and the judge must certify that reasonable grounds exist to warrant authorization.

Despite these codified protections, however, in 2017 Privacy International noted that

> the martial law that was declared after the coup in May 2014 is currently still in place. It grants the military the right "to inspect [any] message, letter, telegraph, package, parcel, or other things transmitting within the area under the Martial Law." On [sic] May 2014, the junta published Order 26/2014 on "the control and surveillance of the use of social media." In this order, the government claims the right to "monitor and access the computer traffic, the use of websites, social media, photos, text, video and audio which are deemed to instigate violence and unrest, which are deemed to be unlawful, and which violate the National Council for Peace and Order's (NCPO) Orders."[23]

In addition, Privacy International notes troubling uses of surveillance:

> The community of Thai Muslims who live in the far south of the country, at the border with Malaysia, has been reported to be under high levels of surveillance. Generally, anyone who criticizes the Royal Family even in a muted way can be considered a criminal and therefore a likely target of surveillance. The number of arrests for lèse-majesté crimes has multiplied since the coup. Since the coup, however, targets of surveillance have included political dissidents and, more particularly, students and young persons.[24]

Despite these problems, political changes in Thailand and shifts between regime types enable a fitful but continuing effort to create meaningful privacy protections and begin to effectively circumscribe mass digital surveillance.

VIETNAM

In contrast, privacy protections and limits on state surveillance do not exist in Vietnam. At the time of this writing, the government continues to expand its powers and its capacity to monitor the entire population's online and public behaviors. Its practice of state surveillance mirrors China's, revealing the similarities between the two regimes. Also as in China, mass surveillance underlies Vietnam's use of repression to squash dissent and maximize political control. The extent and scope of these activities has prompted international human-rights organizations to repeatedly single out Vietnam's especially appalling record in this area. For example, in 2019 Human Rights Watch reported that in Vietnam "basic civil and political rights including freedom of expression, association, and peaceful public assembly are severely restricted. . . . Activists questioning government policies or projects, or seeking to defend local resources or land, face daily harassment, intrusive surveillance, house arrest, travel bans, arbitrary detention, and interrogation."[25]

Evolving digital technologies expand the Vietnamese government's mass-surveillance activities and its repressive capacity. A cybersecurity law passed in June 2018 that went into effect in January 2019 enables increased surveillance while facilitating state repression. The law requires that "service providers must take down offending content within twenty-four hours of receiving a request from the Ministry of Information and Communications or the Ministry of Public Security. Requirements that Internet companies store data locally, 'verify' user information, and disclose user data to authorities without the need for a court order also threaten the right to privacy and could facilitate further suppression of online dissent or activism."[26]

And repercussions for noncompliance are harsh. As Eitay Mack and Vu Quoc Ngu have noted,

> Vietnamese civilians who voice criticism—whether on Facebook, as journalists, or as protesters—are consistently attacked by the security forces: they face arrest, severe torture, criminal charges for draconian offenses. . . . Those activists who are not arrested and suspected of hostility to the regime are under constant surveillance and have severe restrictions on their freedom of occupation and freedom of movement. For example, on 15 November 2019, the regime sentenced Nguyen Nang Tinh, a music teacher, to eleven years in prison for Facebook posts that caused 'negative information about the country' to be circulated.[27]

CONCLUSION

To different degrees and using varying technologies, countries around the world use mass digital surveillance to monitor their populations. And the use of this practice keeps growing. On the other hand, journalists, activists, academics, NGOs, and some political leaders continue to push for the adoption of robust protections covering informational privacy. At present, the race to surveil all, to know all, and to control all is running ahead of efforts to protect privacy. But in many countries groups continue to push for regulation addressing this and other features of the Brave New Digital World.

Governments around the world that lack the requisite domestic technological capacity can acquire the latest surveillance tools and other technologies at international expositions. The most famous and largest of these "surveillance bazaars" occurs annually in Paris's Milipol, held at the Parc des Expositions. While most exhibits showcase military hardware, bringing sellers and buyers together from around the world, Hall 4 focuses on cyber.

Here "the world's biggest gathering of companies [sell] the latest, greatest, and most powerful technology to militaries, police, and intelligence agencies. . . . Some countries have the goods in spades, but most countries lack powerful cyber capacities, and every country wants more." And, of course, NSO exhibits at Milipol, as do the other companies comprising the Israeli surveillance industrial complex. Not surprisingly, "NSO's booth is one of the biggest on the floor but relatively private, with a dark cyberpunk theme. Skyscraper walls keep visitors discreet and conversations private as deals are being made."[28]

Every regime, including those that systematically violate human rights, can find all of the wares it needs at the Parc des Expositions. Indeed, "At Milipol you can buy potent zero-day vulnerabilities or powerful data-interception equipment plus the drones, vehicles, or backpacks to move hacking tools wherever needed."[29] In addition to its signature exposition in Paris, Milipol stages regional events in Kuala Lumpur, where Asian customers can shop for military wares and cyber tools. Another convention is held in Qatar for customers in the Middle East. The targeting of sales to regions with notable histories of egregious human- and civil-rights abuses reveals that all these companies are completely disinterested in preventing the misuse of their products despite their frequent protestations to the contrary.

NOTES

1. Steven Feldstein, "The Global Expansion of AI Surveillance," working paper, Carnegie Endowment for International Peace, September 2019, https://carnegieendowment.org/files/WP-Feldstein-AISurveillance_final1.pdf, p. 8.

2. Azam Ahmed and Nicole Perlroth, "Using Texts as Lures, Government Spyware Targets Mexican Journalists and Their Families," *New York Times*, June 19, 2017, https://www.nytimes.com/2017/06/19/world/americas/mexico-spyware-anticrime.html.

3. Stephen Levitsky and Lucan Way, "The Rise of Competitive Authoritarianism," *Journal of Democracy* 13 no. 2 (April 2002): 51–65.

4. "Moscow Facial Recognition Tech Will Outlast the Coronavirus," *Vice News Tonight*, April 16, 2020.

5. Bethan McKernan and Paul Lewis, "Israel 'Creating a Task Force' to Manage Response to Pegasus Project," *The Guardian*, July 21, 2021, https://www.theguardian.com/world/2021/jul/21/israel-creating-task-force-to-manage-response-to-pegasus-project.

6. Jeffrey Rosen, *The Naked Crowd: Reclaiming Security and Freedom in an Anxious Age* (New York: Random House, 2004).

7. Sanja Kelly, Madeline Earp, Laura Reed, Adrian Shahbaz, and Mai Truong, *Freedom on the Net 2015: Privatizing Censorship, Eroding Privacy* (Washington, DC, and New York: Freedom House, 2015), 2, https://freedomhouse.org/sites/default/files/FH_FOTN_2015Report.pdf.

8. Tyson Barker, "Germany's Angst Is Killing Its Coronavirus Tracing App," Opinion, *Foreign Policy*, May 8, 2020, https://foreignpolicy.com/2020/05/08/germany-coronavirus-contract-tracing-pandemic-app/.

9. Richard Kemeny, "Brazil Is Sliding into Techno-authoritarianism," *MIT Technology Review*, August 19, 2020, https://www.technologyreview.com/2020/08/19/1007094/brazil-bolsonaro-data-privacy-cadastro-base/.

10. Kemeny, "Brazil Is Sliding."

11. Kemeny, "Brazil Is Sliding."

12. Kemeny, "Brazil Is Sliding."

13. For an example of this coverage, see Ahmed and Perlroth, "Using Texts as Lures."

14. Avi Asher-Schapiro and Christine Murray, "'Birds on the Wire'? Concerns over Mexico's Cell Phone Surveillance," Reuters, June 12, 2020, https://www.reuters.com/article/us-mexico-tech-rights-trfn-analysis-idUSKBN23J2CC.

15. O. Emmanuel, "EXCLUSIVE: Jonathan Awards $40 Million Contract to Israeli Company to Monitor Computer, Internet Communication by Nigerians," *Premium Times*, April 25, 2013, https://www.premiumtimesng.com/news/131249-exclusive-jonathan-awards-40million-contract-to-israeli-company-to-monitor-computer-internet-communication-by-nigerians.html.

16. John Dada and Teresa Tafida, "Online Surveillance: Public Concerns Ignored in Nigeria," in *Global Information Society Watch 2014: Communications Surveillance in the Digital Age*, Global Information Society Watch, GISWatch.org, 2014, https://giswatch.org/sites/default/files/online_surveillance_public_concerns_ignored_in_nigeria.pdf.

17. "Nigeria—Data Protection Overview," DataGuidance, September 2019, https://www.dataguidance.com/notes/nigeria-data-protection-overview, parenthetical original.

18. Paradigm Initiative and Privacy International, *The Right to Privacy in Nigeria: Stakeholder Report, Universal Periodic Review, 31st Session—Nigeria*, March 2018, https://www.privacyinternational.org/sites/default/files/2018-05/UPR_The%20Right%20to%20Privacy_Nigeria.pdf.

19. Privacy International, "Bulk Surveillance Is Unlawful, Says the High Court of South Africa," last updated October 7, 2020, https://privacyinternational.org/news-analysis/3212/bulk-surveillance-unlawful-says-high-court-south-africa.

20. See p. 224 of Jane Duncan, "Communications Surveillance in South Africa: The Case of the *Sunday Times* Newspaper," in *Global Information Society Watch 2014: Communications Surveillance in the Digital Age*, Global Information Society Watch, GISWatch.org, 2014, https://giswatch.org/sites/default/files/communications_surveillance_in_south_africa.pdf.

21. Duncan, "Communications Surveillance in South Africa," 224–27.

22. Privacy International, "State of Privacy Thailand," March 14, 2017, https://privacyinternational.org/state-privacy/1011/state-privacy-thailand.

23. Privacy International, "State of Privacy Thailand."

24. Privacy International, "State of Privacy Thailand."

25. Human Rights Watch, "Vietnam: Events of 2018," *World Report 2019*, https://www.hrw.org/world-report/2019/country-chapters/vietnam.

26. Human Rights Watch, "Vietnam: Events of 2018."

27. Eitay Mack and Vu Quoc Ngu, "Arms, Drones and Spy Tech: How Israeli Weapons Power Vietnam's Cruel Surveillance State," Opinion, *Haaretz*, September 23, 2020, https://www.haaretz.com/israel-news/2020-09-23/ty-article-opinion/.premium/arms-drones-and-spy-tech-israeli-weapons-aid-vietnams-cruel-surveillance-stat/0000017f-f505-d47e-a37f-fd3df4130000.

28. All quotations in this paragraph have been drawn from Patrick Howell O'Neill, "Champagne, Shotguns, and Surveillance at Spyware's Grand Bazaar," *MIT Technology Review*, November 25, 2019, https://www.technologyreview.com/2019/11/25/131837/champagne-shotguns-and-surveillance-at-spywares-grand-bazaar/.

29. O'Neill, "Champagne, Shotguns, and Surveillance."

Chapter 11

The Rise of Surveillance Capitalism

Although the power that states acquire over individuals through digital intrusions is especially consequential, corporate surveillance deepens inequalities in important ways given the scope of their capacities.[1] As noted at the outset of this book, digital technologies unleashed a form of capitalist accumulation unlike anything known before while impacting every part of society. Shoshana Zuboff argues that the companies involved in this new economy seek "instrumentarian" power—a power that seeks to replace society with certainty in a world of deeply diminished social trust. Although distinct from earlier totalitarian visions, since it does not rely on violence and has a different utopian understanding of the future, this instrumentarian power has a totalizing end, as it consumes information about everything and everyone. Machine-driven surveillance seeks to create increasingly perfect predictability and, consequently, increase control.

Machine-driven omniscience promises solutions to previously intractable problems as well. The most avid exponents of this new model believe that digital tools will dramatically reduce poverty and disease, promote equality and democracy, and expand the range of the possible in every domain. The same vision inspires advocates of new technological developments such as the metaverse. This promise suffuses the pronouncements of these entrepreneurs, and particularly the founders of Google and Facebook. This vision and its conjoined prospect of new and multiplying economic opportunities animates much of the rest of Silicon Valley and the tech industry.

Sergey Brin and Larry Page founded Google in 1998, initially using the information that the company had gleaned from searches on its site to improve its services. In a decision with enormous repercussions for humanity's future, the founders decided to make Google a free service, in part to eliminate financial barriers to access. This required that they find a different path to profitability. Advertising offered a perfect solution, promising, moreover, to generate profits that an ad-free paid service could never match. Google's market advantage over nondigital ad companies rested on its ability to monetize the personal information that the company could glean from search activities conducted on its website. This enabled the company to offer advertisers the ability to target ads more precisely than ever before.

Amit Patel, one of Google's engineers, earned a place in the pantheon of those who have done most to destroy privacy during the digital age when he identified the enormous value of the "digital exhaust" that each search generated. This exhaust included the search terms that were used, keystroke information, time spent on the search, and other apparent trivialities. However, this exhaust became the fuel of Google's success, since it contained vast amounts of individual data which could be mined and sold to advertisers. So, in order to offer a free service, Google became an advertising company. As Shoshana Zuboff writes,

> Google would no longer mine behavioral data strictly to improve service for users but rather to read users' minds for the purposes of matching ads to their interests, as those interests are deduced from the collateral traces of online behavior. With Google's unique access to behavioral data, it would now be possible to know what a particular individual in a particular time and place was thinking, feeling, and doing.[2]

This model, as computer scientist Jaron Lanier observes in his many public talks, inevitably led to the embrace of surveillance and collection. For her part, Shoshana Zuboff writes that

> Surveillance capitalism commandeered the wonders of the digital world to meet our needs for effective life, promising the magic of unlimited information and a thousand ways to anticipate our needs and ease the complexities of our harried lives. . . . Under this new regime, the precise moment at which our needs are met is also the precise moment at which our lives are plundered for behavioral data, and all for the sake of others' gain.[3]

The founders and executives of Google, perhaps feeling a bit queasy about a business model based on the appropriation of the personal and the private for profit, turned to doublespeak to disguise the company's activities. Indeed, just like the US government, the company used obfuscating terms to minimize the extent of its operations. As Shoshana Zuboff writes, "Google has been careful to camouflage the significance of its behavioral surplus operations in industry jargon. Two popular terms—'digital exhaust' and 'digital breadcrumbs'—connote worthless waste: leftovers lying around for taking. . . . The word 'targeted' is another euphemism. It evokes notions of precision, efficiency, and competence. Who would guess that targeting conceals a new political equation in which Google's concentrations of computational power brush aside users' decision rights as easily as King Kong might shoo away an ant, all accomplished offstage where no one can see?"[4]

Ironically, given the ultimately disempowering consequences of this model, the decision to provide a free service came at least in part from an egalitarian impulse: a free platform would make Google much more generally available, expanding access to the Internet. This egalitarianism, however, had more of a libertarian than a leftist imprint. The founders of these digital companies had an ethos that celebrated individual choice and individualism. Their pursuit of universal access sought to advance typically libertarian ends and reflected free-market fundamentalism rather than more leftist ideas about socioeconomic equality and justice. Paradoxically, it was precisely the libertarian content of their egalitarianism, based on notions about the boundless human capacity for self-government and understandings about broader cognitive equality, that ultimately produced many of the most harmful impacts of their services.

Part of the impulse behind the decision to provide a free service came from the open-source movement, whose members believed it would empower ordinary individuals, reducing entrenched elite power. In the early days of the Internet, many saw free access as a revolutionary way to reduce the power inequalities embedded in widely disparate communicative and informational capacities. A free, open-source digital world promised to rupture elite control over information and communication.

Unfortunately, although not surprisingly, the greatest victims of this model were some of its imagined beneficiaries. For example, many of those who depended on copyright protection experienced a precipitous and extraordinarily rapid change in their circumstances. Musicians and many others who had been able to make a decent living during the analog age saw their sources of income disappear, and entire professions became immiserated or existentially threatened, such as print journalists. The creative destruction that free-market capitalists embrace and celebrate ended up destroying the economic well-being of people in many creative fields. More generally, the Brave New World of open access did not diminish inequality. It only made it more extreme, as the income premium on the possession of certain skills and education rose.

Several odd dichotomies emerged from this business model. As discussed previously, the users of the services were, in reality, not the actual clients of these companies; in fact, they were a product. Shoshana Zuboff objects to the use of the term *product*, writing that it is more precise to say that "we are the *objects* from which raw materials are extracted and expropriated for Google's [and Facebook's] prediction factories. Predictions about our behavior are

Google's [and Facebook's] products, and they are sold to its actual customers but not to us. *We are the means to others' ends.*"[5]

This argument captures the objectification of human beings embedded in Google and Facebook's business models and their treatment of people as sources of a monetizable raw material. And this raw material becomes a product after mining and processing before being sold to an advertiser. The sale of the personal information of users effectively transforms significant portions of their inner selves into a product. Moreover, this is done in ways that undermine real informed consent, given the extent of secrecy and the construction of terms and conditions that seek to obscure and not enlighten.

A particularly intrusive subset of surveillance capitalism revolves around what Augustine Fou calls "surveillance marketing," which he coined in response to a 2006 book written by Chris Anderson—*The Long Tail.*[6] Before its publication, Fou says, "digital media was primarily purchased from large sites that had large human audiences. *The Long Tail* promulgated the idea that collectively a large number of small sites could rival the scale of a small number of large sites." This approach rested on what Fou identified as three myths: The long tail, behavioral targeting, and hypertargeting. Specifically,

> The long tail of sites were all of those tiny, niche sites that had niche content that people would visit. The theory was that with adtech, marketers could reach any person at the right time with the right ad on any site. . . . The theory of behavioral targeting was that, if adtech could track what sites users visited, what pages they looked at, and even what content was on the page, they could figure out who the users were and what they wanted to buy, even if they never logged in or provided any personally identifiable information. . . . Finally, with all of this data collected about users, adtech promised marketers that they could hypertarget them—literally, the right ad to the right person, at the right time, on any site they happen to visit at the time.

Moreover, users paid for all of these things with their privacy.[7]

Beyond all of these problems, people receive no monetary compensation beyond the modest sum represented by a free service for the private information they relinquish. Phrased differently, users are mined for profit but receive no compensation for the essential information that they provide. As Jack Belkin argues,

> the digital age produces two crucial trends: the democratization of digital content and the increasing importance of digital content as a source of wealth and economic power. These trends quickly come into conflict. That conflict, and its consequences for freedom and speech, is the central problem of the digital age. . . . The very same features of the digital age that empower ordinary individuals

also lead businesses continually to expand markets for intellectual property and digital content.[8]

In his public talks, Jaron Lanier frequently uses the case of Google Translate to explain the uncompensated appropriations marking the practices of many digital platforms. Google scours the almost unlimited cache of data on the Internet for new phrases and words to be put into Google Translate. While this makes Google Translate a single, extraordinary compendium, the company's tool is not the source of the data that it uses. Instead, actual human beings who are not part of the company generate this data in their online activities and other communications but do not receive any money in exchange. Instead, Google accrues all the benefits. Lanier argues that the generators of information should receive compensation, even if only a few cents, each time the data they produce is used. Over time, this would create fair compensation for an appropriation while spreading the economic benefits of the platforms beyond their founders, stockholders, and employees to the actual providers of the raw material. This might partially reduce the unprecedented inequality accompanying the rise of the digital age.

The imperative for profound reform is revealed in the common characterization of the personal information of the users of these platforms as "the new oil." This is an especially apt characterization, since these companies are just as rapacious as the famous Seven Sisters that controlled the oil industry during much of the twentieth century. The consortium's business models included the payment of pittances to countries with exploitable oil reserves to maximize profitability. Eventually these countries used expropriation and nationalization to counter the practice; corrupt elites had permitted the appropriation of these natural resources with virtually no compensation.

But however miserable the compensation, the Seven Sisters had at least paid *something* for the resources they'd extracted. Facebook, Google, and others, in contrast, do not pay a cent for the data they harvest. Their entire model reflects the implicit assumption that personal information, their "new oil," is valueless to the users of their services—or of such little value that they will knowingly trade it for a "free service." But if the creators of these companies really believed this, why did they disguise what they were doing?

Users, for their part, lack the power of states and cannot reclaim ownership over their personal information or demand compensation commensurate with the value of the taking. Although the architects of the platforms may not have been able to foresee all the consequences of their business model, they clearly knew that they were engaging in a taking, itself a morally reprehensible act. They knew as well that they were commodifying human beings through the monetization of their private lives. And they knew that the continuing pursuit of their business model depended upon appropriating increasingly minute information about each of their users. In addition, the incentives embedded in this model encouraged the companies to use this information to engage in the behavioral manipulation of their users designed to increase time spent on their platforms.

The regulatory framework—or more accurately the absence of a regulatory framework—that allowed the development of this model came from a little-discussed 1997 Federal Trade Commission decision. Shoshana Zuboff writes about the meeting that preceded this decision in a 2020 opinion piece published in the *New York Times*:

> The debate on privacy and law at the Federal Trade Commission was unusually heated that day. Tech industry executives "argued that they were capable of regulating themselves and that government intervention would be costly and unproductive." Civil libertarians warned that the companies' data capabilities posed an "unprecedented threat to individual freedom." One observed, "We have to decide what human beings are in the electronic age. Are we just going to be chattel for commerce?" A commissioner asked, "Where should we draw the line?" . . . The line was never drawn, and the executives got their way. Twenty-three years later, the evidence is in. . . . The rise of surveillance capitalism over the last two decades went largely unchallenged. "Digital" was fast, we were told, and stragglers would be left behind. . . . [Many] of us rushed to follow the bustling White Rabbit down his tunnel into a promised digital Wonderland where, like Alice, we fell prey to delusion. In Wonderland, we celebrated the new services as free, but now we see that the surveillance capitalists behind those services regard us as a free commodity. . . . We barely questioned why our new TV or mattress had a privacy policy, but we've begun to understand that "privacy" policies are actually surveillance policies.[9]

In part, this FTC decision reflected the continuing political and ideational grip on the American polity of the Reagan administration long after its end. The Democratic Clinton administration, in power at the time of this decision, epitomized the worldview of the so-called "New Democrats" in the United States and the Blairites in Great Britain. During the 1990s, and throughout the first decades of the twenty-first century, much of the Democratic Party in the United States and the Labor Party in Britain moved to the right in response to the popularity of the Reagan and Thatcher administrations, abandoning many historical attachments to social welfare and extensive market regulation. For example, President Bill Clinton, in addition to shrinking the American social safety net through welfare reform and other measures, was almost as much of a free-market fundamentalist as his Republican predecessors, Ronald Reagan and George H. W. Bush. He was, in addition, just as attached as his Republican counterparts to the US private corporate sector and reluctant to do anything that might stifle technological innovation and capital accumulation.

The same rationales that informed the Clinton administration's reluctance to regulate the tech sector governed the behavior of the George W. Bush and Obama administrations that followed, despite their ideological differences on other matters.

GOOGLE/ALPHABET

Google's exalted sense of self and its worldview were revealed in its original motto "to organize the world's information and make it universally accessible and useful." This motto conveniently included the word *organize* but did not mention that the company intended to collect and mine the private data of its users. In a moment of candor, cofounder Larry Page observed of Google's market niche in 2001, "If we did have a category, it would be personal information. . . . The places you've seen. Communications . . . Sensors are really cheap . . . Storage is cheap. Cameras are cheap. People will generate enormous amounts of data. . . . Everything you've ever heard or seen or experienced will become searchable. Your whole life will be searchable."[10] Former Google executive Douglas Edwards recalls, "Larry opposed any path that would reveal our technological secrets or stir the privacy pot and endanger our ability to gather data."[11]

These statements reveal much about the attitudes of Google's founders. Their personal fortunes rested on their willingness to traffic in the personal information of their users. Whatever their other commitments, all were willing, as a result, to violate privacy. From the outset, Google and many of the so-called "interactive computer services" indicated an awareness that their operations could not withstand the light of day.

There were "reasons for concealment and obfuscation," Shoshana Zuboff writes. "Google policies had to enforce secrecy in order to protect operations that were designed to be undetectable because they took things from users without asking and employed those unilaterally claimed resources to work in the service of others' purposes."[12] It is especially troubling that none of these entrepreneurs and engineers evidently had moral qualms about commodifying millions of human beings.

Over time, Google perfected a practice that other digital companies would imitate. As the years passed, it acquired more and more start-ups and other digital entities, exercising dominance over a growing number of digital sectors. This was especially consequential in the first decades of the digital age. Early entrants into the market, like Google, Facebook, and Amazon, acquired especially extensive market control, given the particularly significant advantages of scale embedded in their hold over the personal data of billions of users. Even when competitors arise, these companies possess the resources to buy them out and to move laterally into other activities. The combination of vertical and horizontal integration ushered in a level of market concentration not seen since the latter decades of the nineteenth century and the beginning of the twentieth century. Users, for their part, were largely robbed of meaningful choice, despite bromides from the founders of these companies about their attachment to rights, making them virtual captives of these entities if they wished to use the Internet.

FACEBOOK/META

Facebook appeared in 2004, six years after the founding of Google. Initially the company was a social-networking site targeting university students. In 2007 the company opened its platform to everyone. Facebook followed Google, adopting a free service model. Also like Google, it generates revenue from the monetization of the private information of its users. In 2007, in a foretaste of things to come, the company introduced a tool called Beacon, which automatically shared user transactions on partner websites with the "friends" of users. Designed to drive traffic to these partner websites, Beacon marked Facebook's first foray into advertising. Moreover, in a telling sign of the company's longer-term intentions, users could not opt out of Beacon or have a say in who received these advertised posts.

After only a month, intense user backlash forced Facebook founder Mark Zuckerberg to turn Beacon into an opt-in program. Unfortunately, rather than abandoning this enterprise, the company decided that Beacon had failed because it had been too obvious. Facebook subsequently deployed more subtle and surreptitious tools, including mass surveillance, collection, data mining, and behavioral manipulation to accomplish Beacon's original ends. Rather than interpreting the backlash to Beacon as an indication of the importance of privacy to users, Zuckerberg and his engineers initiated a largely invisible and even more extensive effort to collect, mine, and monetize the data of those using their site.

In the spring of 2008, in an even more fateful decision for the privacy of Facebook's users, Zuckerberg hired Sheryl Sandberg, a Google executive, as Facebook's chief operating officer. Her hiring was a public relations coup, since feminist groups immediately lionized her, praising Zuckerberg for appointing a woman to such a prominent position. Sandberg, however, was an enthusiastic supporter of Google's data-collection and data-mining culture. During subsequent years she would oversee Facebook's transformation into an advertising juggernaut. As Shoshana Zuboff writes about the hiring of Sheryl Sandberg, the talented Sandberg became the "Typhoid Mary" of surveillance capitalism as she led Facebook's transformation from a social-networking site to an advertising behemoth. . . . Sandberg understood that Facebook's social graph represented an awe-inspiring source of behavioral surplus. . . . "We have better information than anyone else. We know gender, age, location, and it's real data as opposed to the stuff that other people infer," Sandberg said.[13]

Over the next decade, under Zuckerberg's and Sandberg's stewardship, a company that touted itself as a way for people to connect and deepen community was transformed into a global purveyor of a host of social and other pathologies. Facebook's design, as will be discussed later, ensured that the platform would become a cesspool of fake news, anger, hatred, political vitriol, propaganda, tribalism, polarization, and various forms of behavioral and other manipulations.

In an additional exercise in deceit, Zuckerberg assured users that the company was deeply committed to protecting privacy and as a result did not use "cookies" to track them on the site. And before people learned differently, many celebrated this commitment. However, in lieu of cookies, Facebook created "likes," designed to function exactly like cookies. The use of likes and the sharing of links enabled the tracking of users and the tailoring of their experience to drive "engagement." Algorithms drove users toward particular content and "news" and "information." The algorithms and likes steered people to others who shared their views, causing the harmful effects of confirmation bias to explode, while creating epistemic bubbles where oft-repeated anecdotes replaced empirical verification as a source of factual knowledge.

From the very outset, Zuckerberg described the company's goals using language that disguised the consequences of its business model. He proclaimed, for example, that Facebook intended to "connect humanity." This grandiloquent claim did not begin to capture and, in fact, disguised the true intent of the company—to become the largest advertising entity in human history. Even more deceptively, Zuckerberg insisted that "the future is private" at a time when his company was involved in a systematic effort to destroy the privacy of all of its users. As Shoshana Zuboff observes,

> Facebook would learn to track, scrape, store, and analyze [user profile information] to fabricate its own targeting algorithms, and like Google it would not restrict extraction operations to what people voluntarily shared with the company. Sandberg understood that through the artful manipulation of Facebook's culture of intimacy and sharing, it would be possible to use behavioral surplus not only to satisfy demand but also to *create* demand.[14]

All of this reveals the deeply deceptive and hypocritical nature of the platform. Facebook deliberately sought to encourage conversation, sharing, intimacy, self-revelation, and trust. It then exploited the especially extensive private information that intimacy and sharing produce. And just like Google, Facebook did not tell its users what it was doing, hiding its activities behind claims of trade secrecy, deliberate obfuscation, pious statements of intent, outright deceptions, and the systematic twisting of language.

AMAZON

Like his counterparts at Google and Facebook, Amazon founder Jeff Bezos issued messianic statements about the goals and purposes of his company in the years after its establishment. At one point, for example, he claimed that Amazon was dedicated to the "empowerment of the individual." However, Amazon treated its workforce, and especially its warehouse workers, in ways that directly belied this vision. In fact, much of Amazon's workforce received very low wages and worked in difficult conditions until widespread external pressures led to reforms.

Despite its historically predatory labor practices, Amazon possesses a much better reputation than Facebook, in particular, and enjoys high levels of consumer trust. However, its business model rests significantly on surveillance as well. Just like Google and Facebook, Amazon systematically commodifies the private information it collects from users. As Emily West writes,

> What about the affective aspects of Alexa, and Amazon more broadly, as a brand that consistently and cheerfully offers us surveillance as a service? . . . Amazon . . . has always been a brand with little explicit emotional content but a powerfully affective relation with its consumers, building trust and relationality with consumers through *interaction.* Fundamentally, Amazon offers to serve us by *knowing* us, including the domestic, private side of ourselves represented by our product searches, our purchases, the media we consume, and now with Alexa, what we say and how we say it. Alexa only deepens this relationship due to the affective nature of the human voice and the real-time experience of personalization in domestic space. In other words, Amazon's tools and techniques of surveillance create tremendous *intimacy* between consumer and brand—achieved through the sensations of being seen, heard, and known.[15]

The affective, ever-helpful components of this model caused people to accept and even welcome this surveillance. The use of a female human voice anthropomorphized Amazon's devices while softening their practice of surveillance. These digital domestic assistants created the same mixture of distance and familiarity characterizing the relationship between lord and servant in an earlier age. As Emily West writes,

Perhaps the closest equivalent we have to understanding the rise of digital assistants and their impacts on the subjectivities of those who use them is the history of domestic service. . . . Now that tech companies like Google and Amazon provide a digital version of personal assistants, the tension between personalized service and the loss of privacy, long a dilemma faced only by the upper and upper-middle classes, is being newly negotiated by people of modest or middle class means.[16]

This is very different from the kind of surveillance that Facebook conducts, which feels much more surreptitious and manipulative, despite the presence of terms and conditions. This may help to explain Amazon's genius: it surveils everything within its reach, but Alexa and its other tools soften the nature of the appropriation.

Moreover, Alexa is noncontroversial, like a good servant. Alexa does not seek to inflame political passions, does her best to answer questions honestly and factually, and does not stoke controversy. Alexa does not allow others to bully users, dox them, direct hate speech at them, or encourage tribalism. Like a good servant, Alexa is always there, awaiting commands, but never overstepping. However, unlike a good servant, Alexa lacks real discretion, understood as the ability to preserve confidences and secrets. Good servants exercise complete discretion. The classic reserve of the English butler and his categoric unwillingness to share the family's secrets make him a perfect archetype of the "good" servant. Living in the same abode, no matter how large and separated, requires the exercise of complete discretion, since proximity destroys privacy.

Alexa, however, does not keep the secrets of her users. Amazon knows them and uses them to advance its economic interests. Thus any user of these services should understand that the company does not exercise true discretion but is monetizing all the personal information that it appropriates. But many do not consider this problem and behave as if they had not placed a surveillance device in their home. "Amazon, personified as Alexa, creates an intimacy of familiarity," says West. "It's the brand that is part of everyday life. Amazon facilitates and encourages the experience of having one's self and one's needs seen by another, of being catered to. . . . At the same time, it normalizes surveillance by a corporate entity made warm and familiar through the persona of Alexa."[17]

TERMS AND CONDITIONS AND THE EXPLOITATION
OF AN OBSOLETE REGULATORY ENVIRONMENT

As noted before, users did not realize and, more importantly, were not told in a direct, clear, straightforward fashion that the price of "free" digital services was their private selves; any disclosure was made through notably opaque terms and conditions. And neither did users begin to think about the long-term implications of a model that enabled a few extraordinarily large and powerful corporate actors to amass the personal information of billions of people. Paradoxically, a free model designed to decrease informational inequality only produced even larger differentials between individuals and huge organizations—whether private corporations or states.

To quote Shoshana Zuboff again,

> The new harms we face entail challenges to the sanctity of the individual, and chief among these challenges I count the elemental rights that bear on individual sovereignty, including *the right to the future tense* and *the right to sanctuary.* Each of these rights invokes claims to individual agency and personal autonomy as essential prerequisites to freedom of will and to the very concept of democratic order. . . . Right now, however, the extreme asymmetries of knowledge and power that have accrued to surveillance capitalism abrogate these elemental rights as our lives are unilaterally rendered as data, expropriated, and repurposed in new forms of social control, all of it in the service of others' interests and in the absence of our awareness or means of combat.[18]

Life in the digital age includes a seemingly inescapable Faustian bargain: There is no way to receive any of the benefits of digital technologies without paying for them with a portion of the self. And this payment only grows with time, since continued online activity requires providing additional personal information while revealing even larger parts of the self. Furthermore, all efforts to avoid this bargain become increasingly futile in societies where credit-rating agencies, information-aggregating vendors, and a plethora of other companies are allowed to mine, share, and sell an individual's information.

All the digital platforms benefited from the passage of the Communications Decency Act of 1996. CDA's Section 230 states, "No provider or user of an interactive computer service shall be treated as the publisher or speaker of any information provided by another information content provider." This effectively exempts entities like Facebook from liability for the content posted on their platforms. As is true of the rest of the legal architecture governing the digital world, Section 230 became obsolete as soon as the ink on the bill was dry.

The drafters of this legislation in the mid-1990s had no way of predicting the growth and evolution of "interactive computer services"; the technologies that came to dominate the first decades of the twenty-first century didn't even exist when this legislation was drafted. Nobody drafting this legislation could have imagined that a "social-networking" company would, in just a few years, become the largest advertising company in human history while serving as the primary source of propaganda, misinformation, and various forms of manipulation throughout much of the world.

Section 230 of the CDA contributed as well to the development of an initially laissez-faire approach to content moderation on social media platforms and other interactive computer services. In part, this reflected Silicon Valley's widespread attachment to the US Constitution's First Amendment, although as private entities the First Amendment did not constrain their actions. The founders of these companies repeatedly proclaimed their attachment to American free-speech norms when resisting efforts to increase content moderation. Although their policing of the sites grew, causing much controversy as different groups and people complained about censorship, this content moderation did not end the ubiquity of fake narratives. Misinformation, rumors, and conspiratorial accounts routinely outran reasoned, empirically grounded arguments. Fake accounts, manufactured identities, and bots added velocity and vitriol to this process.

The first, largely uncontroversial efforts to police content targeted child pornography and animal cruelty. Hate speech proved harder to regulate and remains a particularly contentious issue. Intense value conflicts between free-speech purists and ideologically committed advocates on both the left and the right, who often intersect with identitarians of various stripes, make this type of content moderation especially acrimonious. A fraught and polemical discussion over "political correctness" only added to these conflicts. In this online environment and increasingly in the real world, common norms of politeness, kindness, and respect for others declined.

In addition to Section 230 protections, platforms use terms and conditions to create the legal facade of informed choice. Informed choice, however, especially in an ethical rather than a legal sense, requires the presence of enough information and transparency to permit a genuine decision. As a result, terms and conditions constitute a particularly problematic use of narrow legalism. Rather than being designed to protect users, terms and conditions are designed to obscure the actions and intentions of the company while simultaneously fulfilling the requirement of informed consent.

If they wished to protect users and provide genuine transparency about the impact of their operations on individual privacy, these companies might have included something like the following brief warning for users of their platforms in the United States:

In exchange for receiving this free service, you agree to let us collect, analyze, and sell the personal information that you provide or share. This includes anything you upload, including photographs, and everything you post or write. Supreme Court decisions establish that none of your activities on this platform receive Fourth Amendment protection. You are providing everything that you post or upload to us, a third party. As a result, according to the Supreme Court, you have surrendered a "reasonable expectation of privacy" and have made this information our effective property.

Even if such a warning had existed when these platforms were first adopted, individuals had few choices because the government's approach to antitrust regulation encouraged extreme market concentration. Moreover, even if one could find an alternative and stop using the largest platforms, most of the few alternatives required an equivalent "voluntary surrender" of personal information and cloaked their actions in similar terms and conditions. The fact that many sites sold users' personal information to other platforms made the avoidance of this appropriation even more difficult.

Terms and conditions, in fact, remain part of a larger business model that surreptitiously destroys individual decision-making capacity. As Shoshana Zuboff writes,

> Decision rights confer the power to choose whether to keep something secret or to share it. One can choose the degree of privacy or transparency for each situation. . . . Surveillance capitalism laid claim to these decision rights. The typical complaint is that privacy is eroded, but that is misleading. In the larger societal pattern, privacy is not eroded but redistributed, as decision rights over privacy are claimed for surveillance capital. Instead of many people having the right to decide how and what they will disclose, these rights are concentrated within the domain of surveillance capitalism.[19]

The systematic effort to elide transparency embodied in terms and conditions raises another question. Typically, the most dubious human enterprises employ deception or embrace obfuscation, since clarity and honesty undermine them. As a consequence, it seems clear that the founders of the largest tech enterprises, along with many of those who work for them, were not proud of the core, essential feature of these companies—the appropriation and exploitation of personal information for profit.

CORPORATE SURVEILLANCE AND WORKERS

Yet another form of private corporate digital surveillance merits particular mention. Digital tools enable companies to deploy a raft of surveillance tools to monitor worker productivity. As a result, people lose more and more privacy in their workplaces. During the COVID-19 pandemic, many companies, in an attempt to reduce congregate gatherings, encouraged their employees to work from home. The success of this effort led many companies to decide to continue portions of this practice even after public-health lockdowns had lifted and offices around the world reopened. While technology allows many employees to work from home, employers monitor their productivity, introducing yet another surveillance tool into the last semiprivate sanctuary recognized in law—one's house. Ifeoma Ajunwa writes, "Employers with an interest in monitoring worker productivity can request that employees install productivity applications on devices such as computers or mobile phones."[20]

Several start-ups, in common with other areas of the surveillance industrial complex, have emerged to provide these tools. The most widely used productivity tools at the moment are Avaza, Boomr, Hubstaff, TSheets, GPS Phone Tracker, TrackView, and Where's My Droid. Some of these productivity tools not only monitor location but also record activity, logging keystrokes and capturing screens. To quote Ifeoma Ajunwa further, "The twenty-first century has ushered in new technologies uniquely designed to attend to employers' interests in profit-maximization, but those new technologies also bring with them new concerns about employee privacy. . . . The introduction of productivity applications and wearable technology in the workplace will create more opportunities to capture employee data."[21]

CONCLUSION

Fatefully, not long after its founding, Google decided to offer a "free" service to expand access and use while earning revenues through the collection, mining, and eventual sale of the information of its users to advertisers. This created the basis of the economic paradigm governing the first decades of the digital age—a paradigm that Shoshana Zuboff terms "surveillance capitalism." Other companies, especially Facebook, copied this feature of Google's model, creating a world in which the price of an ostensibly free good was personal, formerly private information.

Restrictions on the sale of this data were modest in the United States, reflecting the government's generally laissez-faire approach to digital regulation. The US government focused instead on preserving its ability to surveil online activities. In the absence of regulatory restraints, the sale and sharing of data exploded. Unsurprisingly, companies emerged to gather and sell data in every imaginable domain. Cuebiq, a company that gathers and analyzes location data for advertisers, provides a notable and representative example of these practices. As Jennifer Valentino-DeVries reports for the *New York Times*,

> Although the data excludes names, phone numbers, and other identifying information, even anonymous information can be revealing. The *Times* has reported on the intrusiveness of such data, which can show intimate details like trips to doctor's offices and outings with romantic partners. . . . Hackers or people with access to raw location data could identify or follow a person without consent, by pinpointing, for example, which phone spent time at that person's home address. . . . Location data on individuals is used for purposes like marketing and analysis for hedge funds and law enforcement. There is no federal law in the United States that limits the use of location data in this way, although some have been proposed.[22]

The absence of regulation has made personal data available to an enormous number of actors, including many with malevolent intent. Everybody from identity thieves and other black-hat hackers to credit-rating agencies, other private corporations, and governments can gain access to this information. Data gathered for one purpose becomes available for another, enabling more and more actors to use this information for profit or the monitoring of individual behavior.

Inequality grew as well. As many observe, the individual users of digital technologies, whose information, knowledge, and talents are the source of the profits for interactive computer services, never receive any real compensation. So some grow fabulously rich off this data while those who provide it receive nothing except for access to a free service. While many factors explain the unprecedented inequality marking the end of the twentieth and the first part of the twenty-first centuries, these digital practices have made matters worse.

Even though 9/11 accelerated the rush of states to know all and see all so they could control all, Google and Facebook's business models and those of the multitude of companies that adopted this same approach created a new gold rush—the drive to appropriate as much private information from as many people as possible—and to mine, manipulate, sell, and otherwise monetize this information. Given the extent of loneliness, alienation, and unhappiness, people rushed to social media platforms in search of connection and community.

Even though the digital age did not create these problems, it did not alleviate them as its devoted acolytes had promised but only made them worse, as many studies document. Isolation and alienation had become omnipresent during the industrial age as traditional meanings and social relations cemented in culture and custom eroded under the impact of industrialization, urbanization, mobility, and other modern forces. The founders of the social media companies, and especially Mark Zuckerberg of Facebook, promised that their platforms would provide the human connection lost during the headlong rush to modernity. However, none of the advocates of the Brave New Digital World advertised their intention to capture all of the attention of their users, atomizing them behind screens. Moreover, very few people understood that parts of themselves paid for the "freeness" of social media activity, online searches, and other novel conveniences.

The continual and, in many cases, obsessive use of social media reveals the persistence of solitude and loneliness and the profundity of the desire to connect with others, while the countless hours spent online undermine face-to-face interactions. People spend more time "connecting," even as they spend more time alone. As a result, digital connections and the nature of online interactions reinforce feelings of solitude, sadness, and depression while they deepen social and political divisions, shattering communities.

Awareness of these problems only emerged slowly and belatedly, but eventually became widespread, especially in Europe and North America. Unfortunately, by the time understanding dawned of the exchange of the self for the use of these platforms, these tools had become embedded into daily life and seemed indispensable. As a result, use did not decline in proportion to growing awareness, and neither did the sharing of personal information; but this awareness did create a constituency for future reforms.

NOTES

1. The term *surveillance capitalism*, as used in this chapter's title, was coined by Shoshana Zuboff. See Shoshana Zuboff, *Age of Surveillance Capitalism: The Fight for a Human Future at the New Frontier of Power* (New York: PublicAffairs, 2019).

2. Zuboff, *Age of Surveillance Capitalism*, 78.

3. Zuboff, *Age of Surveillance Capitalism*, 53.

4. Zuboff, *Age of Surveillance Capitalism*, 90.

5. Zuboff, *Age of Surveillance Capitalism*, 94, emphases original.

6. Chris Anderson, *The Long Tail: Why the Future of Business Selling Less of More* (New York: Hyperion, 2006).

7. All quotations in this discussion of surveillance capitalism are drawn from Augustine Fou, "What Is 'Surveillance Capitalism?' And How Did It Hijack the Internet?" *Linux Journal*, February 6, 2019, https://www.linuxjournal.com/content/what-surveillance-capitalism-and-how-did-it-hijack-internet.

8. Jack Belkin, "Digital Speech and Democratic Culture: A Theory of Freedom of Expression for the Information Society," in *Information Ethics: Privacy, Property and Power*, ed. Adam Moore (Seattle: University of Washington Press, 2005), 307–8.

9. Shoshana Zuboff, "Opinion: You Are Now Remotely Controlled," *New York Times*, January 24, 2020, https://www.nytimes.com/2020/01/24/opinion/sunday/surveillance-capitalism.html.

10. Larry Page as quoted in Douglas Edwards, *I'm Feeling Lucky* (Boston: Houghton, Mifflin, Harcourt, 2011), 291.

11. Douglas Edwards as quoted in Zuboff, *Age of Surveillance Capitalism*, 89.

12. Zuboff, *Age of Surveillance Capitalism*, 89.

13. Sheryl Sandberg as quoted in Zuboff, *Age of Surveillance Capitalism*, 92.

14. Zuboff, *Age of Surveillance Capitalism*, 92, emphasis original.

15. Emily West, "Amazon Surveillance as a Service," *Surveillance and Society* 17, no. 1/2 (2019): 31, https://ojs.library.queensu.ca/index.php/surveillance-and-society/article/view/13008/8472.

16. West, "Amazon Surveillance as a Service," 31.

17. West, "Amazon Surveillance as a Service," 32.

18. Zuboff, *Age of Surveillance Capitalism*, 54–55, emphases original.

19. Zuboff, *Age of Surveillance Capitalism*, 90.

20. Ifeoma Ajunwa, "Algorithms at Work: Productivity Monitoring Applications and Wearable Technology as the New Data-Centric Research Agenda for Employment and Labor Law," *St. Louis University Law Journal* 63, no. 21 (2018): 23.

21. Ajunwa, "Algorithms at Work," 23, and quotation at 53.

22. Jennifer Valentino-DeVries, "How Your Phone Is Used to Track You, and What You Can Do About It," *New York Times*, August 19, 2020, https://www.nytimes.com/2020/08/19/technology/smartphone-location-tracking-opt-out.html.

Chapter 12

Conspiracy Theories and Other Impacts of Social Media Platforms

The tracking of people's behavior to increase "engagement" enables the formation of hermetic online communities. These closed epistemic bubbles ultimately diminish even a minimal social consensus over facts. Increasingly people cannot agree on the most basic information or standards of evidence. This extreme epistemic balkanization further erases the line between fact and opinion—the inevitable result of a society that has lost common understandings about ways of knowing. Increasingly people inhabit informational and perceptual realities confined to those who share their views and "factual" understandings. In an environment that undermines empirical verification and rejects rationality and reason, conspiracy theories flourish. Those inclined to conspiratorial thinking can easily find each other and engage in mutual validation. And the algorithms on Facebook and other platforms drive millions of people with this proclivity toward one another. All of this fractures society, increases political polarization, and creates a form of epistemic madness, given the depth of the collective paranoia informing these conspiracy theories.

The digital age, whatever the promises of tech company founders and promoters, accelerated the decline of social trust in many countries. Social trust reflects the confidence that people feel in members of the society beyond friends, family, and others who are personally known. Social trust binds communities together, facilitates collective action, and diminishes polarization. If social trust was already fraying in many polities before the dawn of the digital age, the introduction of these new technologies has only made things worse.

The United States, given the extent of its diminished social trust and its early and widespread exposure to social media platforms during the first part of the twenty-first century, vividly exhibits these problems. Social media platforms and entities like YouTube (another Google acquisition) and TikTok facilitate the spread of conspiratorial thinking evident throughout the country's history. Perceptual gaps have become unbridgeable, while objective events and pieces of data are interpreted in mutually unintelligible ways. Dialogue and persuasion continue to diminish, and feelings of discomfort after encounters with ideological opponents prompt many to retreat further into their tribes. And because these differences are anchored in real, indeed fundamental, value conflicts, they cannot be reconciled.

Societies always depend upon the preservation of certain norms of discourse, including the minimal collective exercise of politeness, civility, and reticence. When these practices diminish, and eventually disappear, as they have in an increasing number of public fora in the United States, animosity begins to cleave the society and the polity. Unmediated expressions, often in the most vile and accusatory ways, sunder cooperation and compromise. This problem became especially pronounced on the online world and then, inevitably, migrated into "real life" behaviors. The stentorian ventilation of differences includes the deployment of epithets, stereotypes, and other attacks in the effort to negate the legitimacy of dissenting perspectives. Self-righteousness and moral and factual certainty saturate this rhetoric (or invective) as well, adding another notably dogmatic flavor to much of this discourse. Although these issues predated the digital age, its technologies, and especially the social media platforms, give a megaphone to the most committed and frequently most extreme purveyors of these perspectives, adding volume and velocity to invective.

Before the digital age, the press in the United States, and especially the printed press, whatever its limitations, played a central role in helping to create a basic consensus over empirical information. Outside of the "yellow press," editors and journalists acted as curators, verifying facts and narratives before publishing stories. While ideological differences animated editorial and opinion pieces, standards of verification governed the evaluation of news stories. On the other hand, common narratives dominated large parts of this news landscape, most evident in the nightly news shows on television networks. Unsurprisingly, conventional, mainstream views prevailed in this environment, drowning out dissident and novel perspectives. This produced the tendency toward conformity, conventionality, and sameness that John Stuart Mill decried in *On Liberty*.

Even so, the press's curation of news and verification of facts diminished the spread of manifest falsehoods and outright propaganda. In addition, at their very best, journalists, editors, and publishers act as a check on the powerful and expose malfeasance and injustice while facilitating informed discourse. For all these reasons, the press, along with the educational system, play an important role in the construction of civic virtue—a critical feature of a vibrant and functioning democracy. An informed citizenry constitutes the essential core of civic virtue. Preserving, let alone constructing, civic virtue becomes increasingly difficult with the decline of the press as an authoritative source of factual knowledge, especially in a country where strong civic education does not provide a counterweight to tidal waves of misinformation circulating on widely used digital platforms.

The Internet makes it harder for many to discern reliable information, especially in an environment where a profusion of sources push contending narratives. The enormous volume of false, manufactured, and manipulated information on the Internet deepens this problem. In the absence of gatekeepers, ordinary people suddenly must become curators. Not surprisingly, they often fail to adequately perform this task.

Even as the digital world equalizes access to "raw" information, it demands much of its users—perhaps too much. People have to accurately verify and interpret facts, data, and different narratives while lacking the contextual knowledge and background to perform these tasks. Since they cannot do this, they fall back onto the roadmap most closely conforming to their beliefs, biases, prejudices, and assumptions. They then seek out others who hold the same views, finding validation and verification in reiteration. Digital platforms, for all these reasons, promote what Mill most feared—atavistic group emotions anchored in ignorance, prejudice, and bias.

Thus technologies that promised enlightenment, a broadening of human horizons, and connection to others instead helped to fuel ferocious tribalism. The explosion of access to information on social media platforms neither broadens many minds nor increases the tolerance for difference but rather leads to a commonplace retreat into hermetic, self-reinforcing narratives. Fellow travelers constitute the source of knowledge and information while the repetition of anecdotes and "data" establishes the manifest, indeed categoric, truth of shared "factual" and ideological understandings. Although others promote this phenomenon, Facebook stood out in this area given its especially relentless efforts to drive people into these epistemic bubbles to produce greater "engagement" with its platform. This practice inevitably undermined and prevented the connection and community that Facebook founder Mark Zuckerberg repeatedly insisted he desired.

Around the world, politicians exploit the surveillance and tracking features of the platforms to activate and connect their followers. These same features enable demagogues. charlatans, and malign actors of every type to use social media platforms and several other interactive computer services to whip up grievances and resentments. Indeed, Jair Bolsonaro of Brazil, Rodrigo Duterte of the Philippines, and former US president Donald Trump revealed the power of social networks to galvanize the very worst in people. Rather than promoting greater trust, these platforms are more likely to foster the psychology of an aroused mob. Indeed, the design of the social media networks ensures the prominence of the most intense group sentiments while elevating their most virulent expression.

The attachments within these epistemic bubbles are necessarily parochial. While these connections created a sense of belonging and attachment to others in the group, and to those perceived as allies, they prevent the recognition of those on the outside of these circles, who are frequently the objects of obloquy precisely because they are an easily vilified other. This produces a wider social solitude derived from the inability to recognize this "other," fatally undermining a broader sense of community. Charles Taylor brilliantly analyzes this phenomenon in his discussion of the relationship between French-speaking and English-speaking Canadians and between them and the country's other "Founding Society"—aboriginal Canadians.[1]

This reality suffuses social media platforms. Many groups on these platforms engage in an affirmation and a negation, and it is this dialectic that binds their members together while making each group hermetic. The affirmation celebrates the group, its allies, and its ideology, while the negation excoriates outsiders and their views. This process of identity formation deepens "we" feelings anchored in various acquired and ascriptive elements including race, language, culture, religion, gender, sexual preference, and ideological persuasion. The celebration of the self and of the group is often accompanied by denigration of outsiders and the proliferation of stereotypes, labels, and generalizations about them, undermining the possibility of mutual recognition. The inability to truly connect with those outside one's group, to transcend one's epistemic bubble or identitarian and ideological frame, diminishes broader feelings of empathy and common humanity. And it is this inability to connect to a larger whole that constitutes the essence of this type of solitude.

The ever-sharper drawing of lines between groups naturally encourages the assumption that the worst of motives animate others and that these others share undesirable and even despicable traits, attitudes, and perspectives. Expecting insult and injury, people hear attacks where none are intended and take profound offense. This makes interactions more fraught and volatile. In this environment, the best protection is silence, since any utterance may occasion conflict. As people retreat into their epistemic bubbles and surround themselves with fellow travelers, ferocious defensiveness and hermeticism grow along with moral certainty and self-righteousness. And as has always been true, moral certainty and self-righteousness produce missionary proclivities, manifested in the pursuit of efforts to spread and materialize the group's self-evident and categorical truth while excommunicating those who might have the temerity to ask questions or request evidence, let alone resist conversion.

Many of the most avid and frequent user-consumers of these services understood their impacts least and were most subject to manipulation. Especially in the early decades of the twenty-first century, few understood that the service they were using contained algorithms designed to identify and exploit their emotions, especially their fear and anger, given the power of the most intensely limbic sentiments. Those most apt to seek greater connection and convenience or who are subject to the greatest angers, resentments, and fears are the easiest to exploit, although everyone can fall prey to the designers of these algorithms and the expanding capacities embedded in machine learning and AI.

Through the repeated use of these platforms, users become adept at navigating them while remaining ill-informed about their operations or their implications. Many people become ever more skilled at posting and uploading and producing a torrent of memes and videos while simultaneously thinking less and less about the veracity of what they are seeing and hearing, accepting it as self-evident. Those immersed in these tribes accept as categoric truths the underlying assumptions and assertions behind the information that they share. This leads them to reject requests for systematic, factually verified evidence that substantiates their views, seeing such requests as indicative of the worst types of bias and bad intentions. Disconfirming evidence or contrary perspectives are rejected even more ferociously. The psychological satisfaction of being in communion with others who share a point of view, a communion that feelings of superior virtue and moral certainty reinforce, overwhelms concerns about the implicit bargain involved in the use of these platforms. Worries about the amount of information being surrendered to companies (and, by extension, to governments) shrink with every click and keystroke. This declining awareness cannot match the satisfactions, present in groups on both the left and the right, that they are warriors for the categoric truths that they advance and consequently for their vision of justice.

A deep belief in the cognitive equality of ideas and opinions creates a citizenry in the United States that is, contradictorily, more skeptical but simultaneously more subject to behavioral manipulation, since their skepticism frequently rests on anger, scorn, and even hatred of others. In fact, this skepticism is not the fruit of the difficult encounter with compelling disconfirming information but a product of outrage about various matters.

A fideistic understanding of the world expands. *Fideism*, to use Antonio Gramsci's famous term, involves the reification of faith, of what one believes in the belly and the heart, with the simultaneous diminishment of the importance of rigorous empirical verification. Fideism impedes the acceptance of anything that contradicts what is already believed. The social media platforms, since they are based on the reinforcement of confirmation bias, increase fideism, encouraging a disdain for, or disinterest in, empirical evidence or the dispassionate and ecumenical pursuit of knowledge. Shared beliefs and understandings about the world matter more than anything else, and the belief that one has arrived at a moral truth erases interest in or openness to other views and evidence. Categories of believers form, with labels for themselves and others, and sometimes split into subcategories with new labels for themselves and others. In this environment, the concern with proper labels and terms for the self and for each group transforms labeling into an obsessive exercise.

The social media companies' incapacity to address the social and political consequences of their business models only exceeds their enormous technical and behavioral-manipulation skills. Charitably one might imagine that, at least in the early years, naivete about the human capacity to engage in malevolent behavior led them toward unintentionally problematic product design. However, the fact that their algorithms were deliberately designed to exploit the most volatile human emotions fundamentally mutes this charitable interpretation.

Moreover, as evidence grew that these platforms were amplifying the worst in humans, they did little to change their business models. In fact, they doubled down on behavioral manipulation. Facebook in particular proved extraordinarily adept at using the information derived from its tracking and surveillance on its various platforms to drive its users toward desired behavioral outcomes, ensuring that they spent more and more waking hours on the platform.

As a sign of its continuing commitment to this business model, in fact, in early 2022 Facebook warned that it would have to leave the European Union after EU officials determined that EU privacy protections and the GDPR were violated by Facebook's storing—and sharing—of European users' information in the United States, given that US surveillance laws did not protect the privacy of foreigners, including Europeans. In effect, in issuing this threat, Facebook revealed that the preservation of the ways it harvested, stored, and used the personal information of its users was more important than access to the European market.

More generally, Facebook's problems on this score reflected the debility of US privacy protections and the expansiveness of its surveillance regime. Most seriously for Europeans and other "non-US persons," the regulations governing US surveillance practices reject the notion that foreigners haveany right to privacy. The US government insists on preserving its ability to surveil Europeans, among others, even though international law and the GDPR enshrine privacy as a fundamental human right. In response to Facebook's warning, several European leaders expressed their joy at the prospect of its departure.[2]

SOCIAL MEDIA, THE QANON CONSPIRACY THEORY, AND THE SPREAD OF MISINFORMATION ABOUT THE COVID-19 PANDEMIC

As noted at the outset of this chapter, the design of social media platforms, and entities like YouTube and TikTok, are uniquely capable of spreading conspiracy theories. A vast number of users find solace in stories and assertions that make the unknown intelligible. Sometimes, in the case of many conspiracy theories, the fantastical and the rococo prevail over the commonsensical, and elaborate paranoid explanations take flight. The feeling of satisfaction and virtue derived from knowing something hidden that the less enlightened do not understand in part explains the embrace of the fantastical. In the last few years the most well-known, although certainly not the only, of these conspiracy theories has been QAnon.

QAnoners believed that a cabal of Satan-worshiping pedophiles and organ harvesters including Hillary Clinton, the "deep state," and "liberal elite" and Hollywood were waging war on Donald Trump and his virtuous, God-loving supporters while violating the Constitution. QAnoners feverishly read the pronouncements of an anonymous self-professed high-level government official who called himself "Q" and claimed to be helping Donald Trump fight the deep state. For all these people who believed, Q was a modern digital prophet, unseen and unknown but omniscient.[3] And Donald Trump, they felt, was the modern American political equivalent of a biblical figure, fighting to save the virtuous from the evil left. Over time, the QAnon conspiracy theory spread across the Internet like a wildfire.

QAnon found particular support among evangelicals, perhaps because of their already strong preexisting attachment to fideistic understandings of the world conjoined with the extent of their support for Donald Trump. In June 2021 the election for the new leader of the Southern Baptist Convention revealed the appeal of QAnon views within this enormous evangelical organization. Although the membership elected Ed Litton, his denunciation of QAnon ignited an intense and widespread conflict between QAnoners and others within the organization. And polling in 2021 showed that 27 percent of the broader community of evangelicals, a category that includes the Southern Baptists, believed in the conspiracy theory.[4]

From the outset, QAnoners repeatedly and vividly demonstrated the resistance of conspiracy theories to disconfirming information and the extent of the hermeticism characterizing the ideational bubbles on the Internet. A common claim among QAnoners in the lead-up to the 2016 US presidential elections was that Comet Ping Pong, a pizza parlor in Washington, D.C., was the center of a child-exploitation ring run by Hillary Clinton. Religious zealot and dedicated QAnoner Edgar Welch traveled to Comet Ping Pong from North Carolina in December 2016 with an assault rifle and other weapons to "liberate the children." After terrifying the patrons of the restaurant, including families with children, Edgar Welch fired two shots at a lock on the only closed door in the space. QAnoners had claimed that the restaurant's basement held trafficked children. But after blowing off the lock, Edgar Welch found a utility closet. There was no basement, and there were no children being held in captivity. After he was arrested, Welch said that "the intel on this was not 100 percent," even then failing to acknowledge the mendacity of Q's claims. The zealot was sentenced to four years in prison, while despite "Pizzagate," QAnoners' conspiracies continued to spread.

When it was shown that a claim was questionable, as occurred after revelations surfaced that Ron Watkins, the administrator of the 8kun messaging board, was probably Q and not a high-level official who was privy to the secrets of the "deep state," QAnoners did not stop believing in the conspiracy theory or abandon their key understandings. All of this reveals an additional feature of conspiracy theories: their protean, shifting, and amorphous nature and their ability to skirt, ignore, or rationalize disconfirming evidence.

In part, the spread of QAnon comes from the sharing of links, a natural outgrowth of the kind of groups promoted by Facebook's design. Sharing of links meant that QAnon ideas inevitably penetrated seemingly unrelated groups, since users and bots frequently have cross-group affiliations. As a result, these ideas become discussion topics in groups on child rearing, mothering, health care, yoga groups, and men's issues. Seeming distance from fevered obsessions about Satan worshipping and pedophilia did not prevent the spread of this miasma. This, of course, makes it very hard to identify and circumscribe these theories once they have been dispersed. The number of Facebook accounts attributable to QAnon, and not including the groups noted above, eventually numbered in the tens of thousands, as did their presence on other social media sites like Instagram.

QAnon conspiracy theories continued to spread in 2020 after the outbreak of the COVID-19 pandemic. QAnoners claimed that the Satan-worshiping cabal, and especially the deep state, had created the COVID-19 pandemic, spreading the virus through 5G technology with the goal of undermining Donald Trump's valiant battle to protect children and families.

Throughout that year, conspiracy theories attached themselves as well to the measures that public-health authorities and other experts recommended to reduce transmission of the virus. These conspiracy theories led to protests in many American cities and towns. Vilified were both Microsoft founder Bill Gates and the director of the National Institute of Allergy and Infectious Diseases Dr. Anthony Fauci, the country's most visible public-health figure.

Rumors spread, in particular, that Gates had created the virus to profit from the eventual development and sale of vaccines.

During this period, QAnoners, who now numbered in the millions, embraced another outlandish theory, now blaming the US Democratic Party for intentionally causing the pandemic. This line of "thinking" claimed that the Democrats had either created the pandemic or had magnified it and exaggerated its impact to damage Donald Trump's reelection prospects. The "mainstream media" was a coconspirator, believers said, advancing lies about the dangers of the pandemic. Others extended these claims, asserting that COVID-19 did not exist at all and was just a hoax, used as a Democratic public-relations campaign.

Social media platforms facilitated the spread of additional and false public-health information, although they were not the only mechanisms used to transmit the misinformation. False claims spread online about the efficacy of hydroxychloroquine to treat COVID-19, despite the drug's occasionally serious side effects and the absence of clinical evidence that it worked. The persistent claims about the efficacy of the drug primarily came from Donald Trump and Jair Bolsonaro, as well as from some fringe members of the medical community. Hydroxychloroquine, an effective antimalarial, became unavailable as demand skyrocketed. This had terrible consequences for lupus sufferers, who rely on hydroxychloroquine for effective treatment. Subsequently, social media users spread the claim that antiparasitic medication Ivermectin, which has veterinary uses, was an effective treatment for COVID-19. Even though the claims were strongly rejected by Merck, Ivermectin's manufacturer, runs on supplies of the drug continued.

These social media platforms played a key role as well in enabling the organization of protests against public-health lockdown measures—the most dramatic being the occupation of the Michigan state house by armed Trump supporters. The social media companies then became part of the remarkably politicized debate that roiled in the United States over the wearing of face masks. These platforms amplified and spread the Trump administration's many and repeated public pronouncements decrying and criticizing many of the health-care responses to the pandemic, including those of his own administration's experts. For example, on April 20, 2020, on the right-wing *Hugh Hewitt Show*, Trump's attorney general William Barr said, "There are unprecedented burdens on civil liberties right now. The idea that you have to stay in your house is disturbingly close to house arrest." Social media users picked up this inflammatory statement and repeated it. Barr thus joined others on the right calling for an end to public-health measures during the pandemic on the grounds that they either violated or came close to violating constitutional rights. Those against mask wearing typically advanced similar claims, asserting that the required use of masks violated their constitutional rights. Some insisted as well that masks in and of themselves spread the disease.

Regional differences influenced the willingness of people to accept conspiratorial explanations about the pandemic. COVID-19 originally impacted the Northeast, the upper Midwest, and the West Coast of the United States, leaving many other parts of the country essentially untouched. The lack of visible effects of the pandemic in these places, including personal exposure to sick people, conjoined with the economic impact of lockdowns, naturally created a tendency among the conspiratorially inclined to view it as a manufactured crisis. And since the pandemic occurred during a presidential-election year, it seemed equally feasible to assume for those with these inclinations that the pandemic had emerged for political reasons. Particularly in many rural areas, where distrust of government is especially widespread, cases were rare in the first few months—except for those places that contained meatpacking plants, many of which experienced serious outbreaks. Unsurprisingly, rural areas proved most resistant to public health-care measures. In addition, rural areas and rural states contained disproportionately large white evangelical populations and tended to be redoubts of support for Donald Trump.

In addition, a raft of pro-Trump voices on Fox News and other conservative outlets including talk radio advanced many of these conspiratorial claims, adding to the seeming veracity of views circulating on social media. And finally, extraordinarily confused and contradictory messaging from public-health authorities in the early months of the pandemic undermined faith in expert opinion. At first these public-health authorities strongly discouraged mask use, only recommending social distancing and handwashing, while insisting that anything other than medical-grade masks were useless and consequently dangerous. Simultaneously, because of supply shortages, access to medical-grade masks had to be reserved for health-care personnel and first responders. Not many weeks after, however, the first part of this message flipped, and everyone was being urged to make or buy a mask, except for medical-grade ones, of course. Masks consequently became the fundamental symbol of the pandemic—whose use signified political predilections and belief in the authority of experts.

Conspiratorial thinking about the pandemic in late 2020 and 2021 turned to the use of vaccines, especially in the United States. "Anti-vaxxers" used the social media platforms to spread claims that the vaccines developed against the COVID-19 virus produced a raft of dangerous health and other effects. For example, a particularly extreme QAnon variant of the anti-vax movement even asserted that the vaccines were designed to implant chips in people so that the government could control them.

The ubiquity and spread of misinformation and conspiratorial claims about the vaccines on social media and other platforms helped slow immunization to a crawl by the middle of 2021. Even as a Delta variant of the virus emerged that was much more contagious, more than 40 percent of the US population remained unvaccinated. Unsurprisingly, case counts, hospitalizations, and deaths, which had declined in the late spring, began to climb again in the middle of 2021. The even more infectious but fortunately less lethal Omicron variant that emerged at the end of 2021 only managed to raise vaccination rates by a few percentage points, to barely over 64 percent, even though well over two thousand Americans continued to die daily in the first couple of months of 2022. And though the number of Americans who had died from COVID-19 surpassed one million by the middle of 2022, only one hundred million people had taken advantage of the recommended and free booster shots.

A small group of anti-vaxxers were the source of much of this misinformation. Robert Kennedy Jr., son of the former attorney general and presidential candidate, was an especially well-known member of this group. This eventually forced Facebook/Meta to close his Instagram account, although the company only did this after facing a torrent of criticism about its failure to address the falsehoods about the vaccine circulating on its platforms.

Regional differences continued. Rural America and especially the Southern states and portions of the Mountain West and the Plains, whose low case counts and right-wing political predilections led them to question the existence of the pandemic in early 2020, now became the epicenter of vaccine resistance, given the reach of QAnon ideas in these parts of the country. The South and the more rural states consequently became the locus of the lowest rates of inoculation and the most rapidly rising case counts and subsequent hospitalizations and deaths.

The resistance in these areas to vaccination and to other public-health measures reflects deeper attitudes about the relationship between individuals and the state. Throughout the pandemic, fears of government and distrust in its motives and truthfulness were repeatedly voiced. As proclaimed a representative placard at one of the countless demonstrations against public-health measures, "I fear the government more than COVID-19." The sense of vulnerability and attitudes toward the state created a fertile breeding ground for conspiracy theories. As Karen Douglas, Robbie Sutton, and Aleksandra Cichocka observe,

> Studies have shown that people are likely to turn to conspiracy theories when they are anxious and feel powerless. Other research indicates that conspiracy belief is strongly related to lack of sociopolitical control or lack of psychological empowerment. Experiments have shown that, compared with baseline conditions, conspiracy belief is heightened when people feel unable to control outcomes and is reduced when their sense of control is affirmed.[5]

Additionally, repeated revelations over the decades of injurious government actions in a range of areas fuel skepticism about the state and the elite while making many people feel small, voiceless, and inconsequential. The extent of government secrecy and a popular culture that portrays the extent of the state's capacity for violence and its ability to penetrate the lives of individuals only intensifies the distrust that fosters conspiracy thinking. Ultimately, the panopticon cannot escape its internal contradictions: the government's insistence on seeing all and knowing all while remaining impenetrable to its citizens leads just as inevitably to the erosion of its legitimacy and to widespread distrust of its motives and actions among certain groups.

Although all the major social media platforms finally began to address this torrent of misinformation, conspiracies and untruths had already spread widely and taken root among a significant portion of the population throughout the last half of 2020. Once established, these ideas proved as difficult to eradicate as the pandemic. At the time of this writing, conspiracy theories continue to flourish along with widespread skepticism about many public-health measures in the United States.

Taking advantage of the global reach of these platforms and the impact of the United States on attitudes throughout the Western world, anti-vax movements used social media to organize around the world. Especially notable examples of these protests broke out in Canada and France in early 2022, where "freedom convoys" of truckers and others blocked roads and bridges, bringing commerce to a crawl. These demonstrations spread everywhere across the Western world, even touching New Zealand.

SOCIAL MEDIA, CONSPIRACY THEORIES, AND THE JANUARY 6 RIOT IN THE US CAPITOL

Social media platforms played a particularly significant role in the spread of another conspiracy theory after the November 2020 presidential election in the United States. Donald Trump, in the wake of his loss, repeatedly claimed that the Democrats had committed massive fraud to steal the election. The same features of the social media platforms that were spreading QAnon conspiracy theories and COVID-19 misinformation allowed Donald Trump's claims to take flight. In this environment various allegations spread among QAnon followers and other Trump supporters. Yet again the rococo prevailed over the rational. Those inclined to spend the most time on the Internet and on social media sites particularly became unmoored. One widespread claim linked voting machine company Dominion to late former president of Venezuela Hugo Chavez, asserting the company had cooked the electoral results in the state of Georgia. One employee of Dominion had to go into hiding after being subjected to death threats when false claims spread about ballot tampering. After the election, a second equivalently elaborate theory gained currency called "Italygate"; Trump chief of staff Mark Meadows lent credibility to this conspiracy theory when he asked the Justice Department to investigate its claims. QAnon adherents argued that the Italian Ministry of Defense had used its military satellites to penetrate and steal votes for Donald Trump from voting machines, enabling Joe Biden's fraudulent victory.

The conspiracy theory about Venezuela and Dominion and Italygate were part of a much larger "Stop the Steal" campaign led by Trump supporters, which included assertions that ballot dumping, the removal of vote-count observers, and problems with voter rolls had marked the election. According to the bulk of the Republican Party, widespread electoral fraud had enabled the dead and others to improperly cast ballots. Unsurprisingly, given their ideological views and political predilections, they identified cities and especially areas that contained significant numbers of African American voters as the epicenters of fraudulent activity. While some improper activity undoubtedly occurred—as happens in virtually all elections—available evidence indicates that the extent of this fraud was insignificant and consequently incapable of altering the election's results. Numerous court cases and recounts validated the results of the election but did not alter the views of Trump and his supporters.

Instead, their anger only intensified as did the spread of these conspiratorial claims, especially on the Internet and in the right-wing information ecosystem, including Fox News, Newsmax, One America News Network, and the enormous Sinclair Broadcast Group. Trump's refusal to concede the election and his continuing unfounded claims about widespread fraud inflamed passions, as did the support of most Republican leaders for these assertions. After Trump exhausted court challenges to the results, he intensified other efforts to vitiate the election. He directed most of this effort to try to pressure local officials to overturn the results in Arizona, Georgia, and Pennsylvania. When this failed, he began urging his supporters to come to Washington, D.C., on January 6, 2021, to pressure Congress into not certifying the Electoral College's results that gave Joe Biden a decisive victory.

Tens of thousands of Trump's supporters answered this call. After hearing speeches from Trump and others in the morning, they marched on the Capitol, transforming themselves into a riotous mob once they reached the building. Four rioters died in the occupation and vandalization of the Capitol, as did one policeman. Several others were seriously injured as well. Eventually the crowd was forced to retreat and disperse. Among many other effects, the attack on the Capitol had a profound impact on content moderation on social media sites. Twitter excluded Donald Trump "permanently" from its site, and Facebook and Instagram imposed an indefinite ban on him, although all these restrictions were certain to end given the pressures of free-speech advocates. In the immediate aftermath of these decisions, Trump supporters migrated further onto Parler, a conservative social media site funded by the Mercer family, and then onto other similar platforms after Parler ran into difficulties. They also moved onto encrypted platforms like Telegram and others that did not practice content moderation. In addition, they began a strident campaign against "cancel culture." All of this only increased the tendency of people to cluster in epistemic bubbles and reject information that in any way differed from their own beliefs and "factual" understandings. A couple of months after Joe Biden's inauguration, Facebook reviewed its decision and extended its ban on Trump. However, increases or changes in content moderation, or the banning of people, does not address the core of the problem—a business model that uses tracking and surveillance to exploit the most intense emotions of its users to drive engagement. In this world, conspiracy theories are destined to continue to flourish.

FACEBOOK'S IMPACT ON POLITICS
IN THE GLOBAL SOUTH

Although QAnon and other groups are suffused with understandings that can, at the extreme, promote violence, as occurred during the attack on the US Capitol on January 6, 2021, the most virulent expression of this problem and of the negative impacts of social media arose in the Global South. This came from the especially widespread usage of Facebook in many countries, where its size and reach made its impact especially consequential and often devastating. This problem became particularly evident and serious in 2016 in Myanmar. In that year Buddhist extremists, including Buddhist monks and the country's military, the Naypyidaw, used Facebook to wage a campaign of hate against Myanmar's Rohingya Muslim minority. Postings filled the site, accusing the Rohingya of horrific crimes and of being interlopers who did not belong in the society. In effect, Buddhist monks and other activists conducted a far-reaching "blood libel" campaign on Facebook, the source of news for the vast majority of the country's population. Facebook did nothing to stop this torrent of hate. The company had not bothered to hire enough Burmese speakers to identify the vitriolic messages clogging its site. And even more importantly, its design accelerated the spread of these messages. In addition, the company ignored explicit and repeated warnings from journalists and human-rights activists detailing the nature and scope of this campaign of hate.[6]

Facebook had acquired dominance over the Internet in Myanmar using a strategy it employed in many poor countries around the world. In keeping with the rest of its behavior, the company cloaked its activities in pieties, insisting on its philanthropic intent. Facebook proclaimed that its investments in the Global South reflected its desire to reduce global inequality and help close the gap in Internet access around the world. In pursuit of this goal, it entered agreements with national governments across this part of the world to build the backbone of their Internet.

The company was more silent about the quid pro quo embedded in its "philanthropy." In exchange for building this backbone, Facebook became the sole Internet service provider in these countries, granting it overwhelming, arguably unprecedented power. In countries throughout Asia, Africa, and Latin America, Facebook not only became the dominant source of advertising but the primary purveyor of news and information. As a result, in many countries, Myanmar included, Facebook controlled most of the news and media market.

The company consequently played a significant role in the resulting genocide of the Rohingya. Facebook's negligence, conjoined with its failure to heed well-documented warnings about the poisonous quality of the postings on its site, categorically establishes its responsibility. Facebook, at a minimum, owes reparations to the Rohingya. But as one might expect from a company without much of a sense of social responsibility, Facebook refuses to acknowledge that its business model encouraged a mass campaign of vicious hate that spread with explosive rapidity. All Facebook did in the wake of this catastrophe was hire more Burmese speakers, including subcontractors, to engage in content moderation. However, there is no escaping the fact that Facebook played an integral role in a genocide and that it did not pay a price for its actions.

Facebook had a less extreme but still very problematic effect on the Philippines, to mention another example of its most injurious political impacts around the world. As occurred in Myanmar, Facebook provided the Philippines with free Internet access in exchange for the use of its platform as the sole ISP. This enabled the company to establish a virtual monopoly over online content, acquiring extraordinary power and influence. Because of its position, Facebook played a particularly critical role in the 2016 election of Rodrigo Duterte. Throughout his campaign, Duterte used Facebook and the platform's "influencers" to fuel hate—this time against drug users. After his election, Duterte began a policy of state-sponsored summary incarceration and assassination of those identified as drug users, extrajudicially killing thousands. This clear crime against humanity was the fruit of Facebook's business model. Duterte used his influencers on Facebook to attack his political opponents and the press as well.

While Facebook played an enormous role in the campaign for the Philippine presidency, in 2022 Chinese digital company TikTok had an equivalently consequential effect. Filipinos, and young Filipinos in particular, widely used the platform to post and view short videos. TikTok became a centerpiece of the presidential campaign of Bongbong Marcos and his vice presidential running mate, Sara Duterte—daughter of Rodrigo Duterte. Bongbong Marcos is the son of Ferdinand and Imelda Marcos, who led a remarkably brutal and corrupt dictatorship that ruled through martial law. The videos on TikTok completely whitewashed the Marcos dictatorship, portraying it as a time of plenty, and helping to change the popular narrative in the Philippines about this brutal historical period. In so doing, they completely altered Bongbong's history and standing enabling him and Sara Duterte to win the election. Others are likely to learn from this campaign and use TikTok to advance their political ambitions in environments that lack effective countermeasures to, or regulation of, blatantly false information.

In many ways Jair Bolsonaro's 2018 campaign for the Brazilian presidency was similar to the strategy Rodrigo Duterte used in 2016. Rather than using Facebook itself, however, Bolsonaro used the Facebook-owned messaging platform WhatsApp, which has even more broadly penetrated Brazilian society. At the time of the election, WhatsApp had roughly 120 million Brazilian users out of a total population of 210 million. *The Guardian* analyzed a sample of 11,957 viral messages in 296 group chats during Bolsonaro's campaign. It found that "approximately 42 percent of right-wing items contained information found to be false by factcheckers. Less than 3 percent of the left-wing messages analyzed in the study contained externally verified falsehoods." More specifically, analysis showed that "up to 48 percent of the right-wing items containing externally verified falsehoods mentioned a fictional plot to fraudulently manipulate the electronic ballot system, echoing conspiracy theories promoted by Bolsonaro's team and casting suspicion on the democratic process." Also, 16 percent of the right-wing messages during Bolsonaro's campaign for the presidency "tried to dismiss the political system and mainstream media as corrupt, reflecting key elements of Bolsonaro's antiestablishment rhetoric."[7] In this case, as in so many others, social media served to amplify and spread falsehoods along with anger and hate.

Throughout 2020, Brazil was an epicenter of disinformation and conspiracy theories about the COVID-19 pandemic and about public-health measures. WhatsApp played a critical role in the spread of these ideas. Bolsonaro's public declarations and messaging on the platform tried to minimize COVID-19, repeatedly referring to it as a "little flu" while discouraging the implementation of public-health measures, including mask wearing and social distancing.[8] And Bolsonaro, as noted before, promoted the claim that hydroxychloroquine could cure COVID-19. Unsurprisingly, protests against mask wearing and social distancing occurred in Brazil as well.

More generally, countries with populist leaders proved especially subject to conspiratorial explanations of the COVID-19 pandemic. All variants of populism, regardless of their ideological coloration, distrust experts; indeed, the distrust of experts is symptom and cause of populism. These governments usually come to power because they channel deep public disenchantment with the extant system of power, along with its elites and experts. Once in power, these governments disdain and excoriate expert opinion, claiming that it is self-interested and consequently corrupt. This only intensifies the distrust that many ordinary people feel toward "the establishment." All populist leaders share a direct, unmediated connection with "the people," or at least those they define as the "real" people. And social media platforms facilitate exactly this type of relationship. Moreover, the messianic and chiliastic features of populist leaders make them naturally prone to resist scientific approaches. Not surprisingly, countries with populist leaders accounted for a disproportionate share of the world's COVID-19 cases and deaths from the virus.

Although Facebook stands out for its harmful effects on politics and society in the Global South, other platforms share many of its problems. Twitter, like Facebook, is prone to manipulation. For example, in 2015 two employees of the company, who turned out to be Saudi spies, hacked thousands of Twitter accounts. In the years after this Twitter hack, at least six Saudis who ran anonymous or pseudonymous accounts critical of the Saudi government were arrested, almost certainly as a result of this stolen information. As Ryan Gallagher writes in *Bloomberg News*,

> the Justice Department's indictment of Twitter's Saudi infiltrators . . . exposed a more serious issue: The reams of data collected on users by Twitter and other social media companies makes them an ideal target for nation-state spying operations against which there are few effective defenses. . . . The Saudi operation underscores the stakes involved. Government critics in Saudi Arabia have been jailed and even executed.[9]

THE RISE OF OBJECTIONS TO
SOCIAL MEDIA COMPANIES

Facebook's role in the genocide of the Rohingya and the use of its various platforms to elect various human-rights-abusing authoritarians around the world did not occasion much criticism or outrage in the United States. The company's stock price continued to rise, as did use of the platform. This reflected lack of knowledge about these events conjoined with complacency and parochialism.

Objections to Facebook, at least among the American left, only emerged when it became evident that Russian operatives, including both direct agents of the state and hackers working at its behest, were using the platform to try to manipulate the 2016 US presidential elections. Ironically, even those who objected to the platform on this ground either continued to belong to groups on the site or participated in many of the epistemic communities on Instagram and WhatsApp that reflected and echoed their certainties about the world.

However, Russia's use of Facebook in particular during the 2016 elections did finally engender pressures for reform and regulation. Many Democrats suddenly became vociferous critics of the platform. It says much about the world that the Russian use of Facebook to undermine Hillary Clinton and elect Donald Trump fueled more consequential outrage than its facilitation of a genocide in Myanmar. The Russians, of course, were only exploiting Facebook's design and business model.

In a rich twist of irony, even as Mark Zuckerberg and Sheryl Sandberg maximized the ways Facebook appropriated, mined, shared, and monetized the data of users, others were manipulating the platform for their own ends. Over time, it became harder to distinguish the exploiter from the exploited. While Zuckerberg, Sandberg, and their employees were manipulating the personal information and behavior of their user-products, a vast number of actors were manipulating them and their platform in pursuit of their own political, economic, social, and cultural ends.

Despite growing political pressures after the 2016 US general election, Facebook continued to resist efforts to seriously change the platform. Indeed, the company has never acknowledged that its business model is the fundamental source of the problems on the platform. Instead, it has focused more and more attention on content moderation. Ironically, this caused the American right to join in the attack on the platform, albeit from a different angle, in its case through the unsubstantiated claim that Facebook had a political bias and that it targeted conservatives for "deplatforming." For its part, the company insisted that it focused on removing posts that advocated violence and that presented an imminent danger.

Facebook's increasingly comprehensive content moderation led it to create elaborate and sophisticated, although inadequate and problematic, methods of policing the site. Content moderation expanded in the fall of 2020 and after the January 2021 Capitol attack. However, these efforts are unlikely to fix the company's problems. Facebook's problems are structural and will not end until Mark Zuckerberg changes the ways the platform drives "engagement."

Twitter increased content moderation and the policing of its site earlier than Facebook. For example, in early 2020, they decided to place a "fact check" on tweets from Donald Trump that claimed mail-in ballots resulted in widespread voter fraud. Mark Zuckerberg criticized this decision, asserting in an interview on Fox News's May 28 episode of *Daily Briefing* that social media platforms should not be "arbiters of truth."[10]

Twitter CEO Jack Dorsey responded to Zuckerberg, insisting that the company's aim was not to be an "arbiter of truth" but by fact-checking Trump's tweets they were announcing that "we'll continue to point out inaccurate or disputed information about elections globally." In the same interview, Dorsey insisted that Twitter's intention "is to connect the dots of conflicting statements and show the information in dispute so that people can judge for themselves."[11]

Trump's allegations about mail-in voting during the long run-up to the US presidential election in November 2020 were part of a systematic attack on the reliability of the US electoral system. In particular, he repeatedly insisted that he could not lose unless massive fraud occurred, cementing this notion in the minds of his followers. Moreover, he floated various suggestions designed to elongate his presidency, including postponing the election because of the COVID-19 pandemic and holding a "do-over" if he lost. Against all of this obfuscation, blatant falsehoods, and misinformation, the placement of a fact-check label next to a tweet constitutes a mild form of censorship. Moreover, Zuckerberg's criticisms of Twitter were disingenuous, given the steady growth in its own content moderation.

Both Twitter and Facebook, moreover, shared another proclivity: Their decisions about whom to flag or exclude from their platforms reflect calculations of power, consequence, and numbers of followers (who are sources of revenue). Although they ultimately ended up excluding Donald Trump, both agonized over the decision, having profited handsomely from his use of their platforms over the many preceding years. As Roger McNamee told CNN's *Reliable Source*, Facebook "[aligns] with the powerful in every country that it operates, exempting them from its terms of service." The company's behavior, he added, was reminiscent of a chemical company in the days before the regulation of spills: if the company spilled toxins like mercury into the water, Facebook spilled toxins into the body politic while profiting from hate speech.[12]

Facebook's former Global Head of Election Integrity Ops for Political Ads–turned–critic of the company, Yael Eisenstadt, observed in an op-ed in the *Washington Post* on November 4, 2019, that

> The real problem is that Facebook profits partly by amplifying lies and selling dangerous targeting tools that allow political operatives to engage in a new level of information warfare. Its business model exploits our data to let advertisers aim at us, showing each of us a different version of the truth and manipulating us with hypercustomized ads—ads that as of this fall can contain blatantly false and debunked information if they're run by a political campaign.[13]

However, though Twitter was more public and aggressive about policing its site than Facebook, it suffered from the same intrinsic vulnerabilities. Its model encouraged the creation of epistemic bubbles and was designed to drive engagement. QAnon and other conspiracy theories flourished on Twitter as well.

Trump responded to Twitter's use of the fact-check label with his habitual mixture of threats, misinformation, and lies. Presumably to cow Twitter and other platforms, he unveiled a "draft executive order"—which he never signed—ending the liability from immunity that Section 230 of the CDA grants these platforms. He argued that this executive order was required because Twitter had violated the law's "good faith" provisions. For its part, Facebook asserted that Trump's posts about mail-in ballots and voter fraud did not pose an "imminent danger" and consequently did not merit removal. However, as events in January 2021 revealed, these posts did, in fact, pose a considerable threat, which finally forced Facebook to indefinitely suspend Trump's account.

This decision was the inevitable result of a growing backlash from major advertisers that had begun in the middle of 2020. The political climate throughout that year was especially fraught because of the confluence of the COVID-19 pandemic with the Black Lives Matter protests after the killings of George Floyd and Breonna Taylor. The behavior and postings of Trump and his supporters made Facebook an especially poisonous environment throughout the year.

In response to the torrent of racist invective on the site, several organizations, including the Anti-Defamation League, the Color of Change, and the NAACP, successfully pushed corporate advertisers to increase pressure on the social media companies. In June 2020 Verizon announced that it would suspend advertising on Facebook. Other major corporations followed suit, reflecting the tenor of the times and the unwillingness of these companies to have their products appear alongside the hate-filled content that Facebook would not, or could not, effectively police.

Soon Coca-Cola, Unilever, REI, North Face, Patagonia, Eddie Bauer, Hershey's, The Lending Club, and Ben and Jerry's among others announced that they would boycott Facebook absent significant change. While these decisions reflected corporate public-relations considerations in the wake of the death of George Floyd and the widespread support for the Black Lives Matter movement, they nonetheless represented a fundamental challenge to Facebook. These pressures forced the company to accelerate its already substantial content moderation despite its professed reluctance to engage in censorship. By late 2020, Facebook was employing thirty-five thousand "fact-checkers" and content moderators. In addition, with much fanfare Facebook created an independent board made up of "luminaries" from various fields who were to review content-moderation decisions and advise the company. Even with all these efforts, scholarship revealed continuing and extraordinarily serious problems with its approach.[14] At the same time, Facebook continued to insist that its behavior reflected its deep attachment to American free-speech norms—even though it was a private entity.

More fundamentally, it is clear at this point that fact-checkers and content moderators cannot fix Facebook's problems or provide a real remedy to the social and political pathologies it promotes. These problems are intrinsic features of the company's business model and are destined to recur unless Facebook transforms its core, indeed fundamental, modus operandi. However, Facebook shows no inclination to change its algorithms or retreat from the use of behavior manipulation to increase user time spent on the platform. Even though the company continues to face a torrent of public criticism and negative press coverage along with scrutiny from lawmakers, it has not paid an economic price for its behavior. Throughout this period its revenues have continued to grow, as has its dominance of an array of online activities. Changes in its stock price reflected shifting expectations about advertising revenues and the costs of its investment in the metaverse but not a concerted effort to punish its behavior. And even as its user base stagnated—at an extraordinarily high level—in the rich world, it continued to expand in the Global South. The company changed its name to Meta Platforms, indicating its intention to dominate the metaverse as well—and perhaps escape the taint associated with its former name in many quarters. And many investment advisers have continued to recommend holding of the stock. So far stockholders and others have not forced the company to contemplate changes to its business model. However, until it changes its model, its design ensures that it will continue to have an extraordinarily problematic and socially and politically destructive effect on the world.

CONCLUSION

Throughout Donald Trump's presidency, social media platforms matured into hotbeds of conspiracy theories. A foretaste of this phenomenon arose during the Trump-led "birther" movement meant to undermine Barack Obama with false claims that he was a closet Muslim and hadn't been born in the United States. But nothing equaled the reach of conspiracy theories during the Trump administration—many coming from the president himself. The QAnon conspiracy theory, the election-fraud conspiracy theory, and other fantastical allegations could never have taken root and spread to such a large segment of the population without Twitter and Facebook. For that matter, Donald Trump,

Jair Bolsonaro, Rodrigo Duterte, and Bongbong Marcos could never have reached power without social media.

Although always prone to conspiratorial confabulations, the United States has faced a new phenomenon. Unmediated, immediately shared communications on social media sites have not only facilitated conspiratorial thinking but poisonous discourse as well. Intemperate language has flourished. In addition, the resulting epistemic bubbles have encouraged particular forms of othering, along with intensified self-righteousness. These problems have touched all parts of American society, dividing friends and family and affecting places as diverse as universities and local bars. While social media did not initiate the long decline in social trust, it has made this problem significantly worse.

More generally, the tracking and surveillance interactive computer services deploy have driven users into epistemic bubbles. Extant differences have intensified, deepening political polarization. The corollary rupture of a minimal social consensus over "facts" and about ways of knowing has created an increasingly fraught and contentious discursive and personal terrain. Invective has flourished, as has grotesque behaviors like "doxing" (the unauthorized leaking of elements of someone's identity and other personal information) and "trolling" (the online practice of harassment and bullying), among a raft of other destructive practices.

In the contemporary era, it is hard to think of a corporate actor whose behavior produced consequences as harmful as Facebook's spreading of conspiracy theories and its deepening of political polarization. The one company that most immediately comes to mind is Monsanto, which tried to monopolize both the GMO seed market and the herbicide market when it created "Roundup Ready" seeds. And as Monsanto pursued these ends, it insisted that it was bent on "feeding the world" while using a safe and benign herbicide. It fought off critics and lobbied for the adoption of its genetically modified seeds while suing farmers whose crops had been damaged or who violated its efforts to patent and own biological processes. When Roundup's carcinogenic effects were revealed, the company continued to engage in denial—a practice that continued after its acquisition in 2018 by German multinational corporation Bayer, for $66 billion. Monsanto's efforts to manipulate and own ever-greater shares of the world's food supply parallel Facebook's efforts to own and manipulate the private information of much of humanity. Finally, like Monsanto, Facebook insisted that it had a larger teleology and that its intentions were benign, all while trying to avoid fixing its business model. Both as well used all their money and power to elide responsibility for the problems that they created.

NOTES

1. Charles Taylor, *Philosophical Arguments* (Cambridge, MA: Harvard University Press, 1997).

2. Jillian Deutsch and Stephanie Bodoni, "Meta Renews Warning to EU It Will Be Forced to Pull Facebook," *Bloomberg*, February 7, 2022, https://www.bloomberg.com/news/articles/2022-02-07/meta-may-pull-facebook-instagram-from-europe-over-data-rules.

In addition, see David Meyer, "Meta's European Warning Wasn't a Threat—But if It Does Have to Withdraw, US Surveillance Laws Will Be to Blame," *Fortune*, February 9, 2022, https://fortune.com/2022/02/09/meta-european-withdrawal-warning-gdpr-us-surveillance-ceo-daily/.

3. David Gilbert, "Q Accidentally Outed Himself, But QAnon Followers Don't Care," *Vice News*, April 6, 2021, https://www.vice.com/en/article/v7m58a/q-accidentally-outed-himself-but-qanon-followers-dont-care.

4. Dana Hajjaji, "Southern Baptist Leader Ed Litton Says QAnon Conspiracy Theories Are 'Fables,'" *Newsweek*, June 18, 2021, https://www.newsweek.com/southern-baptist-convention-leader-ed-litton-says-qanon-conspiracy-theories-are-fables-1601900.

5. Karen M. Douglas, Robbie M. Sutton, and Aleksandra Cichocka, "The Psychology of Conspiracy Theories," *Current Directions in Psychological Science* 26, no. 6 (December 2017): 539, https://journals.sagepub.com/doi/full/10.1177/0963721417718261, parenthetical citations original, internal citations omitted.

6. Steve Stecklow, "Why Facebook Is Losing the War on Hate Speech in Myanmar," *Inside Facebook's Myanmar Operation: Hatebook, a Reuters Special Report*, Reuters, August 15, 2018, https://www.reuters.com/investigates/special-report/myanmar-facebook-hate/.

In addition, see Paul Mozur, "A Genocide Incited on Facebook, with Posts from Myanmar's Military," *New York Times*, October 15, 2018, https://www.nytimes.com/2018/10/15/technology/myanmar-facebook-genocide.html.

7. All quotations from this paragraph are drawn from Daniel Avelar, "WhatsApp Fake News during Brazil Election 'Favoured Bolsonaro,'" *The Guardian*, October 3, 2019, https://www.theguardian.com/world/2019/oct/30/whatsapp-fake-news-brazil-election-favoured-jair-bolsonaro-analysis-suggests.

8. Felipe Bonow Soares, Raquel Recuero, Taiane Volcan, Giane Fagundes, and Giéle Sodré, "Research Note: Bolsonaro's Firehose: How Covid-19 Disinformation on WhatsApp Was Used to Fight a Government Political Crisis in Brazil," *Harvard Kennedy School Misinformation Review* 2, no. 1 (January 2021): 1–12, https://misinforeview.hks.harvard.edu/wp-content/uploads/2021/01/soares_whatsapp_brazil_20210129.pdf.

9. All quotations and data in this paragraph from Ryan Gallagher, "Spies in Silicon Valley: Twitter Breach Tied to Saudi Dissidents Arrests," *Bloomberg News*, August 18, 2020, https://www.bnnbloomberg.ca/spies-in-silicon-valley-twitter-breach-tied-to-saudi-dissident-arrests-1.1481922.

10. Reuters, "Facebook's Zuckerberg Says Government Censoring Social Media Not the 'Right Reflex,'" Reuters.com, May 27, 2020, https://www.reuters.com/article /us-twitter-trump-facebook-zuckerberg/facebooks-zuckerberg-says-government -censoring-social-media-not-the-right-reflex-idUSKBN234026.

11. Lauren Frias, "Twitter CEO Jack Dorsey Responds to Criticism after Dustup over Adding Fact-Check Labels to Trump's Tweets," *Business Insider*, May 27, 2020, https://www.businessinsider.com/jack-dorsey-responds-criticism-for-fact -check-labels-trump-tweets-2020-5.

12. Roger McNamee, *Reliable Source*, interview, CNN, May 31, 2020.

13. Yael Eisenstadt, "I Worked On Political Ads at Facebook. They Profit by Manipulating Us," *Washington Post*, November 4, 2019, https://www.washingtonpost.com /outlook/2019/11/04/i-worked-political-ads-facebook-they-profit-by-manipulating-us /.

14. See, for example, Faiza Patel and Laura Hecht-Felella, "Facebook's Content Moderation Rules Are a Mess," Brennan Center for Justice, BrennanCenter.org, February 22, 2021, https://www.brennancenter.org/our-work/analysis-opinion/facebooks -content-moderation-rules-are-mess.

For a more positive appraisal of Facebook's activities, see Kate Klonick, "The New Governors: The People, Rules and Processes Governing Online Speech," *Harvard Law Review* 131, no. 6 (April 10, 2018): 1598–1670, https://harvardlawreview.org/ wp-content/uploads/2018/04/1598-1670_Online.pdf.

Chapter 13

Surveillance Tools and the Coronavirus Pandemic

A Case Study

The COVID-19 pandemic that swept the world in 2020 completely transformed daily life. The methods used to fight highly contagious diseases have not changed much over the centuries, revolving primarily around the identification and quarantining of carriers. In modern times, more sophisticated and expansive contact-tracing methods were developed. In addition, vaccines emerged, although their existence, given the time involved in their development and deployment, did not vitiate the need for these older methods of controlling spread. Digital surveillance and the use of other tools promised to facilitate contact tracing and the enforcement of quarantines, making their use even more desirable after the outbreak of the pandemic.

Apps on cell phones, CCTV cameras with facial-recognition capacities, and drones seemed purpose-made to confront the pandemic. These tools could facilitate contact tracing since they could passively catalog all movements and interactions. This surveillance could monitor other behaviors as well, enabling the discovery and sanctioning of violations of public-health orders. The transformations seen in the digital age were vociferously championed by leaders in the tech world—former Google CEO Eric Schmidt foremost among them—appearing publicly to support use of digital surveillance and proclaim that the pandemic was an information problem: governments using these technologies, they said, could at a relatively low cost enforce compliance with prohibitions on public gatherings, track movements, log encounters between people, and monitor those in quarantine, ensuring that they met the terms of their isolation.

However, these same tools placed vast powers in the hands of governments and enabled extraordinary intrusions into the private lives, freedoms, and agency of individuals. This raised questions in a number of democratic countries. Debate emerged over whether the use of surveillance tools should be compulsory or voluntary and about the collection and sharing of information. Not surprisingly, given the variations in attitudes across states, the use of these tools differed—as did public support for these measures.

Every aspect of the effort to fight the pandemic presented challenges to the authorities. Contact tracing, given the speed of transmission and the growth in the number of cases, seemed like an overwhelmingly daunting task. So too did the enforcement of social distancing in public, a key part of efforts to reduce the speed of contagion. The enforcement of quarantine orders, especially when there were very high case counts, presented equivalent difficulties.

This is why digital surveillance seemed a perfect solution to many of these problems. Early in the pandemic, Jeremy Cliffe, among many others, argued that the imperatives behind the construction of this "biosurveillance state" were so powerful that they were difficult to resist. The pressures to engage in biosurveillance grew just as Cliffe had predicted as governments emerged from lockdowns or experienced subsequent outbreaks, particularly because it was framed as an alternative to the extreme form of social distancing that lockdowns represented.[1]

The first and most enthusiastic adopters of digital surveillance tools to fight the pandemic were, in the main, authoritarian regimes, sultanistic (personalistic) governments, and incomplete democracies. But some established democracies deployed these measures as well, among them Israel, Italy, South Korea, Taiwan, and the United Kingdom. While Italy's early adoption of mass surveillance was explicable given the extraordinary magnitude of the crisis it confronted as the virus's epicenter in the first few months of 2020, other states moved in this direction before the same imperative existed. The use of these tools reflected larger understandings about the appropriateness of broad and relatively unconstrained state powers and views about the dangers of the pandemic.

In Europe, Poland's increasingly illiberal government deployed the most intrusive approach. Indeed, in its intrusiveness, this approach more closely resembled Chinese and Israeli methods than those of other European and North American countries. Poland required everyone to download a cellphone app that included facial-recognition capabilities to monitor movement, behavior, contacts, and compliance with health orders, as concerns about the pandemic swept constitutional protections of privacy aside.

Hungary moved in an equivalently authoritarian direction. With a few exceptions, countries that adopted widespread surveillance in the early stages of the pandemic, and especially those that used cell phones as tracking, monitoring, and surveillance devices, tended to violate privacy in additional ways.

For example, countries using these tools often required people to report those who appeared ill, in effect forcing ordinary citizens to spy on each other.

While a very large number of countries, including all the advanced democracies, adopted measures affecting freedom of assembly and freedom of movement, Denmark, unlike many others, explicitly excluded protests from these bans. However, after Black Lives Matter protests broke out in many countries, states that had restricted assembly to fight the pandemic, including the United States and countries in Europe, chose to not enforce these bans.

The International Center for Not-for-Profit Law produced the most comprehensive early reportage of the impact COVID-19–fighting measures were having on civil rights. In April 2020 the ICNL released a Civic Tracker to monitor how governmental responses to the pandemic were affecting civil and human rights. By early April, sixty-nine countries had passed emergency declarations, nine countries had passed measures affecting freedom of expression, seventy-three countries had restricted freedom of assembly, and eleven countries had expanded the legal grounds for surveillance.

For example, immediately after the outbreak of the pandemic, Hungary placed additional restrictions on freedom of the press and freedom of expression. These measures reflected the deeply illiberal, indeed proto-fascist, proclivities of Viktor Orbán's government. Moldova, Thailand, South Africa, Lesotho, Uzbekistan, and Zimbabwe all restricted freedom of the press and freedom of expression as well. Moldova went further still, aggressively expanding surveillance powers. Colombia and India restricted freedom of the press but not freedom of expression. Armenia, Bulgaria, Honduras, and Jordan limited freedom of expression but did not place greater restrictions on the press. Several countries immediately expanded government surveillance powers, including Bulgaria, China, Ecuador, Honduras, Israel, Italy, Montenegro, Poland, South Korea, and the United Kingdom.[2]

With some exceptions, countries that failed to sufficiently slow case numbers during the early months of the pandemic ended efforts to deploy these tools, at least for a time. In these countries, the number of cases made contact tracing impracticable. The refusal of many, and especially the young, to comply with restrictions on public gatherings and the continuation of family and other gatherings vitiated efforts to enforce bans. As a result, the use of these tools was ubiquitous in some countries and virtually nonexistent in others.

To assuage reservations about privacy intrusions, the US government along with its counterparts in other Western countries made the downloading of cell phone contact-tracking and -tracing apps voluntary; but few people chose to actually do so, negating the initiative's efficacy. Despite this, and given the dearth of other options, their allure to governments and health-care authorities continued.

More generally, despite the unwillingness to use these tools in many Western societies, this and future pandemics require contact tracing, the monitoring of movement, and the enforcement of quarantines. Because of their ability to advance these ends, innovations in digital-surveillance tools will generate powerful incentives to require their use and even embed them into phones. Consequently, these measures seemed destined to spread, however fitfully. This made essential the drafting of rigorous legislation that would ban the sharing of this information with anyone except for health-care authorities. While the entities developing these tools insisted that they safeguarded privacy, and Western governments promised to confine access to public-health authorities, there are strong imperatives to enact stringent legislation on this matter given the extent of public distrust and the intrinsic privacy violations embedded in these tools.

The use of surveillance tools to monitor public gatherings enhanced concerns about violations of freedom of assembly. In the United States, the political right and the Trump administration made restrictions on in-person church services the center of legal efforts to overturn limits on public gatherings. Many US states ignored public-health recommendations and encouraged a return to in-person church services. The US Supreme Court supported these states and the Trump administration, ruling that state restriction of the size of in-person church services is unconstitutional. These decisions complicated efforts to restrict gatherings but did not end controversy about them. Questions about freedom of assembly did not fade, emerging again and again in debates over stay-at-home measures.

Moreover, in the United States strongly libertarian strands in the political culture inhibited efforts to fight the pandemic. The nature of American individualism and the way that many Americans framed personal rights undermined cooperative behavior as did intense political polarization. The Trump administration encouraged opposition to public-health orders, making compliance and resistance proxies for larger political attitudes and political affiliations.

Trump's supporters claimed that they were resisting these measures because they violated constitutional rights. His opponents rejected this understanding, arguing that compliance with these measures did not undermine freedom and only reflected compliance with the consensus view of the scientific community. While one side saw masking requirements as an assault on freedom, the other saw them as a relatively minor inconvenience in the face of an enormous threat. In a broader sense, political conflicts over how to respond to the pandemic and comply with public-health orders revealed deeper conflicts over the understanding of the collective good and the relationship between the individual and the community.

However, even those who complied with public-health mandates in Western democracies typically resisted the use of digital-surveillance tools embedded in cell phones. Given the extent of fear during the COVID-19 pandemic, the population's reluctance to voluntarily download digital-surveillance tools revealed people's growing awareness of extant digital intrusions and their unwillingness to surrender even more privacy. While the extent of this reluctance varied across different Western countries, revealing differences in attitudes about the desirability of state surveillance, most liberal democracies exhibited varying degrees of reticence about this particular type of contact tracing.

In contrast, other parts of the world, and especially countries in Asia, immediately embraced the mandatory use of digital-surveillance tools. The complete lack of debate about the impact of these tools on privacy reveals the fundamental impact of cultural and social understandings on this topic. In the main, the most enthusiastic early adopters of these technologies were Confucian societies, even though some other countries, particularly Israel, employed this same approach. At least in part, the Confucian understanding of the relationship between the individual and the collectivity embodied in the state, along with relatively higher levels of social trust, explains the population's acceptance of technologies that were seen in much of the liberal West as intolerably intrusive.

CONCERNS ABOUT PANDEMIC SURVEILLANCE

Journalists were among the many groups expressing concern about the impact of the adoption of new digital-tracking and -surveillance measures to fight the pandemic. For example, Reporters Without Borders' secretary general, Christophe Deloire, noted that

> During a global public health crisis, journalists play a crucial role in guaranteeing the right to information. . . . They must be able to move about and communicate with their sources confidentially. And to cover the crisis, journalists may need to contact carriers of the virus. It is essential that the technological measures deployed by governments [. . .] not endanger this confidentiality.[3]

Privacy advocates and many academics expressed the most comprehensive concerns about the longer-term impacts of a biosurveillance regime. In the spring of 2020, many feared that the pandemic could become another critical moment in the development of mass surveillance, equivalent to 9/11. Surveillance designed to fight the pandemic searched for biological and health information while the approach developed after 9/11 used mass surveillance to find malign actors. The combination of these two types of surveillance in countries that chose to extensively use these tools could create new, all-encompassing monitoring systems designed to not only see and record all of people's behaviors and utterances but their biological states. As Yuval Noah Harari wrote,

> The epidemic might . . . mark an important watershed in the history of surveillance. . . . [I]t might normalise the deployment of mass surveillance tools in countries that have so far rejected them [and] . . . signifies a dramatic transition from "over the skin" to "under the skin" surveillance. Hitherto, when your finger touched the screen of your smartphone and clicked on a link, the government wanted to know what exactly your finger was clicking on. Now the government wants to know the temperature of your finger and the blood pressure under its skin. . . . But if you can monitor what happens to my body temperature, blood pressure, and heart rate . . . you can learn what makes me laugh, what makes me cry, and what makes me really, really angry. It is crucial to remember that anger, joy, boredom, and love are biological phenomena just like fever and a cough. The same technology that identifies coughs could also identify laughs.[4]

At the outset of the pandemic, Edward Snowden also raised concerns about digital surveillance. In an interview with Shane Smith on Vice's *Shelter in Place*, Snowden said, "we are building the architecture of oppression." He argued that in a pandemic, where one is trying to track a large number of outbreaks, there is no way to depersonalize or anonymize the data being collected. Thus, he said, even if companies and governments insist they are only tracking the movements of large groups of people rather than single phones, the data is in fact not anonymized, and in fact cannot be, given problems of scale.[5]

Privacy advocates feared that people might become habituated to the use of a technology that tracked their movements and monitored their contacts and behaviors. And they were concerned as well that the information on social behavior and health gathered through surveillance during the pandemic would join all the other data streams flowing to the state, completing yet another piece of the panopticon. Additionally, the technologies enabling these measures would continue to evolve after the end of the immediate crisis that prompted their adoption, leading to even more intrusive tools in the future. And if history is a guide, the powers granted to governments and their agencies would not likely be rolled back or relinquished. In this area, the temporary tends to become the permanent as the state finds more and more ways to use these tools to become even more powerful and facilitate governability.[6] The allure of having real-time data about the entire population's movements, their encounters with others, and their participation in gatherings is too powerful to resist, especially since the first purpose of government is the preservation of order and stability, which, in turn, influences efforts to expand social control..

THE BIOSURVEILLANCE APPROACH
TO COVID-19 IN THE WEST

Despite widespread resistance throughout the United States to the use of digital surveillance, some communities adopted these technologies. Westport, Connecticut, embraced a surveillance approach early in the pandemic that became an object lesson in how *not* to use these tools. The town had a drone for crime control and decided to employ this same technology to enforce public health-care orders and track and trace outbreaks. The local police, in partnership with the drone's manufacturer, Draganfly Inc., collected the drone's data.[7]

From an altitude of forty feet, the drone used its camera to monitor and enforce social-distancing measures and could detect coughs, sneezes, and fever. The deployment of this technology marked the first time in history that the entire population of an American city was monitored and intimately surveilled from the air. But the largest objections to this program arose because the police, rather than the health-care authorities, were gathering this data. In particular, tasking the police with this data collection reduced the prospect that access to the information would be confined to public health-care needs. Further, reflecting the wider law-enforcement community's view of surveillance, the local police asserted their right to not only collect this information but retain it indefinitely.

Furthermore, the police's involvement in this data collection aggregated health-care data with other information on individuals. Evasion and resistance became commonplace because of the fully warranted distrust of the police in many poor, marginalized, and vulnerable communities of color—the most numerous victims of the pandemic due to health inequities and disproportionate exposure given the jobs they often performed. In fact, it is hard to imagine that anyone would welcome the experience of having a drone controlled by a police officer hovering over their heads and monitoring their behavior—including those who have nothing to fear from the police because of their class and race.

Westport finally abandoned this approach after a storm of criticism. The United States more generally did not use the police to collect data on the pandemic. Instead, it partnered with private companies to perform this task. At the end of March 2020, only a couple of weeks after some states had gone into lockdown, the *Wall Street Journal* reported that

The federal government, through the Centers for Disease Control and Prevention, and state and local governments have started to receive analyses about the presence and movement of people in certain areas of geographic interest drawn from cell phone data. . . . The data comes from the mobile advertising industry rather than cell phone carriers. The aim is to create a portal for federal, state, and local officials that contains geolocation data in what could be as many as five hundred cities across the United States.[8]

This data was ostensibly stripped of identifying information, such as the phone number's owner.

In addition, companies with the capacity to track the movement of cell phone signals in aggregate fashion provided data on the numbers of people moving in and out of hotspots. And with much fanfare, Kinsa, a company that manufactured digital thermometers linked to smartphones which had first been used against the flu in 2018, advertised its capacity to track the presence of temperature clusters. However, the extraordinarily rapid spread of the pandemic soon pushed the United States' paltry contact-tracing efforts even further into the background.

Catastrophic testing failures conjoined with all the other problems mentioned before contributed to exploding case counts, making contact tracing almost impossible. A narrowing set of available options were left to confront the pandemic when the spread of the virus accelerated, in part due to the relaxation of stay-at-home policies during the summer 2020, and the general unwillingness to shut down the economy again. By the middle of the summer, New York, with the assistance of Michael Bloomberg and Johns Hopkins, was the only state that had prioritized contact tracing and hired the requisite number of people to conduct this task.

In April 2020, before the number of cases had risen precipitously across the United States, Apple and Google announced a joint project to create a COVID-19 tracking feature embedded into both iOS and Android phones. The design and adoption of this tool was intended to reassure users about the protection of their privacy. In the first place, people had to opt in to use the feature, making its adoption voluntary.

Apple and Google insisted that they had found a remedy to the problem of anonymizing data that Snowden among others raised. Their approach involved the creation of a unique piece of code linked to Bluetooth and connected to each phone's ID to create a log. Those using this tool would submit their ID code to a central database if they received a positive COVID-19 test. When any phone using this feature connected with the database, it ran a scan that indicated whether the information in its log matched any IDs in the database, indicating exposure.

The system, in an effort to protect privacy, used points of contact rather than location data. Moreover, the limited range of the Bluetooth signal prevented others from capturing this data with Stingray or other devices. Public-health officials could use the data to contact trace and identify those who needed to self-isolate. At the time, Android and iOS were respectively found in 87 percent and 13 percent of smartphones worldwide, while 72 percent of the population of the United States owned a smartphone, improving contact tracing.[9] As was true of the rest of the pandemic, however, those most in need of effective contact tracing—the poor and the marginalized—were the least likely to own smartphones, given their cost.

This digital-tracing tool did not appear in the early months of the pandemic and eventually aroused controversy, especially in the United States. However, the seeming ability of this approach to safeguard privacy prompted its eventual spread to many countries—with one important revision. To further protect privacy, many Western countries came to favor an approach that stored data on people's phones rather than in a central database. By the last months of 2020, people with smartphones could opt in to using apps that had these tracing features. However, the numbers of actual downloads of these apps remained initially modest.

Effective cell phone tracing requires an adoption rate of at least 40 percent. In the United States, the extreme politicization of public-health measures and the extent of social distrust limited downloading of this app to a small fraction of smartphone users. The US government and Big Tech's long history of lying about the extent of mass surveillance and the manifest inadequacy of their privacy protections and security protocols makes skepticism extraordinarily widespread. In these regards, even though he had faded from the headlines after 2013, Edward Snowden achieved his original goal: although it had taken time, many Americans have clearly become aware of and begun strongly objecting to mass digital surveillance, including new forms of biosurveillance.

Furthermore, until a combination of vaccines, social distancing, and masking could reduce the number of new cases, cell phone contact tracing remained impracticable in the United States. During the spring of 2021, an effective inoculation campaign resulted in the vaccination of roughly 50 percent of the US adult population by the middle of the year. However, as noted before, vaccine resistance meant many states lagged far behind this percentage, most notably the red states that supported Donald Trump in the South and the rural states of the Midwest and Rocky Mountain West. The emergence of the Delta variant of the virus—which once again raised the number of cases, hospitalizations, and deaths, this time largely among the unvaccinated—and then of the Omicron variant focused attention on inoculation and masking, and pushing contact tracing through cell phone surveillance into the background. Public discussions about the use of cell phones to contact trace remained very rare, although some institutions like universities used this tool to control outbreaks among their student body, and cities like New York promoted their use, as did a growing number of states. However, the extent of public resistance to cell phone surveillance features continued to inhibit the public-health utility of these tools in most regions of the country. Despite all of this, digital biosurveillance preserves its allure to governments and public-health authorities.

OTHER WESTERN DEMOCRACIES

Iceland created the most effective cell phone contact-tracing program in the West: its Rakning C-19 app rapidly achieving the required voluntary uptake of 40 percent. In fact, during the first year of the pandemic, Iceland was the only democratic country using voluntary downloading to achieve this threshold. The modest size of Iceland's population and very high levels of social trust might explain why it was an outlier in this area. So too did the extent of its privacy protections of digital information and the extent of the public's faith in these protections. In all these regards, it differed markedly from most other Western democracies.

Shortly after the pandemic began, the British government asked O2, one of the country's major telecoms, to analyze aggregate data on social distancing, modes of transportation, and movement. Ostensibly, this data was anonymized and aggregated and could only determine patterns in the flow of people without tracking individuals. However, the British government's poor record of protecting data and its failure to limit its sharing and retention occasioned skepticism among civil libertarians about claims of anonymization.

Fueling these concerns, immediately after the outbreak of the pandemic, the British government rushed the 340-page Coronavirus Act 2020 through Parliament. The legislation created a legal architecture that facilitated emergency measures, including expanded mass surveillance, and granted the government so-called Henry VIII powers. These powers include the ability to ban public gatherings, including political protests, to close borders, and to contain and isolate people for indefinite periods of time. The act extends the duration of surveillance warrants up from a previous maximum of three days to twelve days before requiring a judicial review. There was no clear indication at the time of when such measures would be lifted, raising concerns about whether some or all of them would become permanently institutionalized. However, despite the implications of these measures for privacy and other civil rights, much of the British public supported their adoption.

In addition, the British government developed a contact-tracing cell phone app early in the pandemic. However, this app, designed by the National Health Service, did not work well on Android and Apple devices, leading to its eventual abandonment. Subsequently, the British government announced on June 18, 2020, that it would develop an app in conjunction with Google and Apple based on their approach; it was eventually available for download in the fall of 2020. Throughout early 2021, downloads increased, and by the middle of the year nearly fifteen million Britons were active users of the app.[10] This was a larger proportion of the adult population than the United States, yet again reflecting the greater relative tolerance for surveillance in Great Britain.

However, problems continued to dog the United Kingdom's efforts in this area. A significant controversy erupted in July 2021, revealing the extent and nature of problems with the app. Those whose contacts indicated exposure to the virus were "pinged" by the app and were supposed to self-isolate. By late July, seven hundred thousand people had received this notice. At a time when severe labor shortages were plaguing the United Kingdom, as was happening in many other countries as they began to recover from the economic downturn in 2020, the placement of hundreds of thousands of working-age people in self-isolation complicated economic activities. Moreover, government messaging made it unclear if those who were pinged by the app were required to self-isolate or if quarantining was voluntary. Additionally, the app's anonymity and privacy protections made it impossible to enforce behavior modification in response to pings, leading to a mix of compliance and disobedience. Perhaps for all these reasons, one in five of the Britons who had originally downloaded the app deleted it from their phones by the middle of 2021.

Even places with stronger reservations about state intrusions than existed in the United Kingdom adopted surveillance initiatives in the early months of the pandemic. This reflected generalized panic about the virus, although the subsequent use of these tools later lagged the rate of use in the United Kingdom. On March 25, 2020, in the name of tracking the virus, the European Commission asked telecoms to hand over the data streams of their users. That same month, the German government unveiled a national hackathon, #WirVsVirus, to crowdsource digital solutions to track and contact trace.

Resistance, however, soon developed to these measures. The Robert Koch Institute, Germany's equivalent of the CDC, deployed a symptom-tracking app connected to fitness bands and smartwatches. Roughly four hundred thousand users downloaded this app, giving RKI data about disease incidence as well as heart-rate, activity and body temperature. Subsequent revelations that this data was being shared with Big Tech companies and that the German government could access user information caused many to delete the app, undermining its efficacy.

Widespread participation in #WirVsVirus and willingness to consider downloading a contact-tracing app indicate how worried Germans were about the dangers of COVID-19 given the strong cultural reservations about surveillance. As Tyson Barker writes,

> Across German society, popular willingness surged to reevaluate the country's stringent and popular data-protection rules in favor of solutions to stop the virus in its tracks. The tech euphoria culminated in the launch of the Pan-European Privacy-Preserving Proximity Tracing (PEPP-PT) initiative, which would seek to use Bluetooth technology to trace human-to-human infection contact via smartphones while also adhering to European-level privacy regulations.

However, this effort soon faced substantial criticism and pushback. To quote Tyson Barker again:

> An open letter signed by some three hundred tech experts viciously criticized the centralized processing of [contact] tracing apps. Other critics claimed that PEPP-PT lacked transparency because its founders were unwilling to openly publish their code. Also, and not least, the cybersecurity proved shoddy; the Federal Office for Information Security, Germany's cyberauthority, said the Android version was riddled with vulnerabilities. The criticism led to an exodus among the app's founding supporters.[11]

Separately, the German government continued working on an official app, launching the Corona-Warn-App developed by SAP and Telecom on June 16, 2020. This app used low-energy Bluetooth technology to pseudonymously collect data from phones within two meters. If people remained at this distance for fifteen minutes or longer, the phones exchanged data via Bluetooth, which had been purposely used so the signal could not be remotely captured. If a user tested positive, they put this information into their Corona-Warn-App, which then anonymously informed all stored contacts.[12] As can be seen, this app closely mirrored the approach that Apple and Google proposed.

France, for its part, finally rolled out a COVID-19 contact-tracing app on June 2, 2020. StopCovid, as it was initially called, became available for download on the same day the French lockdown ended. For the first time in many months the French were allowed to go to restaurants, cafés, parks, beaches, museums, and monuments. Unlike the apps developed in the United Kingdom, Germany, Italy, and Switzerland, all of which stored the information that the low-energy Bluetooth collected on each individual phone, the French system uploaded data to government-run central servers.

This system notified users who had tested positive, enabling them to notify those they had encountered so that they in turn could self-isolate and seek treatment if necessary.[13] A month after its launch, voluntary downloads of StopCovid did not even top two million, revealing the initial extent of resistance to this tool across all of the Western democracies, regardless of product design. Of those who downloaded the app, only sixty-eight received reports that they were positive, and only fourteen were notified that they had been in contact with an infected person; resistance to the use of StopCovid increased after evidence surfaced that it was gathering and storing much more contact information than had been advertised.[14] Subsequently, France rebranded the app TousAntiCovid, hoping to increase its use although widespread popular resistance continued.[15]

Poland's original contact-tracing and quarantine-enforcement practices, along with its other measures, violated the minimal provisions of the GDPR and other EU guidelines. As noted before, Poland's first app clearly demonstrated the growing fragility of the country's attachment to liberalism, requiring that those in quarantine submit geotagged selfies to the government. The early version of Poland's ProteGO Safe app did not sufficiently anonymize and protect users either. If someone became infected with COVID-19, they were supposed to be able to change their status on the app "anonymously." However, this data was sent to an external server, which then notified this person's contacts from the previous two weeks. Obviously, this exercise vitiated anonymity despite the government's assurances.

In the broadest terms, Poland's initial approach exemplified Eastern Europe's weaker attachment to liberal civil- and human-rights norms, including privacy rights. But sustained criticism, including from the European Union, forced the Polish government to keep revising their app, which eventually looked like those on the verge of deployment in Germany and other European countries, all based on variations of the Apple/Google initiative.

Poland was the first to release an app based on this design. The new app, still called ProteGO Safe, was intended to be interoperable with others on the verge of appearing elsewhere in Europe. In common with these other apps, ProteGO Safe used Bluetooth short-range signals to log connections between smartphones, keeping a record of contacts on these phones while preventing the transfer of this data to a central database. When a user became sick, they changed their status through an anonymous key that notified contacts. "We paid a lot of attention . . . to secure privacy issues," said Marek Zagórski, Poland's digital minister. "The application does not collect, process, or transfer any data outside, except for the anonymous keys that are used to activate the notification module. It is completely anonymous."[16]

Early apps adopted outside of Europe did not use portions of the Apple/Google approach and were consequently less protective of privacy. For example, in Australia, the government deployed the COVIDSafe app. After initial concerns arose about use of the app's data for other law-enforcement purposes, legislation was passed on May 15, 2020, that made it an offense to use COVIDSafe for anything other than contact tracing. To avoid tracking people with location data, COVIDSafe did not use GPS. Despite this limitation, COVIDSafe's lack of more robust privacy protections undermined any widespread adoption of the tool.

Development of a national contact-tracing app did not occur initially in Canada. Alberta was the lone province to deploy a contract-tracing app in the first few months of the pandemic. Canada's central government, however, subsequently developed an app based on the Apple/Google initiative that was available for download by early July 2020. As in the rest of the Western democratic world, use of this app was voluntary. Here too Snowden's revelations had left a mark.

More generally in the West, most public discussions and downloading of cell phone apps remained relatively rare. Instead, discussions about "vaccine passports," masking, and testing consumed public attention. The government's unwillingness to mandate the downloading of cell phone apps and the population's corollary reluctance to voluntarily use these tools ensured rates too low for efficacy.

THE EAST ASIAN AND CHINESE APPROACHES TO BIOSURVEILLANCE DURING THE PANDEMIC

China, in keeping with the rest of its approach to mass surveillance, deployed the most protean tools in the world to fight the pandemic. Extraordinarily intrusive digital tools tracked all movement and travel among other activities. For example, in February 2020, China's top three telecommunications companies sent out mass text messages offering to provide information to their customers about the cities they had visited during the previous month.

The telecoms provided this "service" because many train stations and neighborhoods, at the behest of the government, were requiring people to provide this information as a way of verifying whether or not they had traveled to a hotspot, particularly the city of Wuhan and the surrounding Hubei province.[17] In addition, several cities, including Shanghai and Shenzhen, began forcing commuters to register their personal information if they wished to use the subway. People had to declare their identity on a phone app before being allowed access to trains.

In addition, and most intrusively of all, China's "super app" WeChat, along with the Alipay payment system, developed color-coded QR codes to be displayed on phones. This system established whether a phone user was safe or not, using a green, yellow, or red QR code, drawn from city and municipal data indicating all movements, behaviors, activities, and contacts. A green QR meant the phone user was safe, a yellow QR mandated a seven-day self-isolation, and a red QR required a fourteen-day quarantine.

The color could change based on travel, movement, and encounters. These QR codes had to be shown prior to engagement in any public activity. As Jeremy Cliffe writes about China's approach, "citizens must show [these codes] to move around and to ensure that they are not violating personalized restrictions. There are even efforts to create a system that combines 'body detection, [and], face detection [with] . . . sensing via infrared cameras and visible light' to identify those prone to infection."[18]

As if these measures were insufficient, the Chinese government promoted the development of additional tools. As June Ko writes, "The state-owned China Electronics Technology Group Corporation (CETC) has also launched a platform called Close Contact Detector, which pulls in traffic, rail, and flight information. According to state media, the platform can accurately pinpoint a passenger's location on a flight or a train to within three rows of a confirmed or suspected virus carrier."[19]

Although no other country equaled China in its intrusiveness, other East Asian governments required cell phone users to install contact-tracing apps. Taiwan was the first country to use cell phone data to enforce quarantines, calling people in quarantine twice a day to make sure that they had not left their phones at home to avoid having their movements tracked.[20] In addition, Taiwan used cell phone contact tracing conjoined with the use of government databases to track the pandemic. But as Andreas Kluth observes,

> Taiwan and its people added a twist. In effect, the whole country voluntarily partnered with the government to create a protean network of databases in which information flows both from the bottom up and from the top down. To make new online and offline tools for fighting the virus, "hacktivists," developers, and citizens have been collaborating with the government on vTaiwan, a sort of online democracy town hall and brainstorming site. One tool, for example, prevented a run on face masks by mapping where the stocks were and allocating them wherever they were most needed. By involving people in the solutions rather than just dictating policies to them, the process is transparent and inspires trust, even civic pride.[21]

While Kluth argues that Taiwan's was the best early reaction to the pandemic because of its grassroots and democratic features, the country's approach still raises a number of issues. Taiwan was the first democracy and first country outside of China to link different data sets together, establishing a very troubling precedent. For example, from the outset Taiwan linked immigration information with public-health information. Fortunately, most democracies outside of East Asia have resisted this initiative. While perhaps acceptable under these circumstances, databases once linked almost never become disentangled, even in countries with strong civil-rights traditions. In fact, all genuinely liberal states recognize the depth of this problem and segregate data bases. Despite its democratic elements, the Taiwanese approach included some remarkably intrusive and coercive elements as well. Most dramatically, those whose cell phone data indicated a lack of compliance with any feature of a quarantine order received an immediate visit from the police.

Like Taiwan, South Korea is a democratic country with a Confucian ethos, which played a part in enabling the South Korean government to immediately deploy a tracking app on cell phones. Shortly after the outbreak of the pandemic, South Korean private developers created contact-tracing apps that monitored movement and contacts.

One of these apps, Corona 100m, was downloaded over a million times in just a few weeks and collected information from public sources that "alert users of the presence of any diagnosed Covid-19 patient within a one hundred–meter radius, along with the patient's diagnosis date, nationality, age, gender, and prior locations." Another South Korean app, Corona Map, "similarly plots locations of diagnosed patients" and shares this data with those who wish to avoid these areas.[22] This data was used in conjunction with footage from CCTV and information from credit card transactions. South Korea used geolocation data on cell phones as well to ensure quarantine compliance—effectively putting the ill under house arrest.[23]

Singapore and Hong Kong's responses to the pandemic parallel the approach used in Taiwan and South Korea. Shortly after the outbreak of COVID-19, Singapore deployed an app called TraceTogether. Meanwhile, Hong Kong used an app called StayHomeSafe to enforce self-isolation of arriving travelers for fourteen days. It also made them wear a wristband, paired to this app, that used so-called geofencing technology to catch those breaking self-isolation. Violators could face prison sentences of up to six months and fines of $3,200.[24]

OTHER EXAMPLES

Israel's response to the pandemic similarly relied heavily on the use of digital surveillance tied to cell phones. Surprisingly and problematically, Shin Bet, their domestic-intelligence agency, was charged with conducting the surveillance designed to track and trace the pandemic. The country's public-health authorities were excluded from this process. Moreover, Shin Bet was under the direct control of Prime Minister Netanyahu and not subject to any external oversight. The choice to use a security agency to contact trace is just another indication of the corrosive effects that perpetual conflict and war have on liberal practices. Netanyahu claimed that health officials had requested the use of "digital" techniques—that is, mass surveillance—"used in the fight against terror" to confront the pandemic. "It's difficult to locate this enemy, because it's stealthy," he added, in an obvious effort to link the pandemic with the fight against terrorism. "But there's no choice, because we're fighting a war that requires special actions."[25] This in turn became the justification to use a domestic spy agency rather than the public-health system to gather data.

Israel's decision to use the most powerfully intrusive mass-surveillance tools available to the government to fight the pandemic made it an extreme outlier among the economically developed non-Asian democracies. So too did its failure to include some protections of privacy rights in its approach. Because it was such an outlier, it is more appropriate to group its response to the pandemic with the Confucian countries. However, it should be emphasized that Israelis—although not Palestinians in the occupied territories—enjoyed much stronger protections from state surveillance than the Chinese. Israeli telecommunications law required law enforcement to secure a warrant before gaining access to the information that cellular networks had gathered. Despite this protection, Israelis experienced cell phone surveillance during the pandemic equivalent to or even greater than that found in Taiwan and South Korea.

For example, shortly after the outbreak of the pandemic, Israel began pulling the cell phone data of those who had tested positive for COVID-19. This data was then used to chart patient movements over previous weeks and then to trace and inform their contacts, who were then ordered into self-isolation. And cell phones were also used to enforce compliance.

All of this caused academics and activists to worry that measures taken in haste to combat the pandemic might linger, as has happened in so many other cases. For example, in March 2020, shortly after the Israeli government deployed these measures, Yuval Noah Harari wrote,

> You could, of course, make the case for biometric surveillance as a temporary measure taken during a state of emergency. It would go away once the emergency is over. But temporary measures have a nasty habit of outlasting emergencies. . . . My home country of Israel, for example, declared a state of emergency during its 1948 War of Independence, which justified a range of temporary measures from press censorship to land confiscation to special regulations for making pudding. . . . Israel never declared the emergency over and has failed to abolish many of the "temporary" measures of 1948 (the emergency pudding decree was mercifully abolished in 2011).[26]

Russia too embraced digital surveillance. As Reporters Without Borders notes of their response to the pandemic, "[the Russian state] has developed a 'Social Monitoring' mobile phone app that assists 'self-discipline' by those who have caught the virus. The app requires [users to grant] every possible permission [to the government], including access to personal and banking data, location, microphone, and camera, and shares this data via unprotected channels."[27]

Turkey launched a contact-tracing app called Hayat Eve Sığar (life fits into the house) to monitor the movement of people diagnosed with COVID-19 and warn users if they had come into contact with an infected person or had entered an area where there were positive cases.[28] Data-sharing and -retention protections did not exist in Turkey, and the Erdoğan government passed legislation in 2020 granting itself carte blanche to online information. Moreover, the Turkish people lacked much of a democratic foothold, or at least a sufficient democratic foothold, to protest the abuse of their data.

Colombia was the only Latin American country to adopt a contact-tracing app early in the pandemic. Over four million users immediately downloaded CoronApp, which was based on technology from a Portuguese company called HypeLabs. However, the Colombian government had to drop the app only a few days after its launch when it failed to accurately log contacts and generated unnecessary alerts.[29] After this failure, Colombia announced that it too was entering into a partnership with Google and Apple to eventually roll out a contact-tracing app based on their initiative. All of this shows that the design of the Apple/Google app and especially its privacy-protecting features had effectively transformed it into the contact-tracing gold standard among democratic countries.

Although they did not launch contact-tracing apps early in the pandemic, other countries in the region used other surveillance techniques to track contagion. For example, Ecuador, a country with a large early outbreak, decided on a notably expansive approach. On March 17, 2020, the government authorized satellite surveillance of cell phones and collection of location data in an effort to contain the pandemic.[30]

In April 2020, in Latin America's largest country, Brazil, as Richard Kameny notes in the *MIT Technology Review*,

> when the governor of Sao Paulo launched a project using phone data to track how well people were adhering to isolation measures, Bolsonaro's son Eduardo called it an "invasion of rights," and the president quickly put a stop to a similar plan from the Science Ministry. Yet he apparently had no such qualms a week later when he signed a decree mandating that telecoms hand over data on 226 million Brazilians to IBGE, the government's statistical agency, ostensibly for surveying households during the pandemic.[31]

Several other countries in the region adopted measures to confront the pandemic that raised additional human-rights issues. To cite the Washington Office on Latin America (WOLA),

> In El Salvador over 1,200 people have been detained in "containment centers" for violating curfew orders. . . . In Honduras, the president issued a decree temporarily restricting freedom of speech rights as guaranteed in the nation's constitution, asserting this was necessary to combat the spread of misinformation related to the pandemic. . . . In Bolivia, the [Inter-American Commission on Human Rights (IACHR)] Special Rapporteur on Freedom of Expression has called for the interim Añez government to withdraw a decree that threatens prison sentences for overly broad and vague charges of "disinforming" and "inciting crimes against health." In Venezuela, the de facto Maduro government has sought to silence criticism of its response to the pandemic, harassing and detaining journalists who question official statistics.[32]

In addition, several governments, including Argentina, Bolivia, El Salvador, Honduras, and Mexico, used the military to enforce compliance with public health-care measures. This included enforcing curfews, patrolling streets, and repressing protesters. Given Latin America's long, fraught history of military abuses of human rights, any involvement of this institution in governance raises serious concerns.[33]

Early in the pandemic, South Africa was the only country in Africa to work on the development of a contact-tracing app. Covi-ID, developed in conjunction with the University of Cape Town, was said to comply with GDPR-based privacy protection, yet the collected data was submitted directly to the government.[34] For these reasons this app had serious implications for the privacy of South Africans.

LIMITS ON THE EFFICACY OF TRACKING AND TRACING APPS ON CELL PHONES

Despite its promise, digital surveillance to monitor and control COVID-19 outbreaks proved less effective than expected in many countries. The number of cases rose more in several countries using intrusive surveillance tools than it did in some that did not deploy these tools or did not employ them to the same extent. For example, although Israel initially succeeded in containing the virus, the country experienced an enormous increase in the number of cases as the late spring of 2020 moved into and through the summer and fall. Israel's experience, although more extreme, did not differ from Singapore's, where the TraceTogether app, although downloaded over a million times, failed to identify half of new cases. This led the app's product lead, Jason

Bay, to write, "If you ask me whether any Bluetooth contact-tracing system deployed or under deployment, anywhere in the world, is ready to replace manual tracing, I will say without qualification that the answer is 'No.' Not now, and even with the benefit of AI/ML and—God forbid—blockchain . . . not for the foreseeable future."[35]

Hong Kong and several other East Asian countries that used widespread surveillance to fight the pandemic experienced an increase in cases as well. While surveillance undoubtedly facilitated contact tracing and the monitoring of quarantines and self-isolation, available evidence suggests that the behavior of the population, and especially its collective willingness to comply with health-care orders and recommendations, was much more important in reducing the spread of the virus than surveillance. Early in the pandemic countries with notably low case counts and deaths, like Norway and Finland, showed that testing, ordinary contact tracing, and compliance with public-health initiatives remained more effective than surveillance.

Israel's vast surveillance apparatus, for example, largely failed to contain the spread of the virus. The large religious population refused to comply with public-health orders and alter their behaviors. Not surprisingly, an explosion in the number of cases resulted from resistance among haredi Jews to public-health measures and continued participation in congregate activities, which involve praying and singing in large groups. By the end of July 2020, Israel's number of cases exceeded seventy thousand. By that point, Israel had a per capita case count equivalent to Spain's and much higher than the United Kingdom's and France's. And revealingly, its per capita case numbers were equivalent to Sweden's, the country in Europe that was taking the most laissez-faire approach to the pandemic in Europe in an effort to reach herd immunity.[36]

Paradoxically, despite its use of a domestic-intelligence agency to intrude into the private lives and behaviors of all of its citizens, the number of Israel's cases was much higher than several countries in the circum-Mediterranean area, including Greece and Croatia, which all had much lower rates of spread during this period.[37] And with the exception, most dramatically of China, and to a lesser degree, South Korea and Taiwan, no state used surveillance nearly as aggressively as Israel. In 2021 Israel's extraordinarily successful vaccine campaign finally reduced hospitalizations and especially deaths. But this reduction was entirely related to the availability of vaccines and the absence of a large anti-vax movement rather than to the government's biosurveillance. This was true elsewhere in the world. In fact, much of the difference between countries in terms of hospitalizations and deaths reflected the availability of vaccines—itself based in substantial measure on the wealth of the society— and the extent of the population's lack of resistance to inoculation rather than the use of cell phone surveillance.

Nonetheless, surveillance has continued to seem like an especially apt way to fight a pandemic. On common-sense grounds, digital surveillance seems capable of discovering those who are transmitting a disease, tracing their contacts, and enforcing self-isolation and quarantines. However, other things including the communitarian or libertarian dispositions of the population, its willingness to comply with public-health orders, and the extent of social and other forms of trust were much more important than surveillance in reducing the spread of the COVID-19 virus. When vaccines became available in the developed countries, social, cultural, and other susceptibilities to anti-vax propaganda and misinformation became one of the most important factors explaining national and subnational variations in case counts.

Nonetheless, more and more countries developed their own cell phone apps along with other digital-surveillance tools to combat the pandemic. Moreover, this type of surveillance promises to expand in the future. Pandemics naturally inflame the governmental and social desire to "see" more in order to predict more and control more, all in a quest for security. Technological innovations will facilitate this end. One can only hope that meaningful privacy protections will accompany the development of these expanding capacities.

CONCLUSION

During the early months of the COVID-19 pandemic, many feared that countries were going to deploy widespread biosurveillance, adding an additional, notably intrusive layer onto existing mass-surveillance practices. However, in the Western democracies widespread biosurveillance did not proliferate as expected. Paradoxically, the explosion in cases in Europe and the United States reduced pressures to deploy these tools, given the inability to conduct effective contact tracing. Even more importantly, very widespread public resistance to these tools forced governments to make the use of cell phone contact-tracing apps, in particular, voluntary.

Continuing resistance, evidenced in very low adoption rates of this feature on cell phones, vitiated efforts to transform these devices, and especially smartphones, into tracing and tracking devices. Moreover, the use of smartphones as contact-tracing devices confronted another problem. The poor, especially people of color, were particularly in need of effective contact tracing because they were most exposed to the pandemic given their concentration in jobs that did not permit them to shelter at home. In addition, the social determinants of health meant that they were the most likely to get very sick and die if they caught COVID-19. At the same time, they were the group least likely to possess smartphones due to the cost of these devices.

Other countries, however, embraced an approach to the pandemic that relied in part on mass surveillance. Taiwan, South Korea, and China used these tools most extensively and experienced enormous successes in reducing the spread of the virus, at least in the very early phases of the pandemic. However, as 2021 progressed, the appearance of new and more contagious variants caused case counts, hospitalizations, and deaths to rise, most dramatically in Hong Kong. The city's extensive surveillance regime could not overcome the inadequacy of its inoculation campaign. The rest of mainland China began exhibiting this same problem in the first quarter of 2022. It responded with complete lockdowns of areas with cases, as it pursued a "zero COVID" approach. These lockdowns paralyzed the most dynamic cities in the country, including Shanghai and Beijing, resulting in serious hardship and economic dislocation, along with evident public dissatisfaction. In part the inadequacies of China's domestically produced vaccines (which for nationalistic reasons it had insisted on using exclusively) along with the "immunological innocence" of much of its population, given its earlier success in reducing the spread of the virus, explain increases in case counts and deaths. So too did its failure to inoculate a sufficiently large portion of its most vulnerable and elderly population.

The extensive use of surveillance tools outside the region, in places as diverse as Russia and Israel, did not even produce the initial reduction in case counts that China achieved. In fact, both Russia and Israel, despite spying especially extensively on their populations, had case counts that equaled or exceeded incidence rates in many countries that resisted these measures. From this evidence, it seems clear that deeper social, cultural, and political factors provide the primary explanation for successes and failures in fighting the pandemic. By 2022, as the pandemic moved into and through its third year, strong management of an increasingly endemic problem reflected the ability of different countries to mount effective inoculation campaigns rather than the use of surveillance technologies. In turn, the efficacy of these campaigns was influenced by the presence or absence of a large anti-vax movement, itself a proxy for other features of the polity and of its social and political divisions.

NOTES

1. Jeremy Cliffe, "The Rise of the Bio-surveillance State," *New Statesman America*, March 25, 2020, https://www.newstatesman.com/long-reads/2020/03/rise-bio-surveillance-state.

2. All statistics in this discussion have been derived from International Center for Not-for-Profit Law, "COVID-19 Civic Freedom Tracker," ICNL.org, introduced April 2020, continually updated, https://www.icnl.org/covid19tracker/.

3. Christophe Deloire as quoted in Reporters Without Borders, "Coronavirus: State Measures Must Not Allow Surveillance of Journalists and Their Sources," RSF. org, April 10, 2020, https://rsf.org/en/coronavirus-state-measures-must-not-allow -surveillance-journalists-and-their-sources.

4. Yuval Noah Harari, "Yuval Noah Harari: The World after Coronavirus," *Financial Times*, March 19, 2020, https://www.ft.com/content/19d90308-6858-11ea-a3c9 -1fe6fedcca75.

5. Edward Snowden, *Shelter in Place*, interview with Shane Smith, Vice.

6. Jennifer Stisa Granick, *American Spies: Modern Surveillance, Why You Should Care, and What to Do about It* (Cambridge: Cambridge University Press, 2017), 9–26.

7. Details of the Westport, Connecticut, incident are drawn from Jake Ward's reportage and interview with Craig Melvin on MSNBC, airing April 23, 2020.

8. Byron Tau, "Government Tracking How People Move Around in Coronavirus Pandemic," *Wall Street Journal*, March 28, 2020, https://www.wsj.com/ articles/government-tracking-how-people-move-around-in-coronavirus-pandemic -11585393202.

9. On Apple and Google's proposed tool, see Zoe LaRock, "Google and Apple Are Collaborating on a Wide Scale Coronavirus Tracking Tool," *Business Insider*, April 14, 2020, https://www.businessinsider.in/science/news/google-and-apple-are -collaborating-on-a-wide-scale-coronavirus-tracking-tool/articleshow/75144239 .cms; and also see Russell Brandon, "Answering the 12 Biggest Questions about Apple and Google's New Coronavirus Tracking Project," *The Verge*, April 11, 2020, https://www.theverge.com/2020/4/11/21216803/apple-google-coronavirus-tracking -app-covid-bluetooth-secure/.

10. Ryan Browne, "UK Contact Tracing App Downloads Spike Despite Fears of a 'Pingdemic' as Covid Cases Surge," CNBC, July 23, 2021, https://www.cnbc.com /2021/07/23/uk-covid-latest-nhs-contact-tracing-app-downloads-spike.html.

11. All quotations in this paragraph are drawn from Tyson Barker, "Germany's Angst Is Killing Its Coronavirus Tracing App," *Foreign Policy*, May 8, 2020, https:// foreignpolicy.com/2020/05/08/germany-coronavirus-contract-tracing-pandemic-app /.

12. Norton Rose Fulbright, "Contact Tracing Apps: A New World for Data Privacy," February 2020, https://www.nortonrosefulbright.com/en/knowledge/publications/ d7a9a296/contact-tracing-apps-a-new-world-for-data-privacy.

13. France 24, "France Rolls Out Covid-19 Tracing App amid Privacy Debate," France24.com, June 2, 2020, https://www.france24.com/en/20200602-france-rolls -out-covid-19-tracing-app-amid-privacy-debate.

14. Norton Rose Fulbright, "Contact Tracing Apps."

15. Romain Dillet, "France Rebrands Contact Tracing App in an Effort to Boost Downloads," *Tech Crunch*, October 23, 2020, https://techcrunch.com/2020/10/22/ france-rebrands-contact-tracing-app-in-an-effort-to-boost-downloads/.

16. Marek Zagórski, as quoted in Reuters staff, "Poland Rolls Out Privacy-Secure Coronavirus Tracking App," Reuters, June 9, 2020, https://www.reuters.com/article/us-health-coronavirus-poland-tech-idUSKBN23G208.

17. June Ko, "How China Used Technology to Combat COVID-19—and Tighten Its Grip on Citizens," Amnesty International, Amnesty.org, April 17, 2020, https://www.amnesty.org/en/latest/news/2020/04/how-china-used-technology-to-combat-covid-19-and-tighten-its-grip-on-citizens/.

18. Cliffe, "Rise of the Bio-surveillance State."

19. Ko, "How China Used Technology," parenthetical original.

20. Yasheng Huang, Meicen Sun, and Yuzi Sui, "How Digital Contact Tracing Slowed Covid-19 in East Asia," *Harvard Business Review*, April 15, 2020, https://hbr.org/2020/04/how-digital-contact-tracing-slowed-covid-19-in-east-asia.

21. Andreas Kluth, "If We Must Build a Surveillance State, Let's Do It Properly," Opinion, *Bloomberg*, April 21, 2020, https://www.bloomberg.com/opinion/articles/2020-04-22/taiwan-offers-the-best-model-for-coronavirus-data-tracking.

22. Huang, Sun, and Sui, "Digital Contact Tracing."

23. Kluth, "If We Must Build."

24. Huang, Sun, and Sui, "Digital Contact Tracing."

25. Benjamin Netanyahu as quoted in Joshua Mitnick, "Better Health through Mass Surveillance?" *Foreign Policy Dispatch*, March 16, 2020, https://foreignpolicy.com/2020/03/16/israel-coronavirus-mass-surveillance-pandemic/.

26. Harari, "World After Coronavirus," parenthetical original.

27. Reporters Without Borders, "Coronavirus: State Measures."

28. Norton Rose Fulbright, "Contact Tracing Apps."

29. Dave Paresh and Stephen Nellis, "Colombia Had to Abandon Contact Tracing from Its Coronavirus App because It Didn't Work Properly," Reuters, published on *Business Insider*, May 7, 2020, https://www.businessinsider.com/colombia-contact-tracing-apple-google-coronavirus-app-2020-5.

30. Reporters Without Borders, "Coronavirus: State Measures."

31. Richard Kameny, "Brazil Is Sliding into Techno-authoritarianism," *MIT Technology Review*, August 19, 2020, https://www.technologyreview.com/2020/08/19/1007094/brazil-bolsonaro-data-privacy-cadastro-base/.

32. WOLA staff, "Commentary: Monitoring Anti-democratic Trends and Human Rights Abuses in the Age of COVID-19," Washington Office on Latin America, WOLA.org, April 13, 2020, https://www.wola.org/analysis/anti-democratic-trends-human-rights-abuses-covid-19-latin-america/.

33. WOLA staff, "Commentary: Monitoring Anti-democratic Trends."

34. Norton Rose Fulbright, "Contact Tracing Apps."

35. Jason Bay, "Automated Contact Tracing Is Not a Coronavirus Panacea," *Medium*, April 10, 2020, https://medium.com/singapore-gds/automated-contact-tracing-is-not-a-coronavirus-panacea-57fb3ce61d98.

36. There are numerous sources for coronavirus case and mortality counts. All, with some variation, contain broadly similar numbers. The cited data were drawn on July 31, 2020, from *Worldometer*, https://worldometers.info. The assertions about

relative success in fighting the pandemic during the first months of the outbreak were drawn from the same source to ensure consistency.

37. Data drawn on July 31, 2020, from *Worldometer*, https://worldometers.info.

Conclusion and Epilogue

The spread of the COVID-19 pandemic during 2020 caused an ever-greater number of activities to be moved online. Novel potential threats to privacy emerged in this environment. Online psychotherapy services, for example, raise new vulnerabilities not because of their design but because of difficulties in preserving the absolute security of online communications even though these companies encrypt. In the United States, two platforms, Talkspace and The Difference, released apps enabling online conversations with licensed therapists through cell phones and other devices. In the summer of 2019, Amazon Alexa began offering this service as well. These services complied with HIPAA guidelines on patient confidentiality and increased the accessibility and affordability of mental-health care but were not invulnerable, in common with other online activities no matter their security protocols, to hacking and surveillance.

While telemedicine has many virtues—increasing ease of access, among other things—black-hat hackers could potentially acquire information shared digitally. As has been true of so much in the digital age, the price for convenience and ease of access has been the diminished ability to protect previously private information. Giant hacks of personal information, including the Equifax attack in 2018 and the SolarWinds hack uncovered in late 2020, along with repeated ransomware and other attacks, to just mention a few out of many, many examples, provide continuing reminders of growing vulnerabilities to nefarious intrusions even as they subject millions to the theft of their identities. Regardless of security protocols, there is no reason to expect that companies like Talkspace and The Difference can prevent attacks from sufficiently sophisticated actors.

Remote work and online education expanded even more rapidly during the pandemic, as did online banking and shopping, to mention just a few examples. Consequently, an even more significant portion of people's lives moved onto digital platforms. And all these interactions required users to provide personal information, spreading parts of themselves all over the Internet.

Quarantines, self-isolations, stay-at-home orders, lockdowns, border closures, and travel restrictions separated families, friends, lovers, and others.

The loss of face-to-face contact and the deep need for social connection forced people to substitute direct encounters with online interactions. Almost everything that had previously occurred in face-to-face conversations moved online. The business model of most platforms enabling these communications, such as Skype and Cisco Webex among many others, meant that people paid for these services with their personal information too. In turn, these corporate entities continued to share and monetize this information. Even more importantly, these online activities were often subject to state penetration and ubiquitous hacking.

Many companies, when they adopted work-from-home policies during the pandemic, deployed monitoring apps to oversee employees working remotely. Employers use these apps to ensure that productivity and hours worked did not decline in a work-from-home environment. Moreover, some employers used these tools to ensure that workers did not leave their "desks" or change their location for too long. When the lockdowns lifted, many companies decided to continue remote work for some employees. Many workers embraced this option, since it ended commuting, enabling one to live far from the workplace and spend more time with family. However, productivity-monitoring apps remain in use. And thus apps designed for the workplace have migrated into the home, joining the other instruments of surveillance populating a previously private place.

Corporate tracking of online activity has increased as well. Before the pandemic, people had grown accustomed to receiving messages and ads with personalization indicating the extent of the tracking, surveilling, monitoring, and collection of their searches and other activities. During the pandemic, these ads and messages became even more ubiquitous. In one of many examples, Netflix began sending messages in real time to its customers as they watched a series, urging continued viewing.

The wide variations in security protocols and in privacy protections became even more manifest in this environment. So too did the extent of hacking. Zoom, a Chinese-owned company, provides a perfect example of all these problems. Zoom's platform came into widespread use immediately after the outbreak of the pandemic. Businesses, universities, and other organizations adopted Zoom, transforming it into a widely used workplace and online-education tool. Zoom's cost, ease of use, and flexibility—arguably greater than Cisco Webex, Google Hangouts, or Skype—encouraged rapid growth in the use of the platform.

Shortly thereafter, however, it became evident that Zoom could be easily penetrated and that hackers had taken over meetings and other online gatherings. Less noted but perhaps even more injurious was the revelation that Zoom was selling user data to Facebook. After American colleges and universities shut down and moved online in the spring of 2020, Zoom became the location of classroom sessions and faculty and administrative meetings. As a result, the communications tool became privy to many conversations between professors, often about research, and between professors and students of all ages, including graduate students involved in cutting-edge scholarship. In early 2020 the platform experienced "Zoombombing," when hackers interrupted meetings with hate speech and porn. Zoom responded to the ensuing outrage over the evident weakness of its security protocols with several measures: it added required passcodes to meetings and tried to reassure users by promising to store the data of its US consumers on US soil. However, international students studying remotely, and especially Chinese students at American universities studying remotely from China, did not enjoy these protections, given Zoom's subordination to the expansive dictates of the Chinese government.

As many companies moved meetings to Zoom and as remote work became the new normal, Zoom acquired corporate information as well. In the immediate rush to respond to the pandemic, the wholesale adoption of Zoom did not undergo the same debate and scrutiny that another Chinese company, Huawei, received. The US government, especially during the Trump administration, tried to create a global boycott against Huawei, with mixed success although some countries embraced this boycott. After the Snowden revelations, other countries knew that American law granted foreigners no protection at all from US mass surveillance; this made them skeptical about US assurances that the government was trying to prevent China from exploiting Huawei's technology to engage in this same activity. Nonetheless, the US government pressed countries around the world to avoid using Huawei's 5G technology or its devices, arguing that its products contained "backdoors" facilitating Chinese government access to its hardware and its 5G backbone. In 2020, for example, Canada announced that it was banning Huawei and ZTE from its 5G network.

The flood of personal, private information shared across digital platforms enabled all these companies to gain further insights into the preferences, desires, interests, impulses, appetites, thoughts, fears, political views, personal lives, and relationships of all those who used their services. Platforms that amassed this information could discern the health, socioeconomic, and financial status of every user, along with virtually every other feature of their personal situation. And the creators of algorithms worked to refine them in ways that produced more complete and faithful portraits of every user. Governments could readily access all this information as well even as continuing innovations in AI and machine learning facilitated appropriations of the formerly private. Even more critically, AI and machine learning allow ever more precise prediction. As Zeynep Tuyfekci writes,

Increasingly, though, artificial intelligence can use surveillance data to infer things that aren't even whispered. . . . [Increasingly], such predictions are made by analyzing big data sets with algorithms (often called "machine learning") that can arrive at conclusions about things that aren't explicitly in the data. For example, algorithmic interpretations of Instagram posts can effectively predict a person's future depressive episodes—performing better than humans assessing the same posts. Similar results have been found for predicting future manic episodes and detecting suicidal ideation, among many other examples. Such predictive systems are already in widespread use, including for hiring, sales, political targeting, education, medicine, and more.[1]

And unless strong privacy protections are put in place before the adoption and spread of the metaverse, all prior intrusions will seem inconsequential. Participation in the metaverse will enable the gathering of complete data on each user in real time. This will not only permit the faithful recording of each person's internal world and emotional, intellectual, and biological state but enable effectively perfect prediction as the technology evolves. Unless data brokers are aggressively restrained through a comprehensive regulatory regime, information gathered in one area will be exploited even more extensively in every other domain. In fact, absent these and other legal restraints, the data surrendered in the metaverse will become a single perfect "data double" of the self, accessible to both governments and private entities.

THE CONTINUED EXPANSION OF
STATE SURVEILLANCE

Although the Chinese government's activities remain an especially extreme manifestation of state surveillance and its consequences for individual privacy, freedom, and agency, all states, as has been repeatedly emphasized throughout this book, assault privacy in ways that were unimaginable before the spread of digital tools during the early decades of the twenty-first century. For the first time in human history truly mass surveillance has been made possible with these tools, enabling the construction of an ever-more-encompassing panopticon.

The already unprecedented powers concentrated in the hands of national governments since the rise of the modern nation-state in the 1930s experienced another quantum leap in their size with the emergence of these digital-surveillance innovations. An organization capable of depriving people of their lives and liberty acquired even greater majesty, making every individual—excepting those with enormous wealth and power—smaller and more inconsequential in comparison. And everywhere these tools enabled states to violate an internationally recognized human right, the right to privacy. With hardly any discussion about the implications of this development, in the frenzied aftermath of the terrorist attacks of September 11, 2001, states, and especially the US government, adopted tools designed to defenestrate everybody to find a few.

Even the most totalitarian regimes that arose in the middle decades of the twentieth century lacked the technological means to monitor their entire populations, let alone ordinary people outside their borders. It is precisely this capacity that the largest and most powerful states in the world, democratic and authoritarian alike, began to acquire and deploy in the first decades of the twenty-first century. And these capacities soon spread to less technologically advanced countries as a growing surveillance industrial complex pursued this novel market opportunity. This surveillance industrial complex sold its wares indiscriminately around the world, providing states with atrocious human-rights records access to these tools.

Democratic states, in the main, placed some modest limits on their ability to use these tools on their own populations, although not on foreigners, differing significantly from their authoritarian counterparts in this regard. However, they often found ways to enable their security apparats to elide these restraints and engage in mass warrantless surveillance. In addition, despite their democratic character, they often singled out protesters, dissenters, ethnic minorities, and immigrants and refugees for especially extensive monitoring.

The Snowden revelations in 2013 created a strong public backlash against the US government's mass-surveillance activities. Unfortunately, although perhaps inevitably, this public outrage faded in a relatively short time, although the legacy of his whistleblowing could be seen in the reluctance to voluntarily download surveillance apps during the first months of the COVID-19 pandemic. Additionally, news and other reports detailing the surveillance practices of private digital companies pushed concerns about government spying activities out of the public mind. In short, even as concerns about the US government's continuing use of mass surveillance began to occasion less and less public commentary, criticisms of the social media companies grew rapidly. The NSA faded from the headlines even though it still surveilled the world in conjunction with its Five Eyes partners.

Moreover, the framing of the attack on the US Capitol on January 6, 2021, as an act of domestic terrorism produced additional desires for expanded government surveillance. This time the targets were not foreign terrorists but far-right nationalist groups, especially White supremacists. Many people clamored for government agencies to increase their capacity to monitor these groups. Inevitably this involved increased surveillance of social media activity and the Internet to locate and track the activities of members of these groups.

After the attack on the US Capitol, law-enforcement agencies, much as they had after 9/11 when pushing for the USA PATRIOT Act, repeatedly lamented the lack of legislation enabling the tracking and arrest of domestic terrorists—conveniently avoiding mention of the fact that finding these "needles in haystacks" would increase surveillance of other "US persons." Leaders of US law enforcement, as they have since the earliest years of the digital age, continue to complain about the existence of encryption and about encrypted platforms, insisting that they undermine security. In short, the Capitol attack generated a new impetus for mass surveillance. The fact that members of Congress were the targets of the rioters ensured their continuing reluctance to enact any kind of legislation that might restrict the law-enforcement community's use of digital-surveillance tools or meaningfully circumscribe its surveillance practices.

Other events fueled arguments in favor of the further expansion of the US government's digital capacities. The Chinese government's hacking of Equifax, the Russian government's SolarWinds hack, and a raft of other cyber intrusions of US government agencies and ransomware attacks against American corporations has led to continuing demands for a more robust US response to its adversaries' incursions. Many Trumanites on media outlets like MSNBC and CNN insist that the United States must move from defense to offense, all while eliding mention of its already extensive and long-standing cyber intrusions against others.

In the aftermath of these hacks, many worried that the United States was falling behind its adversaries and was not devoting sufficient attention to the "cyber domain." This last argument was particularly dubious given that American capacities dwarf those of its adversaries. Just as supporters of increased US military spending claim every few years that neglect has reduced battle readiness, supporters of the NSA and the rest of the US intelligence apparatus insist that their capacities have deteriorated due to insufficient funding. More money must be found to confront adversaries in the cyber domain, they insist. These claims ensure continued lavish funding for the newest branch of the US military, Cyber Command, and ongoing pressures to increase the budgets of the various agencies of the intelligence apparatus, including the NSA. Conveniently forgotten is the fact that the United States far outspends all its potential adversaries in these areas, even during the "leanest" budgetary years.

The worsening of the United States' relationship with Russia and China and the prospect of escalating tensions with these two countries, along with Russia's invasion of Ukraine, fuel the impetus for the United States to expand its cyber capacities and accelerate the arms race that already exists in this area.

So too do continuing conflict with Iran and North Korea and American global activities against various terrorist organizations. President Biden's assertion that the democratic world and the authoritarian world are engaged in a global struggle presages a New Cold War, and with it the need for even more powerful cyber capabilities. Until international treaties are enacted that govern cyber tools and their uses, it is hard to imagine the development of domestic regulatory architectures that genuinely circumscribe state-surveillance activities. Absent such treaties, national-security claims will remain predominant, overwhelming civil-rights and privacy protections. Moreover, in the United States the continuing growth of surveillance is ensured by the presence of real and perceived domestic threats—ranging from White supremacists and criminals to others who are nonviolent but still framed as inimical to "domestic tranquility," such as so-called "Black identity" activists, environmentalists, supporters of animal rights, and other dissidents.

In sum, while it is possible to imagine that the surveillance activities of private corporations will eventually encounter increased regulation, it seems unlikely that the US government will show similar enthusiasm to regulate itself. It is not alone in this regard. Even though Europe's enactment of the GDPR indicates its intention to protect its citizens from the intrusions of private entities, governments in the region retain expansive surveillance capacities. And Russia and China continue to grow their capacities in this area at a febrile pace. At the time of this writing, all states are increasing their abilities to surveil each other and their own populations, making it harder and harder for individuals to protect the remaining vestiges of the formerly private.

SURVEILLANCE AND POLITICS

Among the most enthusiastic users of social media platforms, especially Twitter and Facebook, are politicians. They have embraced these platforms' manipulative capacities, derived from the surveillance of their users, quickly learning that they can use these features to win the hearts of supporters while depressing turnout or votes for their opponents.

Political campaigns have become especially adept at using these tools. The information gathered on voters through tracking and surveillance along with the sale and sharing of data on them can drive mobilization and demobilization efforts alike. This information has permitted political operatives, hackers, trolls, and other states to drive up votes for some while depressing votes for others. Microtargeting—the ability to craft specific messages to specific voters—rests on the surveillance, collection, and data mining of vast amounts of personal information and constitutes an especially effective way to encourage or suppress voting. The information that campaigns can weaponize and exploit often do not come from data that voters voluntarily surrendered. Instead, it is harvested or acquired from other sources, including the social media platforms. Microtargeting focuses on activating and exploiting the strongest and most visceral human emotions, including fear, anger, resentment, and grievance. Less frequently, these efforts target individual hopes for specific changes or the preservation of the status quo. Political campaigns have lost more and more of their already diminishing informative content, becoming increasingly sophisticated engines of behavioral, algorithmic manipulation. In these regards, they mirror the social media companies who they pay to become the central purveyors of microtargeted political advertisements.

This form of political advertising became especially evident during 2016. Trump political advisor Steve Bannon and major Trump contributor Robert Mercer, the billionaire who finances Breitbart News, a hard-right website, among other extremist ventures, in 2013 created the company Cambridge Analytica to gather intelligence that right-wing clients could use in a variety of ways. The Trump campaign for the presidency in the United States and the pro-Brexit campaign in the United Kingdom hired Cambridge Analytica in 2016 to provide the kind of information that would permit microtargeting. And it was Cambridge Analytica that enabled both campaigns to transform this practice into an art form.

Cambridge Analytica harvested information about voters from Facebook to learn their most intense proclivities. Campaigns could then exploit this knowledge to microtarget political ads. Revelations in the aftermath of these elections showed that Cambridge Analytica had taken users' information from Facebook without their knowledge or consent. This forced the resignation of CEO Alexander Nix and the eventual closure of the firm in 2018. However, sophisticated digital microtargeting did not end, becoming a mainstay of campaign advertising during the 2018 midterm elections in the United States and throughout subsequent elections. Given its efficacy, the practice seems certain to remain a centerpiece of electoral campaigns unless regulations emerge that circumscribe the uses of private information.

Microtargeting designed to exploit the most limbic reactions intensifies conflicts and differences and deepens tribal attachments against feared or hated others. Political polarization grows apace. Those on the right, already suffused with anger against the "woke" and against cancel culture, are microtargeted with information, video clips, and links to merchants of outrage designed to fan their ire. And those on the left are fed a diet larded with their view of the world, designed to nourish their anger, increase their identitarian proclivities and self-righteousness, and fuel their contempt for those who differ. In the end, rather than increasing feelings of connection and community, as these platforms have so benevolently promised, the result is the emergence of more ferocious tribalism conjoined to feelings of anger, alienation, sadness, polarization, animus, and anxiety.

All of this occurs in an environment that fetishizes technology and innovation and elevates tech entrepreneurs into demigods. This was especially true of the early years of the digital age. It took a decade for systematic criticism to emerge and even longer still before tech entrepreneurs became the object of widespread opprobrium. Unlike governments, however, corporations cannot wrap their surveillance and collection in legalized secrecy, and neither can they invoke security or the pursuit of the common good, however dubiously on many occasions, as a justification for their actions. All of this makes their digital surveillance and other behaviors more likely to be confronted by regulation than will be the practices of states. By extension, companies selling tools that promise to protect privacy will continue to proliferate, as will technological innovations designed to accomplish this same end.

THE CONTINUING ACCEPTANCE OF CORPORATE SURVEILLANCE DESPITE CRITICISM

Although not as consequential to the individual as state surveillance, given the more limited powers of private companies, corporate surveillance facilitates the concentration of economic power and wealth. As a small number of corporations became larger and larger and have reached into more and more areas of life, individuals, whether as workers or users, became smaller and smaller. Years before the outbreak of the COVID-19 pandemic, the behavioral manipulations designed to promote continual engagement with different platforms was facilitating surveillance. The denatured, impersonal quality of online interactions and activities make it hard for people to imagine the scope and minuteness of surveillance, despite the extent of information available on the topic. In addition, the tendency to not think about these practices reflects the continuing subliminal hold, especially among older people, of behaviors developed when analog technologies predominated. People entered the digital age habituated to listening to the radio, watching TV, or reading a book, possessed of complete agency over an inanimate object: *you* watched TV or listened to the radio, but neither object, and certainly not your refrigerator or thermostat, watched or listened *back*.

Computers, at first blush, seemed as inanimate as typewriters, and cell phones were perceived as new versions of rotary telephones, not as tracking, listening, and monitoring devices. During the analog age, a telephone could be legally wiretapped with a warrant, but was not subject to hacking and could not be remotely transformed into a portable surveillance device. Nor did it contain much personal information. Because of this lag in awareness, most users, particularly during the first decades of the digital age, did not think about the implications of interacting with objects that they no longer controlled but that others could appropriate.

Furthermore, the passive, increasingly universal nature of surveillance—wherein an algorithm rather than a human gathers information—has facilitated the spread of this practice. The impersonality of algorithms and widespread ignorance about their operation has played a role as well. The deceptive proclamations of the technology companies has made matters worse. In their public utterances, these entities have insisted that the data they amass is only gathered to improve consumer convenience and the experience of users on their sites. They conveniently avoid discussing how these algorithms were designed to encourage people to spend more and more of their waking hours on their platforms or the ways that they used the metadata that they are mining.

The behavioral manipulations designed to drive continual engagement succeeded in making consumers perceive these products as indispensable. Even as knowledge grew about the harmful effects of these platforms and the surveillance capacities embedded in digital devices and the "Internet of things," use did not significantly decline. Moreover, few understood that the devices they were placing in their homes were especially vulnerable to hacking, given their routinely weak security.

Stories emerged about the hacking of "baby cams" and "nanny cams," but none of these revelations discouraged use. Devices designed to engage in passive surveillance with weak security protocols could be hacked and transformed into active appropriators of personal information. Because "smart" appliances were generally more expensive—although cost differentials diminished and it became harder and harder to find "nonsmart" appliances—the initial purchasers of these things tended to be more affluent or at least more avid consumers.

Paradoxically, this means that acquisitiveness made those most prone to consume especially subject to surveillance and to the hacking of their personal information, including the theft of their identities. While convenience and the insatiable appetite for the newest gadget drives purchases of these devices, the quotidian failure to think about their embedded surveillance capabilities or their inability to protect information from hacking reflects a particular reality of the digital age. Although these appliances are concrete, material objects, their wireless and hence invisible connection to an equally disembodied entity—the Internet—makes their capacities abstract and therefore unthreatening.

This last element helps attenuate popular outrage whenever revelations about the extent of surveillance occur. This stands in marked contrast to the reaction during the analog age to revelations about an equivalently surreptitious activity—subliminal advertising. People saw subliminal advertising as hidden, dishonest, and manipulative, and their objections caused the banning of the practice. No equivalent reaction and no immediate government response has followed the revelations about the hidden manipulations that many platforms, and especially Facebook, use on their billions of users.

In addition, to avoid cognitive dissonance, many denizens of the first decades of the twenty-first century chose to ignore the continual presence of surveillance and clandestine behavioral manipulation or engaged in gallows humor about the subject. Not thinking about or joking about these things facilitated continual, virtually obsessive use of digital devices and submersion in the content on digital platforms. The irony is that the invisibility and sophistication of the behavioral manipulations on these platforms makes them infinitely more deceptive than subliminal advertising, their primitive predecessor.

The inability to galvanize greater public support and pressure for regulatory reform in part reflects the so-called "privacy paradox," discussed before. Suzanne Barth and Menno de Jong write,

> Users claim to be concerned about their privacy but do very little to protect their personal data. . . . Thus, while many users show theoretical interest in their privacy and maintain a positive attitude towards privacy-protection behavior, this rarely translates into actual protective behavior. Furthermore, while an intention to limit data disclosure exists, actual disclosure often significantly exceeds intention. . . . Although users are aware of privacy risks on the Internet, they tend to share private information in exchange for retail value and personalized services. . . . Privacy concerns should logically lead to restricted provision of information in social networks; however, the reverse effect can be observed as many users provide personal information seemingly without hesitation.[2]

REGULATORY REMEDIES TO SURVEILLANCE CAPITALISM AT THE END OF THE SECOND DECADE OF THE DIGITAL AGE

Privacy activists and those objecting to the market dominance of a few firms continue to try to regulate social media companies and other interactive computer services and to reduce their power, control, and influence. Most commonly, especially given the market dominance of these companies, many people supported antitrust actions to shrink their size. Antitrust measures would not change the most problematic feature of some of these companies—their business model—but would at least lessen their influence. The breakup of these companies would increase consumer choice as well. Others favor revoking or reforming Section 230 of the Communications Decency Act, ending or circumscribing the immunity that the statute grants these companies.

A third approach, favored by many conservatives, would be to regulate these platforms as common carriers. *Common carriers* are monopolies such as utility companies that deliver a public good. Among other things, common carriers are not allowed to discriminate. Many conservatives believe that the social media companies exclude their voices. This remedy would ostensibly prevent content moderation that discriminates against different perspectives.[3] Problematically, this same approach could circumscribe efforts to prevent the spread of misinformation and the proliferation of hate speech.

Several other ideas have arisen during the latter half of the second decade of the twenty-first century about how best to regulate these companies. Among the most interesting is to designate all companies that hold information on users as "information fiduciaries." This would require them to safeguard and adequately protect the information gathered from users while being charged with elevating the protection of privacy into a central operational priority.[4]

A promising approach to the protection of privacy is offered by the Illinois Biometric Privacy Act as well. Passed in 2008, BIPA is designed to prevent companies from gathering biometric information—including such things as the faceprints that lie at the heart of facial recognition—from the residents of Illinois without their knowledge and consent. Several plaintiffs including groups that represented victims of domestic violence and former sex workers, among other vulnerable communities, sued Clearview AI because of the harms resulting from misuse of facial-recognition technology. They won their lawsuit in 2022. To quote the ACLU, under the settlement, "Clearview is permanently banned nationwide from making its faceprint database accessible to most businesses and other private entities. The company will also cease selling access to its database to any entity in Illinois, including state and local police, for five years."[5]

If other states follow Illinois's lead, biometric privacy might begin to gain greater protection, at least from private entities seeking to monetize this information. On the other hand, the suit brought against Clearview under BIPA does not provide much of a break on state uses of invasive technologies like facial recognition. For this reason, legislation like BIPA represents an important but only partial remedy.

The same is true of another measure advocated by many—adoption in the United States of the privacy protections embedded in the EU's General Data Protection Regulation. This would facilitate the GDPR's extension across the world, making it the foundation of a genuinely universal privacy-protection regime. The GDPR does contain several novel regulations designed to protect privacy in the digital age. For example, information systems that collect data must use the highest possible privacy setting as the default option. And "data subjects" who consent to the processing of their personal data can withdraw this consent at any time.

Those who collect data must disclose the legal justification for its collection and their data-retention and -sharing practices. Further, upon request, companies must provide data subjects with a portable copy of the data collected on them. In certain circumstances, data subjects can pursue the "right to be forgotten" and have their data erased. Data breaches that impact user privacy must be reported within seventy-two hours, and companies that fail to comply with these directives can face fines of twenty million euros, or up to 40 percent of their worldwide annual revenues. In addition, all companies that collect data are required to employ a data protection officer, charged with ensuring compliance with the GDPR's directives.

Given the absence of other, more robust regulations, the GDPR constitutes an important step forward in the protection of digital privacy, even as it remains inadequate. For example, the GDPR fails to fully address the numerous problems surrounding consent. Terms and conditions fulfill the GDPR's minimal requirements but continue to lack sufficient transparency to facilitate genuinely informed consent. A different standard would be much more effective than the GDPR's criteria. A step beyond would ban the use of personal information as a primary source of revenue. To get regulatory approval to collect information, a company would have to establish that the data it gathers is indispensable to the provision of its service. It would have to show as well that collection is limited to the fulfillment of this end. Cookies and other highly intrusive practices could be banned, along with the sale of user information to other companies. A more modest approach might require explicit user consent before information could be sold or shared.

Even more stringent limits on data retention need to be enacted as well. In many democratic, economically developed countries, and especially the United States, limits on data retention are insufficient. In a world with plunging data-storage costs, these limitations became more and more essential to prevent the gathering of everything on everyone and the holding of it forever. As a first step, those retaining data would have to establish a time limit on retention. And in all cases, a maximum period would have to be established for each type of data. Practices in several European countries constitute an especially good model in this area, given strict and relatively brief time limits for data retention in much of the region.

Senator Ron Wyden (D-OR) continues to introduce bills that exceed protections found in the GDPR and that impose the kinds of restraints on private corporations advocated herein. For example, in October 2019 he introduced the Mind Your Own Business Act, that, if ever adopted, would establish the gold standard of privacy protection in the world. Among other things, the bill would require genuine transparency of private corporations and give user-consumers complete control over the sale and sharing of their information while stopping a company's ability to track people on the Web.[6] That this bill has languished since its proposal says much about the lobbying powers of the technology sector and of data brokers in the United States and their hold over Congress, along with the resistance of Republicans to the regulation of business.

The failure of this bill and the extent of the lobbying power of this sector is already evident in the fact that the United States has failed to adopt the GDPR, despite the relative modesty of its requirements. At the time adoption was proposed, current and former executives and founders of several Silicon Valley companies responded with contempt. Former Google CEO Eric Schmidt, for example, asserted that the "collision between a right to be forgotten and a right to know . . . the balance was struck wrong" in the proposed legislation.[7] This claim, of course, completely overlooks the reasons for a right to be forgotten and other privacy protections. Why do interactive computer services even have a "right to know"? And *what* exactly do they have the right to know? Does their knowing serve a public interest? And what happens to inaccurate and prejudicial information?

Not surprisingly, Google cofounder Larry Page doubled down on Schmidt's comments, immediately criticizing the GDPR and the European Court of Justice's decision validating the right to be forgotten. He argued that private technology companies are "more reliable repositories of personal data than governments because they care more about their reputations."[8] Even as he said this, however, Google/Alphabet's reputation was declining, although this decline significantly trailed Facebook's. Issues with content moderation on YouTube and the company's aggressive pursuit of monopoly power were the most common of these criticisms.

In fact, from a privacy perspective the problem with the GDPR goes beyond its insufficient regulation of the activities of private corporations. At present, the act only protects individuals from some of the intrusions of the private sector, much like BIPA, while leaving them largely unprotected from governmental assaults on their privacy. As noted earlier in this chapter and throughout this book, it is largely states because of their overwhelming power that require the greatest regulation. The GDPR does relatively little to restrain them, permitting the legal collection of data in a wide range of areas. "Consent, contract, public purpose, vital interest, legitimate interest, or legal requirement" constitute legal grounds for the processing of personal data under the specific carve-outs of the GDPR. The regulation does not adequately define and circumscribe "public purpose, vital interest, legitimate interest, or legal requirement." Absent narrow and precise definitions, the GDPR does little to protect people from expansive state surveillance and collection.

Even though the GDPR remains inadequate, its influence continues to grow. To the surprise of many, given the extent of surveillance in the country, even the Chinese government passed a Data Security Law in August 2021 that contains many of the elements included in the GDPR. However, like other governments, it excluded itself from these limitations. Its efforts to construct the most comprehensive panopticon in human history remain unconstrained and are certain to continue.

Yet again Senator Wyden, this time joined by Rand Paul (R-KY), proposed a bill that would restrain government access to personal data in the hands of data brokers. The Fourth Amendment Is Not for Sale Act, proposed in April 2021, would close a loophole that enables data brokers to sell personal information to law-enforcement agencies.[9] As did other proposed legislation before it, this bill stalled, reflecting the same confluence of interests and forces that have constrained other efforts to create a more robust privacy regime in the United States. In this case, of course, the coercive apparatus added its opposition to any measure that constrained its operations to the resistance of these other interests.

TECHNOLOGY COMPANIES AND ANTITRUST MEASURES

In the United States the cost-freeness of many interactive computer services has shielded them from antitrust legislation for several decades, facilitating their development and preservation of monopoly power. The Reagan administration, in keeping with the pro–big business approach of the Republican Party, redefined antitrust enforcement in the 1980s. Throughout the next forty years, trust busting in the United States largely focused on whether mergers and acquisitions had potentially deleterious price impacts on consumers. Market domination stopped animating antitrust actions during this period. Moreover, even digital companies that charged for certain services, notably Amazon, successfully argued that they reduced prices for consumers, shielding themselves from antitrust enforcement for many years.

In addition, the companies and their supporters and lobbyists asserted that antitrust actions and other regulations stifle innovation. The deep American faith in technological progress, and the country's admiration of wealth, have facilitated the acceptance of these arguments and developments. And finally, the rise of China and its emergence into a technological powerhouse has added a geopolitical dimension to US reluctance to regulate these companies. As "national champions," tech leaders and their products were seen as essential to American dominance of the digital world. The public and private handwringing accompanying the United States' early failures to match

China's development of 5G technology added nationalistic concerns to an environment favoring huge American tech companies. From the vantage point of many, they were the only entities who possessed the capital and human resources to match Chinese investment.

Eventually, however, arguments that extreme market concentration and the corollary absence of competition stifle innovation, conjoined with worries about the outsized power and influence of these companies, led to widespread support for antitrust actions during the second half of the Trump administration. Antitrust pressures grew inexorably, coming from both sides of the US political aisle. For the first time, hearings were initiated before of the House Antitrust Subcommittee on July 29, 2020.

Mark Zuckerberg of Facebook/Meta, Jeff Bezos of Amazon, Tim Cook of Apple, and Sundar Pichai of Alphabet/Google all appeared before the subcommittee—though remotely, due to the COVID-19 pandemic. The hearings lasted six hours and were the culmination of a year-long investigation launched by subcommittee chair Representative David Cicilline (D-RI) in which the subcommittee had obtained millions of documents, interviews, and private messages. The hearings in and of themselves demonstrated something very rare in Washington, D.C.—a bipartisan consensus about the need to confront the size of the largest technology companies.

Tim Cook faced the fewest questions, perhaps because Apple, despite being the largest company in the world at the time, did not control sales of digital devices in different market areas. This was true of its phones, tablets, laptops, and other products, all of which faced serious competition from other manufacturers. The complaints about Apple revolved mostly around claims that its App Store engaged in rent-seeking and monopolistic practices that unfairly impacted app developers and other parties. But these issues paled in comparison to the complaints about the market dominance and practices of the other three companies.

The members of the House who questioned Mark Zuckerberg primarily focused on the company's acquisition of competitors like Instagram, probing claims that Facebook had used strong-arm tactics to drive competitors out of business. Lawmakers used Zuckerberg's own emails to show that he had dissembled when discussing the acquisition of Instagram. They also explored the implications of Facebook's market dominance on innovation and competition.

The Republican members of the subcommittee who questioned Zuckerberg mostly leveled the accusation that the tech community discriminated against conservatives and excluded their voices—despite strong evidence that Facebook's content-moderation algorithms favored conservatives during the 2020 election cycle.[10] The two members raising this argument, Representatives Jim Jordan (R-Ohio) and Matt Gaetz (R-FL), were both reliable supporters of

Donald Trump, and this charge echoed his claims. In the main, Republicans, reflecting the continuing hold of Reaganite understandings, are more reticent to initiate antitrust actions in this area and are more prone to embrace a different form of regulation, in this case through the application of the common carrier standard. Zuckerberg's and the other tech titans' only enthusiastic supporter was Representative James Sensenbrenner (R-WI), who was opposed in general to antitrust actions because he did not wish to "punish success"; as a committed supporter of big-business interests, his position was not surprising. Paradoxically, although not surprisingly, on the same day of the hearings, the Turkish government passed new laws giving it blanket access to the social media accounts of Turkish users of social media platforms, indicating the embedded problems with Facebook's business model.

Jeff Bezos was questioned about Amazon's treatment of third-party vendors on the platform and especially those who competed with the company's products. Nearly 40 percent of all online sales occurred on Amazon's site, clear evidence of its market dominance. Bezos argued that the company was not a monopoly because of competition from huge brick-and-mortar companies, including Walmart, which had a market value even larger than Amazon's, and Costco, Target, and others. But there was no eliding the fact that Amazon dominated online commerce.

In addition, Bezos was asked about the company's extraordinarily lax protection of private data. Although the company had protocols governing how this data could be accessed and used, their use was entirely voluntary, and compliance was not enforced. Representative Pramila Jayapal (D-WA) launched the most incisive critique of the company, using public reports to show that Amazon tapped into data from third-party sellers to increase the sales of its own products. Because this was an antitrust hearing, Amazon escaped scrutiny about its treatment of its warehouse workers or its foray into facial-recognition technology—two especially controversial issues.

Sundar Pichai, for his part, was questioned about Google's acquisitions, its business tactics toward competitors, and its manipulation of searches. In 2020, 90 percent of *all* online searches were conducted on Google, which gave the company complete and overwhelming dominance of its market. The company's treatment of Yelp occasioned particular scrutiny, given the evidence that Google had appropriated Yelp's data while strong-arming the company. Pichai argued that size was not a vice but a virtue and indispensable to the provision of Google's services. All these companies at one time or another have made similar claims—as have other conglomerates—insisting on the importance and even the necessity of enormous size in the name of efficiency and economies of scale. Google has claimed that the provision of certain services requires the kind of metadata that only a huge company can amass.

In response, Expedia Group CEO Peter Kern told CNBC's *Squawk on the Street* that Google continued to conduct an "inequitable auction that favored its own products" when it came to the travel industry. In the same interview Kern applauded the US government's examination of Google's practices and the European Union's scrutiny of the company.[11] In all these regards, he was echoing the complaints of many businesses about Google's manipulation of its site and the manifold ways the company advantaged its own products.

In the United States, antitrust scrutiny continued after the hearings. Representative Cicilline reported the subcommittee's findings in August 2020, and new hearings were scheduled for October. Shortly thereafter, and with largely bipartisan support, the US Department of Justice filed antitrust lawsuits against Facebook and Apple, with several state attorneys general joining as well. For its part, the European Union released draft rules on December 15 directed at Facebook, Google, and the other interactive computer services, which regulated both illegal content and anticompetitive behavior. The proposed fine for violations of these rules was 10 percent of global revenues.

The Biden administration immediately indicated its intention to intensify antitrust scrutiny of these firms. In March 2021, President Biden appointed a professor at Columbia Law School, Tim Wu, who is a leading critic of big tech, and advocate of antitrust actions to the Council of Economic Advisors.[12] And subsequently, President Biden nominated Lina Khan to head the Federal Trade Commission. In 2017, while still a student at Yale Law School, Khan had written a widely discussed article arguing that Amazon's low prices drove competitors out of business and constituted a type of monopolistic behavior. The argument was a direct challenge to received wisdom concerning how to govern antitrust actions that has been held since the Reagan administration.[13]

However, proponents of online privacy met a serious setback at the end of June 2021 when a federal judge dismissed the FTC's antitrust lawsuit against Facebook and a case that a group of state attorneys general had brought challenging the company's acquisition of Instagram and WhatsApp. The judge decided that the FTC's case lacked sufficient factual evidence to support its arguments and gave the agency thirty days to refile its case. The judge dismissed the state attorneys' case entirely, ruling that they had waited too long to challenge the acquisition of Instagram (bought in 2012) and WhatsApp (purchased in 2014). The judge's opinion did suggest, however, that the FTC possessed the authority to file a similar case.[14]

This setback to antitrust efforts against Facebook indicates the future length, cost, and tortuosity of the legal battle to reduce the size and influence of the tech giants. However, the last time pressures to employ antitrust measures were equivalently strong occurred in the mid-1980s, when Ma Bell, the

US telephone monopoly, was broken up. For this reason, antitrust actions are likely to continue.

More generally, the problematic features of some of these tech companies, conjoined with their enormous size, power, and influence, means that efforts to construct a regulatory environment addressing these issues must continue. However, widespread grassroots activism, the impetus behind many other regulatory reform movements, does not drive these initiatives. Instead, they reflect the work of committed but relatively small groups of activists, academics, and politicians. The "privacy paradox" powerfully captures a central feature of the early decades of the digital age: rising awareness of privacy intrusions conjoined with continuing willingness, often in the interest of convenience, to surrender personal information. Nonetheless, the persisting conflict between the desire for privacy and the desire for convenience promises to continue to reward companies that are responsible stewards of data and that behave as de facto information fiduciaries.

Despite the privacy paradox and the absence of a significant grassroots movement pushing for change, pressures for reform continue. Although privacy protections have gradually increased in some countries, modeled largely on the GDPR, like the GDPR they remain inadequate and lag far behind the development of new technologies. Even more unfortunately for the protection of privacy, the extraordinarily problematic business models undergirding the worst features of technologies developed in the digital age remain unreformed. In the absence of the transformation and regulation of these business models, no amount of content moderation can fix the problems inherent in the use of interactive computer services, since these services are founded on commodification of the personal. And most states, given extant threat perceptions, will continue to resist efforts that restrain their operations in the security realm while pursuing technologies that enable them to see everything and know everything. The totalizing, indeed totalitarian, impetus behind "Total Information Awareness" has not diminished since 9/11. And superpower rivalries and the febrile race to dominate the cyber domain promise its acceleration.

EPILOGUE

The close connection between digital technologies and mass surveillance and other practices that destroy privacy and consequently diminish the power and agency of individuals raises the question as to whether or not digital tools *in and of themselves* undermine liberalism absent significant restrictions on their use. The question is especially urgent regarding state uses of these technologies, given the ways governments use this technology to magnify their existing powers while creating new capacities. The vast powers these digital tools give states constitutes one of the greatest assaults in history on limited government.

A totalizing and centralized conception of power underlies all panopticons. For this reason, panopticons created through the mass deployment of digital-surveillance tools destroy a central liberal remedy to tyranny—the diffusion of power. Moreover, these technologies alter beyond all recognition the line between the public and the private and between the self and the state. And surveillance, in whatever size or form, diminishes individuals and empowers huge organizations—and especially states.

Above all, however, liberalism rests on choice and, consequently, unpredictability. Indeterminacy marches hand in hand with choice and freedom. The architects of the digital world seek to use information to erase uncertainty, replacing it with predictability and assurance. All totalitarian states and totalizing visions in human history have had the same goal. Liberalism stops being liberal the moment indeterminacy and, consequently, freedom, disappear.

Privacy constitutes a fundamental element of liberalism as well. Without privacy, the individual loses all agency and any remaining vestiges of personal power. A person who cannot control information about themselves, the locus of their greatest individual sovereignty, has surrendered freedom and choice. This loss makes the individual smaller, particularly in comparison to the huge organizations appropriating ever-larger swathes of their private and personal self. The power gap between the individual and these entities widens relentlessly, worsening another vector of inequality. And states around the world insist on their right to potentially know everything about everyone in the name of advancing the common good while simultaneously cloaking more and more of their own activities in secrecy. For example, the US government, despite having a Freedom of Information Act, continues to classify more and more information, impeding the transparency FOIA was designed to advance. Simultaneously the US government claims that it is using its surveillance capacities judiciously and in a precise and targeted fashion. However, the secrecy covering its operations makes it difficult to evaluate these claims, although whistleblowers and occasional leaks throw them into question. In this environment, the individual becomes smaller and more exposed even as the government becomes more opaque and powerful. This fundamentally, and perhaps fatally, undermines the essence of liberalism—limited government and zones of protection for individual sovereignty.

More broadly, human dignity rests on the control and choice that privacy confers, as philosophers and other scholars have noted throughout the centuries. The cavalier destruction of privacy accompanying the adoption of digital activities consequently embodies nothing less than a massive and systematic human-rights violation. Digital technologies turn the individual inside-out, making their inner self increasingly legible, while erasing, through facial recognition, their "right to be let alone," undisturbed and unrecognized.

Other attacks on individual sovereignty continue. Previously unknown pathologies including hacking and large-scale identity theft are systematic attacks on the essential self, adding new uncertainties to human existence. And this assault will only grow if new digital arenas such as the metaverse are not regulated in advance, since they promise to involve the appropriation of the personal in previously unimagined ways. One can only hope that the experience with digital technologies during the first decades of the twenty-first century will eventually encourage the emergence of a digital ethics modeled on bioethics. Such an ethic would seek to constrain the most damaging practices before they emerge, enabling humanity to finally escape some of the worst features of the digital age.

NOTES

1. Zeynep Tuyfekci, "We Need to Take Back Our Privacy," Opinion, *New York Times*, May 19, 2022, https://www.nytimes.com/2022/05/19/opinion/privacy-technology-data.html.

2. Suzanne Barth and Menno D. T. de Jong, "The Privacy Paradox: Investigating Discrepancies between Expressed Privacy Concerns and Online Behavior—A Systematic Literature Review," *Telematics and Informatics* 34, no. 7 (November 2017): 1039–40, https://doi.org/10.1016/j.tele.2017.04.013.

3. Matthew Feeney, "Are Social Media Companies Common Carriers?" Cato Institute, Cato.org, March 24, 2021, https://www.cato.org/blog/are-social-media-companies-common-carriers.

4. Senator Mark Warner, "Potential Policy Proposals for Regulation of Social Media and Technology Firms," white paper (draft), summer 2018, published at https://graphics.axios.com/pdf/PlatformPolicyPaper.pdf.

5. American Civil Liberties Union, "In Big Win, Settlement Ensures Clearview AI Complies with Groundbreaking Illinois Biometric Privacy Law," ACLU.org, May 9, 2022, https://www.aclu.org/press-releases/big-win-settlement-ensures-clearview-ai-complies-with-groundbreaking-illinois.

6. Senator Ron Wyden, "Wyden Introduces Comprehensive Bill to Secure Americans' Personal Information and Hold Corporations Accountable," Wyden.Senate.gov, October 17, 2019, https://www.wyden.senate.gov/news/press-releases/wyden-introduces-comprehensive-bill-to-secure-americans-personal-information-and-hold-corporations-accountable.

7. Eric Schmidt as quoted in Shoshana Zuboff, *Age of Surveillance Capitalism: The Fight for a Human Future at the New Frontier of Power* (New York: PublicAffairs, 2019), 60.

8. As recounted in Zuboff, *Age of Surveillance Capitalism*, 60.

9. Taylor Hatmaker, "New Privacy Bill Would End Law Enforcement Practice of Buying Data from Brokers," *Tech Crunch*, April 21, 2021, https://www.wyden.senate .gov/news/press-releases/wyden-paul-and-bipartisan-members-of-congress-introduce -the-fourth-amendment-is-not-for-sale-act-.

10. Isaac Stanley-Becker and Elizabeth Dwoskin, "Trump Allies, Largely Unconstrained by Facebook's Rules against Repeated Falsehoods, Cement Pre-election Dominance," *Washington Post*, November 1, 2020, https://www.washingtonpost.com /technology/2020/11/01/facebook-election-misinformation/.

11. Peter Kern, *Squawk on the Street*, interview, CNBC, July 31, 2020.

12. Cecilia Kang, "A Leading Critic of Big Tech Will Join the White House," *New York Times*, March 5, 2021, https://www.nytimes.com/2021/03/05/technology/tim-wu -white-house.html.

13. Lina M. Khan, "Amazon's Antitrust Paradox," *Yale Law Journal* 126, no. 3 (January 2017): 710–805, https://www.yalelawjournal.org/pdf/e.710.Khan.805 _zuvfyyeh.pdf.

14. Cat Zakrzewski and Rachel Lerman, "Court Says FTC Hasn't Provided Evidence Facebook Is a Monopoly, Dismisses Lawsuit," *Washington Post*, June 28, 2021, https://www.washingtonpost.com/technology/2021/06/28/ftc-facebook -antitrust-complaint-dismissed/.

Index

Oculus, 140
Office of Legal Counsel
(OLC), 101, 105
Official Secrets Act, 185
OLC. *See* Office of Legal Counsel
Olmstead v. US, 57, 78
Oneida Community, 44
On Liberty (Mill, J.), 44, 220–21
open-source movement, 203
Operation Intercept, 168
Orbán, Viktor, 159, 245
Orwell, George, 7
Owen, Robert, 44
Oxygen Forensics, 132

Page, Carter, 95
Page, Larry, 201–2, 207, 282
Pakistan, 118, 160
Palantir, 129, 164
Palestine, xvii, 259
Palmer, A. Mitchell, 145, 146
PAN. *See* National Action Party
Panetta, Leon, 95
Pan-European Privacy-Preserving
Proximity Tracing (PEPP-PT), 254
panopticon and panoptic effect:
academia and, 133; in COVID-19
pandemic, 248; origins and definition
of, 78–80; people of color and, 144,
152; power and, 79, 288; smart
cities/safe cities and, 166; state
surveillance and, 79–80, 144, 152,
178, 230, 272, 283, 288; television
shows on dangers of, 171
paranoid style, 9
Parent, William, 46–47
parent-teachers associations
(PTAs), 14, 15
Parler, 232
Patel, Amit, 202
patriotism, xii, 84, 95
Paul, Rand, 283
Paz, Octavio, 29
PCLOB. *See* Privacy and Civil Liberties
Oversight Board

Peeping Tom, 77
Pegasus, 181–82; in Mexico, 192
Peissl, Walter, 7, 86
Peña Nieto, Enrique, 192
"pen registers," 59
Peru, 169
the Philippines, 221, 233–34
Pichai, Sundar, 284, 285
plausible deniability, 123
Poindexter, John, xv
Poitras, Laura, 110, 111
Poland, 244, 245, 255
Polanyi, Karl, 5
"political correctness," 213
politics, social media and, 275–77
Posner, Richard, 39, 62–64
power: of metadata, 82; in panopticon
and panoptic effect, 79, 288; privacy
and, 23, 27, 32–33, 48, 282, 287–88;
surveillance and, 79–80, 287–88; in
surveillance capitalism, 205, 279,
282, 283, 284, 287
Power, Samantha, 90
predator-prey relationship, 6, 7
"predictive policing," 144, 167
press: conspiracy theories in, 220–21;
in COVID-19 pandemic, 245, 247;
in Mexico, 192; privacy from, 56; in
South Africa, 194
PRI. *See* Institutional
Revolutionary Party
PRISM, 110
privacy: accountability and, 50–51;
of Apple iPhones, 126; in Brazil,
67, 190–91; of children, 25–26; in
China, 30, 67, 161–62, 163–64; in
Cold War, 45–46; consent in, 47–48;
control in, 46–48; in COVID-19
pandemic, 68, 245, 246, 247, 254,
263; defense of loss of, 39–40;
"digital exhaust" and, 202; discretion
with, 25, 71–72; in EU, 66, 111,
224, 282–83; on Facebook, 23–24,
208–9; with facial recognition,
129–30, 158; feminism on, 50–51; in

About the Author

Juan D. Lindau is professor of political science at Colorado College. He has been teaching about state secrecy and surveillance since 2003, when it became evident that mass surveillance constituted a core, defining feature of the information age and the reaction to 9/11. In addition to his work on this topic, Dr. Lindau's scholarship primarily focuses on the drug war and its impacts on Mexico and Latin America.